A NOT-SO-DISTANT HORROR

A NOT-SO-DISTANT HORROR

MASS VIOLENCE IN EAST TIMOR

JOSEPH NEVINS

Cornell University Press
Ithaca and London

Portions of chapters 3 and 8 are reprinted from "East Timor, the United Nations, and the International Community: Force Feeding Human Rights into the Institutionalized Jaws of Failure," *Pacifica Review* (now *Global Change, Peace and Security*) 12, no. 1 (2000): 47–62. Reprinted with permission from Taylor and Francis.

Portions of chapter 6 are from "The Making of 'Ground Zero' in East Timor in 1999: An Analysis of International Complicity in Indonesia's Crimes." © 2002 by The Regents of the University of California. Adapted from *Asian Survey* 42, no. 4 (July/August 2002): 623–41, by permission of the Regents.

Portions of chapters 7 and 8 are reprinted from "(Mis) representing East Timor's Past: Structural-Symbolic Violence, International Law, and the Institutionalization of Injustice," *Journal of Human Rights* 1, no. 4 (2002): 523–540, with permission from Taylor and Francis.

Portions of chapter 8 are reprinted from "Restitution over Coffee: Truth, Reconciliation and Environmental Violence in East Timor," *Political Geography* 22, no. 6 (2003): 677–701, with permission from Elsevier.

•

First published 2005 by Cornell University Press
First printing, Cornell Paperbacks, 2005

Printed in the United States of America

Library of Congress Cataloging-in-Publication Data

Nevins, Joseph.
 A not-so-distant horror : mass violence in East Timor / Joseph Nevins.
    p.   cm.
 Includes bibliographical references and index.
 ISBN 0-8014-4306-7 (cloth : alk. paper) — ISBN 0-8014-8984-9 (pbk. : alk. paper)
    1. East Timor—History—Autonomy and independence movements.   2. Political atrocities—East Timor.   3. Violence—East Timor.   I. Title.
 DS649.6.N47   2005
 959.87′032—dc22

                                                                   2004030952

Cornell University Press strives to use environmentally responsible suppliers and materials to the fullest extent possible in the publishing of its books. Such materials include vegetable-based, low-VOC inks and acid-free papers that are recycled, totally chlorine-free, or partly composed of nonwood fibers. For further information, visit our website at www.cornellpress.cornell.edu.

Cloth printing   10 9 8 7 6 5 4 3 2 1
Paperback printing   10 9 8 7 6 5 4 3 2 1

To João Guterres
and all those "disappeared" in East Timor from 1975 to 1999,
and to their families and friends

CONTENTS

ACKNOWLEDGMENTS

No work of this size is produced in isolation. It is the result of knowledge, insights, ways of seeing the world, and experiences gained through interactions with countless individuals over many years in a variety of countries. For such reasons, along with limitations of my memory, I can acknowledge only a small number of those who merit recognition for their contributions.

First, I thank many friends in East Timor for sharing their stories and thoughts with me—often at great personal risk during the years of the Indonesian occupation—and providing insight into the myriad aspects of the war and occupation. These include: Eduardo Belo Soares, José Antonio Belo, Emanuel "Bere" Tilman and his family, Juana and Pedro Lebre and their children, and Gabriela and Constancio Pinto. My East Timorese colleagues at *La'o Hamutuk* — Sr. Maria Dias, Tomas Freitas, Fr. Jovito Rego de Jesus Araujo, Inês Martins, and Jesuina (Delly) Soares Cabral—were very helpful in this regard. Friends at the Sa'he Institute in Dili—especially Paulo Alves Cabral, Mateus Goncalves, Ajiza Magno, Nuno Rodrigues, and Aderito de Jesus Soares—and at neighboring Perkumpulan/Yayasan HAK—most notably Joachim Fonseca, Aniceto Guterres Lopes, Titi Irawati, Nug Katjasungkana, and José Luis de Oliveira—were also of great assistance.

Many individuals generously provided me with key information, articles and documents, and analysis at various points. They include Russell Anderson, Paul Barber, Francis Boyle, Carmel Budiardjo, Scott Burchill, Noam Chomsky, Roger Clark, James Dunn, Paulo Gorjao, Geoffrey Gunn, Bruno Kahn, Maire Leadbeater, William Liddle, the late Andrew McNaughtan,

John Miller, Karen Orenstein, Mark Purcell, Reynaldo Reyes, Geoffrey Robinson, Brad Simpson, Stephen Shalom, Kristin Sundell, Ron Takaki, and Max White. A special thanks goes to Arnold Kohen, not only for his help with this particular project but also for his efforts over the years to keep me honest.

Various friends and colleagues read chapters or portions of the book, and constructively critiqued and commented on them. For this I extend my deep appreciation to Mizue Aizeki, Anthony Arnove, Clare Campbell, Robin De-Lugan, Bill Hayes, Susana Kaiser, Ian Martin, Joshua Muldavin, Susan Shepler, and Fred Seavey.

John Agnew, Amy Gurowitz, and Himadeep Muppidi read and commented on the sections of chapter 1 relating to international relations. In doing so, they taught me much.

Friends also heroically waded through much or all of the manuscript, and made extensive comments and offered fabulous suggestions. To them I owe a great debt. They are John Chamberlin, Charles Scheiner, and Ben Terrall. Similarly two anonymous readers — part of the review process at Cornell University Press — read and constructively critiqued previous versions of what is now this book. In doing so, they undoubtedly helped to improve the accuracy, breadth, and overall quality of the final product. One person deserves special mention: John Roosa, my unofficial editor. A longtime student of, and solidarity activist with, Indonesia and East Timor, John read through at least the first two drafts of each chapter. Editorially, conceptually, and intellectually, he selflessly provided immeasurable assistance (and some great jokes) as I struggled with the book.

Roger Haydon at Cornell University Press has been a joy to work with. Flexible, responsible, easy-going, and full of good ideas and constructive criticisms, he has been a great editor during this process. A few other people at Cornell merit special mention: Karen Hwa, the production editor, and Susan Barnett, copy supervisor, both of whom were most helpful in the latter stages of the book's production. It was Karen Hwa who secured Rita Bernhard to copyedit the manuscript. Rita was an excellent choice as she did a fantastic job of improving the prose.

Much of the research and most of the writing of this book took place while I was at the University of California at Berkeley from 2000 to 2003. A Rockefeller Foundation Postdoctoral Fellowship in the Humanities brought me to the Institute of International Studies at Berkeley for the first year. In addition to thanking the Rockefeller Foundation, I send my deep appreciation to Michael Watts, the director of IIS during my stay, for his myriad forms of support, mentorship, and inspiration over my three years on campus. In addition, I thank Nancy Peluso, my faculty mentor during my second and third years at Berkeley as an S. V. Ciriacy-Wantrup Postdoctoral Fellow — not least for carefully reading an early draft of the entire manuscript and offering highly constructive comments. Nancy was always generous with her time, advice, and good humor. During my time at Berkeley, Eric Stover and Harvey Weinstein of the Human Rights Center were also of great help. For this I am most grateful.

Prior to Berkeley I spent many years at the University of California, Los Angeles. It was in the Department of Geography that I began to research and become politically involved in matters related to East Timor. I thank my two principal advisers during graduate school — Gerry Hale and Mark Ellis — for intellectual, academic, and political support that was instrumental in enabling me to work on East Timor in various ways, ways that sometimes did not conform to the requirements of the program.

Vassar College, my academic home since the fall of 2003, provided a hospitable place for me to put the final touches on the book. I thank Darcy Nelson, my very capable research assistant in 2003–4, for her careful reading of the manuscript, helpful comments, and various tasks well done, and Melissa Sepe, my assistant in 2004–5, for so capably reviewing the page proofs. I thank the college for providing me with a faculty research grant to purchase photos and to pay for production-related expenses. I also extend my appreciation to the faculty and staff of the Department of Geology and Geography for making me feel so at home and for providing multiple forms of support: Candice Cunningham, Mary Ann Cunningham, Harvey Flad, Brian Godfrey, Lois Horst, Brian McAdoo, Kirsten Menking, Alison Tumarkin-Deratzian, Jill Schneiderman, Meg Stewart, Jeff Walker, and Yu Zhou. I also thank Bill Hoynes, my faculty associate at Vassar, who has also been of generous assistance.

For more than a decade I have had the good fortune to work with many people in the East Timor solidarity movement in the United States, and also with individuals from across the world. My base for this activism during most of this time was Los Angeles. I greatly appreciate the chance to work with some great activists as part of the East Timor Action Network. They include Zara Benosa, Ravinder Bhatia, Brendan Crill, Bob Frang, Joann Lo, Peter Mao, Rudy Pisani, Byron Philhour, Mark Rhomberg, Lisa Rosen, Garrick Ruiz, Liz Ryder, Sarah Smith, Helmi Wattimena, Don White, and Juhani Yli-Vakkuri.

From July through September 1999 I worked with a terrific cast of individuals from across the world — ranging from Australia, Brazil, Canada, Indonesia, Japan, and Norway to the United Kingdom and the United States — as part of the International Federation for East Timor Observer Project for the United Nations–run vote. I had the pleasure and honor of getting to know and working closely with inspired and inspiring individuals — often under very trying conditions. I thank all of you—you know who you are—for your work and for putting up with me.

Special thanks also go to Carol Nevins, Mark Salzer, Pam Sexton, and Will Seaman for all sorts of things. And lastly to Mizue and Sayako for bringing so much joy and love into my life and helping to make the world a more beautiful place.

J. N.

Poughkeepsie, New York

ABBREVIATIONS

APEC	Asia Pacific Economic Cooperation
Apodeti	Timorese Popular Democratic Association
ASDT	Association of Timorese Social Democrats (later to become Fretilin)
AusAID	Australian Agency for International Development
CIA	Central Intelligence Agency (U.S.)
CivPols	civilian police officers
CNRT	National Council of Timorese Resistance
CRPs	Community Reconciliation Procedures
CAVR	Commission for Reception, Truth, and Reconciliation
DSD	Defence Signals Directorate (Australia)
ELSAM	Institute for Policy Research and Advocacy (Indonesia)
Falintil	Armed Forces of National Liberation of East Timor
Fretilin	Revolutionary Front for an Independent East Timor
ICJ	International Court of Justice
IDPs	internally displaced persons
IFET-OP	International Federation for East Timor Observer Project
IMF	International Monetary Fund
InterFET	International Force East Timor
IOM	International Organisation for Migration

JSMP   Judicial System Monitoring Project (East Timor)
NGO   nongovernmental organization
PKI   Indonesian Communist Party
SCU   Serious Crimes Unit
TNI   Indonesian military
TRC   Truth and Reconciliation Commission (South Africa)
KPS   Commission on Peace and Stability
UDT   Timorese Democratic Union
UNAMET   United Nations Mission in East Timor
UNCHR   United Nations Commission on Human Rights
UNCLOS   United Nations Convention on the Law of the Sea
UNDP   United Nations Development Programme
UNHCR   United Nations High Commission for Refugees
UNMISET United Nation Mission of Support in East Timor
UNTAET   United Nations Transitional Administration in East
                 Timor

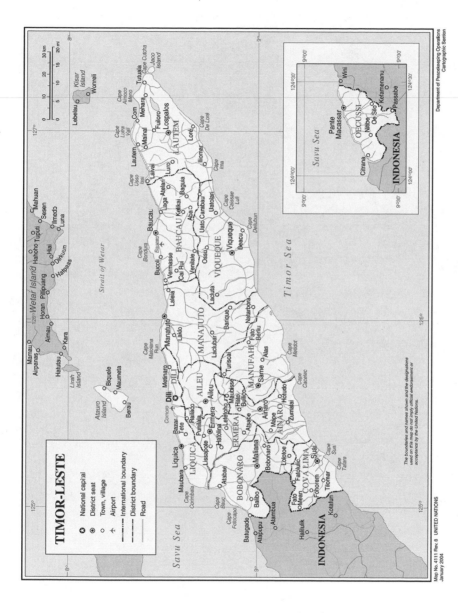

Map of East Timor. Timor-Leste no. 4111 Rev. 8. *Produced by and published with the permission of the United Nations Cartographic Section.*

Map of Southeast Asia. *From U.S. Central Intelligence Agency* Factbook.

A NOT-SO-DISTANT HORROR

Forgetting the extermination is part of the extermination itself.

    —JEAN BAUDRILLARD

The one who gives the blow forgets, the one who gets hurt remembers.

    —HAITIAN PROVERB

A Dili neighborhood in the aftermath of the September 1999 terror campaign. *Photo by the author.*

T he terror had been over for several months by the time I arrived. Most people were already well on the way to putting their lives back together. But the devastation was still all around, reminding me -- and, more important, those who had actually witnessed, experienced, and survived the horror — of what had transpired.

Homes and buildings reduced to piles of rubble. Whole residential areas flattened, reminiscent of Dresden or Tokyo following World War II. Charred remains of clothing and other personal belongings strewn amid the ruins. Pieces of deformed and blackened corrugated steel, formerly rooftops, thrown on the ground, among which stray dogs and an occasional pig foraged for scraps. These are some of the images imprinted on my mind from my first days there.

I remember sitting in a small, modest, open-air restaurant in the midst of the destruction. It was painted an unusual shade of blue, and its square, concrete floor was spotlessly clean. The restaurant was devoid of any decoration except for a national map hanging lopsided on the back wall. The other walls were only waist-high, and from which vertical beams arose that supported a thatched roof. Green plastic chairs surrounded the small number of tables, which held candles to help patrons read the sparse options on the one-page, photocopied menu.

It was a Saturday evening. I was the only customer. Although hot, a light breeze was coming off the ocean. As I waited for my food, a girl of thirteen and her mother entered. While her mother spoke with one of the workers, the girl sat down at my table. She had dark hair, piercing eyes, and a warm smile. Her name was Liliana.

Despite her youth, she was outgoing and self-assured. She spoke some words of English. Because she was learning it at school, she insisted on trying to speak with me in my mother tongue. Soon, however, we reverted to Indonesian. Liliana spoke slowly, clearly, and simply to ensure that I understood, given my elementary level in the language.

Liliana was a witness and a survivor, I soon learned. She had seen terror and death up close. And she had vivid memories.

She recalled seeing heads, severed from their bodies, rolling on the ground. Many hundreds of people were there with her, witnessing the horror. They were screaming and attempting to flee those who were attacking, stabbing, hacking, and beheading her compatriots. But the heads on the ground created a different sort of scene. It was "as if they were playing soccer," she recounted.

What was striking about this young girl was how she told the story — in a manner that made it seem as if the happening was something somewhat normal to her. She expressed quiet outrage at what she had witnessed, but for a thirteen-year-old—or, for that matter, any human being recounting such an experience—she seemed amazingly composed.

Her mother soon joined us. Probably in her mid-thirties, she told me that she had closed her eyes when the killings began, as she could not bear to watch, but that Liliana and her siblings had kept theirs opened. Yes, the experience had traumatized the children, she reported. "They didn't eat for a number of days afterward." Still today, according to her mother, Liliana sometimes has nightmares related to what she saw.

Less than two weeks after the terrifying scene described by Liliana took place, Seth Mydans of *The New York Times* quoted an international aid worker who employed the phrase "ground zero" to characterize the situation in Liliana's devastated homeland: East Timor.

Entering the territory on September 20, 1999, with an Australian-led international military force charged by the United Nations with restoring order, Mydans described the scene in the former Portuguese colony as the quiet after an annihilating storm: "There was no resistance—but no welcome—for the peacekeepers, who arrived with all the firepower and high technology of modern war. There is no peace to keep: East Timor's tiny capital is a dead city, burned, looted, evacuated."[1]

Maggie O'Kane of the London-based newspaper *The Guardian* also returned with the peacekeeping troops. Arriving at the airport in Dili, the territory's capital, she noted that the small terminal, "like the rest of this city, has been trashed. [It] is littered with rubbish, charred clothes and abandoned books."

Many of the perpetrators of the destruction and terror—members of the Indonesian military (TNI) and its paramilitary allies[2]—were still present, but there was little threat to the peacekeepers. As O'Kane wrote, their work "is already complete. They don't want any trouble. Why bother? East Timor has been sacked, looted and emptied."

The only way for the reporter to get from the airport to the city center was on a child's abandoned bicycle. "The cars were stolen long ago. The houses of the wealthy, with their wide white verandas along the airport road, have been torched with the same zeal with which the militias and army flattened the corrugated roofs of the poor. The schools, the hospital, the telephone exchange, the university: all have been destroyed. There's no water, electricity or telephone lines."

This in what was already one of the world's poorest places.

As for the people, the only ones "left here now are those too frightened to move. They are women with children, and they have become beach people.

"In Dili they are everywhere. They live in the open, under sheets on scorched grass. Along the sea shore the stench of excrement mingles with the smell of hundreds of bubbling pots of rice. Some camp in the grounds of the burned-out bishop's mansion. Inside, a statue of the Virgin Mary has the mark of a machete through her face."[3]

What Maggie O'Kane and Seth Mydans portrayed, however, was the result of only the final act of more than two decades of atrocities and destruction perpetrated by the Indonesian military in the former Portuguese colony. Indonesia invaded East Timor in December 1975 and formally annexed the territory less than six months later. Human rights organizations and the half-island's Catholic Church estimate that more than two hundred thousand East Timorese — about one-third of the 1975 population — lost their lives as a result of Indonesia's invasion, and the violence and deprivation associated with its almost twenty-four-year occupation,[4] an outcome that many scholars have characterized as genocidal in nature.[5]

As in New York City in September 2001, so in East Timor many hundreds perished in September 1999 due to acts of horrific terror. While the attacks in New York occurred within a twenty-minute span, most of the violence in East Timor took place over approximately three weeks after the population voted overwhelmingly in a U.N.-run ballot in favor of independence from Indonesia. In its aftermath, the Indonesian military and its paramilitary (or militia) proxies destroyed about 70 percent of the country's buildings and infrastructure, raped untold numbers of women and girls, and massacred an estimated 1,000 people. These military forces also displaced hundreds of thousands within East Timor, and forcibly deported and compelled to flee to Indonesia about 250,000 people — including Liliana and her family.[6]

The climax of the terror was preceded by a concerted and successful effort to drive out almost all international media and foreign observers, a campaign that ultimately succeeded in forcing the United Nations Mission in East Timor (UNAMET) to abandon the territory as well.

Often one cannot know with full certainty why those who commit mass atrocities do what they do. They rarely offer candid and extensive explanations for their crimes. Instead, they tend to say nothing, deny their guilt or argue that their accusers exaggerate or lie, or justify their horrific acts by invoking self-defense or some sort of high-minded responsibility.[7] One is therefore forced to look behind official rhetoric — or silence — for the answers, an enterprise that typically involves a certain amount of educated guesswork.

In the case of East Timor it is likely that the killings, rapes, and destruction were intended as an example, a message sent to restless regions within Indonesia's sprawling archipelago and to that country's dynamic pro-democracy, workers' rights, and human rights movements that challenging the authority of the military would exact a very high cost. For the people of East Timor, these acts of terror were intended largely as a parting blow, a punishment against a population that had the audacity to vote for independence from its brutal colonial overseers. The scorched-earth nature of the TNI-militia rampage made it clear that the Indonesian military had no intention of staying in the territory. There was also a message for international consumption: the massive destruction and the "flight" of much of the population to West Timor was intended to give substance to the lie that most East Timorese wanted to remain part of Indonesia, and that the U.N.-run ballot had been a farce.

●

"If you want independence, six months from now you will be eating rocks." These are the translated words of one of the first of many pieces of Indonesian-language graffiti that I saw staining Dili's ruins as I walked through the flattened neighborhoods of the East Timorese capital. I had returned in May 2000 to the former Portuguese colony for the first time since having fled the territory on September 4, 1999.

With a heavy heart mixed with a sense both of worry and relief, I — along with two other Westerners — had made my way overland to Indonesian West Timor as the killing and destruction began. On the edge of Dili, militia members armed with automatic weapons checked our papers to ensure that we had official permission to leave overland and inspected our vehicle to make certain that no East Timorese without authorization from the TNI or militia were traveling with us. Indonesian police officers were present at the roadblock, and uniformed soldiers in trucks passed by, belying the claim that the paramilitaries were independent of Indonesia's security apparatus. We were part of a convoy of hundreds of vehicles containing mostly fleeing Indonesian civil servants and their families, several hours after United Nations Secretary-General Kofi Annan had announced the result of the U.N.-run "popular consultation." As we drove along the coast-hugging road toward the boundary with West Timor, through the lush, picturesque countryside, we saw homes burning in the distance. Passing through roadblocks on the outskirts of villages, I furtively looked in the eyes of bewildered East Timorese standing on the roadside, ashamed of my ability to leave and afraid of what might happen to them.

Undoubtedly they, too, feared what was to come, what I knew — in an intellectual sense — was a real possibility but did not feel in my heart would actually happen. It was not that I was unaware of what the Indonesian military was capable of doing: I had long known about the tragic history of the territory and the bloody record of the TNI and the political leadership in Jakarta. Moreover, I had already lost East Timorese friends and acquaintances to the TNI's brutality. And I was cognizant of the frequent warnings made by Indonesian authorities, military leaders, and militia spokespersons. Throughout the months and weeks preceding the vote of August 30, 1999, not-so-thinly-veiled threats were issued, in the form of predictions as well as explicit warnings that blood would flow if continued "integration" were to lose at the ballot box.

Nevertheless I guessed that the worst the Indonesian military and its militia proxies would do in the aftermath of the pro-independence vote would be to burn and kill at the margins — indeed, they had already started doing so in the days leading up to my departure. But it was unlikely that the TNI terror campaign would go much beyond that, or so I thought. After all, I reasoned, what would the Indonesian military have to gain by destroying the territory and engaging in a killing spree? Moreover, there was no way that the international community, given the presence of a United Nations mission in the territory, would allow the Indonesians to go *too* far, so I assumed, or perhaps hoped.

In retrospect, the problem was that I was thinking rationally or, should I say, from a perspective I deemed rational. My intellectual and ideological blinders as well as conflicting and confusing developments on the ground — in addition to the human difficulty of imagining someone in your presence actually carrying out horrific acts — prevented me from seeing what was to come. And I was not alone. Numerous international observers and many East Timorese felt the same way. But most East Timorese and many internationals also knew that they had to assume the worst and could not count on the promises of the United Nations to stay with them following the vote and, implicitly, to protect them. The failure to heed such voices exacted a terrible cost.

Indonesia's scorched-earth campaign was unprecedented in terms of its degree of destruction in the context of departing colonial powers in the twentieth century. What made such violence all the more outrageous — at least in international eyes — was that it occurred in the presence of a U.N. mission charged with organizing and running the August 30, 1999, plebiscite that allowed the people of East Timor to express their wishes regarding their political-territorial status. Furthermore, the Indonesian government had pledged to maintain peace and security as part of the international accord that led to the vote. On the face of it — given the illegal nature of Indonesia's very presence and the military's horrific record in the territory — the accord was a pact with the devil and, in hindsight, a fatal one. But that was the best deal the "international community" could secure, or so its spokespersons frequently told us.

●

The purveyors of what we commonly see as terror lack logic — their most vociferous critics often tell us. They are crazy, beyond reason. But such an analysis — especially when applied to gross violence carried out by organized groups of people as opposed to deranged individuals — is facile, an outgrowth of a refusal to try to truly understand terror. Sometimes it becomes a thinly disguised ploy to avoid looking at ourselves and the status quo, and how our own actions and society might have contributed — indirectly or directly — to the horrific acts and events. It is also often a result of various notions of racial, ethnic, or cultural superiority that sees "our" way of life, behavior, and acts of violence that we perpetrate as far better than "theirs" — "they" being those who engage in violence of which the powerful do not approve. And many times such a perspective flows from a narrow conception of the acts that constitute mass violence, as well as of when such violence is legitimate and acceptable, and when it is not.

Collective terror almost always has a logic, but it is precisely because we see it as terror (as opposed to just simple, everyday violence), and thus so extraordinary, that we cannot understand it through conventional lenses. And it is also for this reason why terror is so difficult for us to anticipate — even when warnings of the pending horror are all around us.

We have difficulty understanding mass violence because, among other reasons, it seems so foreign to and distant from our own reality. However, we are often not as unconnected as we might think to the horrific images from seemingly remote corners of the earth that we watch on our television screens — especially if we live in relatively powerful and affluent countries. In a world of ties that transcend the boundaries drawn on maps, terror does not emerge in a global vacuum.

People in the United States and others were reminded of this truth with the attacks on the World Trade Center on September 11, 2001. The U.S. Central Intelligence Agency (CIA) armed and provided other various forms of support to the *mujahadin,* which Osama bin Laden later joined, beginning in 1979 and during the 1980s, as part of its proxy war in Afghanistan against the Soviet Union. In 1996 Washington gave a behind-the-scenes endorsement to the Taliban's seizure of power, going so far as to urge Pakistan and Saudi Arabia to support the group for reasons of regional "stability" and access to the oil riches of Central Asia.[8] To state this is not to suggest that Washington is responsible for the 9/11 terror attacks. The responsibility rests squarely with those who planned them and carried them out. Yet it does raise important issues that should force Washington and the U.S. public to reconsider U.S. policy and practice abroad.

Such an observation does not at all change the nature of what happened in New York City on that day in September. By almost anyone's definition, what occurred were crimes against humanity. And so were the events in East Timor two years earlier — to say nothing of the horrors that took place there in the previous twenty-four or so years. Few commentators in the world's most powerful countries, however, treat them in a manner that gives them anything approaching comparable weight.

●

Drawing comparisons between cases of gross human suffering and crimes against humanity—such as those embodied by the respective ground zeros of New York and Liliana's East Timor—is a tricky enterprise, one that often invites the accusation that one is showing insufficient respect for those who died and suffered during a horror deemed by others to be worse, or to be the pinnacle of horrors. Thus for many, for example, any comparison with the Nazi-perpetrated Holocaust is a sacrilege, a denial of the uniquely evil nature of that mass slaughter. But to make such an argument, regardless of intentions, is to elevate one set of atrocities above all others, to privilege the profound suffering of one group while relegating that of others to (at best) a second-class status, and, as such, to engage in a highly problematic venture—morally and politically. As historian Peter Novick argues about the Nazi-made genocide in his much acclaimed book, *The Holocaust in American Life,*

> Insistence on its uniqueness (or denial of its uniqueness) is an intellectually empty enterprise for reasons having nothing to do with the Holocaust itself and everything to do with "uniqueness." A moment's reflection makes clear that the notion of uniqueness is quite vacuous. Every historical event, including the Holocaust, in some ways resembles events to which it might be compared and differs from them in some ways. These resemblances and differences are a perfectly proper subject for discussion. But to single out those aspects of the Holocaust that were distinctive (there certainly were such), and to ignore those aspects that it shares with other atrocities, and on the basis of this gerrymandering to declare the Holocaust unique—like the claim that it is singularly incomprehensible or unrepresentable—is, in practice, deeply offensive. What else can all of this possibly mean except "your catastrophe, unlike ours, is ordinary; unlike ours is comprehensible; unlike ours is representable."[9]

Hence an approach to mass killings that highlights the unique characteristics of a specific set of events is not inherently mutually exclusive to an approach that looks for similarities with other cases of slaughter. They are equally valid and complementary.[10] Indeed, if we assume that a horror is unique, it is not possible to draw any lessons, to learn anything that we might apply to other times, places, and contexts. Of course, given the highly extreme nature of the immediate causes of ground zero–like atrocities, we must be careful not to exaggerate the relevance of such lessons to our everyday lives. But to the extent that what we learn enables us to better understand our own roles, and the roles of institutions and agents that we are in a position to influence, in producing gross crimes, these lessons empower us to reduce the possibility of similar violence reoccurring.

Episodes of mass killings, even when very different, can also be related in a broader sense. Western imperialism and the associated slaughter of "inferior races" in the nineteenth and early twentieth centuries, for example, laid the groundwork for Hitler's genocide of millions of Jews and the mass extermination of Roma (or Gypsies) and others deemed as lesser or undesirable peoples in Europe. "European world expansion, accompanied as it was by a shameless defense of extermination," according to Sven Lindqvist, "created habits of thought and political precedents that made way for new outrages."[11]

The Holocaust is undoubtedly the most known and memorialized of these "new outrages." And despite the invocation of "never again," the myriad horrors of the post–World War II world remind us that "never again" is, at best, wishful thinking (if not merely an empty slogan) rather than a promise of resolve.

Mass killings also differ in terms of what we know about them. And what we do not know is often just as important as what we do. What we remember and forget, what we learn and do not learn, and what we hear and do not hear say a lot about who we are and where we are going. As Adam Hochschild observed in his outstanding chronicle of Belgium's appalling crimes in its colony of the Congo, "The world we live in—its divisions and conflicts, its widening gap between rich and poor, its seemingly inexplicable outbursts of violence—is shaped far less by what we celebrate and mythologize [or mourn, for that matter] than by the painful events we try to forget."[12] In the case of September 11, 2001, it has undoubtedly become—like Imperial Japan's attack on Pearl Harbor on December 7, 1941—a "date which will live in infamy" in the collective U.S. memory. And outside the United States church bells now toll, and many observe moments of silence and attend memorial events in cities and towns in various parts of the world on September 11.

As for the "painful events we try to forget" or those we never even learned about, the list of horrors is long. The modern world that Christopher Columbus's first voyage to the Americas helped bring about, the renowned intellectual Eqbal Ahmad once observed, "is a time of extraordinary unrecorded holocausts."[13] How many of us, for instance, are familiar with the deaths of as many as ten million in the Belgian-controlled Congo in the late nineteenth and early twentieth centuries? How many of us have even heard of Australia's extermination of the indigenous population of Tasmania?[14]

But even if the slaughter is known and recorded, do we confront or even commemorate it? Who among us, after all, mourns the victims of the 1994 genocide in Rwanda that saw close to one million killed in roughly one hundred days?[15] And how many of us memorialize the conquest-related deaths of tens of millions of native peoples in the United States and throughout the Americas?[16]

One might say, of course, that there have been too many tragedies and gross crimes for us to know all of them and pay tribute to those fallen. And that would be true. But numerical challenges do not explain why we know about and commemorate one group of victims and not another.

And then there are those large death tolls that we do not see as the outcome of violence — at least as commonly conceived — but as the outcomes of normal, albeit unfortunate, everyday components and practices of the contemporary world. Almost eleven million children across the globe die every year, for example, from malnutrition and disease — phenomena that are preventable given the world's abundant resources but that are also inevitable given the unequal distribution of and access to these resources.[17] In this regard, these deaths are not accidents or even surprises. While the deaths of specific children in this overwhelming number are not predictable, the deaths as a collectivity are. They are deaths that are destined to occur as a result of structures and actions of violence not viewed as such. It is for such reasons that, in thinking about violence, we should focus on outcomes and consequences — especially those that are foreseeable — rather than concern ourselves with means. If we do this, we realize that a death caused by a bullet is no more morally reprehensible than one caused by practices and social structures that predictably result in otherwise avoidable hunger-induced fatalities.[18]

●

Why do we pay greater heed to some atrocities and not others? The most important reason is perhaps perceived social distance — how closely one identifies with a particular group of people or a particular place. In the case of ground zero in New York, for example, it is understandable that people in the United States know so much about the event and memorialize the deaths so profoundly. Among other reasons, involved in the devastating attack were key symbols of U.S. power in the country's most populous city, with almost three thousand killed in the span of less than two terrifying hours — the time between the first attack and the collapse of the second World Trade Center tower. And many perceive the victims as part of an "imagined community"[19] — the United States — with which they strongly identify, and can envision that they themselves could easily have been in the same predicament as those who suffered. In addition, the spectacular nature of the attacks invites, if not demands, intense attention.

For similar reasons — along with the awesome power and reach of U.S. corporate-owned media to shape the images and stories received by people across the globe — it makes sense that downtown Manhattan, rather than East Timor, has become, for so many throughout the world, the ultimate embodiment of ground zero — defined here as a geographical location of extreme violence, devastation, and human suffering. Moreover, the United States is the world's most powerful and influential country, whereas East Timor is one of the most marginal. Most people outside the United States "know" the world's sole superpower. As for "knowing" East Timor, the vast majority of us are fortunate if we can find it on a world map.

Whose suffering becomes newsworthy is thus not simply a matter of geographic proximity but one of power and social distance, and the ability to make what otherwise might be very remote seem close or to make what is actually relatively nearby seem far away. Many of us — including those who have few if any ties to Britain — might know a lot more about Princess Diana's death, for example, than we know about, say, the death of someone who lives one street away. And it is those who wield the most power who are best positioned to bridge the social distances that separate us or to obfuscate the ties that connect us, to determine what is important and what is not, to shape what we know and what we do not know.

Because of the power of technology and the geographic reach of our actions, we are able to operate over great distances but often with little actual interface with those affected by what we do. In the most extreme cases, we can seemingly act by remote control. We can buy and sell goods through the Internet, without directly interacting with a human being in any sensory manner, for example, and we can shoot missiles at points on computer screens and, in the process, kill unseen, faraway enemies. More indirectly, we can act through transnational structures and relationships to shape livelihoods across the world. Decisions made in corporate boardrooms or on the floors of commodity exchanges in places such as London and New York, for instance, significantly affect the living conditions of coffee farmers in Nicaragua, Rwanda, and Vietnam. But despite the social proximity manifested by this relationship, ideology — one aided by the political geography of a world divided into supposedly distinct nation-states and a complex set of social relations that helps to obfuscate cause and effect — allows those of us who wield relatively large amounts of power to deny or understate our responsibility for the plight of those on the receiving end of our actions. This reflects a paradox of the modern world: modernity brings people around the world closer together while at the same time increasing our ability to deny our responsibility for the effects we have on others — especially those geographically distant. Modernity thus maintains an illusion of social distance that, in reality, it is helping to erase.

The fact is, whether we recognize it or not, our lives influence those who live far from us — and do so increasingly. But because of the hidden nature of our ties and the geographical distance, we know little about these anonymous, invisible "relatives."

After all, who makes the sneakers we wear, produces the coffee we drink, assembles the radio we listen to? Where do they live? What are their wages and standard of living? Typically we do not know the answers to these questions, even though these people are our neighbors in this increasingly globalized world, people to whom we are intensely tied despite our not knowing who they are. Similarly East Timor's ground zero — and the violence that created it and terrorized Liliana and her family — may seem very distant from us but, in truth, it is not; it is actually quite close. And it is primarily to "us" — those who live in the relatively wealthy, powerful countries of the "West," such as the United States, Japan, Australia, the United Kingdom, Canada, and France — that I address this book.

We live close to ground zero in East Timor for it was our actions — or, more precisely, those of our governments — that helped to make it. But rarely do we hear of their roles — whether in the pronouncements of politicians or government officials, in journalistic accounts, or in academic works. And on the infrequent occasion that such issues are raised, typically they are grossly understated or misrepresented. Thus the role of powerful foreign governments in East Timor's suffering is presented in its worst light as one in which they were bad Samaritans, bystanders to a horror who did nothing.[20] But, at best, this is a mistaken view. Washington, London, Ottawa, Canberra, Tokyo, and others were not mere bystanders; they were actively complicit in Jakarta's crimes. Indeed, without their help, Indonesia's military could not have accomplished its horrendous deeds.

Erasing this history of complicity — like forgetting a mass killing itself — is a part of the crime, as it facilitates impunity for those culpable of bringing about gross levels of human suffering while undermining efforts to ensure restitution for the victimized population. Such erasure takes many forms. It is largely one of silence, but when challenged and, on rare occasion, compelled to respond, those responsible employ a whole variety of tactics to justify their actions or to deny the charges. Like the direct perpetrators, the complicit parties argue that their accusers exaggerate, that they lack an understanding of the context in which the perpetrators undertook their actions, or that it does no good to focus on the past as doing so might undermine the present and the future. And sometimes they attack their accusers, contending that they have a hidden and implicitly nefarious agenda.

Social proximity — or, more important, a perception of such proximity — helps to explain why some know so much about and react especially intensely to one set of crimes and are relatively unconcerned about another with comparable outcomes. But it does not explain why the world as a whole — especially those populations and institutions that disproportionately benefit from and shape the global environment in which we live — remembers and has reacted to the tragedies of New York and East Timor in such different fashions.

This is a function of power, of who exerts it and to what ends. Power relations are never stagnant. That said, given the persistent, growing, and profound socioeconomic inequalities that plague the world, there is gross disparity in terms of who wields effective power on the global stage. And those who exercise such power usually endeavor to maintain or enhance this disparity. In doing so, the powerful help to define what is important and what is not, and what is possible and pragmatic.[21] Hence they largely determine which issues become problems in need of radical global redress. And what has so far proven to be not terribly important in the global hierarchy is remembering fully what happened in East Timor and why, and, on that basis, holding those responsible accountable for that country's plight.

Nevertheless ground zero in East Timor should matter just as much as any other. Underlying this assertion is a normative position that we have a moral (as well as political) obligation to remember horrors that have taken place—especially those which our involvement has helped bring about—and to act accordingly in a manner informed by an ethic of justice.[22] For if we assume that all human lives are equally worthy and that international law is universal, should we not be equally concerned with and knowledgeable about the devastation of Liliana's homeland and the crimes against humanity committed there as we are about New York City's ground zero? And to the extent that we are not as troubled and far less well-informed, what does that say about our intellectual and political cultures and the world as a whole?

●

This book is about connections and how we remember, represent, and account for them, connections that transcend the usual temporal, spatial, and social categories and entities that make up the world and our efforts to understand it. The late anthropologist Eric Wolf helped us to appreciate that the history of the world has always been one of connections, a totality of interrelated processes. We tend to disassemble this totality when seeking to understand specific developments in space and time. Unless we situate that which we isolate back into the disassembled whole, our understanding is significantly less than it otherwise can be. Indeed, failure to do so leads to a falsification of reality and to the creation of misleading inferences.[23]

That said, all inquiries into and representations of reality are partial. Only reality itself, and all that comprises it, represents a whole. Thus, for all sorts of reasons—and not least our own intellectual limitations—it is not possible to comprehend and explain fully all the myriad bundles of relationships that bring about any one particular phenomenon. But it is not simply the impossibility of the task that explains how and why one frames an inquiry or explanation, and what information and perspectives one includes or excludes, emphasizes or downplays. Nor is such an endeavor merely an intellectual exercise; rather, it is typically a profoundly political one—even if one does not consciously conceive of it as such—in that the process of picking and choosing reflects and reproduces certain biases, worldviews, and interests.[24] Stating this is not to reduce all representations to bias and the merely subjective. Although subjective and biased they are, that does not mean that representations are necessarily dishonest. They are, however, unavoidably partial. The question is, what do they include and leave out, why, and to what effect?[25]

Although striving to be scrupulously honest, this book, too, is biased and partial, and its boundaries are informed by politics: while it discusses Liliana's experiences and memories and those of her neighbors within East Timor, its primary goal is to understand the role of her more distant neighbors in the international community, and thus that is its focus. It is a story about the making of Liliana's ground zero and, more specifically, our participation in it. It is a tale of terror, death, betrayal, hypocrisy, and simple yet extraordinary survival in a world of cynical power relations. It shows us what we remember, what we forget, and why and how our memory is selective, and, on that basis, what we do in response.

Thus the book illustrates the process by which we draw social, historical, and geographical boundaries around the stories we tell ourselves, boundaries that help mask our role in the making of Liliana's nightmares. This process has profound implications for our own countries and, given our collective power to influence that which takes place beyond our national boundaries, for Liliana and her compatriots, and the world as a whole.

●

The description and explanation of mass violence have long been of interest to academics in various fields. Many have developed theories of, or generalized explanations for, collective violence in their efforts to understand the conditions under which bloody conflict or mass killings take place, and what motivates individuals and groups to participate.[26]

This book does not seek to provide a generalized explanation for collective violence nor even to expound on why the Indonesian military carried out the atrocities it did in East Timor — beyond the conventional understanding. Instead, my effort is to address the question "Who?" — as in who (beyond the Indonesian military and the political leadership in Jakarta) is responsible for the terror experienced by the East Timorese people. This, in turn, will contribute to the question "Why?" — as well as "How?" — by helping to illustrate the ways that various countries supported Indonesia's crimes, why they did so, and how their support enabled the Indonesian military to carry out its actions. In so doing the book contributes to a framework for analyzing international conflict.

Within universities, most markedly in the United States and Britain, explanations emanating from within political science — variants of the realist and liberal schools of thought especially—dominated analyses of international relations and interstate conflict for many decades. These perspectives no longer enjoy their relatively unchallenged positions in the academy. Nevertheless their underlying assumptions are still pervasive among political elites outside university walls, as evidenced by the numerous accounts of Indonesia's war with East Timor by mainstream journalists, pundits, and politicians.[27]

Although Indonesia's invasion and occupation of East Timor are, in many ways, archetypal manifestations of an "old war" of conquest,[28] one that conventional approaches to international affairs are well equipped to explain, the resulting accounts typically obscure more than they elucidate as they ignore or downplay international complicity. To the extent that they discuss the support afforded by various countries to Indonesia's crimes, they usually do so in realist terms, arguing that lucrative relations with Indonesia left these countries little choice but to acquiesce to Jakarta lest they hurt their respective "national interests."[29] In making such an argument, analysts mistakenly present states as internally unified and as representing some homogeneous interest group (i.e., "the nation") rather than a variety of interest groups, some of which are in a position to influence foreign policy far more than others. At the same time they do not appreciate the significance of the international complicity, especially that of the West, which was crucial in facilitating Jakarta's invasion and occupation. Nor do they exhibit an understanding that such complicity was part of a larger complex of efforts aimed at maintaining and enhancing Western dominance and weakening the emerging "Third World."

This analytical poverty is in no small part the result of their tendency to assume that Western countries are relatively high-minded and righteous in their international conduct—a position seemingly supported by the fact that none of the wealthy liberal democracies has engaged in armed conflict with one another in the post–World War II era (and this way of being, many argue, is an extension of their relatively benign conduct toward their own populations).[30]

What this line of argument ignores, however, is that many of these very same countries—in addition to having huge militaries that help to further the sense of insecurity of would-be adversaries and to being collectively responsible for the vast bulk of the international trade in weaponry—have directly and indirectly perpetrated acts of gross violence in numerous instances. These have been largely against far less powerful and relatively poor countries (some of which have been political democracies) in an effort to protect and maintain a narrowly defined set of "national interests."[31] East Timor—as part of a larger, post–World War II endeavor to limit the influence and independence of the Third World—is only one of the more tragic examples of such conduct.[32]

This deficient analysis of collective violence is also a manifestation of a tendency not to pay sufficient attention to extraterritorial factors in trying to explicate interstate relations. Like much of international relations theory, most accounts of the horrors experienced by East Timor are "territorially trapped," because they implicitly assume that national territorial states (i.e., countries) are synonymous with society or with the social relations that shape and reflect the foreign policies and practices of any particular national political entity.[33] Thus they typically do not give adequate weight to the role of social actors and institutions outside the countries directly involved in an interstate conflict in facilitating, and aiding and abetting or allowing it to unfold or both.

States, by interacting with other states, help to build one another to varying degrees—despite their supposedly sovereign nature. And when these interactions involve states whose levels of power differ dramatically, the practices of relatively strong states have the effect of shaping, to a disproportionate degree, the relatively weak states and thus the former are at least partially, and often significantly, responsible for the latter's internal conditions and practices. As a result, some states are far more "sovereign" than others.

What today is termed "globalization"—the making of international and transnational relations, and the global flows of finance, weaponry, investment capital, people, and other social phenomena—embodies much of what is missing in the analysis of mass violence. The construction of the modern world has long been a global endeavor—albeit one that has involved and affected places and peoples in profoundly unequal ways. The world is not simply the sum of its nominally independent parts but rather the outgrowth of historically constructed international and transnational relationships. Hence there is a systemic aspect to the international order, which defies the division of the world into discrete territories defined by sharp boundaries and which compels us to attempt to comprehend how geographic areas mutually constitute one another.[34] Thus, for example, it is folly to try to understand the existence of spatial concentrations of poverty—or wealth, for that matter—by analyzing factors only contained within those particular areas, just as it would be wrong to limit such an inquiry to a narrow time frame that ignored history. Poverty and wealth are the outcomes of highly complex processes that transcend narrow notions of history and geography.[35] Similarly it is simplistic to draw sharp distinctions between countries or regions at war and those at peace, especially when the latter are intimately involved in numerous ways in supporting direct protagonists in an armed conflict. The geography of conflict is far more complicated than what such distinctions suggest.

In terms of the modern world map, the most obvious manifestation of globalization was in the making of territorial empires. Just as these empires reflected and produced international political and economic relationships—

ones frequently predicated on the use of direct force—the world order that has grown out of formal empires and that exists today reflects and replicates such relationships in various ways. States do not simply project power onto the international stage from within their territories. They also do so through international institutions and mechanisms, and allied actors abroad. At the same time transnational forces also deploy such power.[36]

As a result of their collective political, economic, and military strength, powerful states are generally far more active and influential internationally than relatively weak states. Their state power is "internationalized."[37] The most important manifestation of this internationalization of state power is a Western bloc—an entity implicitly or explicitly defined by many analysts as one centered on the states of Western Europe, Australia, New Zealand, Canada, the United States, and Japan.[38] Because the states that comprise this bloc collectively dominate global affairs, they are involved to varying degrees in a disproportionate number of the cases of war and mass violence through-out the world. Thus the effect of underplaying international and transnational factors in the making of war and mass violence, of failing to bring to light "behind-the-scenes" actors, and, in the process, obfuscating responsibility over time and space, is to bolster a global status quo that disproportionately reflects Western interests.

A political-economy approach to international relations, along with an appreciation for the complexity of territorial spaces, helps to overcome the shortcomings of mainstream perspectives on international conflict. The political-economy approach focuses on relationships of power between economic and political actors and institutions on multiple geographical levels. Within states, even those commonly seen as democracies, political-economy concentrates on power relations between interest groups and institutions—ones typically allied (directly or indirectly) with the economically powerful—and analyzes how certain actors dominate societies and transform narrow agendas that largely serve the interests of small groups into national agendas. Between states, it emphasizes material inequality, the social construction of this disparity across time and geographic space, and its maintenance through various international mechanisms—largely dominated by a handful of countries such as the United States, Japan, and those of Western Europe. Thus, rather than seeing countries as unified rational actors carrying out foreign policies for reasons of national interest, those employing a political-economy approach focus on how elite groups shape national agendas to a degree disproportionate to their numbers and project national power onto the world stage—in part by working through international and transnational mechanisms, military, political, and economic elites, and institutions abroad.[39] These expressions of national power mainly serve interests below and beyond the level of the nation-state rather than those of the national populaces in whose names the policies are carried out.[40] Imperialism, or the making and maintenance of international relationships based on domination and subordination of people and places, is the concrete expression of such efforts. As was forcefully demonstrated by the terror inflicted on East Timor, imperialism is often a team effort, one involving a number of states, agents, and institutions in various countries playing different roles in a common project.[41] Thus it is not only states that engage in war making. So, too, do blocs, regions, and various types of international and transnational alliances that defy traditional spatial configurations.

The relationship between those who are the principal protagonists in such a project and those who play a supporting role is frequently complex. Powerful countries, in addition to having potent allies that generally share their worldviews and goals, often have less influential "client states" that serve their interests.[42] Although, in many ways, the Indonesia that invaded and occupied East Timor was a client state of the West — and especially of the United States — the term "client state" implies a master-puppet relationship that probably obfuscates at least as much as it clarifies the complex nature of the ties between Washington (and its powerful allies) and Jakarta. Whereas the Indonesia ruled by Suharto (from the mid-1960s until May 1998) undoubtedly served the interests of Washington in myriad ways, Jakarta's interests and those of Washington, although significantly overlapping, were never simply one and the same. Thus Washington and its allies did not simply dictate Jakarta's actions; the relationship was far more nuanced. That said, Washington, Tokyo, London, and Canberra (among others) — especially in 1975 — did indeed wield considerable influence over Jakarta. This was particularly true in international security and military matters given Indonesia's heavy reliance on its Western partners for military equipment, in addition to development assistance, economic investment, trade preferences, and the like. Regarding matters Jakarta perceived and could justifiably construe as strictly national prerogatives, or those tied more deeply to the well-being of Indonesian society as a whole or to powerful segments of the population or to both — for example, economic liberalization — Jakarta has been able to exercise a greater deal of sovereignty.

In the case of East Timor, the initiative and decision to invade the then Portuguese colony was Jakarta's. Yet, given the unequal power relations between Jakarta and its potent patrons, the Indonesian regime felt compelled to consult some of them about the wisdom of its intentions and to seek permission from the United States to carry out its plan. Thus Indonesia was not following the direct bidding of others in attacking East Timor. Nevertheless militarily powerful or wealthy countries like Japan, the United States, Australia, and Britain were willing to acquiesce to Indonesia's designs on its tiny neighbor and support its war of conquest because—in significant part—Jakarta's efforts to "stabilize" the region by annexing East Timor happened to dovetail with their own geo-strategic agendas. As these same countries wielded disproportionate influence within the so-called international community, their complicity—which continued until the bitter end in September 1999—not only provided many of the necessary resources and space for Indonesia to enact its crimes with impunity but also circumscribed the ability of the United Nations to bring about a peaceful and just resolution of the conflict.

Although the overt violence of the Indonesian military—and, by extension, that of its patrons—has ended, many injustices associated with the invasion and occupation of East Timor endure. If, as Carl von Clausewitz once observed, war is the continuation of politics by other means, the obverse is true as well: politics can be—among other things—the continuation of war by other means. What primarily determines whether the post-conflict politics are warlike is the extent to which the parties responsible for wrongdoing are held accountable for their actions and the resulting injustices redressed. And whether accountability takes place is informed in large part by how various parties perceive and represent the conflict.

As with any experience or event, the terror that transpired in East Timor can be represented in numerous ways. While just depictions of the experiences of those victimized by the war cannot take away their pain, such descriptions can validate and give moral weight to their deeply felt recollections. Similarly, the nature of the portrayals of the roles played by those responsible for the suffering has important implications for how others view them and how they perceive themselves. For these reasons, struggles over representations of the past are inherently tied into struggles over identity, that of individuals and, more important, militaries, national governments, and the citizenries they represent, political leaders and parties, as well as other entities, depending on the nature of the events in question.

Many use the term "collective memory" to characterize group consciousness of the past; others use the terms "popular memory" or "social memory."[43] Such collective memories are often composed of simplified, emotionally and politically charged depictions that cast those they represent as either inherently good or as tragic members of a victimized population. Thus collective memories are often selective and inaccurate, but they are not necessarily so. Indeed, such memories can also be highly exact. While collective memory, of course, is not the same as history, the two are not unrelated: one can, and often does, inform the other. That said, history, as the purview of scholars, is, at least in terms of what they profess, open to rigorous scrutiny, whereas collective memory—as the repository of a group's identity—is typically not amenable to examination. Nevertheless collective memory is hardly stagnant. As present-day concerns inform group memories, these memories evolve to meet current needs, and are subject to challenges or manipulation or both by individuals and groups. At the same time the collectivities represented by these memories are never as monolithic, unified, and homogeneous as the actors dominating or championing them like to pretend. Hence struggles over memories from within particular groups and outside these groups can and often do inform the shape and content of popular recollections of tragic pasts. But given the vested interests of those committed to particular memories and the unequal power relations between dominant and subordinate groups, effectively challenging established, hegemonic memories is a tall task.[44]

Just as international power relations shaped the parameters within which the United Nations and the Indonesian military were able to act, so do they help construct our collective memories—memories bounded historically, socially, and geographically—of what transpired in East Timor, and why. Memories thus have significant power to influence what we "know" and do not know, what and whom we think is good and bad, and, on that basis, how we live our lives. In this manner, these "memories of power" both shape and reflect efforts to realize justice and accountability in the aftermath of gross atrocities. And just as imperialism provided the favorable international environment for Indonesia's crimes in East Timor to take place, imperial power profoundly informs the biases, content, and effectiveness of international law and its associated mechanisms, and thus efforts to ensure justice for the horror experienced by the East Timorese people. A dialectical relationship therefore exists between (unequal) power relations, international law and its associated institutions, mass violence, and collective memories—subjects I examine in the context of East Timor's specific experience in the chapters that follow.

More concretely I provide an overview of East Timor's history, especially from 1975 to 1999, the years of the Indonesian invasion and occupation, focusing on the final year when the U.N.-run vote took place and when the TNI and its allies created "ground zero." In so doing, I examine the context and the actors that helped to make the vote possible as well as the TNI's final wave of terror. I also offer an account of the role of the "international community" throughout the time of Indonesia's aggression toward East Timor, and discuss how and why almost all the world's most powerful countries aided, abetted, or facilitated the crimes of Indonesia's military and political establishment. Finally, I look at how we remember, forget, and frame what transpired in East Timor and responsibility for those events, as well as its implications for matters of justice, accountability, and international relations.

POR PORTUGAL

CONTRA O INVASOR

Oppression helps to forge in the oppressed the very qualities that eventually bring about the downfall of the oppressor.

—RICHARD WRIGHT, *"The Psychological Reactions of Oppressed People"*

The resistance to terror is what makes the world habitable.

—CAROLYN FORCHÉ, Against Forgetting: Twentieth-Century Poetry of Witness

To be free, you have to sacrifice.

—JOSÉ ANTONIO BELO, *2003*

João, Maubisse, July 1992. *Photo by the author.*

João saw me almost as soon as I got off the bus. He saluted and, bowing, kissed my hand. I had just arrived in Maubisse, a coffee-growing town in the mountainous central area of East Timor. João was barefoot and disheveled, and it quickly became obvious that he was also mentally ill.

The middle-aged man spoke to me in a combination of barely intelligible English, broken Portuguese, Mambai (the local language of the area), and some Indonesian. Following me around from time to time, he would rant endlessly about his father, the Australians, Jesus Christ, the English (I never could figure out why), the Portuguese, the Indonesians, and Fretilin[1] — a reference to East Timor's largest and, at the time, underground pro-independence party. At times he would laugh at his own jokes — he had a very endearing smile — or at me; it was not always clear.

I later learned that during World War II João had been a *criado,* the name given to the local guides and personal servants who assisted a few hundred Australian troops that had invaded East Timor ten days after Imperial Japan's December 7, 1941, attack on Pearl Harbor. The Australians' goal was to inhibit Tokyo's feared southward advance. In response, Japan attacked two months later with twenty-thousand soldiers. With the help of the *criados,* the Australian soldiers kept the Japanese soldiers at bay for about a year, after which time the Aussies abandoned the island.

The East Timorese population paid a high price for having the poor fortune of being caught in the middle of the Pacific War. Between 40,000 and 70,000 East Timorese (out of a prewar population of approximately 450,000) lost their lives — primarily as a result of Japanese atrocities and politically induced famine and disease, and, secondarily, Allied bombing. When the Portuguese returned in 1945, the territory was devastated. Had the Australians left the then-Portuguese Timor alone, it is likely that the Japanese would not have invaded or would have sent a small, token force at most.[2]

Local people told me that, three decades later, João joined Falintil[3] — the East Timorese guerilla army — in the mountains in the aftermath of Indonesia's 1975 invasion of his homeland. Captured sometime thereafter, João was reportedly forced by the Indonesian military to fight against his own comrades. His wife and all his children died during the course of the war. It was for these reasons, people said, that he went crazy.

João was the one person who fully and loudly spoke his mind in public during my first visit to the former Portuguese colony in mid-1992. "Viva Timor Leste" (Long live [an independent] East Timor), "Viva Fretilin," João would yell in the middle of the town. He would also sing Fretilin's anthem while marching in position and yell about the glories of the "povo maubere" — a nationalist expression used by Fretilin to characterize the East Timorese people.[4] When Indonesian soldiers on patrol would pass, he would either bow submissively or spit in front of them as he yelled "Indonesia" in disgust. The soldiers, either out of pity or scorn, would ignore him.

The locals loved his antics. João was their collective conscience, their Greek chorus. In playing this role he showed the fuzzy nature of the boundary between sanity and psychosis—at least in a clinical sense. Being able to speak his heart and mind openly, João was, in many ways, one of the few sane, public voices to be heard. Or perhaps he was the only one that the circumstances would allow to be fully human.

João subsisted, I learned, through the help of a local priest who gave him a place to stay and sufficient food. João insisted that I take his picture before I departed Maubisse. I took it as he desired: in front of an old Portuguese monument as he stood at attention like a soldier.

●

Despite the immunity João enjoyed, East Timor at that time was hardly a safe place to speak one's mind. This became almost immediately apparent to me when I arrived in Dili, about two weeks prior to traveling to Maubisse.

Before my arrival my image of Dili, at the time a town of about 150,000 inhabitants, was of a place of darkness. In many ways, however, it was very attractive—especially along the length of its extensive, gracefully curving waterfront that displayed a predominance of Portuguese architecture, a legacy of the more than four hundred years, to varying degrees, of colonial presence on the half-island. Also, the town seemed, at least on the surface, to have a much more relaxed atmosphere than other places within the Indonesian sphere of influence. A place where the siesta is still in practice, much of the town closes down for a few hours in the afternoons.

At the same time I quickly became aware of the climate of profound fear pervading the territory. I had traveled to other places with repressive governments—to Poland in the mid-1980s, and Guatemala and Honduras in the latter part of the same decade. But the level of fear among the populace was far more palpable in East Timor than anywhere else I had been. Unlike in Indonesia proper, few on the street would even say hello to a stranger. People passing an obvious foreigner on the street often averted their eyes, risking only a furtive glance, so as not to give the impression to anyone watching that they might be trying to communicate. Some even crossed to the other side of the street so as not to walk nearby a foreigner, lest they invite the scrutiny of military intelligence.

On my first day in Dili I stopped a young man on the street for directions to the nearest restaurant, and asked how things were going in East Timor. His vague, hushed reply—that it was not safe and there were many problems—warned me not to press further.

Shortly thereafter Father Ricardo, a Catholic priest whom I had gone to see on the advice of a friend who had been to East Timor the year before, told me that he could not talk to me, that it wasn't safe, that there were "eyes and ears" everywhere. The Indonesians had coerced and paid off people in his own congregation to report on his activities, he told me. "Trust no one," he cautioned, as I was leaving.

Within a few days of that encounter I went to the town of Ermera, another coffee-growing area. There, at the top of a hill, was a beautiful Catholic church painted pale yellow with a blue and white Portuguese fresco on the front of the edifice. Coffee beans were drying on the side of the road leading up to the church. But the seemingly bucolic setting belied the harsh reality of the town. A Catholic seminarian there described life under the Indonesian military as "hell." "We live in a prison," he told me, as his eyes darted around nervously to see if anyone was watching. "We are slaves of the Indonesians." Three young men who had gathered around us nodded in agreement. After two hours in Ermera, it was only when I reached the local Catholic church that anyone opened up to me.

The seminarian then introduced me to the local priest, Father Mario, who showed me where spying Indonesian soldiers positioned themselves at night outside his house. He assured me that military authorities were watching us at that very moment from the TNT post overlooking his home and that they would later question him about our conversation.

Some days later, walking along the waterfront in Dili, just down the road from Father Ricardo's Motael Church, I approached Dili's only lighthouse and knocked on the closed door to see if I could climb to the top for the view. A middle-aged man opened the door. He appeared startled to see me, obviously a foreigner, but nervously agreed to let me climb to the top. I tried to engage him in conversation, but he was visibly afraid to talk, literally shaking. As it happened, the headquarters of the Indonesian military intelligence were right across the road. Only when we were descending the stairs and could not be seen from the outside did he say anything of substance. He informed me that he had been working at the lighthouse for almost seventeen years and had begun his job just a few months prior to December 7, 1975 — the day Indonesian troops launched their full-scale invasion of East Timor.[5] "Everyone wants Indonesia to leave," he said. "It's impossible even to talk in East Timor." He was afraid to go out at night, and his fears appeared justified: sometimes groups of soldiers, he reported, would beat him up. In Dili alone, dozens of military installations and unmarked detention and torture houses littered the streets of the capital.

The first Indonesian troops, it turns out, had parachuted into Dili precisely in the area of the lighthouse. As described by Monsignor Costa Lopes, the former head of the territory's Catholic Church, the scene was a terrifying one:

"The soldiers who landed started killing everyone they could find. There were many dead bodies in the streets—all we could see were the soldiers killing, killing, killing."[6] In the first two days of the invasion, about two thousand people lost their lives at the hands of the marauding Indonesian troops in Dili alone.[7] The man at the lighthouse—whose name I do not recall—surely must have witnessed much of the bloodletting.

After the initial mass killings, the soldiers began looting homes and churches, loading cars, motorcycles, furniture, and even windows onto ships destined for Indonesia. Shortly thereafter the invading troops compelled young women, especially those related to Fretilin activists and members of the Fretilin-associated women's and students' organizations, to join them in a victory celebration. The soldiers arrested and imprisoned most of the women, many of whom they repeatedly tortured and raped.[8]

From an Indonesian military perspective, however, the invasion was hardly a masterpiece. In addition to Indonesian warships shelling their own troops, the TNI dropped some elite paratroopers on top of Falintil forces retreating from Dili and dropped others into the sea where they drowned under the weight of their equipment.[9] The TNI also suffered heavy casualties at the hands of Falintil. Australian intelligence analysts estimated more than 450 Indonesian military casualties within only a few weeks after the invasion of Dili.[10] In the first four months of 1976 alone, as many as 2,000 Indonesian troops were killed.[11]

For the East Timorese, the situation was considerably worse. Following the initial assault, the TNI advanced inland from its bases in places such as Dili and Baucau. The TNI's brutal campaign and Fretilin's strong resistance resulted in large numbers of East Timorese killed. In a statement of February 13, 1976, Francisco Lopes da Cruz, Jakarta's appointee to the position of Vice Chairman of the "Provisional Government of East Timor," stated that fifty thousand East Timorese had already died at the hands of the Indonesian military. Nevertheless, despite support in the form of heavy naval and aerial bombardment, in the first few months of the invasion the TNI's territorial control progressed at "a snail's pace," in the words of the U.S. Defense Intelligence Agency.[12]

In the early stages of the war, Fretilin had a number of advantages over the Indonesian military. For months Fretilin had prepared for the invasion, setting up bases in the interior of the country to which many East Timorese retreated on or before December 7, 1975.[13] The TNI had great difficulties in gaining control over large areas of the country. By August 1976 Indonesia only controlled the major towns, some regional centers and villages in the territory, and several "corridors" that connected some of the areas. Most of the rural areas, where the vast majority of the people lived, were still under the control of the resistance.[14] As of March 1977 the U.S. State Department estimated that two-thirds of the East Timorese population was still in Fretilin-dominated areas.[15]

Falintil had about twenty thousand former soldiers, reservists, and trainees of the colonial army as well as many who had received military training from Falintil prior to Jakarta's invasion. Thus Fretilin's military wing was quite formidable. Falintil also had large supplies of weapons left by the Portuguese and detailed knowledge of East Timor's topography, and was thus able to retain effective control of East Timorese territory, with the exception of the major towns and a few administrative centers. Fretilin radio continued to broadcast throughout the territory. Within the liberated areas, schools, agricultural co-operatives, and the like, functioned under Fretilin's administration. Its control was so secure that it was able to hold a national conference in a town in the center of the territory from May 20 to June 2, 1976, that transpired without disturbance.[16]

This situation began to change dramatically in late 1977. In the face of a military stalemate, mounting international publicity about the brutality of the occupation in the form of press reports and refugee testimony, and growing criticism of the Indonesian occupation in the United States and Western Europe, Jakarta decided it was to time to wipe out the resistance once and for all and put an end to any hopes for an independent East Timor.[17] Emboldened by the acquisition of advanced military technology, especially counter-insurgency aircraft like U.S. "Broncos" (OV-10F's) and Australian "Sabres," the TNI began an eighteen–month campaign characterized by Catholic sources within East Timor as one of "encirclement" and "annihilation."

Using tens of thousands of ground troops and aerial bombardment, TNI forces penetrated toward the center from the border and the coasts. As part of the operation, Indonesia bombed forested areas, hoping to defoliate ground cover, and used chemical sprays to destroy crops and livestock. The objective was to push the resistance into a small area of the country where they could be killed or captured and to drive the population in the interior to the coastal lowlands where the Indonesians could more easily control people.[18]

The campaign had devastating effects on the resistance and the civilian population, killing many thousands.[19] As the situation worsened, Falintil was compelled to instruct the civilian population under its protection to surrender to Indonesian troops nearby, urging a buildup of resistance within the areas under Indonesian control. When the campaign ended in March 1979 many top Fretilin leaders were dead, captured, or had surrendered. Falintil lost an estimated 80 percent of its troops and more than 90 percent of its weapons; its internal and international lines of communication had been completely severed.[20]

The Indonesian authorities herded many of the surrendering civilians into a growing number of large, guarded camps. According to a July 1979 report by the Australian Council for Overseas Aid, fifteen such centers were occupied by 318,921 "displaced persons" (almost half the pre-invasion population). Located in both towns and rural areas, the camps were part of a counter-insurgency strategy composed of techniques similar to those employed against guerrilla movements in Rhodesia and Vietnam. Apart from security needs, the TNI used the camps to "Indonesianize" the population, which included Indonesian-language instruction and political education. Forced labor, including the carrying of ammunition and supplies into combat areas, was common.[21]

The combined effects of Jakarta's brutal military campaign, the forced relocation program, and the undermining of local food production resulted in famine. Conditions were so dire in one camp (in which 80 percent of its eight thousand inhabitants suffered from malnutrition) that a visiting delegate from the International Committee of the Red Cross stated that the situation was "as bad as Biafra and potentially as serious as Kampuchea."[22]

Despite these daunting conditions, the East Timorese resistance was able to reorganize, under the leadership of Xanana Gusmão. By 1980 individual Falintil units were attacking a number of Indonesian garrisons, and even infrastructure and positions around Dili. In response to the resurgence of the guerrilla army, the TNI launched Operation Security (*Operasi Keamanan*) in mid-1981, employing a brutal tactic called the "fence of legs" (*pagar betis*) in which the military forced about eighty thousand East Timorese males to form human chains that would walk across the countryside in front of Indonesian troops in order to flush out Falintil guerrillas or to surround them at points where they could be massacred.[23]

While many Falintil groups surrendered or were slaughtered during the operation, many evaded capture. The operation as a whole had extremely detrimental effects on the population as it greatly disrupted agricultural production, leading to severe food shortages in most regions of the country. Many of those forced to participate starved to death during the campaign, given the meager food allotments provided by the Indonesian military.[24]

Massacres of civilians were commonplace, one of the most infamous ones occurring in a place called Lacluta, southeast of Dili in 1981. There, Jakarta's soldiers killed about five hundred civilians, mostly woman and children. One eyewitness described how soldiers threw children up in the air and smashed their heads on a rock. The witness recounted the words of an Indonesian soldier who participated in the slaughter: "When you clean your field, don't you kill all the snakes, small and large alike?" In 1983 Indonesian troops killed several hundred in the village of Kraras, on the south coast. The soldiers murdered scores of people by burning alive many sick and elderly in their homes.[25]

As before, the resistance was able to reorganize. By late 1982 Falintil was launching a number of attacks in many parts of the country, especially in the east and the south. By that time an estimated two hundred thousand East Timorese had lost their lives due to Indonesia's war.[26]

From that time on the military equation changed little, with the two sides effectively in a stalemate. The war would continue, however, but at a much lower level, with anywhere from fifteen thousand to thirty thousand Indonesian troops controlling the major towns and strategic points, while facing several hundred Falintil guerrillas, divided into small bands active across the country in the forests, jungles, and mountainous areas. The two sides would occasionally attack the other, with the TNI launching offensives aimed at eradicating the guerrillas, while Falintil would engage in much lower-level actions attacking Indonesian troops as they moved between towns or through the countryside, as well as rural military posts.

•

Key to the resurgence of the resistance, and to East Timor's international profile, was the emergence of an extensive underground network in the villages and towns that developed over the course of the 1980s. While much of its activities were focused on supporting the guerrilla army and sending information abroad to human rights and advocacy groups, the underground also engaged in actions in the towns aimed at embarrassing the Indonesian authorities and giving lie to the claim that the East Timorese people had embraced "integration" with Indonesia—save for small bands of hardcore radicals. These public actions began to take place in 1989 when Jakarta, eager to present to the outside world an image of normalcy in the former Portuguese colony and confident that Indonesia's military had the territory and its population under sufficient control, opened up East Timor to the outside world. Prior to that time one needed official permission to enter, even if one were Indonesian.

The first high-profile visitor was Pope John Paul II, who said mass for tens of thousands of East Timor's Catholics in Dili. While Jakarta hoped that the Pope's presence would effectively bless Indonesia's annexation, the East Timorese underground took advantage of the trip to stage a pro-independence demonstration at the end of the Catholic pontiff's public mass. With many representatives of the international media outlets present, the October 1989 trip proved to be an embarrassment for Indonesia.[27]

But most significant in focusing critical attention on Jakarta and its occupation of the territory was what Indonesian government officials referred to as the "Santa Cruz incident." Santa Cruz is the name of the neighborhood containing Dili's main cemetery, which, in many ways, was the geographical impetus for my 1992 trip.

For many years East Timor had seemed like a lost cause. As the title of John

Taylor's 1991 book suggests, East Timor was "Indonesia's Forgotten War" — at least in much of the West.[28] Reports on East Timor in the U.S. corporate-owned media, for instance, were almost nonexistent. From March 1976 to November 1979, for example, there was not a single mention of East Timor in the *Los Angeles Times*. Major American television networks were even more negligent. ABC news did not carry its first report until September 1992, and NBC not until a few years later.[29] And to the extent that media outlets did report on East Timor, they often reproduced misinformation from the Indonesian government and their powerful allies in Washington and Canberra, for example.[30] Although there were some outstanding exceptions in the mainstream media, anyone wanting to learn about East Timor was largely limited to the writings of Noam Chomsky, a handful of books on the topic, various Left-leaning publications, or reports by organizations like Amnesty International.

What happened at the Santa Cruz cemetery on November 12, 1991, was decisive in helping East Timor to break out of its international isolation.[31]

Early that morning Father Ricardo officiated a memorial mass for Sebastião Gomes, a young pro-independence activist killed by Indonesian soldiers two weeks earlier at the Motael Church. Sebastião and a number of other young people had taken refuge from the Indonesian military in late October. In preparation for the arrival of an official Portuguese delegation to East Timor (which, in the end, never came), the TNI had begun rounding up many young people suspected of harboring pro-independence sentiments. And so many fled to what they thought would be the safety of the church. On October 28 the military attacked the church shortly after midnight, shooting Sebastião to death.[32]

After the memorial mass two weeks later the attendees marched to the Santa Cruz cemetery where Sebastião was buried. As the crowd flowed through Dili's streets, the marchers unfurled banners and shouted pro-independence slogans. Many left their workplaces and homes and joined what had turned into the first mass demonstration against Indonesian rule since Jakarta's bloody invasion in 1975.

By the time the procession reached its destination, the throng had swelled to thousands. There, the crowd held a brief ceremony. As the peaceful gathering was beginning to disperse, the Indonesian military arrived and blocked one end of the road. Without warning and, according to eyewitnesses, without provocation, the soldiers marched in formation toward the crowd and opened fire with their U.S.-made M-16 rifles, killing more than 250 people.[33]

In a country where about one-third of the pre-invasion population had lost their lives to the Indonesian invasion and occupation, massacres were not unknown. What made Santa Cruz so different was that members of the Western media were present to witness and report on it, for example, freelance journalist Allan Nairn and Pacifica Radio's Amy Goodman from the United States, and Russell Anderson from Australia. Max Stahl, a British journalist with Yorkshire Television, was also there and filmed part of the massacre. Stahl buried the film in a freshly dug grave and, after Indonesian soldiers arrested and interrogated him for many hours, returned that same night to retrieve it. With the assistance of Saskia Kouwenberg, a Dutch solidarity activist who smuggled the film out, Stahl's efforts helped to bring the horrors of East Timor to television screens throughout the world.

Internationally major newspapers reacted to the eyewitness accounts and the video footage of Jakarta's latest atrocity in East Timor and quickly condemned the massacre. The powerful reporting also helped to reinvigorate what had been a largely dormant international solidarity movement and to greatly heighten the scrutiny by Western governments of Jakarta's illegal occupation. Demonstrations in the United States, Canada, and Western Europe plagued Indonesia's foreign minister, Ali Alatas, wherever he traveled in a tour aimed at damage control. Newspapers throughout the West editorialized in favor of East Timorese self-determination.

In response to the international uproar, Jakarta swiftly moved to stifle the criticism by expressing its official "regret" for what had happened, relieving the two top military commanders (sending them to the United States for university study), and setting up an official investigation of the "incident." Some of Indonesia's top military officials, however, quickly exposed the hollowness of Jakarta's voiced regrets.

General Try Sutrisno, who at the time was the commander of the Indonesian armed forces and soon thereafter became the country's vice president, called the East Timorese who had gathered at the cemetery "disruptors" who "must be crushed." "These ill-bred people have to be shot . . . and we will shoot them," he declaimed while speaking in front of Indonesia's parliament. And General Mantiri, the new regional commander for East Timor, characterized the massacre as "proper," and added, "We don't regret anything."[34]

Jakarta at first claimed that only nineteen had died. In the face of international expressions of incredulity, its official commission of inquiry later upped the figure to fifty-three. Eyewitness accounts of the massacre found this revised number to be ridiculously low, given the scores of bodies seen strewn on the street in front of the cemetery and those within scattered between the graves, in addition to the military trucks filled with corpses leaving the scene of the crime. A detailed investigation by the East Timorese underground subsequently put the figure at 273, a number it characterized as a conservative estimate.[35]

Later, about two years after the Santa Cruz massacre, Max Stahl, on a clandestine return visit to East Timor, learned of a second wave of killings. According to a lab technician at the military hospital in Dili and a massacre survivor, both of whom Stahl interviewed, Indonesian soldiers had killed many of the injured at the hospital. The soldiers "crushed the skulls of the wounded with large rocks, ran over them with trucks, stabbed them and administered — with doctors present — poisonous disinfecting chemicals as medicines to 'finish off' scores of wounded demonstrators in the wake of the massacre." Stahl estimated that anywhere from fifty to two hundred of the wounded died in this manner.[36]

In the aftermath of the massacre, responding to international pressure, Jakarta tried and sentenced a few low-ranking military officers to terms of no more than eighteen months for disobeying orders. According to the official Indonesian line, the massacre was not the result of a concerted policy. Rather, so the line went, a few rogue soldiers had acted on their own. Meanwhile, Jakarta meted out sentences ranging from five years to life imprisonment to some of those who had organized and participated in the Santa Cruz march, and to some who took part, one week later, in a demonstration in Jakarta by East Timorese university students in Indonesia proper to protest the massacre.

A 1994 inquiry by Bacre Waly Ndiaye of Senegal, Special Rapporteur of

Julho Sarmento at the grave of his brother, shot by Indonesian troops at the Santa Cruz cemetery in Dili on November 12, 1991; Maubisse, July 1992. *Photo by the author.*

the U.N. Commission on Human Rights in charge of investigating extraju-dicial, summary, or arbitrary executions, found no evidence that the East Timorese demonstrators had carried weaponry — contrary to the assertions of some Indonesian officials — and characterized the associated claims that In-donesian troops had fired in self-defense as "unsubstantiated." For these rea-sons he wrote that the TNI's actions "were not a spontaneous reaction to a riotous mob, but rather a planned military operation designed to deal with a public expression of political dissent in a way not in accordance with inter-national human rights standards."[37] In the diplomacy of U.N.-speak, the re-port was damning.

●

I arrived in East Timor several months after the killings at the Santa Cruz cemetery. Officially there as a tourist, but with the intention of writing some magazine articles, I traveled to the occupied territory to see firsthand what life was like under the yoke of the Indonesian military and learn how the East Timorese resistance was faring. Once there, I found that many people were still traumatized from what had happened at Santa Cruz; this was hardly sur-prising, given that a number of years had passed since a massacre on that scale had taken place in East Timor — especially in the area of Dili. This is why, in part, the killings stood out so much in the minds of many.

Although the tension in East Timor was undoubtedly palpable, most strik-ing, perhaps, was how utterly normal, almost boringly so, East Timor seemed. There were lots of soldiers, of course — about thirty thousand, ac-cording to East Timorese sources, in a territory the size of Northern Ireland or the U.S. state of Connecticut — and many intelligence agents. At the same time, however, there were many spaces of apparent normalcy. I saw a wed-ding, children playing, women and men going to the market, people praying at churches, and teenagers participating in a volleyball match — in other words, people were going about their lives as one would see almost anywhere else in the world.

But East Timor in 1992 was undeniably a terrifying place, but not, in a spec-tacular sense, fit for the evening news. Rather, the brutality in East Timor was of an established sort, one that comes about when a purveyor of violence has sufficiently won the upper hand, when the stronger party can implement its policies through seemingly normal practices without having frequently to re-vert to direct, physical violence. Only on rare occasions, when the dominated, in significant, organized numbers, refuse to accept their plight and decide to actively resist the permanency of their conquest, does large-scale direct vio-lence become necessary. The occupation had become institutionalized. The violence was in the structures built upon the corpses of the dead and the col-lective trauma of those who had survived.

In her well-known account of the Israeli government's 1961 trial of Adolf Eichmann, the infamous German official who played a major role in planning and implementing Hitler's "Final Solution," Hannah Arendt notes that, despite the best efforts of the prosecutor, none of the spectators saw Eichmann as a monster. Indeed, most striking was how normal, how unassuming, he appeared — and thus Arendt, in the subtitle of her book, evokes "the banality of evil."[38] In many ways East Timor illustrated such banality writ-large.

That said, there was little, in reality, that was normal about East Timor. Yet, when one is surrounded by insanity, that which is perverse can come to seem ordinary. At the same time, however, there are always some who will perceive the insanity for just what it is. In the case of East Timor, those of that view included almost everyone with whom I came in contact. But recognizing the insanity is one matter; being able to deal with it, to challenge it, is quite another.

Nonetheless many did challenge the reality that Indonesia's military was trying to impose. One such person, Eduardo Belo Soares, made contact with me toward the end of my trip. He was in his early thirties, and spoke Portuguese and some English. Eduardo claimed to be an underground correspondent for the BBC and a volunteer with the International Committee of the Red Cross. Assuming that a Western "tourist" would be partial to the East Timorese cause (a fair assumption, given the political sympathies of the small number of foreign visitors to the territory), he told me that he wanted to give me some materials to carry abroad. After a friend confirmed Eduardo's trustworthiness a few days later, I agreed to do so.

On a Sunday evening at precisely 6:30 P.M. I began walking down a particular road as Eduardo had instructed. He had given me the license number of a vehicle — one of the many old, decrepit, blue station wagons that served as taxis and were driven by East Timorese, as opposed to the newer taxis driven largely by some of the many Indonesian settlers. Within one or two minutes of my setting off down the assigned street, a blue taxi with the correct license plate stopped in front of me. In the passenger's seat was Eduardo, and driving was an East Timorese man whom Eduardo introduced me to only by his nom de guerre, or pseudonym.

The vehicle weaved through Dili's streets to make sure no one was following. Eduardo spoke quickly and nervously as he surveyed the road trailing us. He gave me strips of negative film, instructing me to hide them in my shoe as they contained important photos of the guerrillas. He also gave me a letter for the international solidarity movement that contained a request for a specific type of video camera. Falintil wanted to produce videos for propaganda purposes within East Timor, Indonesia, and abroad.

Before dropping me off in front of the main postal and telecommunications office so I could pretend to make a long-distance phone call and thus have an excuse for being out at night, Eduardo asked me for some money to pay the owner of the taxi who had lent him and his comrade the vehicle. I gave him ten thousand *rupiah* — about four dollars at the time — and wished him well, wondering if I would ever see him again.[39]

Eduardo's ability to communicate in Portuguese was an obvious manifestation of the lingering Lusophone influence in the territory. Overall, however, Portugal's mark on East Timor's landscape was not as visible as one might expect, given more than four centuries of its presence. In part this was a manifestation of colonial Portugal's poverty and East Timor's marginal status within Lisbon's dispersed empire. Until very late in Portugal's colonial administration, Lisbon invested very little in the territory. As Alfred Russel Wallace, a British scientist and explorer who visited in the late 1860s, described it, "The Portuguese government in Timor is a most miserable one. Nobody seems to care the least about the improvement of the country, and at this time, after three hundred years of occupation, there has not been a mile of road made beyond the town [Dili], and there is not a solitary European residence in the interior."[40] While Portuguese development of the colony increased significantly over the next several decades, Dili still had no electricity, water supply, paved roads, wharf for handling cargo, or telephone service — except in the homes and offices of high-level colonial officials — on the eve of the Second World War.[41]

The war resulted in the destruction of much of the colony's infrastructure and severe damage to many of its principal towns, while ruining its commercial economy. Upon their return the Portuguese authorities resorted to forced labor to rebuild the colonial infrastructure and to revive the production of agricultural commodities for export.[42] As a member of the Australian War Graves unit who visited the colony in 1947 wrote, "After centuries of colonial rule the natives are as backward and helpless as ever, forced labor under the whip goes on from dawn to dusk, and the Portuguese colonists, including those exiled from Salazar's Portugal, maintain the same attitudes and live with the same mixture of civility and brutality as they had 350 years ago."[43]

All in all, however, the Portuguese had relatively little effect on most people's daily lives. By the time the Portuguese abandoned the colony in 1975, the vast majority of the population continued to live in small, rural hamlets, similar to how they had lived for centuries. And while formal educational levels increased significantly beginning in the 1950s, an estimated 93 percent of the population remained illiterate in 1973.[44]

If there was one legacy of Portuguese rule that left a lasting imprint on East Timorese society, however, it was that of the Catholic Church. The Church continues to be perhaps the most visible legacy of Portugal's empire in Southeast Asia. It played an important role in Lisbon's "civilizing mission" — especially in the last century of Portuguese rule. Although the Church had played a role in Lisbon's colonial project since the Portuguese first arrived on the island of Timor, its relationship with the colonial authorities was not always a smooth one. Nevertheless it always shared the basic assumptions and vision of the colonial regime.

Indigenous, animist religious practices long dominated the spiritual life of the population of Portuguese Timor. Slowly, however, the Catholic Church recruited members — especially among the society's elites. The horrifying experience of World War II greatly helped to facilitate the growth of the Church. By 1973 church membership had reached 196,570 — roughly 30 percent of the population.[45] By this time Catholicism had become the de facto religion of the elite and of nearly all those with some formal education, in addition to thousands of others.

As in all social processes, church activities brought about unintended consequences. Many East Timorese pro-independence activists who assumed positions of leadership within the emerging political parties following the overthrow of Portugal's fascist military regime in April 1974 were graduates of the church's educational system as well as former seminarians.[46]

The experience of the Indonesian invasion and occupation, combined with growing "Timorization" of the religious entity, changed the relationship of the Church to the East Timorese people. During the Portuguese era the Church had been generally very much in favor of the status quo, and very critical of what it saw as the radical tendencies of the pro-independence movement. The Church was the only independent, above-ground institution that survived the Indonesian onslaught. While it remained very conservative on social issues, it provided essential space for the indigenous population to maintain its culture, in addition to attending to spiritual needs. The Church also played an important role in supporting resistance to the occupation and pro-independence activism. All these factors resulted in massive growth for the Church in the years following Jakarta's invasion, with well over 90 percent of the population calling itself Catholic by the 1980s.[47] Some members of the clergy became among the most outspoken critics of Indonesia's crimes in the territory, and a number of them were secretly active in the clandestine resistance.

Such factors incurred the suspicions and wrath of Indonesia's occupation authorities. According to Prabowo, the infamous son-in-law of Suharto — Indonesia's long-time dictator — and, at the time, a regional military commander in the territory, "The church, the priests, and the religious are the three factors which threaten East Timor's integration with Indonesia."[48]

•

Following my 1992 visit more than four years would pass before I returned to East Timor. Continuing efforts by the population to resist Indonesia's illegal occupation, combined with growing international scrutiny and criticism of Jakarta's colonial project in the territory, had culminated in the awarding of the 1996 Nobel Peace Prize to two East Timorese: Bishop Carlos Belo, the leader of the Catholic Church in the territory, and José Ramos-Horta, head of the diplomatic wing of the East Timorese resistance. In its official announcement of the award, the Norwegian Nobel Committee expressed its hope that the prize would "spur efforts to find a diplomatic solution to the conflict in East Timor based on the people's right to self-determination."[49]

The award sent shockwaves through Jakarta's ruling elite, and gave a great boost to an East Timorese population struggling to break the chains of Indonesia's occupation. Internationally the prize gave significant legitimacy to those working to end the complicity of Western governments with Indonesia's annexation of East Timor.

As my taxi left Dili's airport in November 1996, just a few weeks after the announcement, I saw immediate evidence of change since 1992 and one of the effects of the conferring of the Nobel Peace Prize to two sons of East Timor: on a wall near the airport entrance someone had boldly spray-painted "Viva Bishop Belo."

While most East Timorese seemed too afraid to make direct eye contact with me during my 1992 visit, many people greeted me as I walked the streets in Dili in late 1996. Some, particularly younger people, flashed a "V" for victory sign, a display of their nationalist sympathies.

Despite these openings, East Timor remained a place where few dared to speak their minds in public and even fewer dared to invite foreigners into their homes. "We are very happy that, with the Nobel Prize, the world has recognized our suffering," a middle-aged woman told me in a brief conversation on a shady street, "but we still live in a prison." Our talk ended abruptly when a stranger appeared.

Dili's streets were empty by nine o'clock in the evening. Many people reported that Indonesian soldiers randomly attacked people, especially youths, who dared to venture outside after nightfall. And in rural areas matters were much worse. "Outside the towns, people are at the total mercy of the Indonesian military," one priest recounted.[50]

While Indonesia maintained a certain order through a highly visible military force of twenty thousand to thirty thousand troops and an extensive administrative apparatus, the resistance was also becoming increasingly bold and effective. I saw this firsthand when members of the underground smuggled me into a rural safe house, and then into the mountains to meet with Falintil leader David Alex, the number 3 person in the guerilla hierarchy at the time, along with 10 of the 150 fighters under his command.

The success and relative ease with which the resistance smuggled me in and out of the eastern region of the country provided a strong counterweight to official Indonesian assertions that the resistance was marginalized and isolated. And my experience seemed to substantiate what I had often heard from underground activists: the resistance is everyone and everywhere.

During my twenty-four-hour stay at the guerrilla camp, numerous *estafetas,* or couriers, visited to deliver supplies and messages from other Falintil groups and resistance activists in the towns. A number of *seguranças,* men and women who served as the eyes and ears of Falintil, also passed by to brief the guerrillas on the activities of the nearest Indonesian soldiers, reportedly five kilometers away, and on local Indonesian intelligence assets. The driver of the vehicle from Dili worked for the Indonesian military and, at least one of the guides, had documentation identifying him as working with Indonesian intelligence, while the driver on the way back from the safe house was a Catholic priest.[51]

But despite the extensive nature of the underground and its success in penetrating Indonesia's infrastructure of control, resistance work was still a highly dangerous enterprise. Several months after my departure I would learn that TNI troops had captured David Alex, along with José Antonio Belo, who had served as my main guide to the mountains.

While pursuing him the TNI shot David Alex in the leg. The next day the Indonesians announced that David Alex had died while in custody, reportedly from the wound he sustained while trying to flee, although witnesses had said that his injury was minor. The Indonesians said that they buried him in a small cemetery in Dili. But no one, including his family members, ever saw his body.[52]

The previous month — in May 1997 — the authorities had arrested João Guterres in Dili. João had served as an *estafeta* to David Alex and was one of the principal people with whom I had contact during my 1996 visit.

When I returned to East Timor for a few days in early 1998 I inquired about the whereabouts of both José and João. But no one with whom I spoke during my brief stay had firm news about either one. It was not until I was on the plane back to Jakarta that I found someone who appeared to know something. He was Swiss and an official of the International Committee of the Red Cross in Geneva. The man had never heard of João, but he did know about José. The Red Cross official was quite certain that he was in good health but only because José had turned out to be a double agent. The Swiss man informed me that he had credible information that José had long been working for the Indonesian military, which was how the TNI had ultimately captured David Alex.

I knew that this information could not be true. After all, José had led me and many other journalists into the mountains. He had been a prisoner of the Indonesians on previous occasions and had suffered unspeakable torture. And he was trusted and admired by the highest elements of the resistance. But despite my certainty, inwardly I had seeds of doubt. East Timor was a land of fear, terror, and duplicity. One could never be completely sure with whom one was dealing.

It would later turn out that the report was indeed false. For reasons that are unclear the Indonesians released José in August 1998, after torturing him and holding him incommunicado for more than a year — on the condition that he report to the authorities every two days. Perhaps it was because José was well known within the international solidarity movement that helped save him. Indeed, along with Amnesty International, solidarity groups campaigned for José's release, much to the chagrin of the Indonesian authorities.[53]

João Guterres was not so lucky. Unlike José, he spoke neither English nor Portuguese, kept a very low profile, and was a relatively low-level member of the underground.[54] As such, he was not known by many of the journalists and political tourists who visited East Timor in the 1990s. Hence his capture did not elicit much attention, thus allowing the Indonesian authorities more leeway to deal with him as they saw fit.[55] Soon after his arrest they informed his family that he was dead, but in fact he was alive. The Indonesians held João incommunicado for at least several months, badly abusing him, and eventually, it appears, they killed him and dumped his body at sea.[56]

Through such atrocities Jakarta was making it perfectly clear to the East Timorese and to the outside world that it was not going to give up East Timor easily, regardless of what the Nobel Peace Prize Committee or anyone else thought of the matter.

America stands as it always has, against aggression, against those who would use force to replace the rule of law.

—U.S. PRESIDENT GEORGE H. W. BUSH, *1990, in reference to the Iraqi invasion of Kuwait*

It's important for Australia that the world understand that big countries cannot invade small countries and get away with it.

—AUSTRALIAN PRIME MINISTER BOB HAWKE, *1990, in reference to the Iraqi invasion of Kuwait*

President Ronald Reagan and President Suharto at the White House, October 12, 1982. *Photo courtesy of the Ronald Reagan Library.*

He walked confidently into the room. Well-groomed and in his mid-fifties, smiling broadly, he vigorously shook the hands of many of those present. They called him "Ambassador" as they greeted him. The man was Paul Wolfowitz. He would emerge a few years later as undersecretary of defense for the administration of George W. Bush and one of the primary architects of the 2003 U.S. invasion of Iraq. At the time, however, he was serving as dean of the prestigious School of Advanced International Studies of The Johns Hopkins University. Prior to that Wolfowitz had been the assistant secretary of state for East Asian and Pacific affairs from 1982 to 1986 and then ambassador to Jakarta during the last three years of the Reagan administration. After that he served in the George H. W. Bush administration as undersecretary of defense for policy. He had also established himself as an Indonesia expert in Washington circles.

The date was May 7, 1997, and I was in Room 2172 of the Rayburn House Office Building on Capitol Hill. The occasion was a hearing of the Subcommittee on Asia and the Pacific of the Committee on International Relations, House of Representatives. The subject was "United States Policy toward Indonesia."

From the time of Indonesia's invasion, Washington had been the Suharto regime's most important international backer. While a few congressional hearings on developments in East Timor and U.S. policy toward Jakarta had taken place in the late 1970s and one in 1982, there had not been another until 1992, which only came about because of increasing scrutiny in the aftermath of the Santa Cruz massacre. That another congressional hearing on Indonesia and East Timor was taking place was an indication of how far official debate on U.S. policy toward the occupied country had come since 1992. U.S. policy was coming under increasing attack from a greatly strengthened solidarity network, human rights groups, and religious bodies, and from within Congress itself. Despite the progress, however, the rhetoric of Washington officialdom on display at the hearing was indicative of how far U.S policy still had to go.

Douglas Bereuter, a Republican representative from Nebraska, presided over the proceedings as chair of the subcommittee. A longtime supporter of Suharto's "New Order" government, Bereuter had proven to be one of the staunchest opponents of efforts to cut off military aid to Jakarta. He opened the hearing by extolling Indonesia's virtues, saying that it had "done much to preserve peace in Southeast Asia" and that it had "welcomed the U.S. security presence in the region and . . . granted U.S. forces access to Indonesian facilities." While Bereuter acknowledged Indonesia's less-than-shining human rights record — including that in East Timor — he argued for "continued military interaction" with Indonesia through American training and for "the sale of appropriately limited military equipment." Such "interaction," he opined, would "advance U.S. security interests as well as the cause of democracy and human rights."[1]

Wolfowitz's testimony struck a similar tone, while explicitly arguing against any talk in Washington of support for East Timorese independence — talk he characterized as "destructive." His testimony stressed Indonesia's many "achievements."

> In the 7 years since I left Indonesia," he declaimed, "on the positive side, there has been significantly greater openness in a number of respects. There is more open questioning of public officials on government decisions that have gone against the government, although in most cases, the government eventually prevailed. There have been court martials of military officers for the massacre in East Timor in 1991. And I might note that I think for any military to court martial its officers for that kind of action takes an effort.[2]

The former ambassador was referring to Jakarta's prosecution and sentencing of a few low-ranking TNI officers for the Santa Cruz massacre in response to international pressure. The handful of prosecutions and convictions dovetailed neatly with the official Indonesian line that the killings were not the result of a concerted policy but rather of the actions of a few rogue soldiers.

In his prepared written statement submitted to the subcommittee, Wolfowitz was even more effusive in his praise of the Suharto regime. "Any balanced judgment of the situation in Indonesia today," he wrote, "including the very important and sensitive issue of human rights, needs to take account of the significant progress that Indonesia has already made and needs to acknowledge that much of this progress has to be credited to the strong and remarkable leadership of President Soeharto."[3]

Wolfowitz's testimony followed on the heels of the statement of the Clinton administration's representative, Aurelia Brazeal, the deputy assistant secretary of state in the State Department's Bureau of East Asian and Pacific Affairs. She was proud to report that, vis-à-vis East Timor, the administration did "not hesitate to speak out" and pointed to its support for a resolution "that expressed deep concerns over Indonesian policies in East Timor" at the most recent meeting of the U.N. Commission on Human Rights in Geneva. The administration had also called upon Jakarta to reduce troop levels and to allow increased access to the territory. But in a classic case of equating the resistance of a colonized people to the terror of its oppressor, Brazeal reported that the Clinton White House had "also called on the East Timor resistance to foreswear violence and join efforts to achieve a peaceful resolution of the conflict."[4] What she did not mention was that the East Timorese resistance had long offered to engage in direct negotiations with the Suharto regime to achieve a just and peaceful resolution of the conflict but that Jakarta had refused to do so.

Implicitly Washington supported Jakarta's refusal to negotiate with representatives of the overwhelming majority of the East Timorese people. As Brazeal explained in response to a question from Bereuter, the administration (like its predecessors) "recognized the incorporation of East Timor into Indonesia." She then went on to say that "we want to be very supportive of the U.N. efforts." But support for such efforts was limited to mere formalities, such as negotiations between Jakarta and Lisbon that were going nowhere and an "intra-Timorese dialog" between representatives of the East Timorese resistance and some ostensibly "pro-integration" East Timorese that had recently come about—an effort Indonesia had supported as a way of undermining more serious discussion. Jakarta explicitly forbade its representatives from inside East Timor from discussing the contested territory's political status. As for the more important aspects of the U.N. agenda—in the form of Security Council resolutions calling upon all states to respect East Timor's territorial integrity and inalienable right to self-determination—Washington was far less than supportive. When Bereuter inquired about the administration's position on a referendum, Brazeal responded, "We have not taken a position on that." She even went so far as to misrepresent the position of Portugal on such a vote, saying that it was "difficult to characterize what the Portuguese have in mind for East Timor, except that we detect an interest in allowing the people to have more political freedoms."[5] Surely Brazeal was well aware that Lisbon had long advocated exactly such a referendum. Indeed, its constitution contained an article binding Portugal to "her responsibilities under international law to promote and safeguard the right to self-determination and independence of East Timor."

In many ways Washington was out of step with a growing international consensus favoring East Timorese self-determination. Several months earlier the Norwegian Nobel Committee had awarded its Peace Prize to Bishop Belo and José Ramos-Horta and expressed its support for East Timorese self-determination. As for the Clinton administration, it was championing a solution that would "incorporate proposals that give East Timorese themselves greater control over their economic and political life in keeping with their unique history and culture"[6]—a proposal sufficiently vague to seem somewhat critical of the status quo yet guaranteed not to offend Jakarta's sensibilities as it fell far short of allowing the East Timorese the right to determine their political geographical status.

●

Washington's approach to the question of East Timor grew out of a realpolitik-like analysis of U.S. economic and strategic interests and an associated set of practices, ones with deep roots in American policy in the Asia-Pacific region. The United States had long sought to dominate the region, given its immense mineral wealth and vast commercial opportunities. The U.S. war against and its subsequent colonization of the Philippines at the turn of the twentieth century was an early, blatant, and extremely bloody part of this project.[7] The presence of Japan and European colonial powers in the region, however, limited Washington's ability to realize its imperial ambitions. World War II and the disruption of colonial rule radically changed the situation as the United States emerged as the dominant power of the region, allowing Washington to turn it into what one set of commentators characterized as an "American Lake."[8] The U.S. war in Vietnam, as American officials often made clear, was in large part about maintaining and enhancing privileged access to the wealth of resources of the larger region.[9] For many, the centerpiece of the region's wealth was Indonesia, which *U.S. News & World Report,* in interpreting the thinking of the administration of then U.S. president Dwight Eisenhower, characterized in 1954 as "the richest prize in all Southeast Asia."[10]

For these reasons Washington was less than satisfied when the Sukarno-led government that emerged following the end of Dutch colonial rule espoused a nationalist, nonaligned, and anti-imperialist approach to both domestic and foreign policy. As such, the United States began to cultivate relationships with anti-Sukarno elements of the Indonesian military, going so far as to support and foster regional secessionist movements in an effort to destabilize the country's central government.[11] These efforts paid off in the mid-1960s, when Indonesia's military establishment horrifically seized power. As part of its effort to overthrow the Sukarno regime, the Indonesian military — led by General Suharto — and the civilian militia that it armed and directed engaged in one of the worst bloodlettings of the post–World War II era. Over the course of several months in 1965–66 they slaughtered many tens of thousands of members of the Indonesian Communist Party (PKI) along with members of loosely affiliated organizations (woman's groups, labor unions, etc.).

Although Indonesia's holocaust does not meet the strict guidelines of the genocide convention, the scale and nature of the killing spree were undoubtedly genocide-like — similar to the bulk of crimes committed by the Khmer Rouge in Cambodia.[12] Amnesty International estimated that "many more than one million" were killed. The head of the Indonesia state security system approximated the toll at half a million, with another 750,000 jailed or sent to concentration camps.[13] While even the CIA described the massacres "as one of the worst mass murders of the 20th century," the American political establishment welcomed the slaughter and the emergence of Suharto's "New Order," with *Time* magazine hailing it as "the West's best news for years in Asia."[14]

The United States had effectively helped lay the groundwork for the military's seizure of power through U.S. interference in Indonesian affairs and support for the military over the years preceding the coup, and through intelligence operations aimed at weakening the PKI and drawing the party into conflict with the army. Washington had also long urged the military to move against the PKI. So when the military did exactly that, the local U.S. embassy—according to Marshal Green, American ambassador to Indonesia at the time—"made clear" to the army that Washington was "generally sympathetic with and admiring" of its actions.[15] Accordingly the United States supplied weaponry, telecommunications equipment, as well as food and other forms of aid to the Indonesian army in the early weeks of the killings.[16] The embassy in Jakarta also provided the military with the names of thousands of PKI cadre who were subsequently executed.[17]

It was this military-dominated regime that was in power in Jakarta in April 1974 when a relatively nonviolent coup d'état overthrew Portugal's fascist Caetano government. A group of Left-leaning military officials known as the Armed Forces Movement took power and immediately announced a policy of democracy within Portugal and decolonization of all its overseas territories, including East Timor. The coup took ruling circles in Jakarta by surprise. Prior to that time Indonesia had shown only occasional interest in the territory, while often publicly stating that Jakarta had no claim on the then Portuguese colony. Indonesian intelligence reportedly made an assessment in late 1972 or 1973, however, that it could not allow an independent East Timor to exist were the Portuguese to withdraw. Given the U.S. withdrawal from Vietnam, so went the thinking in Jakarta, an independent East Timor could create security problems for Indonesia. This view grew in strength in the aftermath of the coup in Lisbon—leading elements of the New Order intelligence and security apparatuses feared that an independent East Timor would compound the problems at the archipelago's periphery by strengthening already problematic separatist sentiments, and possibly serving as a base for leftist subversion. Months later a small number of top Indonesia's military officials and elements of military intelligence decided to launch a campaign of subversion—code-named *Operasi Komodo* or Operation Komodo Dragon—aimed at convincing the East Timorese of the wisdom of "integrating" with Indonesia or, failing that, forcibly annexing the territory. An important component of the operation was to win over ruling elites in Western capitals to Jakarta's position on East Timor.[18]

This goal was undoubtedly on Suharto's mind when he visited with U.S. president Gerald Ford at Camp David, Maryland, the presidential retreat, on July 5, 1975. During their conversation Suharto informed Ford that Indonesia respected the process of decolonization and self-determination in East

Timor and that his country would not commit aggression against any other. At the same time he opined that those within the Portuguese colony championing independence were "Communist-influenced." In any case, he averred, independence for East Timor did not make sense as the would-be country "would hardly be viable" given its small size and scant resources. Thus "the only way" for East Timor to survive was "to integrate into Indonesia." Ford responded by thanking his Indonesian counterpart for informing him of his views, without saying anything specific about Suharto's framing of the situation in the then Portuguese Timor.[19] At various points in the conversation, both Ford and Suharto situated their remarks in the context of a larger project of combating "Communism" throughout Southeast Asia, an endeavor they saw as all the more pressing in light of the recent U.S. setback in the former French Indochina. Suharto's trip to the United States and Ford's nonresponse made the Indonesian leader sufficiently confident that he made his first public statement ruling out the viability of an independent East Timor upon his return to Jakarta on July 8, 1975.[20]

A diplomatic cable of August 17, 1975, from Australia's ambassador to Indonesia, Richard Woolcott, made clear just how little Washington cared about Indonesian aggression toward East Timor as well as the potential for the U.S. government to affect Jakarta's course of action. As Woolcott wrote, "The United States might have some influence on Indonesia at present as Indonesia wants and needs US assistance in its military re-equipment program. The State Department has, we understand, instructed the embassy to cut down its reporting on Timor. But [U.S.] Ambassador Newsom told me last night that he is under instructions from Kissinger personally not to involve himself in discussions on Timor with the Indonesians. . . . [Newsom's] present attitude is that the US should keep out of the Portuguese Timor situation and allow events to take their course."[21]

Despite the lack of reporting from its embassy in Jakarta, Washington was well aware of Jakarta's plans and activities. In September 1975, for example, the CIA was closely monitoring Indonesian military incursions into East Timor in the aftermath of a brief civil war between the then Portuguese colony's two largest political parties — both pro-independence — Fretilin and the UDT, or Timorese Democratic Union. Instigated by false Indonesian intelligence reports of an imminent Fretilin power grab, clandestine Chinese arms deliveries, and "Vietnamese terrorists" entering the territory to aid Fretilin, the UDT decided to try to seize power in the territory and thus launched a coup on August 12, 1975. On the basis of meetings in Jakarta with Indonesian officials, UDT leaders were convinced that Indonesia would not allow East Timorese independence under Fretilin leadership and probably not even under the UDT. The UDT felt that only by purging the territory of "communist" influence would it have any chance of preventing an Indonesian invasion.[22]

The UDT greatly underestimated the strength of Fretilin, which quickly turned the tide. On September 24, 1975, the short-lived civil war ended when Fretilin drove approximately five hundred UDT soldiers, along with twenty-five hundred refugees (most of whom were family members of UDT leaders and soldiers) westward into West (Indonesian) Timor. During this time the Portuguese authorities fled the territory. Well aware of Indonesia's designs on the territory, and more concerned about its other colonies in Africa and developments at home, Lisbon acquiesced to Jakarta, effectively doing nothing in the face of growing Indonesian interference in the decolonization process and of intensifying acts of military aggression.[23]

As Fretilin was overcoming the last of the UDT at the end of the civil war, incursions by the Indonesian military began in the regions close to the border with West Timor. As early as September 4, 1975, the CIA noted the entry of two Indonesian special force groups (about two hundred men) into Portuguese Timor.[24]

To give the appearance of an ongoing civil war, which would facilitate the acceptance of Indonesia's propagandistic claim that it was intervening on behalf of East Timorese suffering from Fretilin-led brutality, Indonesia maintained a cross-boundary strategy. This consisted of frequent incursions into the then Portuguese Timor with the intent of establishing bases along the territorial divide with Indonesia, as confirmed by the CIA's *National Intelligence Daily*[25] — the highly classified intelligence briefing delivered each day to the White House. Indonesian troops captured a number of towns in the border region. The aggression culminated in mid-November when the Indonesians mounted a land, air, and sea attack for about two weeks against the town of Atabae, which finally fell on November 28, 1975.[26] On that same day Fretilin declared independence from Portugal and the founding of the Democratic Republic of East Timor. Nine days later, on December 7, Indonesia launched its full-scale invasion.

President Gerald Ford and his secretary of state, Henry Kissinger, met with Suharto in Jakarta the day prior to the invasion. They were fully cognizant of Indonesia's plans to invade. According to the transcript of the meeting, Ford assured Suharto that, with regard to East Timor, "[We] will not press you on the issue. We understand . . . the intentions you have."[27]

In previous months the Ford administration had cautioned Indonesia against using American weaponry in any planned aggression. (According to the State Department, about 90 percent of Indonesia's military equipment at the time was from the United States.)[28] As laid out in a 1958 agreement with the U.S. government, Indonesia assured the United States that it would use U.S.-origin weaponry "solely for legitimate national self-defense" as defined by the U.N. Charter.[29] But any reservations that the administration may have had previously about the employment of U.S. weaponry seems to have disappeared by December 1975. However, there was still the problem of perception and public opinion. It was therefore necessary to cast the pending invasion of tiny, impoverished East Timor as something other than aggression. As Kissinger explained to Suharto at the December 6, 1975, meeting in Jakarta, "You appreciate that the use of U.S.-made arms could create problems." The secretary of state thus stated, "It depends on how we construe it, whether it is in self-defense or is a foreign operation." Kissinger then expressed understanding for Indonesia's "need to move quickly" and advised "that it would be better if it were done after we [he and Ford] returned [to the United States]."[30] About fourteen hours after their departure, Indonesian forces invaded.

In response, some individual members of Congress tried to cut off Washington's military largess. Tom Harkin, at the time a member of the House of Representatives from the state of Iowa, for example, introduced an amendment in early 1976 to eliminate a $19.4 million grant in military assistance to Indonesia. Twenty-four of the Iowa Democrat's colleagues supported the measure, but forty-six voted against it, sending it down to defeat. Speaking against the measure, William Broomfield (a Republican from Michigan) predicted that its passage would be "a serious blow" to relations with Jakarta. "Here is a strong anti-Communist nation which is just getting on its feet," he asserted. And the timing of the aid cut, less than one year after the "fall" of Saigon, Broomfield opined, "would be most unfortunate." Another colleague, Morgan Murphy (Democrat from Illinois), justified his negative vote by pointing out that Indonesia "is a rich source of minerals for western markets, and is on a key oil transport route between Japan and the Middle East."[31]

An exasperated Harkin later wrote of his dismay with U.S. policy toward East Timor:

> It is no surprise that the United States has been an apologist for the government of Indonesia, given the country's staunchly anti-communist politics, rich oil reserves, and open-armed acceptance of multinational investment. It is a shock, however, to see how utterly expendable human rights considerations are in our dealings with the government of Indonesia.[32]

The invasion and the illegal use of U.S. weapons required a cutoff of U.S. military assistance. But the administration only imposed an administrative delay of additional military aid to Jakarta while continuing to deliver military equipment "already in the pipeline."[33] As Philip Habib, the assistant secretary of state described during a meeting of Kissinger's staff in June 1976, "[the Indonesians are] quite happy with the position we've taken. We've resumed, as you know, all of our normal relations with them." In reference to the deception of Congress, to Indonesia's invasion and occupation, or to both, Kissinger responded: "Illegally and beautifully."[34]

Soon thereafter the Ford administration ended even the pretense of limiting military sales to Indonesia, using as an excuse Suharto's signing into law East Timor's formal integration into Indonesia on July 17, 1976. From then on, the official U.S. position was to accept Indonesia's annexation of East Timor as a fait accompli, and therefore as a de facto (but not de jure) part of Indonesia — a situation the United States would not contest. The advantage of this position was that it put an end to any discussion regarding the use of American arms in East Timor, as the 1958 "mutual defense agreement" between the United States and Indonesia allowed Jakarta to employ U.S. weaponry "to maintain its internal security." And East Timor was now an internal Indonesian matter — at least from the perspective of the White House. Thus the Ford administration had few qualms about delivering to Indonesia in September 1976 a squadron of U.S.-made OV-10 Bronco ground-attack planes,[35] Vietnam War–era aircraft that were highly useful for counterinsurgency operations, especially against those without effective antiaircraft weaponry.

Only a few months earlier an unnamed State Department official had explained why Washington condoned Jakarta's actions: "We regard Indonesia as a friendly, non-aligned nation — a nation we do a lot of business with."[36]

●

The essence of U.S. policy toward Indonesia and East Timor did not change during the administration of Jimmy Carter (1977–80), a man who, in a 1980 speech to the Organization of American States, described the cause of human rights as the "cause that has been closest to my own heart."[37] Despite such lofty words, the same set of political-economic and geo-strategic concerns that shaped Ford's and Kissinger's behavior also governed Carter's policy, one that gave primacy to good relations with Jakarta over the lives of the East Timorese. The administration thus provided weaponry to Jakarta from the outset, including two additional OV-10 Broncos, six of which were already in use in East Timor according to the Pentagon.[38] In late 1977, when Indonesia was actually running out of military equipment because of its activities in East Timor,[39] the Carter administration responded by authorizing $112 million worth of arms sales for fiscal 1978 to Jakarta, up from $13 million the previous year. In February 1978 the administration announced a decision to sell Jakarta sixteen F-5 fighter jets. And in May of that year Carter sent his vice president, Walter Mondale, to Jakarta where he finalized a deal that led to the release of a few thousand of the twenty thousand Indonesian political prisoners held by Suharto in relation to the 1965–66 terror. In return, the regime received a squadron of A-4 ground-attack bombers. *The New York Times* described Mondale's role in the transaction in fawning terms without mentioning what the planes might be used for.[40] An editorial in the newsletter of the British Campaign for the Release of Indonesian Political Prisoners, in sharp contrast, offered the following: "It is certainly just that the [political prisoners] are receiving the attention of the American President after all these years, but in reality they have simply become pawns in cynical government bargaining over weapons of death."[41]

Carter administration officials facilitated U.S. complicity by often misleading Congress through understatements of the number of East Timorese killed, the level of ongoing resistance to Indonesia's occupation, and even the nature of the "integration" process. In a 1977 hearing, for example, a member of Congress asked Robert Oakley, Deputy Assistant Secretary for East Asian and Pacific Affairs, if the East Timorese people had elected to integrate with Indonesia.

"That is a difficult question to answer," Oakley responded. "There was a referendum which was conducted by the Indonesian Government. Now to what degree that referendum indicated accurately the will of all the people of East Timor, I am not in a position to judge."

The "referendum" to which Oakley was referring was actually a vote by the twenty-eight-member "People's Representative Assembly," a body described by Jakarta as comprised of "prominent citizens of East Timor" selected by the East Timorese people in the traditional method of consensus (rather than universal suffrage). In reality, Indonesian intelligence officers, with the help of pro-Indonesia locals, handpicked the delegates after checking that the candidates had no previous ties to Fretilin or the UDT. Not surprisingly the assembly's members unanimously approved the "Act of Integration" on May 31, 1976. Many of the small number of observers (and, later, even some of the assembly members) reported that the Indonesian authorities had completely staged the event.[42] The few journalists and Jakarta-based junior diplomats that attended the proceedings were not even permitted to speak with the assembly delegates. As one journalist present stated, "Immediately after the council meeting, all were led back into their cars and briefly driven around the town before going straight back to the airport and taking off for Kupang [the capital of Indonesian West Timor]. No one had a chance even to shake hands with council members, and executive members of the Provisional Government refused to answer press questions, climbing immediately into their new Volvo cars."[43]

Richard Holbrooke, along with the bureau he headed in the Department of State, was the primary architect of U.S. policy toward East Timor during

Carter's tenure. Despite this position, Holbrooke typically elected not to participate in congressional hearings that dealt with East Timor. As one reporter explained, regarding his failure to show up at one such meeting in 1980, "Mr. Holbrooke let it be known he was too busy preparing for a trip to appear at the Feb. 6 hearing. He did have the time, however, to play host at a black-tie dinner later the same day."[44] In March 1977 Holbrooke told Australian diplomat James Dunn that Indonesia's geographical location and oil wealth were "of considerable strategic importance to the U.S. As we see it," Holbrooke explained, "the Suharto regime is the best of possible alternatives, and we will do nothing to destabilize it," meaning that the Carter administration would not support East Timor but would back Indonesia instead.[45] Although the results of this policy were horrific for the East Timorese, Holbrooke asserted in a 1979 prepared statement to Congress that "the welfare of the Timorese people is the major objective of our policy toward East Timor."[46]

For the Carter administration, the matter of East Timor was not one of self-determination. As George Aldrich, deputy legal adviser of the State Department, explained, "the policy judgment has been made by this administration . . . that our interests would not be served by seeking to reopen the question of Indonesian annexation of East Timor. Instead, we have directed our efforts to urging Indonesia to institute a humane administration in East Timor and to accept an impartial inspection of its administration by the International Committee of the Red Cross."[47]

Despite the claim to humanitarianism, the Carter White House made little effort to reach out to the East Timorese. It failed, for example, to interview East Timorese refugees to ascertain conditions within the occupied territory. Even near the end of the administration's term of office, when the plight of East Timor was better known, East Timorese refugees going directly to the State Department received a cold reception. As one refugee recounted from his meeting with a State Department official, "He acted like a lawyer for the Indonesians."[48]

It was for such reasons that Representative Tony Hall, a Democrat from Ohio and perhaps the most persistent defender of the East Timorese in the House, opined that the Carter State Department (as well as that of Ford) had "engaged in a consistent pattern of discounting reports of Indonesian-inflicted suffering upon the people of East Timor." The administration had shown itself to be "adverse to congressional pressure about East Timor. Their attitude traditionally has been: 'Leave us alone, we know best. Leave the conduct of foreign policy to the professionals.'"[49]

In the memoirs of his presidency Carter writes how, prior to becoming a candidate for the White House, he was "deeply troubled by the lies our people had been told; our exclusion from the shaping of American political and military policy in Vietnam, Cambodia, Chile and other countries; and other embarrassing activities of our government, such as the CIA's role in plotting murder and other crimes." He goes on to reiterate the "dream" that he announced upon declaring his candidacy in December 1974: "That this country set a standard within the community of nations of courage, compassion, integrity, and dedication to basic human rights and freedoms."[50] The words "East Timor" do not appear in the almost six hundred pages of text.

The blank-check approach to U.S. policy toward Indonesia and East Timor continued in the Reagan and Bush administrations. This is hardly surprising, however, since, in comparison with Carter's presidency, in the presidencies of Reagan and Bush there was barely a pretense of human rights surrounding their foreign policies, which were characterized largely by unwavering support for any regime, no matter how authoritarian, that cast its behavior in anticommunist terms and supported Washington's global agenda. U.S. military sales to Indonesia thus peaked during the Reagan administration, exceeding U.S.$500 million from 1981 to 1986.[51] Such sales dropped somewhat during the George H. W. Bush administration (1989–92), averaging about $28 million annually.[52]

This was a time of growing political repression in East Timor as the Indonesian military violently countered peaceful demonstrations by the increasingly effective underground resistance. In response, 223 members of Congress signed a November 1990 letter to James Baker, secretary of state in the Bush administration, expressing their concerns over the repression and calling on the White House to support peace talks among all concerned parties without preconditions. The letter pushed *The New York Times* to publish one of its rare editorials on East Timor. This U.S. paper of record used the occasion of the fifteen-year anniversary of Indonesia's invasion to issue a strong statement in which it drew a parallel with Iraq's invasion of Kuwait and Indonesia's 1975 invasion of the former Portuguese colony. The *Times* condemned Jakarta's aggression and subsequent record as the occupying power, while calling on Bush to "serve America's principles and honor by raising his voice."[53]

The significant diplomatic and political cover that the Bush administration provided to Jakarta in the aftermath of the 1991 Santa Cruz massacre demonstrated, however, that such words fell largely on deaf ears. While the State Department officially deplored the "overreaction" of Indonesian troops at Santa Cruz, it rejected any attempts to cut military assistance to Jakarta. And, privately, administration officials assisted Jakarta in its efforts to limit the political fallout. According to State Department documents, U.S. officials met with their Indonesian counterparts in Surabaya (Indonesia) on December 10, 1991, which was International Human Rights Day. The administration's envoys explained to Jakarta's representatives that Washington "understand[s]

[that] Indonesia is under considerable pressure from the world at large" and that "we do not believe that friends should abandon friends in times of adversity." Two weeks later Washington's ambassador to Jakarta, John Monjo, met with Dr. Widjojo, Suharto's senior adviser, who, according to the documents, "thanked the ambassador for the stance adopted by the USG [United States government] thus far."[54] Around that same time the State Department characterized the report of the Suharto regime's white-washed investigation as "serious and responsible." And in a January 1992 visit to Indonesia, Senators Daniel Inouye, Democrat of Hawaii, and Alaska Republican Ted Stevens said that they were "impressed" with Jakarta's handling of the matter.[55]

Jakarta was especially concerned about calls by representatives of various national governments to link aid levels to Indonesia's human rights records. The Bush State Department and Pentagon obliged Jakarta by proposing to double military aid to Indonesia while continuing the sale of weapons. The aid took the form of what is called IMET (International Military Education and Training), a program that brings foreign military officers to the United States for training. More than twenty-six hundred Indonesian military officers had received IMET training from the time of the invasion until the end of 1991.[56] According to the then State Department spokesperson Richard Boucher, "these kinds of programs expose the trainee to democratic ideas and humanitarian standards." The State Department supported its argument by pointing out that none of the Indonesian military officers present at Santa Cruz had received U.S. training.[57]

Despite such declarations, the ground under the White House and the Washington-Jakarta partnership was shifting. The Santa Cruz massacre and its publicity had led to a groundswell of outrage toward Indonesia and a dramatic rise in pro–East Timor activism—both at the grassroots level and within various national governments. This was especially true in the United States.

In May 1992 Tony Hall introduced a bill in the House of Representatives to terminate all U.S. economic and military assistance to Indonesia until Jakarta complied with the U.N. resolutions calling on it to withdraw from East Timor and to allow a U.N.-supervised referendum on self-determination. And, in September, members of Congress and the Japanese Diet sent a joint appeal to U.N. Secretary General Boutros Boutros-Ghali calling upon the United Nations to take concrete measures to realize a U.N.-run vote on self-determination in East Timor. Led by Tony Hall and Representative Ronald Machtley of Rhode Island, 150 members of Congress signed the appeal. While such actions were largely symbolic—at least in terms of their short-term impacts—they were manifestations of a marked departure from what had been effectively unquestioning support for Jakarta.

Thus, on October 2, 1992, Congress cut $2.3 million in IMET funding for

Indonesia from the Foreign Aid appropriations bill for fiscal year 1993, despite strong opposition from major U.S. corporations such as AT&T and the State and Defense Departments. The cutoff marked the first time in seventeen years that Congress had cut aid to Indonesia over the issue of East Timor.

●

Such developments seemed to bode well for the future. And Bill Clinton's winning of the American presidency in late 1992 only served to bolster the hopes of many East Timor advocates. In a book he coauthored to boost his election campaign, Clinton had pledged that his administration would "never forge strategic relationships with dangerous, despotic regimes. [My administration] will understand that our foreign policy must promote democracy as well as stability."[58] And during a campaign press conference, in response to a journalist's question, he had stated: "I am very concerned about the situation in East Timor. We have ignored it so far in ways that are unconscionable." Although the problem was not that Washington had "ignored" East Timor but, rather, that it had aided and abetted Jakarta's war of conquest, the perceived sentiment behind the words seemed to be a positive sign—especially to those desperate for such omens.

Certainly the administration made steps in the right direction upon Clinton's swearing-in—in large part as a result of grassroots and congressional pressure. At the March 1993 meeting of the U.N. Human Rights Commission, the U.S. delegation reversed its historical obstructionism and cosponsored a resolution condemning Indonesian human rights violations in East Timor. (That a number of Western countries supported the resolution—including Australia, which would otherwise have voted against it—was indicative of the preeminent position of the United States in international politics, in addition to the key role of Washington in East Timor's plight.) Later that year Clinton's State Department also blocked a proposed sale by the Jordanian government of four U.S.-made F-5E fighter jets to Jakarta. And, in early 1994, the State Department announced a ban on the sale of small arms to Indonesia.

But Jakarta's continuing economic and strategic importance quickly exposed the limits of Clinton's concern for human rights and international law. As reported by columnist Mark Baker in the August 26, 1993, edition of *The Age,* in Melbourne, Australia, "[a] U.S. official said the extent to which the administration was prepared to press Indonesia on human rights was tempered by the continuing economic and strategic importance of Jakarta."

The contradictions of the Clinton policy soon came to an embarrassing head. On November 12, 1994, twenty-nine East Timorese students and workers jumped out of taxis and scaled the spiked fence of the U.S. Embassy in Jakarta, unfurling banners and shouting pro-independence slogans. Camped out in the embassy parking lot, the demonstrators called for East Timorese self-determination and the withdrawal of Indonesian troops from their country. In a written petition to Bill Clinton, who was scheduled to arrive the next day in Jakarta, the protesters made a number of demands. These included that Clinton call upon Indonesia to release jailed East Timorese resistance leader Xanana Gusmão and all other East Timorese political prisoners, to enter into direct negotiations with the different elements of the resistance, and to allow for "an independent and impartial mission" to investigate the Santa Cruz massacre.

The date of the embassy invasion marked the third anniversary of the killings at the Santa Cruz cemetery and the beginning of the annual meeting of the Asia-Pacific Economic Conference, a consortium of Pacific Rim countries that seeks to increase and liberalize intraregional trade and investment.[59] The timing and location of the meeting could not have been worse for Jakarta, nor better from the perspective of the East Timorese. Whoever was in charge of scheduling the meeting, one news report asserted, "must have rocks in his head."[60] In what turned out to be an ingenious public relations coup, the embassy occupation and a series of events in and around East Timor effectively diverted the international media spotlight away from Clinton's and Indonesian President Suharto's free trade showcase in Jakarta toward East Timor.

On November 12 an Indonesian businessman stabbed to death an East Timorese trader in Dili. The murder led to rioting by hundreds of youths, with attacks on Indonesian-owned homes, stores, and hotels, the burning of cars, and clashes with riot police who responded with tear gas. Frequent and violent protests continued for at least two weeks. Several were reported dead and hundreds arrested. And on November 13, in Dili, a small pro-independence rally took place after a Sunday morning Catholic mass to commemorate the Santa Cruz massacre. Several dozen young people marched with Fretilin flags and banners calling for independence and President Clinton's support. Dozens of foreign journalists were present in Dili in preparation for the APEC conference in Jakarta and thus witnessed the demonstration as well as the rioting.

During this time coverage of events relating to East Timor by the three major American television networks was nonexistent (with the exception of one brief report by ABC News on November 14). Most major newspapers in the United States (and throughout the West), however, carried reports, and many, including *USA Today, The New York Times,* and the *Wall St. Journal,* ran editorials criticizing Jakarta's heavy-handedness in the former Portuguese colony, with some even calling for East Timorese self-determination.

But the reporting was often shallow and misleading, and understated the importance of what was taking place. *The New York Times,* for example, led its first report on the embassy occupation by characterizing it as "an incident that raises questions about the security of American diplomatic outposts," a concern the article raised throughout. As for why the demonstrators chose the U.S. Embassy, the *Times* said that it was "an attempt to get President Clinton . . . to put pressure on the [Indonesian] Government over the reported repression in East Timor."[61] Although not entirely false, the statement was only partially true and was indicative of the larger tendency of the American media to soft-peddle the issue of U.S. involvement in what was — proportionately speaking — one of the worst genocides since World War II. At the same time the tone of the editorials was hardly befitting the scale of Indonesia's crimes in East Timor. One *New York Times* editorial of November 14, entitled "Now Myanmar Must Choose," offered stern advice to the Burmese military junta, informing the oligarchy that it had to choose between softening its tyranny and better relations with Washington, on the one hand, and increased economic and political pressure from Washington, on the other. In contrast, in an editorial on the following day, entitled "Indonesia's Embarrassment," the *Times* did not call for increased pressure on Jakarta. Instead, it suggested a few "reasonable demands" that Clinton could make, including a guarantee of safety for the East Timorese in the embassy compound, a scaled-down military presence in East Timor, and an end to human rights violations there, but nothing about ending the very occupation that inevitably caused those human rights violations.

The East Timorese vowed not to leave the embassy compound until the United States met their demands, including a meeting with Secretary of State Warren Christopher or President Clinton himself. (They turned down an offer of a meeting with the U.S. ambassador to Jakarta, Robert Barry.) While both Clinton and Christopher promised that the demonstrators were welcome to stay in the compound for as long as they desired and that they would not be pressured to leave the embassy grounds, the behavior of the embassy staff suggested otherwise.

Embassy officials refused the demonstrators water for the first two days. After that they would only provide water and two servings of white rice once a day. The embassy also denied the demonstrators shelter and access to sanitary facilities. These conditions, combined with the Clinton administration's lack of compliance with their demands along with the repeated exposure to taunts and death threats from the hundreds of Indonesian military personnel ringing the fence around the compound, finally convinced the protesters to accept Portugal's offer of political asylum. Twelve days after the occupation began, the twenty-nine protestors left for exile in Portugal by which time the U.S. media had long lost interest in the story.

For its part, the Clinton administration tried to put the most positive spin on the APEC meeting, emphasizing Clinton's supposedly stern lecture on human rights to Suharto as well as the signing of fifteen separate business deals totaling $40 billion over the next decade (including a $30 billion deal for exploitation of natural gas reserves by Exxon). Undoubtedly it was for reasons similar to such talk of billion dollar deals that inspired a senior administration official, during a visit to the Clinton White House about a year later, to refer effusively to Suharto as "our kind of guy."[62]

In the course of its eight years in office Clinton's administration provided more than $500 million in economic assistance, and sold and licensed the sales of hundreds of millions of dollars in weaponry to Jakarta. The Clinton administration even side-stepped the congressional ban on IMET by allowing Indonesia to purchase the training while continuing joint U.S.-Indonesia military exercises. The administration further circumvented the intent of Congress and provided lethal training to Indonesia's military. At least twenty-eight training exercises in sniper tactics, urban warfare, explosives, psychological operations, and other techniques took place between 1993 and 1998 in Indonesia through a Pentagon program. The primary beneficiary was the Kopassus, Indonesia's special forces troops responsible for many of the worst human rights violations in East Timor.[63] While such revelations served to fuel further grassroots and congressional efforts to close military aid loopholes as well as congressional resolutions supporting self-determination for the East Timorese, various forms of economic and military assistance continued through 1999.

As political instability grew in Indonesia in the second half of 1997 and early 1998 in the context of the regional economic meltdown known as the "Asian Crisis," the Clinton administration continued to back the increasingly embattled Suharto regime. In January 1998 William Cohen, the administration's secretary of defense, went to Jakarta where he explicitly refused to call upon the Indonesian military to exercise restraint in responding to street demonstrations. While there, he also spent three hours at Kopassus headquarters watching the elite troops undertake maneuvers. Sitting by his side was Prabowo, the commander of Kostrad, the presidential guard. He had served for many years in East Timor where he developed his reputation as the military's most ruthless field commander.[64]

If such behavior did not expose the limits of Clinton's professed concerns for the plight of the East Timorese and his willingness to put an end to American backing of Jakarta, the June 1997 visit of Bishop Carlos Belo to Washington did. Despite Belo having received the Nobel Peace Prize more than a year earlier, Clinton refused to meet with him in the Oval Office. Instead, Clinton "dropped by" for fifteen minutes while Belo met with National Security Adviser Sandy Berger. (Such "drop-bys" are of lower status, and thus the meeting represented less of an affront to Jakarta.) After listening to Belo, Clinton promised that "we will try to be more helpful." The next day Belo received eight color photographs of the meeting.[65]

These photos, however, did not appear in any newspapers, as the administration repeatedly refused to release the images to the various wire services that requested them—a fact not known at the time. As to why the photos were withheld, Arnold Kohen, Belo's biographer, explains, "it seemed obvious that, like the 'drop-by' in the first place, this was another way of downplaying the importance of the meeting. By refusing to release the photos to the press in the first two days after the meeting took place, the White House press office ensured they would never receive wide circulation; the news value of such material is generally based on its timeliness."[66]

•

The U.S. government certainly was not alone in backing Indonesia's invasion and occupation of East Timor. Almost all the world's most powerful and wealthy capitalist countries did so to varying extents. While the list of accomplices includes countries ranging from Canada to France and Germany,[67] the activities of Australia, Japan, New Zealand, and the United Kingdom are especially relevant. Along with the United States, these latter four countries emerged in 1999 as the members of the "Core Group" of countries that acted as an informal advisory body to the U.N. secretary-general during the last stages of the negotiations that led to Indonesia agreeing to the "popular consultation" and the subsequent electoral process.

Of all these countries, Australia was perhaps the one whose support for Indonesia's occupation was most steadfast. Given its geographic proximity, wealth of resources, and sheer size, Indonesia has long been important to Australia. It was for such reasons that many Australian policy makers and opinion leaders celebrated Suharto's bloody seizure of power in 1965–66.[68] Recent disclosures prove that Australia's government was well aware in 1974–75 of Indonesia's plans of aggression against East Timor. Officially Canberra expressed support for self-determination in East Timor. In reality, however, the Australian government effectively encouraged Indonesia's action by consulting with Jakarta about its plans for East Timor, and saying and doing nothing to indicate any significant opposition to Indonesia's planned takeover of the former Portuguese colony. In fact, Australian officials, including Prime Minister Gough Whitlam, often expressed their preference for an Indonesian-controlled East Timor rather than an independent one, while communicating to Jakarta that Australia valued its bilateral relationship to such an extent that it would not let events surrounding East Timor get in the way. A September 1974 meeting in Wonosobo, Java, between Whitlam and Suharto was reportedly decisive in pushing Suharto to support the plans of some leading Indonesian generals to annex Portuguese Timor. Until that point Suharto had been apprehensive for fear that aggression toward East Timor would hurt his standing in the capitals of Western Europe and North America. Whitlam's statement that it would be in East Timor's best interest to join Indonesia—albeit one made in conjunction with a less emphatic assertion that Jakarta should respect the wishes of the East Timorese and that Australian public opinion would oppose the use of force by Indonesia—reportedly encouraged Suharto to move away from his cautious stance. The next month *Operasi Komodo* was born.[69]

As other Western powers did, Australia made a decision to effectively sacrifice the people of East Timor for its far more beneficial relationship with Indonesia. As a high-level Australian official responsible for policy on East Timor complained to an Australian diplomat critical of Canberra's policy in 1975 after Jakarta's invasion, "I don't see what you're getting all excited about! The plain fact is that there are only seven hundred thousand East Timorese; what we are really concerned about is our relationship with one hundred thirty million Indonesians!"[70] Thus, despite officially condemning Jakarta's invasion, Canberra doubled its military assistance to Indonesia between 1975 and 1981, during a time when its own Parliament Legislative Research Service described the situation in East Timor as "indiscriminate killing on a scale unprecedented in post–World War II history."[71] The government of Malcolm Fraser (which followed that of Gough Whitlam) also shut down the only radio link between the East Timorese resistance and the outside world, located in Darwin in northern Australia.[72] In 1995 Australian prime minister Paul Keating signed a security agreement with the Suharto regime that facilitated closer ties between the two country's military establishments. And through 1999 Canberra provided significant military training and weaponry, regularly exchanged intelligence information, and engaged in joint military maneuvers with Jakarta.

Australia worked harder probably than any other Western country to provide diplomatic cover for Indonesia's atrocities in East Timor. Perhaps no statement better exemplified the almost slavish nature of the attitude of much of Australia's political establishment toward Suharto than that of Deputy Prime Minister Tim Fischer in early 1998. Regarding the long-reigning dictator, Fischer opined that, "when magazines look for the man of the world of the second half of this century, they should perhaps look no further than Jakarta."[73] Canberra went so far as to extend de jure recognition in January 1979 of Indonesia's annexation of East Timor—a necessary step to enter into negotiations with Jakarta over the rights to the seabed of oil and natural gas deposits between northern Australia and the south coast of East Timor.[74] In 1993, while visiting the United States, Prime Minister Paul Keating urged the

Clinton administration to lessen its criticisms of Suharto's human rights record in East Timor.[75] This stance represented a role reversal of sorts. An August 1976 report in a leading Australia daily cited anonymous "U.S. officials stationed in South-East Asia" as reporting that high-ranking members of the Ford administration had warned Canberra's Fraser government to back down from his criticism of Indonesia's takeover of East Timor for fear that such criticism could hurt overall U.S. and Allied interests vis-à-vis Indonesia.[76] While Canberra had expressed some public criticism following the invasion, its actions — as already shown — spoke differently. In this regard, Washington's chiding was ultimately not especially important, although it did further expose the level of U.S. complicity.

Along with the United States, Britain was one of Indonesia's largest arms suppliers during the 1990s. The roots of British support for the Indonesian military, however, go back to the mid-1960s, when Sukarno was engaged in a military campaign aimed at destabilizing Malaysia. Sukarno perceived Malaysia and the process by which it became independent (in 1963) as evidence of a British plot to maintain a neocolonial foothold in the region. Jakarta's saber rattling led London to send tens of thousands of troops to its former colony. In the months leading up to the 1965–66 bloodbath in Indonesia, the British military and intelligence conspired with elements allied with Suharto to lessen tensions along the country's boundary with Malaysia. The high command of the Indonesian army wanted to undermine Sukarno's policy of escalating hostilities with Malaysia and avoid a full-scale war, a desire that London shared. At the same time the British wanted to see the TNI take action against the Indonesian Communist Party (PKI). The British thus assured the TNI that they would not attack while it was moving against the PKI. To the contrary, the British, in addition to encouraging Suharto to take action against the PKI, helped to transport Indonesian soldiers from outlying areas to Jakarta in the early days of the slaughter, and engaged in anti-Sukarno and anti-PKI propaganda operations.[77]

About ten years later, in the early stages of *Operasi Komodo,* Britain took a similar position to that of the United States and Australia regarding East Timorese independence. Aware of Jakarta's plans and activities, the United Kingdom, like many other countries, decided that it was in its best interest to say and do nothing in protest. As was written in a secret Australian cable from Jakarta dated July 21, 1975, matters relating to Portuguese Timor were becoming "almost a taboo subject for key Embassies here — Singapore and other ASEAN countries, the United States and Netherlands. Few Embassies now even bother to raise the subject with us. The British Embassy's views are also interesting. . . . They know what is inevitable, and they attach a higher importance to their long-term interests in Indonesia."[78] In the same month

Sir John Archibald Ford, British ambassador to Jakarta, wrote to the Foreign Office, "the people of Portuguese Timor are in no condition to exercise their right to self-determination." It was in British interest, he opined, "that Indonesia should absorb the territory as soon as and as unobtrusively as possible; and that if it comes to the crunch and there is a row in the U.N. we should keep our heads down and avoid siding with the Indonesian government."[79] Accordingly Great Britain abstained on all eight votes on East Timor in the General Assembly from 1975 to 1982. In general, London's diplomatic role vis-à-vis East Timor was similar to that of Washington. As one East Timorese resistance representative put it in 1992, the British government was "the single worst obstructionist of any industrialized country."[80]

While Britain sold a variety of military equipment to Indonesia, it was the sale of British-manufactured Hawk ground-attack jets that is most noteworthy. The sale of eight Hawks in 1978 proved useful to the Indonesian military's saturation bombing of the occupied territory. In 1993 the British government approved the sale of twenty-four additional such aircraft to Jakarta, and in 1996 approved the sale of sixteen more. When asked in 1994 about his knowledge of the use of U.K.-origin weapons in occupied East Timor, Alan Clark, who served as British defense minister under Prime Minister Margaret Thatcher, responded by saying, "I don't really fill my mind much with what one set of foreigners is doing to another."[81]

In 1978 a young Labour member of the British Parliament, Robin Cook, wrote a scathing critique of British arms sales to repressive regimes. Such sales, he argued, were wrongheaded for two reasons. First, such regimes "invariably resort to the most brutal method of crushing dissent." And, second, while the recipient country might justify the purchase on the basis of national defense, "arms imports are far more likely to be used by such regimes against their own people than their neighbours." What Cook found "particularly disturbing" was the then current sale of Hawk aircraft to Jakarta—not only because Indonesia practiced repression at home but also because it was waging war in East Timor and in West Papua (what Indonesia called at the time "Irian Jaya").[82] That same year the Labour Party's foreign minister, David Owen, who approved the sale of the Hawks, characterized estimates of the death toll in East Timor as "exaggerated."[83]

In 1994 Cook told Parliament that Hawk aircraft had been "observed on bombing runs in East Timor in most years since 1984." Three years later Robin Cook became Prime Minister Tony Blair's foreign minister (the first from Labour since David Owen). But now in government Cook sang a new tune, denying he had ever stated that British Hawks were operational in East Timor. And his Foreign Office staff continued to claim misleadingly that the TNI was not using British military aircraft in the occupied territory.[84]

Although Blair and Cook publicly championed what they called an "ethical foreign policy"—having run on a party platform which pledged that it would "not permit the sale of arms to regimes that might use them for internal repression or external aggression"[85]—their government proceeded with the sale of the Hawks, water cannons, and armored trucks, exports approved under the previous government, with Cook arguing that it was not "realistic or practical" to stop sales approved before the Blair government came into power.[86] That same government agreed to sixty-four new arms export licenses for Indonesia in its first year in office. By the late 1990s Britain, in addition to being one of Indonesia's top suppliers of weaponry, was the country's second-largest foreign investor, having invested more than $30 billion since 1967.[87] In addition, Blair's Labour government strengthened direct ties with Indonesia's military. Twenty-four senior members of Indonesia's forces received training in British military colleges between 1997 and September 1999, and another twenty-nine officers studied at nonmilitary academic establishments in the United Kingdom. Government representatives defended the training as a form of "constructive engagement," one that ensures "professionalism" and "encourages higher standards, good governance, and greater respect for human rights."[88]

That said, the Blair government did help to raise East Timor's diplomatic profile on the international stage and endeavored to pressure Indonesia to respect the human rights of the East Timorese. In August 1997, for example, Robin Cook visited Indonesia, where he linked Indonesia's human rights record to future arms sales and proposed a high-level delegation from the European Union (EU) to visit East Timor. This visit, facilitated by the British presidency of the EU, took place in June 1998 and resulted in a very strong EU position on the occupied country. The ambassadorial report called for, among other things, a withdrawal of the Indonesian military from East Timor, an immediate ceasefire between the TNI and Falintil, the release of political prisoners, including Xanana Gusmão, and direct East Timorese participation in negotiations aimed at resolving the conflict.[89] Although such developments were significant, London's continuing military and economic support for Jakarta during this period undoubtedly had the effect of sending what were, at best, confusing signals to Jakarta and, at worst (and a more likely outcome), a message that it was business as usual. In a September 1999 opinion essay meant to absolve the Blair government of any wrongdoing, Robin Cook reported that London had licensed 16 million pounds worth of arms exports to Jakarta the previous year, "nearly all of it spares and services for historic contracts and a mere £1 million for new contracts."[90]

While London abstained on most of the General Assembly votes, Tokyo cast negative ballots on all the Assembly resolutions concerning East Timor.

Japanese diplomats did not even pretend to have concern for the suffering of the East Timorese. Instead, they would often simply mouth Jakarta's self-serving claim that Indonesia had been obliged to intervene in the former Portuguese colony to stop the bloodletting from the civil war between Fretilin and the UDT, and to assist East Timor's process of decolonization.[91]

The high level of economic interdependence between Indonesia and Japan is probably the most important factor in explaining Tokyo's uncritical support. As the Japanese government's 1992 Diplomatic White Paper explained, "Indonesia has a strong, mutually dependent relation with Japan through provision of oil and natural gas, and acceptance of direct investment. And Indonesia is a very important country for Japan because it is located in an area with important international sea routes and because it has a large political influence in Southeast Asia."[92]

Whereas in 1975 Japan was the second largest foreign investor in Indonesia, it occupied the first position in the late 1990s. According to a 1992 International Monetary Fund report, Japan received 37 percent of Indonesia's exports in 1991 and provided Indonesia with 25 percent of its imports. By the 1990s Japan was providing the bulk of Indonesia's bilateral assistance, and Jakarta was Tokyo's largest recipient of such aid. In 1996 Tokyo's aid package to Jakarta was worth $965 million.[93]

As international scrutiny and criticism of Jakarta's occupation mounted beginning in the 1990s, Japan remained one of Indonesia's most unwavering supporters among the wealthy capitalist countries. At the time of the 1991 Santa Cruz massacre, for example, Japan's Defense Agency had accepted a number of Indonesian officers to its Defense College. While the United States and some European countries reviewed aspects of their military relationships with Indonesia following the videotaped killings, Japan's Defense Agency refused to review even this minor program, stating that it "did not consider that there were any particular problems in Indonesia."[94] And following the 1996 awarding of the Nobel Peace Prize to two East Timorese, the Japanese government refused to meet with one of the laureates, diplomat José Ramos-Horta, when he visited Tokyo so as not to upset Jakarta.[95]

As for New Zealand, its assistance to Indonesia was small in an absolute sense but important nonetheless. Like the governments of many of its Western allies, that of New Zealand was well aware of Indonesia's plans to invade East Timor but remained silent. In the United Nations Wellington abstained on the first four General Assembly resolutions on East Timor (1975–1978), and voted no on the next four, including the final one in 1982, which merely instructed the secretary general to initiate discussions with all concerned parties with the goal of exploring possible avenues to a comprehensive settlement. New Zealand was also the only Western country whose government agreed to send an envoy to the sham "Act of Integration" that took place on May 31, 1976, in Dili.[96]

The types of attitudes that served as part of the foundation underlying New Zealand's policy of complicity were on display when Wellington's ambassador to Jakarta, Roger Peren, visited East Timor in early 1978. In his report on the chaperoned visit, Peren described the East Timorese as "poor, small, and riddled with disease, and almost totally illiterate." He continued: "Considered as human stock they are not at all impressive and this is something to think about when judging their capacity to take part in [an] act of self-determination or even perform as responsible citizens of an independent country."[97]

Wellington also provided resources to Jakarta's propaganda arsenal by undermining the ability of representatives of the East Timorese resistance to publicize their cause in New Zealand. In the late 1970s, for example, Wellington denied a visa to José Ramos-Horta.[98] More typically successive governments refused to meet with such resistance emissaries. Labor Prime Minister David Lange, much praised in many quarters for his stance against nuclear weapons, for instance, justified his refusal to meet with Ramos-Horta in 1985 by stating, "I do not believe that keeping alive the issue of independence will do anything to help the East Timorese people." The previous year Lange had opined that the human rights situation in East Timor was improving.[99]

A December 10, 1975, memorandum from the secretary of foreign affairs to the prime minister explained Wellington's thinking: "New Zealand has a strong interest in maintaining good relations with Indonesia even if this might on occasion require some measure of compromise on matters of principle." In 1984 the Ministry of Foreign Affairs spoke of New Zealand's "very considerable national interest in maintaining good relations with Indonesia," which it characterized as "unquestionably the single most important country in South East Asia."[100]

From the time of the invasion through 1999 New Zealand hosted and provided annual training to about ten to twenty-five members of the Indonesian military through its "military assistance program." Wellington also frequently participated in joint military maneuvers with Jakarta. And New Zealand allowed Indonesia to have its Skyhawk fighter jets refurbished in the country.[101]

Even when its own citizens lost their lives in East Timor at the hands of the Indonesian military, the government of New Zealand did not protest strongly. In October 1975 TNI troops attacked the East Timorese town of Balibo, near the border with Indonesian West Timor, brutally murdering in cold blood five Australia-based journalists (two from Australia, two from Britain, and one from New Zealand). Wellington did not even issue a protest over the murder of the New Zealander, Gary Cunningham.[102] (The United Kingdom did little as well, apart from making a pro forma inquiry. Australia, for its part, pursued the matter somewhat, but instead of employing its knowledge of what happened to ensure justice, it helped cover up Indonesian responsibility for the killings.)[103] A little more than sixteen years later a nineteen–year-old New Zealander, Kamal Bamadhaj, was among the many killed at the Santa Cruz Cemetery on November 12, 1991. Wellington's protest was so weak that Jakarta praised its "balanced response."[104]

•

The support that its powerful allies provided to Jakarta ensured that the United Nations — the world body whose founding mission dedicated itself to saving "succeeding generations from the scourge of war" — would be impotent to reverse Indonesia's annexation and protect the human rights of the East Timorese from the time of the invasion until 1999.

As the primary international political organization, the United Nations had long served as the most significant arena of debate on the East Timor issue. U.N. discussions on the problem of East Timor began when Portugal first became a member of the world body in 1955. But until the fall of the Portuguese military dictatorship in 1974, Lisbon refused to comply with the U.N. Charter regarding the administration of non-self-governing territories. Claiming that it administered no non-self-governing territories and that its colonies were, in reality, "overseas provinces," Lisbon asserted that the United Nations was exceeding its authority in trying to push decolonization in territories such as Portuguese Timor.[105] Nevertheless, through the early 1970s, East Timor was "the subject of only infrequent and cursory interest in the United Nations."[106] This began to change in April 1974 with the overthrow of Portugal's military dictatorship.

It was not until more than one year later, however, that the United Nations paid significant attention to the situation in Portuguese Timor. In June 1975 the U.N. Special Committee on Decolonization met in Lisbon but merely called upon Portugal to create the conditions "to enable the people of that territory to attain the goals set forth in the Charter of the United Nations and the Declaration [on the Granting of Independence to Colonial Countries and Peoples]."[107] And despite the onset of the Indonesian-instigated civil war in August 1975 and, following that, the beginning of Indonesian military incursions from West Timor, the United Nations did not intervene. Had it done so, the conflict could very well have been resolved prior to Jakarta's invasion. A number of reasons explain the world body's inaction — most notably Indonesian opposition to, and a lack of Western government support for, such involvement. By the time the United Nations did begin to address the issue, it was too late to stop Indonesia's invasion.[108]

Indonesia's full-scale attack on December 7, 1975, led to a flurry of activity in the General Assembly's Fourth Committee (which is responsible for matters relating to decolonization), within which a number of draft resolutions began to circulate. One put forth by Indonesia's allies (the most active among whom were India, Japan, and Malaysia) ignored the invasion and sought to criticize Lisbon for its negligence and to blame it for causing disunity among the different East Timorese political factions.

Algeria, Cuba, Guyana, Senegal, Sierra Leone, and Trinidad and Tobago, on the other hand, introduced an alternative resolution, which came to be known as the "Algerian draft." The Fourth Committee approved the Algerian draft and forwarded it to the General Assembly, which adopted the resolution on December 12, 1975, by a vote of 72 in favor, 10 against, and 43 abstentions.[109] The abstentions included the United States, Canada, and most Western European countries. The resolution "strongly deplored" Indonesia's invasion, demanded that Jakarta withdraw its troops "without delay" to enable the territory's inhabitants "freely to exercise their right to self-determination and independence." Furthermore, it called upon all states to respect East Timor's right to self-determination, and requested that Portugal make every effort to achieve a peaceful settlement of the conflict. Finally, the resolution asked the Security Council to take urgent action to protect East Timor's territorial integrity and its people's right to self-determination, and requested that the international body send a fact-finding mission to the territory as soon as possible.[110] While the East Timorese had hoped for a stronger vote, the outcome marked a first for the United Nations: never before had the General Assembly singled out a leading member of the anticolonial bloc for criticism usually directed at countries such as Portugal, Israel, and South Africa.[111]

Ten days after the first General Assembly resolution, on December 22, 1975, the Security Council met and unanimously passed a resolution similar to the Assembly's. The Council's resolution called upon the secretary-general "to send urgently a special representative to East Timor for the purpose of making an on-the-spot assessment of the existing situation and of establishing contact with all the parties in the Territory and all States concerned in order to ensure the implementation of the present resolution."[112] The high-profile nature of the Security Council, whose resolutions are binding on all member-states, made it more difficult for the United States, Britain, and France to abstain as they had on the first General Assembly resolution.[113]

In the General Assembly the recently independent, former Portuguese colonies in Africa vigorously defended East Timor and were able to gain the support of the majority of African countries. Most Latin American countries and almost all communist states (Yugoslavia abstained) also sided with East Timor. With the exception of Singapore, which, to Jakarta's surprise, abstained, only the ASEAN countries (Malaysia, the Philippines, and Thailand) along with India, Iran, Japan, Qatar, and Saudi Arabia sided with the Suharto regime in voting against the resolution.[114] Indonesia was quite surprised at the level of opposition incurred by its military assault on East Timor, and responded with anger and defiance.

Shortly after the passage of the first Security Council resolution, Kurt Waldheim, secretary-general at the time, sent a special envoy, Vittorio Winspeare Guicciardi, to make the requested "on-the-spot assessment" of the territory's situation. Although the Indonesian military finally agreed to Guicciardi's visit, it only permitted him to stay for two days, limiting him to Dili and three other towns, while controlling every aspect of his visit. After his visit the envoy then tried to return to the territory—specifically to areas held by Fretilin—from Darwin, Australia. Fretilin had designated four possible airfields at which Guicciardi's aircraft could land. But the Indonesian military bombed all four airstrips the evening before his departure. Fretilin then informed the envoy that they could not guarantee his safety. While the Australian government voiced support for Guicciardi's efforts, Canberra was unwilling to challenge Jakarta's obstructionism. At one point, for example, the U.N. envoy was considering using a Portuguese corvette—a highly maneuverable warship smaller than a destroyer—to travel by sea to Fretilin areas. U.S. intelligence sources reported that Indonesia was prepared to sink the vessel. According to James Dunn, the former Australian consul in Dili, however, this certainly would not have happened had Australia been willing to send along an escort vessel. Without such an offer, Guicciardi soon ended his efforts to gain access to Fretilin-held territory and returned to New York where he reported to the secretary-general that "any accurate assessment of the situation in East Timor remained elusive."[115]

The Security Council discussed the special envoy's report at a meeting in April 1976. This resulted in the passage of another Council resolution, sponsored by Tanzania and Guyana, which basically restated the substance of the one approved on December 22, 1975. The resolution also requested that the secretary-general have his special envoy continue the mission entrusted to him by the previous resolution and to submit a report of his findings "as soon as possible."[116] The vote for the resolution was 12 to 0. This time, most significantly, the United States and Japan abstained from voting.

Indonesia's defiance of the resolution, combined with the United States working behind the scenes to convince other Security Council members to accept the "irreversible" nature of Indonesia's occupation, resulted in the effective termination of the Security Council's weak efforts to play a role in ending the East Timor conflict.[117] Of the other permanent members of the Security Council, France and the United Kingdom did nothing to ensure implementation of the resolutions. Even the Soviet Union was rather passive in its support for Fretilin, perhaps partially because China was presiding over the Council at the time. China, however, while never able to supply resources to the resistance within East Timor, provided significant diplomatic support, and even some financial assistance, to the Fretilin-led government in exile of the Democratic Republic of East Timor.[118]

Had further and stronger Security Council resolutions been proposed — ones that, for example, would have required U.N. member-states to take some sort of action in response to Indonesia's flouting of the previous Council resolutions — the United States would have most probably blocked their approval.[119] A statement by Daniel Patrick Moynihan, U.S. ambassador to the United Nations during the Ford administration, bears out such an analysis. In talking about East Timor in his memoirs, Moynihan boasted of his skill as a diplomat in preventing the world body from taking effective action: "The Department of State desired that the United Nations prove utterly ineffective in whatever measures it undertook. This task was given to me, and I carried it forward with no inconsiderable success."[120]

●

Despite such efforts, Indonesia and its allies were not able to erase opposition to its illegal annexation of the former Portuguese colony. From 1976 to 1982 there were annual votes in the U.N. General Assembly leading to the passage of resolutions reaffirming East Timor's right to self-determination. Most powerful capitalist countries, the effective ruling powers of the United Nations, either abstained from the voting (France, Germany, the United Kingdom) or voted no (Japan, the United States, Australia) on all or most of the seven subsequent resolutions that attempted either to condemn Indonesia's occupation of East Timor or merely to instruct the secretary-general to investigate the situation.[121]

Gradually support for East Timor began to weaken in the General Assembly as a result of Indonesia's diplomatic arm-twisting, the commercial and geopolitical interests of many countries, and, perhaps, because of decreasing optimism about the prospects for East Timorese self-determination.[122] The 1982 vote, for instance, barely passed with 50 votes in favor, 46 against, and 50 abstentions; it was the final vote in the Assembly on the matter. But the resolution did set in motion efforts by the secretary-general to realize negotiations between Indonesia and Portugal, which, under international law, remained the "administering power" of the territory.[123]

As chief administrative officer of the United Nations, the secretary-general played an important role in determining the level of attention focused on the East Timor issue within the international body. Kurt Waldheim, who led the world body at the time of the invasion, reportedly had little interest in the East Timor conflict, perceiving it as a "minor problem." Following the second Security Council resolution in 1976, for example, Waldheim basically exerted no effort to ensure that his Special Envoy made any serious attempts to investigate the situation in the occupied territory.[124]

Javier Pérez de Cuéllar, Waldheim's successor, responded to the General Assembly's 1982 resolution by forming a taskforce on East Timor. Pérez de Cuéllar interpreted the resolution's call to "initiate consultations with all parties directly concerned," however, to include only Portugal and Indonesia, not Fretilin, despite its enjoying widespread recognition within the United Nations at the time as representing the people of East Timor. Nevertheless Pérez de Cuellar did help initiate direct diplomatic contact between Jakarta and Lisbon.[125] But because of Jakarta's obstructionism, the resulting talks achieved little, focusing exclusively on "humanitarian issues" while failing to address the fundamental matters, largely that of self-determination, dividing the two sides.

Through the 1980s, the visibility of the East Timor issue faded on the international stage. This was in part due to Portugal's very poor advocacy on East Timor's behalf from the beginning of Indonesian aggression in 1975 through the mid-1980s.[126] Portugal's support for East Timorese self-determination was so weak that Lisbon reportedly seriously considered a deal with Jakarta that would have made permanent East Timor's status as an Indonesian province, in exchange for some minor concessions. (Because the "integration" of East Timor into Indonesia did not conform to U.N. standards for self-determination, the international body officially listed East Timor as a non-self-governing territory.)[127] A letter of February 6, 1989, from Bishop Belo, in which he requested that Pérez de Cuéllar "initiate a genuine and democratic process of decolonisation in East Timor to be realised through a [U.N.-sponsored] referendum,"[128] combined with a significant change in Lisbon's attitude and practice toward East Timor, helped put to rest any attempts at reaching such a Faustian bargain, however.[129] While many have pointed out that Pérez de Cuéllar never even responded to Belo's brief missive, the letter — combined with the October 1989 demonstration in Dili during the Pope's visit — had the effect of raising East Timor's international profile.

The resulting energy helped facilitate the United Nations' brokering of an agreement between Jakarta and Lisbon that an official Portuguese delegation would visit East Timor in 1991. Last-minute obstacles thrown up by Jakarta — and Lisbon's refusal to budge — led to the cancellation of the planned visit, however. The deep disappointment brought about by the cancellation — along with a desire to exploit the presence in Dili of the U.N.'s Special Rapporteur on Torture, Peter Koojimans, and foreign reporters — were significant factors in the decision of the East Timorese resistance to hold a pro-independence demonstration on November 12, 1991, the aftermath of which was the massacre at the Santa Cruz cemetery.[130]

But rather than energizing activity on East Timor within the United Nations, the massacre had the immediate effect of slowing down matters as Portugal broke off talks with Indonesia to protest the killings. It would take several more years of steady work by U.N. diplomats and, more important, various changes within Indonesia and beyond before there would be a context that would allow the United Nations to help break the stalemate over East Timor.

•

The subjugation of, and the commission of mass atrocities in, East Timor were very much a multilateral effort. Although the United States was by far Jakarta's most important partner-in-crime, the web of complicity involved many of the world's wealthiest and most powerful national governments, ones that also purport to be democracies that support human rights and rule of law in international affairs. This complicity not only undermined the ability of the United Nations to resolve the conflict, resulting in what was effectively inaction on the part of the world body through the mid-1990s, but also made the very invasion and occupation possible.

Implicit in such an argument is that Western countries could have prevented Jakarta's invasion and put an end to the subsequent occupation. Such an assertion is inevitably an exercise in speculation in that it involves asking what-if questions. The challenge, therefore, is to base speculation on informed opinion.

Given Indonesia's dependence on foreign assistance and investment and trade, the support or at least acquiescence of its Western allies was key to its plans of aggression against East Timor. Militarily Indonesia was completely dependent on the outside world for weaponry and spare parts. As discussed earlier, 90 percent of its weapons at the time of the invasion came from the United States. Nevertheless there are prominent Indonesia specialists that assert that the likes of Washington and Canberra could not have "saved" East Timor from the Suharto regime's 1975 invasion.[131] Yet, in the months before the December 7, 1975, invasion, Jakarta was sufficiently unsure of the wisdom of its plans for a full-scale attack on East Timor in terms of international opinion that it felt compelled to consult Australia (and probably New Zealand and Japan, among others)[132] and ask permission from the United States before going forward with its all-out aggression. Indeed, according to formerly classified CIA reports, Suharto had vetoed a call by his top military advisers in September 1974 to attack East Timor for fear of the reaction such a move would engender on the international stage, especially in the United States and Australia. Similarly Suharto vetoed Indonesian military intervention when East Timor's brief civil war broke out in August 1975. As the CIA reported at the time, Suharto was "acutely aware" that he would have to justify such a move as one in defense of Indonesian security given the conditions attached to U.S. military equipment.[133] According to an August 22, 1975, secret cable from the Australian Embassy in Jakarta, the local U.S. Embassy had just communicated to the Indonesian military that if it were to use American-supplied equipment in East Timor, it "could place the United States Military Assistance Programme in Indonesia in jeopardy."[134] A 1958 agreement with Washington obligated Jakarta to limit the use of U.S.-origin weaponry to "legitimate self-defense" as defined by the U.N. Charter. Ford and Kissinger thus had to agree to Indonesia's framing of an invasion of East Timor as an act of self-defense, which they ultimately did.

As evidenced by such support, Indonesia was a stalwart ally of the West at the time of the invasion. But the alliance was not one between equals: Indonesia was very much a lesser partner. Thus, had various Western countries — especially the United States — said no to Jakarta's invasion prior to its launching, the Suharto regime would have been in a very difficult bind and likely have reversed course. And given the profound anticommunism of the regime, it could hardly have turned to the likes of the Soviet Union as an alternative. As William Colby, the head of the CIA in 1975, told an interviewer during the 1990s, if the United States had vetoed Indonesia's plan to invade, "we certainly would have had a little diplomatic strain there," but nothing beyond that, the implication being that Jakarta would have backed down. He went on to suggest that Jakarta had no other options apart from securing Washington's compliance and to ask rhetorically, "where would [Suharto] have gone" had the Indonesian ruler not been happy with the U.S. position?[135]

In terms of international diplomacy, Indonesia's Western allies could have worked through the United Nations to bring about an internationally supervised referendum on independence for East Timor following the change of government in Lisbon in April 1974. Similarly they could have called upon the United Nations to take charge of the decolonization process in the territory while insisting that Fretilin and other East Timorese political parties be effective participants in any such process. Such actions would have most likely had the effect of denying Indonesia the space it needed to invade East Timor.[136]

Once the invasion occurred there were also courses of action Indonesia's patrons could have pursued had the desire been present to pressure Jakarta to end its occupation. The most obvious act was simply to stop providing the various forms of material support that enabled the Suharto regime to carry out and solidify its annexation of East Timor. As discussed earlier, for example, the Carter administration had to bail out Jakarta through increased arms shipments as the Indonesian military was running out of weaponry as a result of its activities in East Timor in 1977. What would have happened had Washington refused to provide that equipment because of Indonesia's presence in

East Timor? There probably would have been domestic costs in the form of pressure from U.S. weapons manufacturers, the Pentagon, and elements in Congress. In terms of U.S.-Indonesia relations, there undoubtedly would have been some tensions, but Jakarta could have done little of substance in response. It is highly unlikely, for instance, that there would have been any economic repercussions (in terms of trade or foreign investment). Indonesia was insufficiently strong and too much in need of external capital and commercial ties to take punitive actions. And had other countries followed Washington's lead — either in terms of bilateral relations or in a multilateral manner through support for concerted U.N. pressure — it is similarly hard to imagine that Jakarta would have been able to do anything of significance in response.

It is impossible to know with certainty what Indonesia would have done had its Western allies let it be known in unambiguous terms that they did not approve of the plans to invade East Timor or had made moves to cut off military and economic assistance once the invasion took place. What is certain, however, is that the actions of the countries in question greatly assisted Indonesia's aggression and occupation, and enabled — through the provision of military, economic, and politico-diplomatic resources — the commission of war crimes and crimes against humanity on a scale that would not have been possible otherwise. In this regard, the responsibility for the atrocities that took place in East Timor is very much collective. It is important to highlight this responsibility not merely for reasons of historical accuracy but also because it has significant implications for contemporary matters of justice and restitution vis-à-vis East Timor, how we perceive and act toward the governments of the countries in question, and how they behave today on the international stage.

The assistance to Indonesia was active, not passive. Thus there is little to suggest that Jakarta's Western supporters had any desire to pressure the Suharto regime to reverse its course of action, particularly from the time of the invasion through the early 1990s. To the contrary, the behavior of Jakarta's patrons demonstrated that they simply did not care about East Timor. What mattered was their relationship with Indonesia. As the U.S. State Department advised President Gerald Ford in December 1975, the United States "has no interests in Portuguese Timor" and should "follow Indonesia's lead on the issue."[137] With such reasoning, Washington and its allies were fully willing to indulge Indonesia's desires vis-à-vis the former Portuguese colony. It is difficult to prove this assertion in a full sense given the secretive nature of foreign policy formulation and the tendency of policy makers to be less than forthcoming about the motives informing their behavior. What "proves" this contention most, perhaps, is their silence about the horrors taking place in the Indonesian-occupied territory at that time, the continuing and growing commercial, intelligence, and military ties between Indonesia and the West in the years following the invasion, the diplomatic cover they provided to Jakarta in the United Nations to shelter the Suharto regime from criticism and concerted international pressure, and the lack of any meaningful bilateral actions aimed at ending Jakarta's aggression and illegal presence in East Timor.

Although there were numerous and diverse reasons for the various countries' support for Jakarta, the principal rationale was simple: Indonesia was a populous country with great market potential and a very wealthy resource base and occupied a strategic location. It was for such reasons that Richard Nixon, not long before he was elected president of the United States, characterized Indonesia as "by far the greatest prize in the Southeast Asian area."[138] Two years earlier, in a 1965 speech in Asia, Nixon had argued in favor of bombing North Vietnam to protect Indonesia's "immense mineral potential."[139]

The importance of Indonesia continued to be the overriding objective in determining the policies of the powerful toward East Timor throughout the course of the occupation. But matters surrounding the former Portuguese colony evolved significantly in the late 1990s, creating openings that were unimaginable only a few years earlier. These openings finally provided the East Timorese people with the opportunity they had long demanded: the right to express their political will through an internationally supervised ballot.

I cannot hide my apprehensions regarding the course on which we are about to embark.

—A SENIOR U.N. OFFICIAL *a few days before the signing of the May 5, 1999, accords on the East Timor ballot*

One of the first voters at UNAMET polling site near the Santa Cruz cemetery, August 30, 1999. *Photo by the author.*

"Thank you so much for coming here to help us achieve our human rights," the middle-aged woman gushed as she tightly grabbed our hands. "For twenty-four years we have suffered. Now we have hope." As she excitedly spoke in Portuguese, a small crowd of people gathered around us, the only two visible foreigners in sight. Many of them — those able to understand some Portuguese — nodded in agreement and smiled. That people felt sufficiently safe to express such sentiments openly was unprecedented — at least since December 1975 — suggesting that a new day had arrived in occupied East Timor.

A companion and I were in Manatuto, a coastal town east of Dili. I had first passed through there in July 1992, seven years earlier. At that time the town was crawling with Indonesian soldiers and had a stifling climate of fear. Few people would even make direct eye contact with a visible outsider. It was partially for this reason that I wanted to return.

The date of my return was July 17, "Integration Day," the Indonesian government holiday that marked East Timor's supposedly voluntary union with Indonesia. I had been to an Integration Day ceremony in 1992. Government officials compelled thousands of East Timorese civilians to join soldiers, police, and civil servants under a stifling sun in front of the governor's office in Dili. The monotonous speeches extolling the virtues of Indonesia and the glories of integration, combined with the long faces of the East Timorese in attendance, made it less than inspiring.

I expected a similar scene in Manatuto. But the Integration Day ceremony in that town in 1999 was surprisingly different. While members of the Indonesian security apparatus and civil service employees lined up in formation for the official ceremony outside the district government office, there were no civilians present. Local people reported that, unlike previous years, the Indonesian authorities had made no effort to ensure the attendance of the populace. For that day, at least, it almost seemed as if the Indonesian government had given up.

An article on the holiday from Antara, the Indonesian government's official news agency, released later that day reinforced this perception. The title of the piece daringly asked if 1999 would be the final year that East Timor would celebrate integration. The report also included strong pro-independence statements from various individuals. Dili, the report stated, "seemed not too festive for the occasion. Only a simple ceremony led by Governor Abilio Osorio Soares took place, attended by hundreds of civil servants while a crowd of ordinary residents watched from a distance." Although the article ended with assurances from pro-integration East Timorese that the answer to the provocative title was negative, the very fact that Antara would pose such a question — something unthinkable prior to 1999 — was astonishing.[1]

I had only arrived in East Timor a few days earlier. I was there to help set up and coordinate the International Federation for East Timor Observer Project (IFET-OP), a body established by a coalition of East Timor support groups from around the world to monitor and accompany a U.N.-run "popular consultation" through which the East Timorese people would finally have the opportunity to formally express their political aspirations. The choice was to be one between continued association with Indonesia through "special autonomy" or independence.

The joy and excitement I experienced in Manatuto that day proved to be common over the next several weeks. The vast majority of East Timorese expressed delight at the sight of foreigners whom they saw as the embodiment of the United Nations and as the realization of their long-awaited opportunity to decide their political fate. But the road to the August vote would prove to be far more perilous than was in evidence on that day in Manatuto.

•

Trying to make sense of the past in retrospect is always a tricky matter. Hence it would be foolhardy to reduce the proverbial "beginning of the end" of Indonesia's occupation to a narrow time span or just one set of events. Nevertheless, there was something discernibly different in the air during a brief visit to East Timor in March 1998. It was a time of political and economic crisis in Indonesia. There was a strong sense among many East Timorese that the end of Jakarta's colonial project was imminent as the Suharto regime seemed to be on the ropes. And, indeed, in May of that year, a rising tide of anti–status quo sentiment forced Suharto, one of the world's longest-reigning dictators, to step down.

With Suharto's ouster, fissures within the Indonesian political establishment became more apparent, allowing for initiatives toward East Timor that previously would have been difficult to imagine. After less than three weeks in office — on June 9, 1998 — and facing political instability, economic collapse, and intense international scrutiny on a variety of fronts, including that of East Timor, B. J. Habibie, the new president, announced that Jakarta would offer the East Timorese "special status," a form of autonomy. The autonomy proposal had been "gathering dust" for a number of years at the Indonesian foreign ministry, but Suharto had not allowed it to go forward.[2] Under the plan East Timor would run many of its internal affairs but would remain part of Indonesia. While far short of meeting the demands of the East Timorese, this was the first time that Jakarta had even publicly discussed altering East Timor's political status.

For the first time pro-independence groups, which had recently reorganized into the National Council of Timorese Resistance (CNRT), the umbrella grouping of all the major factions of the East Timorese resistance, were able to operate openly. East Timorese student groups organized open forums in Dili and throughout the occupied territory to discuss and debate East Timor's political status. The CNRT even opened an office in Dili. Beginning in June 1998 huge, pro-independence demonstrations took place, including one of several thousand on November 12 at the Santa Cruz cemetery to mark the seventh anniversary of the massacre. These events quickly made it clear that most East Timorese rejected Jakarta's offer of autonomy and instead demanded the holding of a referendum through which they could decide their political fate—in other words, their right to self-determination.[3]

That the TNI allowed such demonstrations to take place was shocking. Significant elements of the TNI opposed Habibie's proposal for fear that autonomy would set a precedent for disaffected regions within Indonesia proper and would possibly open the door to East Timorese independence. But given the intensifying international spotlight on East Timor, the military could not be as openly brutal as it had been in the past. In addition, the TNI wanted to give a semblance of veracity to the lie that the conflict was, first and foremost, one between East Timorese. So it began organizing and arming paramilitary death squads, or "civilian militia," in the last few months of 1998. The TNI and militia soon began a campaign of terror against East Timorese with pro-independence sympathies, killing hundreds over the next several months.[4]

●

It was hardly a coincidence that TNI-militia terror greatly intensified in the first few months of 1999. It was a time of unprecedented flexibility on the part of the political leadership in Jakarta toward East Timor. A combination of Habibie's eccentric, idiosyncratic, and populist style as well as his desire to distinguish himself from his autocratic predecessor; ongoing pressure from the pro-democracy, labor, and human rights movements within Indonesia; the resistance within East Timor, and pressure from foreign governments and international organizations; and reformist tendencies among some of the advisers closest to the new president all led to a democratic opening.[5] In late January 1999, in a stunning announcement, Habibie declared that he would grant independence to East Timor if its people rejected Indonesia's offer of autonomy. At the same time he proclaimed that the resistance leader Xanana Gusmão would be transferred from Jakarta's Cipinang Prison to a house in the city that, although officially an extension of the prison, would serve as a site from which Xanana could conduct his affairs as head of the pro-independence movement. Internationally Habibie's announcement led to a rapid escalation of U.N.-mediated negotiations between Indonesia and Portugal (which was still legally the administering power of the territory).[6]

Despite these developments Habibie's words were met with skepticism and concern within East Timor. Many prominent East Timorese, and the resistance as well, had long proposed a gradual transition to independence, stretching over a number of years, to prepare the traumatized society adequately for the challenges of independent statehood. Now they feared that Indonesia had decided to cut its losses and would abandon the territory, leaving a wake of chaos and violence in its wake. Indeed, it was during this time that TNI-militia violence dramatically increased.[7]

José Ramos-Horta presciently saw the terror as the realization of a longtime menacing pledge of the Indonesians. "Before [Indonesia] withdraws it wants to wreak major havoc and destabilization, as it has always promised," he explained on February 2, 1999. "We have consistently heard that over the years from the Indonesian military in Timor. They told our people that if one day they had to leave they would lay waste to the whole of Timor."[8]

The worst incident in the pre-ballot period took place two months later in Liquiça, a coastal town about a forty-five-minute drive west of Dili. On Tuesday, April 6, at one o'clock in the afternoon, members of Brimob, the Indonesian riot police, and the local militia, Besi Merah Putih,[9] surrounded the Catholic Church compound in the town. More than two thousand refugees had fled there from TNI-militia terror in nearby villages. The Brimob fired tear gas into the buildings where refugees sought shelter, forcing them to exit. At that point the militia and, according to eyewitness accounts, Brimob members and Indonesian soldiers dressed in civilian clothing entered the compound, firing arms and shooting arrows at the fleeing refugees while also hacking them with machetes. Estimates of the death toll range from twenty-five to fifty-seven. Indonesian soldiers later picked up the corpses and buried them in an undisclosed location.[10] Only a few days earlier Major-General Adam Damiri, the TNI commander of the region containing East Timor, had openly endorsed the militia and acknowledged the provision of arms and training.[11]

On the Sunday following the massacre, Bishop Belo went to Liquiça to say mass and found a deserted church. Only after the bells tolled did several hundred of the town's terrified souls venture to the religious service. Following the mass about thirty militia members attacked the Bishop's convoy, which included several foreign reporters, as it was returning to Dili, pelting the vehicles with rocks and metal pipes.[12]

The next Saturday, April 17, the TNI-militia terror campaign arrived in Dili. A large rally by militia members from all over the territory took place that morning in front of the governor's office. In attendance were the governor, Abilio Osorio Soares, Tono Suratman, the military commander for East Timor, police chief Timbul Silaen, and other government and military officials. They looked on approvingly as militia members fired their weapons in the air and their nominal leaders issued dire warnings. "I order all pro-integration militia to clean up the defilers of integration," shouted Eurico Guterres, chief of the Dili-based Aitarak ("thorn" in Tetum) militia. "Arrest and kill them if necessary." Guterres then mentioned the home of Manuel Carrascalão as a specific target. A member of one of East Timor's handful of elite families, Carrascalão had emerged in the previous few years as one of the more high-profile advocates of independence. His outspokenness, in the eyes of the TNI and pro-integration East Timorese, was all the more unacceptable given that he had served in the local assembly for many years as a pro-Indonesia figure.

Following the rally the militia convoyed around Dili, firing their weapons and terrorizing the capital's population, while targeting the homes of high-level resistance officials as well as CNRT headquarters, which had only recently closed down in the aftermath of the massacre in Liquiça. Soon thereafter they moved onto Manuel Carrascalão's home to where approximately 170 individuals from outlying areas had fled and were living because of the similar terror in their home villages. Invading Carrascalão's home, the militia members attacked the occupants, killing many in cold blood. Members of the TNI and the police joined in the attack.[13]

Not long before the militia had arrived at his home, Manuel Carrascalão and his daughter had gone to TNI headquarters to ask Suratman to intervene to stop the militia rampage and the feared attack on his home. "We have to be neutral," the local TNI commander told Carrascalão. "You Timorese must sort this out yourselves."[14]

During the rampage the military and police did nothing other than stand along the road and cheer the militia on while giving them "high-fives" as they passed. Among those killed was Carrascalão's adopted seventeen-year-old son, Manuelito, whom the paramilitaries shot in the head and stabbed in the stomach. The execution of Manuelito was "punishment for his father's activism," according to Herminio da Costa, chief of staff of East Timor's thirteen militia groups. "If he hadn't been the son of Manuel, he wouldn't have died."[15]

In response to international outrage over the carnage, TNI head General Wiranto flew to Dili and presided over an April 21 meeting that led to the creation of the Commission on Peace and Stability (KPS). In early 1999 the United Nations had proposed to set up a peace commission to resolve conflicts within East Timor under the auspices of the territory's two Catholic bishops. While the Catholic Church, the CNRT, pro-integrationists, and the political leadership in Jakarta voiced support for the proposal, the TNI dragged its feet, fearing the existence of a body convened by the United Nations, and instead launched the KPS. Echoing the long-standing military line that the conflict in East Timor was an internal one between pro-integration and pro-independence locals (a civil war in which the TNI was caught in the middle), the KPS defined the CNRT/Falintil and the militia, along with their political allies, as the two warring parties, while excluding the United Nations and East Timorese civil society groups from participation as originally envisioned. Along with a downtrodden Manuel Carrascalão, the only CNRT representative present at the signing of the document, one in which the supposedly warring factions pledged to cease hostilities, was Leandro Issac, who had to be brought there from the Dili police headquarters to where he had fled after militia attacked his home on April 17.[16] (The KPS would prove to be a worthless mechanism for realizing peace and stability. To the contrary, the Indonesian side used it to divert any serious efforts to create real conditions of security.)

●

It was in this context that the governments of Indonesia and Portugal con-. cluded negotiations that resulted in a series of historic accords signed at the United Nations in New York City on May 5, 1999. What came to be known as the "5 May Agreement" empowered the United Nations to put before the East Timorese people Jakarta's "special autonomy" proposal "for their consideration and acceptance or rejection through a popular consultation on the basis of a direct, secret and universal ballot." If the East Timorese voters were to reject the proposal, the accords required that "the Government of Indonesia shall take the constitutional steps necessary to terminate its links with East Timor . . . enabling East Timor to begin a process of transition towards independence." The accords also provided that "the Government of Indonesia will be responsible for maintaining peace and security in East Timor in order to ensure that the popular consultation is carried out in a fair and peaceful way in an atmosphere free of intimidation, violence or interference from any side."[17] Following the signing, Kofi Annan welcomed "the assurances given by President Habibie that his Government will fulfill effectively its responsibility for law and order and the protection of civilians."[18]

In retrospect, the security provisions, despite the signed agreement and Jakarta's verbal assurances, were clearly far from adequate. But even at the time of the formal approval of the May 5 Agreement, making the Indonesian military and police responsible for peace and security did not at all seem like a wise proposition — at least to those familiar with the history of Indonesia's annexation of East Timor. However, for the United Nations to have pushed more than it did for stronger security provisions, many argued at the time (and continue to assert), would have been a "deal breaker," thus eliminating a historic chance for the East Timorese people to express their political wishes. To accept foreign troops on what it regarded as its soil, from Jakarta's perspective, would have been to admit to being an illegitimate occupying power, something Indonesia's political elite was not willing to do. And the East Timorese leadership certainly did not want to risk losing the opportunity offered by the May 5 Agreement.[19]

Given Jakarta's obstructionism and the failure of Indonesia's powerful economic and military backers to pressure their ally sufficiently, the best the United Nations could do at the time was to attach a memorandum (dated May 4) to the accords specifying what needed to be in place before the secretary-general could determine that the necessary security conditions had been established for the consultation process to begin. Among the conditions were "the bringing of armed civilian groups under strict control and discipline"; a ban on rallies by armed groups; the arrest and prosecution of all who incite or threaten violence; a redeployment of the TNI — the details of which were unspecified; and "the immediate institution of a process of laying down of arms by all armed groups, to be completed well in advance of the holding of the ballot."[20]

Jakarta never complied with any of these conditions.

●

The costs of the resulting security arrangement quickly became obvious in East Timor following the signing of the accords. Just before dawn on Sunday morning, May 16, about sixty paramilitaries and Indonesian soldiers arrived in the village of Atara in the central highlands and attacked a number of the modest homes there, killing unarmed men they suspected of pro-independence sympathies. Many of the other villagers fled into a nearby coffee plantation that surrounds the settlement, pursued by their assailants who continued to fire their assault rifles. According to the Australia-based East Timor Human Rights Centre, sixteen were confirmed dead, and another twenty-one missing and presumed killed.[21]

If any doubts lingered about the role of the Indonesian military in such events, they were dispelled several days later when a U.N. team tried to travel to Atara to investigate what had happened, only to be prevented from doing so by the TNI for supposed reasons of security. Before leaving the nearby town of Atsabe to return to Dili, however, the U.N. officials happened upon a local military base where they witnessed an Indonesian military officer in the process of training local militia members.[22]

While U.N. personnel began arriving in East Timor within days of the signing of the May 5 accords, the official opening of the United Nations Mission in East Timor took place on June 4. Militia leaders and their political allies quickly began publicly accusing UNAMET of pro-independence bias, creating a menacing atmosphere for the mission's work. On June 29 about one hundred pro-Indonesia paramilitary members attacked the UNAMET office in the town of Maliana near the West Timor border, injuring several civilians and a U.N. official from South Africa. Eyewitnesses in Maliana reported seeing at least two TNI members dressed as civilians participating in the attack against the U.N. compound. Two days later about fifteen armed paramilitaries gathered in front of the local UNAMET post in the town of Viqueque, threatening the people inside with death. As a result the United Nations temporarily withdrew seven electoral officers from the area. In both incidents the Indonesian police — charged with security under the May 5 Agreement — did nothing to stop the violence. Eurico Guterres, leader of Aitarak, singled out UNAMET spokesperson David Wimhurst, who had incurred the wrath of the pro-Indonesians for reporting on the militia training in Atsabe, among other things. "I hate David Wimhurst," Guterres stated. "I want him to go away immediately, otherwise I don't know what will happen to him."[23]

And on July 4 militia in Liquiça attacked a humanitarian aid convoy of eight vehicles and seventy-seven persons in the middle of the town as it was departing for Dili. The aid convoy — comprised of representatives from six East Timorese nongovernmental organizations and accompanied by a representative of the United Nations High Commission for Refugees (UNHCR) and a UNAMET official — had just brought food and medicine to a few thousand of what was estimated to be between thirty thousand and fifty thousand internally displaced persons who had been forced to flee their homes over the preceding several months because of attacks by pro-Indonesia militia. As the convoy was stopped at an intersection where the local military headquarters stood and which was located just up the road from a police station, about thirty militia members — armed with pistols, homemade rifles, swords, and stones — attacked the aid workers. The Indonesian authorities allowed the attackers to carry out their actions unimpeded.

Two days prior the police had promised to furnish an escort to the convoy but later informed the organizers that they could not do so. And on July 4 police again declined to provide accompaniment. While Indonesian authorities in Jakarta officially deplored the attack, many government officials tried to cast the blame on the convoy participants. Defense minister and TNI head General Wiranto, for example, stated that a lack of discipline among both pro-integration and pro-independence groups was the cause of the incident. TNI headquarters in Jakarta alleged that the convoy was carrying three armed Falintil guerrillas in one of their vehicles. And Indonesian police officials in East Timor blamed the UNAMET official present for firing shots from a pistol that he allegedly had and provoking the attack. Eyewitness accounts and subsequent investigations showed all such accusations to be baseless.[24]

The violence and intimidation caused grave doubts about the wisdom of proceeding with the "popular consultation" — just as they were intended to do. At the same time pro-autonomy groups, militia, and the Indonesian authorities were aggressively "socializing" the autonomy proposal, forcing villagers to fly the "red and white" in front of their homes and swear allegiance to Indonesia. The May 5 accords banned such activities, limiting any political campaigning to a strictly delimited period after voter registration. The agreement also excluded government officials from political campaigning (except in their personal capacity) and required "absolute neutrality" from the TNI and police. Nevertheless, in the early weeks of the mission, UNAMET officials witnessed public ceremonies at which government and TNI officials were present and at which villagers were compelled to affirm their support for Indonesia and, in a perversion of a local custom, sometimes to drink animal blood. It was also discovered that the local government had diverted millions of dollars in World Bank funds for "social safety net" programs to autonomy propaganda activities and militia terror.[25]

For such reasons the United Nations decided to twice delay the beginning of the voter registration process and to postpone the ballot, which had been scheduled to take place on August 8.[26] Such delays were one of the few points of leverage the United Nations possessed as they highlighted Indonesia's failure to comply with its obligations and caused Jakarta international embarrassment. But such leverage was limited as the United Nations could not afford too long a delay given the fear that Habibie would not last as president much beyond the end of August — a concern that became even more realistic after the general elections on June 9 gave the opposition a plurality of the votes. And although Megawati Sukarnoputri, the de facto leader of the opposition and, as such, the person expected to succeed Habibie, had assured that she would respect the government's commitments, many in the international community (and in the leadership of the East Timorese resistance) feared that the nationalistic Megawati and her supporters in the military would not do so, especially given their vociferous criticisms of Habibie for having agreed to the ballot.[27]

When voter registration actually began on July 16, it did so in an ominous environment. There were profound fears that few would feel sufficiently secure or be able to muster the necessary courage to go to one of the two hundred UNAMET registration sites. But tens of thousands did so in the first week of registration alone. And such enthusiastic participation proved to be the rule rather than the exception. Throughout East Timor, would-be voters flocked to the UNAMET sites. By the time registration finished in the first week of August, more than 430,000 people had enrolled for the vote, far in excess of the most optimistic projections. In addition to serving as a concrete sign of the competence and hard work of UNAMET, the outcome was a demonstration of the East Timorese people's tremendous resolve to see the ballot happen. It was also a manifestation of a security situation on the ground that improved in a number of ways with the growing presence of foreigners in East Timor and an accompanying increase in international scrutiny.

The goal of the Indonesian military and its supporters in East Timor was not to prevent the ballot from going forward. It was to ensure that they won, and they were confident that they would—both because they grossly overestimated the level of pro-Indonesia sentiment in the territory and because of their tendency to see the East Timorese masses as an ignorant, backward lot that could easily be swayed. And because reports received from their colleagues within East Timor were generally positive, the political and military leadership in Jakarta shared this assessment.[28] At the same time they all appreciated the need to make serious efforts to realize the desired outcome.

For this reason, intimidation and physical violence during this period remained pervasive throughout many parts of the territory. Thus the security situation, although it had definitely improved since the arrival of UNAMET and the related increase in international scrutiny, was far from what was needed to ensure a free and fair process; moreover, the problem was magnified by the fact that the start of the political campaign phase of the consultation process was rapidly approaching. As Kofi Annan wrote in a July 27, 1999, letter to the U.N. Security Council, "conditions required for a largely technical exercise such as registration are notably less stringent than those which will be necessary for campaigning in the run-up to the consultation."[29]

In many ways the two-week campaign period was one of elation. On Sunday, July 15, the CNRT publicly raised its flag for the first time at the official openings of its national office in Dili in a moving ceremony attended by many thousands. And in numerous locations throughout East Timor pro-independence demonstrations took place, culminating in a final rally of tens of thousands in Dili a few days before the vote. And as the date of the ballot neared, Indonesian settlers were packing up their belongings and returning to their home regions. Even various Indonesian (noncombat) military installations were closing down. All in all, there was much evidence to suggest that the end of Indonesia's brutal colonial reign was imminent.

But another mood prevailed as well, one of profound fear, even terror.

"They've told us that they will kill us all if independence wins," Francisco solemnly informed me two weeks before the vote, as we sat in the front room of his modest home. Living in a poor neighborhood in central Dili, Francisco, his family, and thirty refugees who had fled paramilitary violence in the area of Liquiça resided across the street from a post of Aitarak, the local militia group. The family, well-known supporters of independence, was under constant threat. Francisco's wife, Ana, would often rock nervously and, in constant fear of an attack, would rarely raise her quivering voice above a whisper.

Aitarak members frequently carried machetes and automatic weapons around the neighborhood, unencumbered by the Indonesian security apparatus charged with protecting civilians. They also occasionally sported T-shirts, bearing the warning that a "bloodbath" would ensue if East Timor's voters rejected continued association with Indonesia.

Such intimidation and threats were common and pervasive. Often Indonesian government officials would express them. Francisco Lopes da Cruz, for example, Indonesia's "roving ambassador" for East Timor and a longtime local supporter of "integration," warned, "If people choose autonomy blood will drip. If people reject autonomy there is the possibility blood will flow in East Timor."[30] As a result of such intimidation, a mood of paranoia was rife among the East Timorese. Rumors abounded of pending attacks by paramilitaries against specific neighborhoods in Dili or against outlying towns, and more often than not they were wrong.

But many people had good reasons for believing the rumors. Although the level of violence had declined significantly following the establishment of UNAMET in East Timor, attacks against pro-independence supporters were still frequent. The TNI and their militia proxies were no longer engaging in high-profile, large-scale massacres; nor were they attacking foreigners or internationals associated with the UNAMET process. Instead, a relatively low-intensity form of terror — one less likely to invite international criticism — was taking place. As a result, pro-independence forces were not able to campaign publicly in many areas of East Timor. In numerous towns the TNI-backed militia attacked the offices of pro-independence groups or prevented them from opening. And various forms of intimidation and coercion were pervasive. Even Bishop Belo came under threat. "Be careful," proclaimed an unsigned flyer circulating around the territory. "For now your robe is white, but one day it will be stained with your own blood."[31]

One of the worst areas was that of Bobonaro, which hugs the boundary with West Timor. I stopped briefly in Maliana, its principal population center, eight days before the vote. It almost resembled a ghost town, the majority of the population having fled to the mountains and nearby villages. UNAMET officials there had told a visiting delegation of American lawmakers the day before that the ballot should be called off there because "too many people will die." Senator Tom Harkin, one of the delegation members, stated in quoting a U.N. official that "this could be a bloodbath down here." Harkin received strong evidence of TNI-militia ties aimed at sabotaging the vote. The U.S. delegation then moved on to the town of Suai on the south coast, where members visited with an estimated twenty-five hundred pro-independence refugees holed up in a Catholic Church compound. Militia and TNI had driven the refugees from their homes and villages as part of their effort to terrorize supporters of independence. "We're going to be asking our Government and the United Nations to be providing some peacekeeping forces here," Harkin promised the refugees. "From what we've seen it's necessary to have somebody here to stop the intimidation." At the same time sources associated with the United Nations reported that senior TNI officers in Dili were making secret plans to evacuate fifty thousand civilians from areas near the West Timor border.[32]

"We share the concerns expressed by Senator Harkin and others about continued violence and intimidation on the part of the pro-integration militias in the campaign before next Monday's autonomy vote," answered James Foley, U.S. State Department spokesperson. But, he continued, "We don't believe that the dispatch of armed UN peacekeepers before August 30 is possible at this point. . . . Moreover, in a more fundamental sense, we believe this is the responsibility of the government of Indonesia, and we don't want to take that responsibility away from them."[33]

How seriously the Indonesian authorities took their responsibility was on display in the days that followed. On August 27, the final day of the fourteen-day campaign period, the militia, its supporters, and the many they coerced to participate held a rally of thousands in Dili at which Eurico Guterres predicted "massive fighting" if the pro-integration side were to lose. East Timor, he warned, would "become a sea of fire."[34] After circulating throughout the capital in a convoy of motorcycles and trucks, the paramilitary groups rampaged through the city, attacking pro-independence youths and foreign journalists, destroying the main office of the CNRT, and engaging in random violence. At least six people died as a result, one of whom was shot in the back of the head by members of Brimob, the Indonesian riot police. After one wave of the militia attack, witnesses saw Indonesian police shaking hands with the paramilitaries.

On the same day militia members attacked Memo, a small village near Maliana. The village was reportedly targeted because its inhabitants had disobeyed the order of the *bupati* (district administrator) to attend a pro-Indonesia campaign earlier that day in Maliana. Militia, with the help of the Indonesian police, shot numerous residents, killing two, and set fire to at least twenty-five homes.

That evening militia members armed with machetes and automatic weapons attacked and fire-bombed the CNRT office in Lospalos, in the eastern section of the territory. Indonesian police took one and a quarter hours to arrive on the scene, even though the police station was located only five hundred meters away. I had visited Lospalos in 1992, staying in the house of the local *liurai* (traditional king), Verissimo Quintas. A man in his sixties, Verissimo had survived Japan's brutal occupation of his homeland during World War II. He would not, however, survive the dying days of Indonesia's bloody colonial project: machete-wielding paramilitaries attacked his family's house as part of their several-hour-long rampage against independence supporters in the town and hacked him to death.

Late that same night militia members also attacked and set fire to the CNRT office in Oecussi, the East Timorese enclave in West Timor.[35] The rampaging militia burned down at least twenty-four houses and destroyed about fifty motor vehicles. Only several hours after the violence began did the police respond.[36]

The terror that came at the end of the campaign was only one of many foreboding signs that led numerous local and international observer missions, the CNRT, and the local Catholic hierarchy to call upon the United Nations and the countries that dominate the world body to greatly increase UNAMET's mandate and resources relating to security. Many, in fact, called for the introduction of a U.N.-led force before the holding of the ballot. But while there was some discussion in the days leading up to the vote about the wisdom of proceeding, there was a consensus among the East Timorese that the ballot had to go forward, lest the people of East Timor lose a historic opportunity to display their collective political sentiment through an internationally sanctioned and organized process.

Nonetheless the fear of what the consequence would be of such political expression was palpable. Many independence leaders were in hiding, and large numbers of families had fled to outlying areas of population centers, including Dili, in the days preceding the ballot. An August 29 press release from João Carrascalão, CNRT vice president living in exile in Australia, ominously foresaw that the TNI and militia would engage in large-scale killings on the day of the vote or shortly thereafter. First, he predicted, they would focus on internationals working with UNAMET or foreign media as part of an effort to force the United Nations and others out of East Timor. The departure of internationals would then allow the military and militia to "go on a rampage of genocidal slaughter of East Timorese independence supporters which will make the Liquiça and Dili massacres look like Sunday school picnics." The model for the TNI-militia, Carrascalão asserted, was Rwanda where, only four years earlier, Hutu militia had succeeded in driving out a U.N. peacekeeping force after killing ten Belgian soldiers, allowing them to continue their mass killings of the Tutsi and moderate Hutu unhindered.[37]

●

The day before the vote Dili was quiet—eerily so. Few people were on the streets. The city was rife with rumors of pending violence.

Late that morning the political officer and the military attaché from the German Embassy in Jakarta dropped by the IFET-OP office, where I was working, to receive a briefing. They were in East Timor to observe the ballot.

I informed them of the violence that had unfolded the previous two days. I then asked them if the German government had plans to help facilitate the introduction of international troops immediately after the vote to prevent the feared campaign of post-ballot terror.

"It's too early to consider such matters," one of them responded. "Let's wait and see how things go."

I, like probably almost everyone else in East Timor, went to bed that evening in great fear of what lay over the horizon.

UNAMET will stay after the vote.

—*Text of poster of the United Nations Assistance Mission in East Timor*

Let me say the United Nations was not naive about the history of violence in East Timor during the past 24 years. . . . [N]obody in their wildest dreams thought what we are witnessing could have happened. We are no fools.

—U.N. SECRETARY-GENERAL KOFI ANNAN, *September 1999*

Pro-independence demonstration, Dili, August 25, 1999. *Photo by the author.*

T he woman was with her young son, on her way to vote at a polling station very close to Dili's Santa Cruz cemetery. She carefully unrolled the picture of Jesus Christ in her hand to show me the UNAMET registration certificate hidden within—"for protection," she said. "It is the happiest day of my life, but it is also my day of greatest fear. I've never been so afraid that someone is going to kill me."

When the woman found out that I was from the United States, she asked if the U.S. government would come to the assistance of the East Timorese. "Will the United Nations send troops soon?" I frequently heard such questions. It pained me to tell people that I doubted this would happen "in time"—in time to avoid what everyone feared. Nevertheless many people maintained a strong faith, or perhaps desperate hope masquerading as faith, that the international community—shorthand for the Western powers—would not allow Indonesia's military to engage in a wave of terror following the vote.

The day of balloting started off auspiciously. At 5:30 A.M.—an hour before polls were scheduled to open—a few hundred would-be voters had already gathered across the street from the headquarters of IFET-OP at Primary School #4, the largest voting site in Dili. And throughout the capital voters defied militia and TNI threats, and overcame their own fears, by turning out in huge numbers. By early afternoon almost all the registered voters had already cast their ballots at most of the polling stations in Dili. Traveling around the city, my fellow international observers and I found them almost empty. At one such station near Dili's Catholic cathedral, UNAMET officials reported at around 2:30 in the afternoon that only three of the registered voters had failed to show up, and two of them had reportedly died since registering. Similar results unfolded throughout East Timor as an astonishing 98.6 percent of registered voters actually voted. Those that had fled their villages and towns bravely returned to exercise the right to franchise and then quickly returned to their places of refuge.

In most places the militia were not invisible. But in some areas, such as Oecussi and Liquiça, militia forces maintained intimidating presences near voting sites. Having told many that they would be able to determine how votes were cast while having created a larger climate of terror, intimidation, and fear, the TNI and militia undoubtedly increased the number of those opting for "special autonomy" within Indonesia. And in the town of Gleno, in the central part of the territory, militia members — shooting homemade weapons into the air and throwing rocks – attacked a polling station, injuring three and forcing UNAMET to close the station for two hours. All together, seven polling stations (out of a total of two hundred) had to suspend voting for some time—largely because of militia threats against local (East Timorese)

UNAMET staff. But all sites reopened and completed the voting, and such incidences proved to be rare exceptions.

The overall success of the day made many East Timorese joyous. It was clear to anyone with a realistic grasp of East Timor that such a voter turnout could only spell defeat for Indonesia. Stopping by a friend's house in the Becora section of Dili that afternoon as I was visiting various polling sites, I watched on the television as José Ramos-Horta cast his ballot in Sydney, Australia—at one of thirteen polling places set up by UNAMET outside East Timor.[1] My friend's young children cheered as the resistance leader voted. (Jakarta had barred the Nobel laureate from returning to East Timor to campaign under the justification that it would incite violence between pro-Indonesia and pro-independence groups.)[2] And they began singing a familiar song, but they had adapted the lyrics to say that East Timor would be independent by day's end.

The massive voter turnout, combined with the relative quiet of the day, gave rise to an impression that Indonesia was finally defeated, and that perhaps the country's political and military leaders had seen the light and had decided to give up gracefully. Large numbers of people, however, were not willing to take any chances. Many, in fact, voted as early as possible to maximize their ability to go to areas deemed safer. One family I interviewed a year later was among the first to vote in Dili so that they would have plenty of time to catch transportation to Baucau—about three hours to the east of Dili—where militia-TNI violence had been almost nonexistent.

●

Before the day was over it became clear that such precautions were well taken. As the day of balloting was drawing to a close, the climate of fear reemerged, especially in areas outside Dili. In the town of Atsabe in the district of Ermera militia members accompanied by TNI soldiers and the local military commander, and armed with swords, knives, and homemade guns, appeared at the polling station around 5:00 P.M. and demanded that UNAMET surrender all the local staff persons to them. They then proceeded to beat, kick, and stab local staffers. One, João Lopes Gomes, died soon thereafter from stab wounds to the back suffered while he was loading ballot boxes onto a U.N. vehicle. (The band also kidnapped two other local staff at Atsabe who were found dead a few days later.) In Gleno, Ermera's administrative center, armed militia reemerged in the evening and patrolled in the center of the town, threatening international observers.

The next morning UNAMET and many of the international observers present in the town tried to withdraw in an increasingly menacing atmosphere as militia fired shots and burned ten houses. But militia blocked the seventeen-vehicle UNAMET convoy, comprised of 150 people, from leaving, demanding that the United Nations surrender the 50 East Timorese in the convoy. In what was to prove to be routine, the Indonesian police failed to take any remedial action. Militia even attacked a U.N. helicopter and prevented it from picking up the district's marked ballots. Only after several hours of negotiation was the convoy able to leave.[3]

That same day militia roadblocks sprung up in many parts of the territory. Between the western border of Liquiça district and Dili alone there were five such roadblocks, including one just west of the capital's airport. Only with a *surat jalan,* or permission-to-travel letter, from the militia or with a police escort could one get through. Police officials escorting international observers through made no efforts to get the militia members to disband the posts. Instead they waved and gave them a "thumbs-up" sign as they passed. Such behavior would consistently manifest itself over the next few days: foreigners were generally off-limits to the militia and their sponsors in the TNI, but they were free to terrorize East Timorese.

At the same time the militia and their TNI sponsors made it clear that foreigners were no longer welcome in the occupied territory. On Wednesday, September 1, militia attacked people in Dili's streets and fired at buildings. And later in the day, as UNAMET began counting the ballots in Dili — in an empty museum building that the Indonesians had built to showcase the development triumphs brought about through "integration" — dozens of armed militia, many of them wearing masks, blocked the road in front of UNAMET headquarters, across the road from which stood an Indonesian police station and a TNI barracks. Using their homemade firearms, as well as some M-16 rifles, they went on a two-hour rampage, firing on vehicles trying to enter the U.N. compound, attacking local residents, and setting fire to houses in the area. In full view of the media, militia members killed one man, hacking him to death with machetes.

Journalists were not immune from attack during the day's violence. One militia member attacked a *Washington Post* correspondent, striking him in the back with the flat side of his machete blade. Others broke the arm of a BBC reporter. Mysteriously a plainclothes Indonesian official prevented the assailants from going further, making it clear that the intent was to spread fear within the international press corps, not to injure journalists to the extent that it might invite a strong reaction by the powers-that-be in the international community. The attacks, however, had the desired effect. That evening the Indonesian government sent in a plane that evacuated dozens of Indonesian journalists. And over the next couple of days foreign news outlets chartered aircraft to evacuate their correspondents and supporting staff as well as anyone else who could afford the price of a ticket — as long as they were not East Timorese. As the militia had publicly threatened, Aitarak members were patrolling entry and exit points to and from the territory, blocking East Timorese from departing, unencumbered by the Indonesian authorities.[4]

In most outlying areas the violence and intimidation were far greater than in Dili. Much of Same, a town in the central highlands, was already burning. The great part of Maliana was also engulfed in flames. UNAMET and international observers abandoned the town in a convoy on September 3 as militia and TNI soldiers taunted them while shooting over their vehicles. U.N. workers there reported seeing bloodied corpses as they fled. UNAMET officials also saw TNI officers directing militia to torch buildings associated with the United Nations and with pro-independence groups. Meanwhile the police in Maliana, charged with local security, remained in their station singing songs.[5]

Businesses in Dili and throughout the territory were closing up shop in the days immediately following the ballot. Most being owned by non–East Timorese, large numbers of their Indonesian proprietors were packing up and returning to Indonesia. IFET-OP lost one of its best computers — one rented from one of the first Indonesians born in East Timor after the invasion — as the owner shut down his small business and moved to Java. Even all the banks in Dili and the few outside the city closed down. It was as if the business class knew something terrible was going to happen. Thus, by the time Ian Martin announced the result of the ballot at 9:00 A.M. on Saturday, September 4, in Dili, there was a sense of foreboding in East Timor. Few journalists remained in the territory. And apart from Dili and a few areas in the eastern part of what was officially still an Indonesian province, the various international observer missions had no presence. As for UNAMET, its regional offices were still open, but the number of U.N. personnel left in these areas was small as all the electoral staff had already departed (as planned), leaving only CivPols (civilian police officers), military liaison officers, some other security personnel, and a few international staffers.

Dili was eerily quiet that morning. The streets were largely deserted. Many Dili residents — especially those from the eastern parts of the city — had already fled from their homes. So when Ian Martin let it be known that 78.5 percent of voters had opted for independence, there were small, private rejoicings. Many sobbed, shedding tears of joy and pain — as if purging themselves of all the suffering imposed on them over twenty-four years of war and occupation. But there was very little of the public displays of celebration that one might expect after such a momentous announcement.

●

Militia, armed with automatic weapons, began cruising Dili's streets within two hours of the announcement of the ballot result, terrorizing the capital's population. Soon thereafter in Liquiça — around the time I was passing through in the convoy heading toward West Timor — militias attacked the post where the last few UNAMET personnel were staying, forcing them to flee. A uniformed soldier fired his AK-47 on the departing vehicle carrying an American CivPol, hitting him once in the lung and once in the stomach.[6] By that evening fires were burning in many areas of Dili, and automatic gunfire was heard incessantly throughout the night—part of the TNI's psychological warfare aimed at driving everyone out of the city.

By the next day, the campaign to empty, loot, and destroy Dili and East Timor as a whole was well under way. Indonesian foreign minister Ali Alatas and TNI commander Wiranto both flew into Dili, where each had tense meetings with Ian Martin at the airport. Wiranto then went to a meeting with the TNI commander for East Timor. This required that he travel to the center of Dili. Thus the military chief surely witnessed the orchestrated chaos and devastation. Nonetheless he claimed that the situation in Dili was under control when he returned to Jakarta.

Tens of thousands had already fled Dili, many to the area of Dare in the hills to the south overlooking the capital. Militia and the TNI compelled those who had not yet fled to leave their homes, often leading them at gunpoint to the waterfront and police stations—locations that had become refugee centers from where they would later be forced to evacuate to West Timor and other parts of Indonesia. But they were hardly refuges in the conventional sense, as militia members freely came in and out, often looking for well-known pro-independence activists, a number of whom were taken out and never seen again.

One international monitor who, along with East Timorese human rights workers and some Indonesian solidarity activists, had been forced by militia to flee to the main police station, described how Eurico Guterres, armed with a machine gun, freely entered the grounds of the police headquarters in Dili. Guterres was looking to see if there were any high-profile independence supporters among the refugees. Meanwhile, militia members were bringing looted goods, including motor vehicles, into the station to store there.[7]

"For those of us staying in East Timor, it was always a bit of a joke to be asked if the military was directly supporting the militias," the observer wrote. "The militias were directly integrated into the military. It was not as if the militias had an autonomous organization of their own. The government publicly announced in May that militia for Dili, Aitarak, was an official 'civil defense squad' (*PAM Swakarsa*). The top military commanders for East Timor were on its 'advisory board.' The militia leaders openly bragged of their connections with military officers. They walked around with walkie-talkies on which they received hourly orders from the military, as some of us confirmed by listening with our own walkie-talkies. Most nights they were seen en masse going in and out of the military headquarters . . . and the police station."[8]

Many who appeared to be militia members, in fact, were actually policemen or TNI soldiers and officers who simply changed their clothes. An American reporter arrested in Dili on September 13, for example, shared an airplane to West Timor with Indonesian police intelligence agents dressed in the black T-shirts of the militia. They were returning to their homes in Indonesia after having completed their tour of duty.[9]

Apart from a few members of Australia's diplomatic contingent holed up at their fortress-like consulate, almost all the foreigners remaining in the territory were in the UNAMET compound along with fifteen hundred to two thousand East Timorese, including many, and their families, who had worked for the U.N. mission. But even these asylums were far from safe as Indonesian forces raked the areas surrounding them with gunfire—especially at night. No area of Dili was free from the shooting. In the midst of it, TNI trucks equipped with loudspeakers were circulating throughout the city, telling people to leave for West Timor in the morning lest they be killed.[10]

Foreigners were among the targets of the psychological warfare. And the effort was largely successful. UNAMET was evacuating its "nonessential" staff in Dili but presenting it as a redeployment (to Darwin, Australia) within the mission's zone of operations. The resulting lack of foreign witnesses made the TNI-militia terror campaign all the easier.

No place was immune from the efforts of the Indonesian police, military, and militia members to systematically ravage the territory, going from house to house, building to building, burning them down. Some even reported seeing trucks with industrial hoses circulating through the neighborhoods, spraying the abandoned buildings with gasoline and then setting entire areas ablaze. But this usually did not take place until the agents of devastation had a chance to loot people's private belongings, including household possessions and, among the more privileged, motorcycles and cars.[11] They then drove many of the vehicles across the border with West Timor, loaded with the possessions of those they had driven from their homes. Towns and villages near the West Timor border were hardest hit, as the proximity made thorough looting much easier. Oecussi was virtually emptied of anything that could be carted off. In Suai, by far East Timor's most prosperous town, all the corrugated steel roofing was taken. The looters went so far as to pry all the porcelain squat toilets in the town's schools out of their concrete bases and take them to Indonesia. But the destruction and looting were hardly the worst of it.

On the afternoon of Sunday, September 5, a combination of TNI soldiers, Brimob, and militia members attacked the Dili Diocese (the headquarters of the Catholic Church), where hundreds had sought refuge, killing upward of twenty-five and wounding many more. The next day militia and soldiers dressed as paramilitaries attacked the residence of Bishop Belo and the compound of the International Committee of the Red Cross next door, firing at the thousands of refugees who had fled there, killing at least thirteen, and then pouring gasoline on the buildings and setting fire to them, just as they had done to the diocese.[12]

Just down the road was the city's harbor. It was there that Liliana and her family had sought temporary refuge. Many had gone there in the hope of finding a ship to relative safety. It was rumored that a passenger ship from Java would arrive around midnight on September 5 and then head to Indonesia's eastern islands. At first there were no militia there, but within a few hours many arrived and began terrorizing the refugees, threatening to rape young women and kill the men, while extorting money for promises of protection. By the time the ship finally arrived at 10:00 A.M., there were throngs of people gathered, all cowering in fear. When the ship's doors opened, a group of East Timorese students from Jakarta were among those who disembarked. They were carrying a Falintil flag and yelling slogans championing East Timorese independence. It is not clear why they were doing so. Eyewitnesses surmise that perhaps they were unaware of what had transpired since the ballot result had been announced, as they had been on the ship for a few days, or maybe they knew what was going on and were bravely confronting the terror. In any case the militia attacked the students with machetes, reportedly cutting off the heads of some. Seeing the bloodletting, the terrorized refugees swarmed toward the ship and boarded.[13]

Later that same afternoon TNI members and militia attacked refugees at the church compound in Suai. They shot and hacked to death almost one hundred people, including three Catholic priests, one of whom was Indonesian. Then they kidnapped many women and girls, and took them to West Timor where they were forced to serve as sexual slaves of the militia. When I returned to Suai in July 2000, an East Timorese friend pointed out his sister-in-law sitting by herself on a porch. She had only been able to return to East Timor within the previous few weeks. Militia had raped her repeatedly, sometimes many times a day. The physical or psychological trauma or both was so severe that she was not able to walk for some time after returning.

And on September 8 TNI soldiers and militia slaughtered pro-independence activists at the police station in Maliana — killing dozens. The next day the TNI hunted down and slew a dozen people who had escaped from the station as the massacre was taking place, including the local head of the CNRT, Manuel Malgalhães, whom I had briefly met in July.[14]

During this time Falintil did little to respond. Since early August the national guerrilla army had been in four cantonment areas throughout the country as a way of undermining Indonesia's attempt to derail the ballot by denying the TNI the opportunity to engage them militarily or to blame them for any atrocities or acts of violence that the TNI or its militia had committed. Falintil also wanted to avoid being drawn into a full battle with the TNI for fear that the military and its militia would use the occasion as an excuse to commit far more atrocities against the civilian population. With only approximately seven hundred experienced guerrillas, Falintil simply did not have the resources to directly and fully confront the TNI. And the resistance feared that if the guerrilla army did engage in conflict with the TNI, it would diminish the chances of the United Nations establishing the hoped-for peacekeeping force. In the weeks preceding the August 30 ballot, the TNI had promised to reciprocate Falintil's cantonment by withdrawing its troops to the district or subdistrict level and ensuring that militia would also redeploy its forces into cantonment areas. This reciprocity never occurred.[15]

●

Meanwhile in New York at the United Nations and in the capitals of various national governments and, most important, many governments of the so-called West, diplomatic activity was rapidly increasing, although still none of the leaders of the U.N.'s powerful member-states supported an international military force for East Timor. On Sunday morning Security Council president Peter van Walsum of the Netherlands canvassed support for sending a mission of Security Council ambassadors to Jakarta, an idea that, only a few days earlier, had not received sufficient support from the five permanent members. Still, several national delegations were reluctant to support the proposed mission unless Jakarta provided authorization, which it did on that same evening. At a late-night emergency session of the Security Council, the members voted to send the delegation.[16] The next evening five ambassadors—from Malaysia, Namibia, the Netherlands, Slovenia, and the United Kingdom—left for Jakarta, charged with delivering a blunt message to Indonesia's political and military leadership and with trying to convince them to accept an international military force.

The ambassadorial delegation arrived in Jakarta on Wednesday, September 8, amid rumors that Wiranto would soon force Habibie to resign and take over as president. When the ambassadors finally met with Habibie the next day, the president's well-known eccentric behavior—the same eccentricity that had led him to authorize the ballot—was on display. As David Usborne, a British journalist accompanying the delegation described it, "Mr. Habibie opened with an hour-long monologue, spoken through a microphone even though his guests were only feet away. He launched into irrelevant tangents. He interrupted ambassadors when they were at last allowed to speak." When asked about reports of widespread destruction and mass atrocities, Habibie characterized them as "fantasies" and "lies." And while he agreed to allow the ambassadors to visit Dili and promised security along with food and water for the besieged UNAMET compound, the president rejected the delegation's offer to provide peacekeepers to help Indonesia "restore order."[17] "You would have to fight your way onto the beach," said foreign minister Ali Alatas in response to the suggestion.[18]

While Wiranto had been present at the meeting with Habibie, he received the ministers the following day at TNI headquarters. Joined by twenty other generals, Wiranto assured the ambassadors of Indonesia's commitment to respect the ballot and, with martial law now imposed, that the TNI was making significant progress in restoring order.

Habibie's government had imposed martial law just hours after the U.N. delegation had left New York, granting the military, instead of the police, the power and responsibility to restore order. It was the proverbial moving of the deck chairs on the *Titanic,* but the United Nations played along, if only to call Jakarta's bluff. Annan told Habibie that the TNI had forty-eight hours to restore order, and, if it did not, the world body would consider other measures. One of the first moves the military made was to cut off the town's electricity and water supplies. The TNI also disabled the regular phone system. Thus satellite phones — for the very few that had them — were the only link to the outside world. UNAMET's vehicle workshop, and along with it the mission's main satellite dish — its principle means for communication — were also destroyed.[19]

"Our commitment to handling the problem should not be doubted," Wiranto told the Security Council envoys. The person Wiranto introduced as his "General of Information" then gave an Orwellian presentation to the ambassadors, complete with graphs, one of which portrayed the number of "attacks, burnings, and destructions" for each of the ten days since August 30. The worst day, according to the presentation, was September 2, when five attacks took place. The previous day, the general reported, there were only two burnings in all of East Timor. While Wiranto agreed to accompany the U.N. mission to Dili on the following day, he again refused the introduction of foreign troops, invoking the "dignity of the TNI" and arguing that it would only encourage the pro-independence side to attack the minority favoring integration with Indonesia.

When the U.N. delegation finally had a chance to respond, the leader of the group, Namibian ambassador Martin Andjaba, forewent diplomatic niceties and directly stated that, despite the repeated promises of Indonesia's government and the TNI to protect the East Timorese, they had not followed through. "We do not believe them," the former SWAPO guerilla fighter declared.[20] "The violence has continued, the oppression, the destruction of property has continued unabated. The killing continues even as we sit here. In fact, the situation has worsened."

Instead of responding, Wiranto spoke about how the TNI alone understood the people of East Timor and was the only institution that could facil-itate reconciliation among its divided people. He also promised that the very military responsible for all the death and destruction would repair the physi-cal damage and "hand over East Timor in good condition."

During the monologue a cell phone belonging to one of the delegates rang. The call was from UNAMET staff inside the compound in Dili. They reported that gun- and grenade-wielding militias had been allowed to pene-trate the TNI cordon and were preventing the evacuation of nonessential per-sonnel to the airport while trying to force their way into the compound. Wiranto assured the delegates that the report was false. "There is no trouble, the situation is peaceful," the defense minister proclaimed after phoning his commander in Dili. A second phone call from UNAMET confirmed that the siege was ongoing. Confronted with the report Wiranto called Dili again, but this time he informed his guests that there was a minor disturbance: some military veterans were protesting, he announced, because of the proposed evacuation of local (East Timorese) U.N. staff, but the situation was not se-rious. "You must believe me," he stated.

Defying the surreal, Wiranto then invited the ambassadors to join him for a round of golf on the new "Cobra Course" that he had helped to design on the grounds of the TNI compound. The ambassadors declined.[21]

●

The delegation's military flight to Dili on the next morning, Saturday, Sep-tember 11, featured a Madonna video with a topless woman shimmying down a pole.[22] Arriving in a city that was calm, the delegation heard no gunfire nor saw any militia on the streets during its visit. While the intention of the TNI was to present the apparent quiet as proof of the effectiveness of martial law, it demonstrated instead that the TNI could turn off the terror any time it wanted to, giving lie to the representation of the militia as an autonomous force or the claim that "rogue elements" of the TNI were the source of the problems.

Once again, a general provided a slide show to the visitors, this one show-ing that the number of incidents of "lootings, killings, kidnappings, burn-ings, and terror" had diminished dramatically since the imposition of martial law. "Isn't all that perhaps due to the fact that the people of Dili have all been driven out of the city?" asked Jeremy Greenstock, the British ambassador.

As David Usborne wrote, "the killings, the deportations and the destruc-tion have already been committed. The city has been laid waste, and the peo-ple are gone. Outside the [UNAMET] compound there is virtually no one left to terrorise in Dili and precious little left to burn or loot. It is not a few buildings that are destroyed: it is hundreds of them."[23]

One of the places the envoys visited was the UNAMET warehouse at Dili's harbor. A few days earlier a UNAMET team with a TNI escort had gone there to access their supplies as food and water were running low. The TNI escort notwithstanding, militia members threatened the UNAMET representatives with firearms and vandalized their vehicles, forcing the team to return empty-handed to the beleaguered compound.[24] By the time the Security Council delegation arrived, the UNAMET warehouse was empty. Outside was a UN-AMET vehicle overflowing with looted goods; the U.N. insignias were painted over and "Aitarak" was painted on the hood.

While visiting the besieged UNAMET compound, refugees there begged the envoys for help. Usborne described the desperate pleas of a woman named Maria. "The woman, perhaps 40 years old, was beside herself with terror, tears streaming down her face. 'Please, stay with us, please,' she gasped, her body twisting with sobs. 'I am so afraid, you have to protect us, please. Tonight, when you are gone, they are going to attack us. They kill us tonight. Stay.'"

But the ambassadors and their entourage could not stay, as they were obligated to return later in the day to Jakarta. Yet the visit made a profound impression on the delegation members, with one ambassador characterizing it on the flight back as "Worse than Kosovo and Bosnia."[25]

Just as the TNI had done on the flight earlier in the day, the military provided video entertainment for their foreign guests on the return flight. This time, however, it was a feature film, one on a serial killer.[26]

●

The next morning General Wiranto attended an event for military wives in Jakarta. Speaking to the TNI spouses and a much larger television audience, the defense minister told them, "You have the same feelings like me about East Timor." The karaoke-loving general then proceeded to a small stage, grabbed the microphone, and began singing in English the 1970s hit, "Feelings."[27] (Just over a year later Wiranto would release an album of his favorite ballads, entitled *For You, My Indonesia*. The proceeds of the album were supposedly to benefit the country's hundreds of thousands of refugees, including what at the time was approximately 120,000 East Timorese in West Timor — most of them being held as virtual hostages.)[28]

Nevertheless Wiranto had already reversed his opposition to an internationally mandated force entering East Timor. According to members of the U.N. delegation, even Wiranto seemed surprised by the level of devastation in Dili. That he was witnessing it firsthand in the company of a delegation of the United Nations' most powerful organ made it much more difficult for him to deny requests for Indonesia's permission for international intervention. More important, rapidly escalating international pressure on Jakarta had forced the Indonesian government's hand: over the weekend the TNI's key patrons — the United States and Britain — had cut ties with their Indonesian counterparts, while the World Bank and the International Monetary Fund (IMF) had threatened economic sanctions earlier in the week.[29] Thus, on the evening of Sunday, September 12, Habibie officially accepted an international peacekeeping force.[30]

But the agreement to allow international military intervention did not mark the end of the TNI's scorched-earth campaign, as indicated by the on-going siege of the UNAMET compound. A few days later, on September 14, all but twelve of the UNAMET staff evacuated to Darwin, taking with them the East Timorese refugees who were in the compound. This was only after the United Nations — raising the horrific specter of its tragic desertion, and the subsequent slaughter, of Rwandan refugees in 1994 and Bosnian refugees at Srebenica in 1995[31] — had come close, only six days earlier, to abandoning all the East Timorese in its Dili compound (with the exception of those working for UNAMET).[32]

Following the evacuation, the TNI and those militia still left in the territory continued to attack civilians and to engage in looting what little was left in the ravaged territory. For its part, Falintil largely remained in its cantonment areas for fear that engaging in a military conflict would undermine international support for a peacekeeping operation.[33] Nevertheless scattered battles raged between the guerrillas and the TNI-militia forces in various locales, especially in the east. On a number of occasions the TNI and militias tried to attack the cantonment areas and refugee concentrations in the countryside.[34]

The International Force East Timor, or InterFET, entered a destroyed Dili on September 20. The Australia-led force, according to the agreement negotiated with Jakarta, was there to assist the Indonesian military and police in restoring order as they withdrew from the territory.

Along with a flood of international agencies and organizations, InterFET brought much-needed relief to the hundreds of thousands of displaced East Timorese hiding in the countryside, averting potential large-scale starvation. But while an international peacekeeping force had never established itself so quickly, it was far too late. And it spread out through the territory very slowly. Soldiers from the international force did not secure Maliana until October 10, for example, and they did not enter the ruins of Oecussi until October 23. Such a sluggish pace allowed ample time and space for militia and TNI to continue killing, looting, and destroying — even in Dili, right under the noses of the InterFET troops.[35]

On September 23, for instance, the Mahidi militia attacked the village of Maununu, near the town of Cassa, shooting twelve dead. On October 3 they attacked the village of Hata Hudo, killing six while decapitating an elderly woman whose head they left on top of a barrel in the middle of the road.[36]

The Mahidi militia was led by the notorious Cançio de Carvalho, a wealthy landowner and an official in the Indonesian ministry of justice, who had quickly established himself as a cold-blooded murderer shortly after the TNI had given him and his men twenty automatic weapons around Christmas 1998.[37] One of his worst early crimes took place during a TNI-militia attack on the village of Galitas, near the town of Zumalai, on January 25, 1999. Cançio shot and killed a pregnant women, Angelina de Jesus, and then sliced open her belly. Cançio justified the brutality, saying that the woman was the wife of a Falintil commander.[38]

Journalists passing through the environs of Cançio's town in early October found "deserted villages where the stench of decomposing corpses was interspersed with the fresh smell of the tall grass and the trees. We didn't stop to look; it had become commonplace — in even the smallest hamlet or village, you'd find at least one body. That seemed to be the pattern. As they arrived, the troops or militia killed at least one person to terrorise the rest into getting on the trucks going to West Timor."[39]

The withdrawal of TNI Battalion 745 — one of only two battalions based in East Timor — was typical of the scorched-earth approach taken by departing Indonesian soldiers and their militia allies. Working together, the Lospalos-based battalion and the local militia sought out and murdered many independence activists in the aftermath of the announcement of the ballot result.[40] By the time InterFET had entered Dili, most of the battalion's members had already withdrawn from the area. Late in the afternoon of September 20 the remaining soldiers began their drive to the West Timor border from a TNI compound in nearby Lautem, where they had all gathered. They spent the night in Laga, about forty miles to the west. When they left Laga the next morning the soldiers torched their barracks. Heading west, the thirty-vehicle convoy of about one hundred soldiers and officers, in addition to some family members and a small number of refugees, came upon two East Timorese brothers returning home. The soldiers shot and stabbed the two brothers to death.[41] Over the next ten miles, soldiers — openly enjoying the sport of it — randomly shot and killed four other civilians as they proceeded down the road.[42]

Prior to their departure from Laga a battalion lieutenant had told his soldiers, "If you find anything on the way, just shoot it." Before the ballot the U.S.-trained battalion commander Lt. Col. Yacob Sarosa had informed his troops that they would have to "destroy everything" if the independence option prevailed. The troops followed their instructions well. Passing through Laleia, the troops brutally murdered at least two other civilians.[43] Entering Dili later in the afternoon they apprehended a British journalist and an American photographer, as well as their East Timorese interpreter, Anacleto Bendito da Silva, on the eastern outskirts of the city. Although they eventually released the two Westerners, the soldiers brought Mr. da Silva to TNI head-quarters where an eyewitness saw soldiers beating him. Da Silva would never be seen again. Proceeding further into the devastated capital, they shot a man in the back as he fled down a side street. They then ran into a Dutch reporter and his East Timorese driver. Upon seeing the TNI, the driver quickly turned around their motorcycle, but he could not escape the soldiers, who caused the bike to wipe out. Although the driver escaped on foot into the brush along the roadside, the thirty-year-old reporter, Sander Thoenes, did not. Soldiers killed him, shooting him in the neck and then cutting off his left ear and part of his face. Thoenes, a journalist with the *Financial Times* of London and a contributor to *The Christian Science Monitor,* a Boston-based paper, had only returned to Dili earlier that afternoon after fleeing the post-ballot terror with other foreign journalists.

Shortly thereafter the convoy arrived in central Dili at TNI headquarters. While briefing the soldiers, Col. Muhammad Noer Muis, commander of the TNI headquarters in Dili, told them, "You don't need to tell anyone about what you have done on your way here. Don't even tell your wives." Later that evening, after refueling, the remnants of Battalion 745 left for West Timor. On the way they passed through an Australian military checkpoint on the west-ern outskirts of Dili.[44] The Australians simply waved them on.

The ease with which the battalion's remaining members departed was in-dicative of the protocol that governed InterFET-TNI relations in East Timor's transition from an Indonesian-occupied land to one administered in the name of the international community. While some confrontations took place be-tween InterFET and the TNI, they were relatively minor, with no shots ex-changed between the two military forces.[45] Instead of treating the TNI as a criminal outfit, InterFET was obligated by political imperatives to treat its In-donesian counterparts with martial deference and thus impunity.[46]

The last of the Indonesian soldiers left East Timor just after midnight on October 31, 1999. Australian troops kept a jeering crowd of thousands at bay as the last troops boarded their ships. One of history's most brutal colonial occupations was over. Historians would have a difficult time identifying as vi-olent a withdrawal by any other colonial power in the twentieth century.

•

Jakarta had hoped, and indeed had believed, that the U.N.-run vote would provide the legitimacy to its annexation of East Timor that it had long sought, the assumption being that the population would vote to remain part of In-donesia. Following the establishment of UNAMET, however, it soon became apparent that the cause of the "red and white" did not enjoy anywhere near the level of support that Jakarta's intelligence apparatus in East Timor had been reporting.[47] But it was too late to back out of the U.N.-brokered arrangement. The TNI and its political partners thus intensified their campaign of dirty and often deadly tricks, in the hope that they could convince enough voters of the dangers of voting for independence. In the end, this, too, failed. So the TNI gave the East Timorese what they had threatened would happen if independence were to win: a return to 1975 and the death and destruction of the Indonesian invasion.

Just as in 1975, and the more than two decades that followed, Jakarta did not act alone in 1999. It had supporters behind the scenes, in the form of powerful national governments whose military, economic, and diplomatic assistance to Indonesia — and whose unwillingness to do anything that would upset the lucrative political-economic relationships underlying such assistance — proved vital in facilitating the commission of war crimes and crimes against humanity against the East Timorese people, and the making of East Timor's ground zero. Appreciating this complicity is essential to understanding the context in which the horrors of 1999 took place.

I think we did the best that could be done under extremely difficult circumstances.

—JAMES RUBIN, U.S. STATE DEPARTMENT SPOKESPERSON, *October 1999*

[People] in East Timor . . . know they would not now be independent without the help of an international coalition of which Britain was a prominent member.

—ROBIN COOK, BRITISH FOREIGN SECRETARY, *January 2000*

I think we behaved most honourably throughout 1999. In fact, it's one of the most honourable periods in Australian foreign policy, where we did everything we possibly could to ensure the ballot took place. . . . At the end of the day, we handled it just right and the proof of that is in the result.

—ALEXANDER DOWNER, AUSTRALIAN FOREIGN AFFAIRS MINISTER, *May 2001*

Signing of May 5 accords at the United Nations. From left to right: Indonesian foreign minister Ali Alatas, Secretary-General Kofi Annan, and Portuguese foreign minister Jaime Gama. *Photo by Eskinder Debebe, courtesy of the United Nations Department of Public Information.*

The dinner in the U.S. State Department's well-appointed James Madison Room featured grilled pear, endive and blue cheese salad, along with crab cakes, artichoke flan timbale, roasted vegetables, and sauvignon blanc to help wash down the meal. Held in the private dining room of the secretary of state, the February 17, 1999, gathering in Washington, D.C., was a working dinner called by its hostess, Madeleine Albright. The invited guests were academics, all of whom were Indonesia specialists, and included former ambassador to Indonesia Paul Wolfowitz. After a dessert of apple crisp and rum-raisin ice cream, the secretary of state asked the guests specific questions about developments in Indonesia, a country she was preparing to visit in March. The last topic of discussion was East Timor.

Geoffrey Robinson, a historian at the University of California, Los Angeles, had been designated to speak on the matter. A State Department representative had told Robinson that he was to discuss alternatives to a referendum in East Timor, to explain what would be viable options other than a one-person, one-vote process, as there were elements within the State Department that did not support that concept. Despite those instructions, Robinson made it clear in his remarks that only a legitimate act of self-determination — in the form of some sort of universal ballot organized and run by the United Nations — would satisfy the East Timorese population, and that there were no viable alternatives.

Sitting at the other end of the table, Paul Wolfowitz quickly responded, informing Albright and the other guests that independence for East Timor was simply not a realistic option. Employing language long utilized by Jakarta, he argued that East Timor would descend into civil war if Indonesia were to withdraw, leading to the same sort of chaos that unfolded in 1975. The problem in East Timor, he contended, was one of tribal and clan-based differences. Only the Indonesian military had been able to put an end to the fighting.

A State Department official politely called the evening to a close as soon as Robinson informed the former ambassador to Indonesia of the wrongheaded nature of his analysis.

Immediately following the formal breakup of the gathering, another State Department official approached Robinson. "Is there really no alternative to a referendum?" she asked. "A referendum is so problematic." When he asked the official to explain her position, she pointed out that Indonesian foreign minister Ali Alatas was against a referendum in that it implied Indonesia was a colonial power, and that its presence in East Timor was illegitimate.[1]

Indonesia's very presence in East Timor was indeed illegitimate, at least under international law. But as the dinner that evening showed, at least some key players in the State Department and in positions of influence in the Beltway did not think so, or at least were unwilling to admit it and act accordingly. More important, the evening demonstrated the overriding weight many still gave to maintaining cozy relations with Jakarta, regardless of the implications for the basic human rights of the East Timorese.

Such thinking within the State Department, and, among many in the political establishment, vis-à-vis East Timorese self-determination, would play a highly significant, if not decisive, role over the next several months. Undoubtedly such a view was one of the many factors that informed Washington's response to the negotiations that culminated in the May 5 accords and to the events that followed.

As before, the United States was not alone in having a significant effect on events in and around East Timor. But its policies and actions would prove to be of vital importance, as would those of the so-called East Timor Core Group, an informal body put together by Secretary-General Kofi Annan as the U.N. negotiations unfolded in 1999. Such "core groups" are collections of interested countries that assist the U.N. Secretariat in a particular matter.[2] In the case of East Timor, the countries had good relations and were deemed to be influential with Jakarta, while not being perceived as biased in favor of East Timorese independence. The five members were Australia, Japan, New Zealand, the United Kingdom, and the United States. Together they would play a crucial role in shaping the activities of the United Nations toward East Timor in 1999.[3]

The May 5 accords provided the procedural framework within which the United Nations organized the August 30, 1999, ballot in East Timor. To a decisive degree, the United Nations is the embodiment of its member-states — especially its most powerful ones. Thus the May 5 agreements and the subsequent efforts to ensure security for the East Timorese serve as a reflection of the power-laden context within which U.N. staff had to function. That the agreements were highly flawed was well known at the time they were signed.

The United Nations team around the negotiations, however, had already decided that trying to get Indonesia to relinquish security during the consultation would have been a "deal breaker."[4] But U.N. officials in New York did try hard to persuade Jakarta to accept stronger security measures. The original U.N. draft of what became the May 5 Agreement for example, required the Indonesian government to disarm all militia groups, to engage in an early and substantial withdrawal of its troops from East Timor, and to confine its remaining soldiers to barracks one month before the ballot. Jakarta, however, deleted these sections, and the Indonesian military leadership refused to meet with a U.N. negotiating team sent to Jakarta in April by Secretary-General Kofi Annan. During this time both Australia and the United States pressured the U.N. negotiators not to push Indonesia any further, with Washington warning the United Nations on April 29 not even to mention the issues of disarmament or the deployment of military observers lest Jakarta withdraw from the whole process. On April 30 Annan wrote a letter to President Habibie, laying out seven security-related elements that would have to be in place for the United Nations to be able to organize a free and fair vote. Jakarta rejected the letter.[5] Nevertheless the United Nations — with the apprehensive support of the East Timorese resistance — proceeded with the negotiations that culminated in the signing of the agreements.

Xanana Gusmão and José Ramos-Horta strenuously protested Jakarta's refusal to agree to an arrangement that would have provided real security for the East Timorese population. In an April 28 letter to Kofi Annan, Ramos-Horta, after voicing his deep gratitude for the secretary-general's efforts, expressed outrage at the prospect of Indonesia being responsible for security for the ballot. "Our people, terrorized and traumatized for 23 years," he wrote, "are expected to vote on their future with 'protection' provided by the very same army and gang of criminals that have turned the country into a hell far worse than Kosovo and apartheid's South Africa." The vote, he continued, "will be a farce and the credibility of the UN will be seriously damaged if firm preventive measures are not considered now. It is necessary that the SC [Security Council] is seized of the question." Ramos-Horta went on to call for a reduction of both the Indonesian military presence to one thousand soldiers and their cantonment, a condition that would also apply to the guerrillas of Falintil. He also insisted on the disarmament and disbandment of the militias and that only the United Nations be responsible for security. "Failure to implement these fundamental measures," the Nobel laureate wrote with unfortunate accuracy about the future, "is recipe for disaster."[6]

Despite such sentiment, the leadership of the East Timorese resistance was not willing to risk losing the opportunity to have the ballot and thus advocated that the accords go forward. The resistance leaders were well aware that this was the best deal the East Timorese could get in the foreseeable future, given the refusal of Indonesia's powerful allies to push Jakarta to accept a more favorable (and secure) arrangement. In this regard, the East Timorese were ambivalent about the agreement.

For this reason Ramos-Horta boycotted the May 5 signing of the accords. The day before he had phoned Jamsheed Marker, Annan's personal representative for East Timor, and told him that entrusting security to Indonesia was like giving responsibility for security in Chicago to Al Capone or, more accurately, putting the Khmer Rouge in charge of election security in Cambodia.[7]

On the same day an op-ed piece by Aniceto Guterres Lopes, East Timor's leading human rights lawyer who, at the time, was hiding in Dili from militia threatening to kill him, appeared in *The New York Times*. "With arms, money and a license [from the TNI] for reckless rampages, the dozen or so militia leaders have openly threatened death to anyone opposed to continued Indonesian occupation," he wrote. "Their spokesman, Basilio Araujo, told an Australian television crew, 'We will kill as many people as we want.'" Guterres called upon the United States and Portugal "to insist on a disarming of the militias and a substantial withdrawal of Indonesia's all-pervasive troops. The United States, holding considerable leverage over bankrupt Indonesia," he continued, "should take strong action, like cutting off all military aid and training until a valid vote on independence is held in East Timor."[8]

Members of the Core Group were also aware of the necessity for a stronger security arrangement prior to the signing of the May 5 accords and in the subsequent months leading up to August 30, 1999. Australian Prime Minister John Howard even met with Habibie on April 27 in Bali where Howard urged his Indonesian counterpart — to no avail — to accept an international peacekeeping force before the ballot. Overall, however, mirroring the language employed by U.N. officials, Core Group representatives argued during the time, and continue to assert today, that to have pushed for some sort of effective force independent of Indonesia would have been a "deal breaker." To quote an American diplomat, "There was no way we could have got the Indonesians to agree to it. We couldn't get it through the Council otherwise. Our question was would we proceed with the consultation or not."[9] Australian foreign minister Alexander Downer has expressed a similar opinion:

> It was clear that Indonesia . . . would not agree to the establishment of an international security/peacekeeping presence in East Timor before the ballot. President Habibie categorically rejected Australian calls for him to invite a peacekeeping force into East Timor in the lead-up to the vote. In these circumstances, there was no prospect of persuading Indonesia under Habibie to agree to accept a UN-run election in East Timor along with an international force. . . . [T]o have pushed the idea with Jakarta would have resulted in the cancellation of the 30 August vote. . . . Jakarta's political sensitivities to this proposition meant this was always a non-starter.[10]

But there is nothing to suggest that the member-states of the Core Croup or any permanent members of the Security Council made any serious attempt to convince Jakarta to change its position. Had such efforts been made, significant security measures might very well have been forthcoming. As Geoffrey Robinson has argued about the "deal-breaker" analysis, "Like most arguments about realism in politics, this is a dubious one. So many previously 'impossible' things happened in 1999, that one cannot say with confidence whether, if vigorously advocated, the idea of international forces might have been accepted."[11] Robinson's analysis highlights the importance of distinguishing between a recognition of a particular constellation of factors at a given time and a subsequent acceptance of those factors, as opposed to a desire and willingness to endeavor to alter them to bring about a different configuration. Only by taking the latter approach can one move beyond the status quo. In the context surrounding the May 5 accords, insistence on an alternative security arrangement was most likely a "deal breaker." But that context, like any other social context, was not immutable. Had the Western powers exerted greater levels of pressure on the TNI while exhibiting strong support for the Habibie government in the face of military and political opposition to its East Timor opening, a new context might have come about allowing for what had been hitherto deemed impossible.

Given Jakarta's refusal to allow an international armed presence in East Timor, the only other option would have been to invoke Chapter 7 of the U.N. Charter, by which the Security Council is allowed to employ force to maintain international peace and security. But the prevailing thinking within the United Nations was that such an option was also a nonstarter. In any case it would take several months at least, according to U.N. officials in New York, to secure authorization for, organize, and deploy any sort of armed force to East Timor. Given the tight schedule of the vote, such a force was therefore nonviable. Thus it was deemed more practical and cost-effective to pressure Jakarta to live up to its security obligations under the May 5 accords. Within the United Nations the Department of Peacekeeping Operations put forth this line of argument most forcefully, with the strong support of the United States and Britain.[12] Nevertheless Kofi Annan began secret negotiations in May 1999 with countries willing to deploy troops in East Timor, if necessary. According to Annan, Australia accepted the principle of such a force and even agreed to consider leading it, but only if Jakarta authorized that course of action. As Annan explained, "No country, I mean no country, would accept to deploy its forces without Indonesia's agreement."[13]

Such a point begs the question of what action was taken by various countries — specifically the members of the Core Group, which collectively provided the bulk of Jakarta's international economic and military aid — to try to secure Indonesia's "agreement" following the signing of the accords, a time during which the TNI and its militia were actively engaging in acts of violence and thus breaching the very same accords. The answer, it appears, is little to no action at all — at least not until *after* the results of the ballot were known and the scorched-earth campaign of the Indonesian military and its militia was already well under way. The British, for example, never even threatened to cut off military aid and sales to Jakarta before the announcement of the ballot result.[14] Similarly the Americans did not threaten to break military ties or cut economic assistance prior to the post-referendum explosion of violence. Nor did President Clinton make any sort of presidential statement warning Jakarta of the dangers of not complying with its obligations under the U.N.-brokered agreements.[15]

There was certainly ample reason—not least Jakarta's conduct over the previous twenty-three years—to expect that Indonesia would not abide by its obligations under the international pact. Core Group members were aware in the months preceding the vote that they had to do something to increase the security mechanisms available to the East Timorese while lessening the possibility of Indonesian attempts to derail the consultation process through violence. But the thinking seems to have been that, by getting Indonesia to agree to allow the presence of a U.N. mission in East Timor, it would give the Security Council a foothold that Jakarta would have to respect. The agreement, according to Core Group diplomats, allowed their respective national governments to pressure Jakarta to abide by their commitments—specifically the provisions relating to security. Moreover, there was an assumption that the Indonesian authorities understood the costs (internationally) that a spree of killing and destruction would entail and would thus restrain themselves.

But the numerous incidents of gross violence in the weeks and months preceding the ballot, along with the flagrant impunity enjoyed by the pro-Indonesia militias, made it clear that, at best, the Indonesian security forces had no intention of living up to the spirit, if not the letter, of their international obligations.[16] In addition, Western intelligence agencies had a great deal of information on what was going on in East Timor behind the scenes, and what the TNI and its militias were planning.

In 1948 the United States and Britain, along with some of their main allies in the Second World War (Australia, Canada, and New Zealand), had signed an agreement establishing a coordination mechanism for the acquisition and distribution of electronic intelligence. The UKUSA agreement, also known as the UK-USA Security Agreement or "Secret Treaty," divided the world into five zones of responsibility, with the United States being accountable for the biggest area by far. Responsibility for Indonesia and East Timor, among other areas, rested with Australia.[17]

From its monitoring of Indonesian communications and information garnered from East Timorese defectors, Canberra was well aware of a strong likelihood that the Indonesian military would engage in a campaign of terror and destruction around the time of the ballot. Alexander Downer, along with other principals of the Australian government, was fully apprised (and was cognizant in early 1999) that the Indonesian military—including the senior command structure—was responsible for organizing, arming, and directing the militia violence.[18] Canberra also had gathered intelligence which showed that the TNI intended to launch a widespread campaign of terror and destruction in the event of a pro-independence result. For this reason Canberra had tried to get Jakarta to accept some sort of international peacekeeping force under Australian leadership in the May–June period. It appears, however, that Prime Minister John Howard and officials in Australia's Department of Foreign Affairs and Trade did not take the warnings from Canberra's intelligence apparatus sufficiently seriously and were under strong delusions about their ability to influence the Indonesian military through conventional and relatively polite diplomatic and military channels. Publicly the Howard government — despite overwhelming evidence to the contrary — continued to pretend that the violence perpetrated by pro-Indonesia forces was not the result of official policy in Jakarta or within the military high command but, instead, was the work of "rogue elements." Such divisions within the Australian state undoubtedly undermined any attempt by various elements of the government to gain Jakarta's acceptance of an international peacekeeping force.[19] Further, from July 24 to August 16 Australia hosted Exercise Kakadu — joint military maneuvers involving six countries, including Indonesia and New Zealand — no doubt strengthening Jakarta's perception that it was business as usual in terms of its military ties with the West.[20]

More specifically, credible allegations that Canberra concealed evidence that could have saved many lives were made by an Australian army intelligence officer, who had access to electronic intelligence prior to the August 30, 1999, vote and also by an Australian federal police officer who served the UNAMET mission in Maliana and prepared intelligence reports. The documents predicted that the TNI would engage in widespread killings in Maliana in the event of a victory by pro-independence forces. But instead of passing these materials on to U.N. staffers in East Timor so that they could forewarn the population, Canberra effectively squelched them. One of the results was the September 8, 1999, massacre in Maliana at the local police station to where thousands, following the instructions of U.N. officials, had fled seeking sanctuary upon the outbreak of widespread violence.[21]

The U.S. government was also aware of much of what its counterparts in Australia knew, given the intense levels of intelligence cooperation between the two countries — in addition to Washington's own highly advanced intelligence-gathering capabilities, many of which were enhanced in the run-up to the ballot so as to strengthen the American capacity to monitor the goings-on in East Timor and Indonesia.[22] Moreover, a U.S. National Security Agency liaison officer is always present in the headquarters of Australia's Defence Signals Directorate (DSD), the agency that intercepted most of Indonesia's electronic communications. The British also have a liaison officer present at DSD headquarters and thus also would have been well informed.

It is likely as well that the New Zealand government was apprised, given its intense cooperation with Canberra on intelligence matters.[23]

That said, the situation on the ground on East Timor was not crystal clear. There were, as Australian foreign minister Alexander Downer contends, "developments [that] provided real cause for optimism that the ballot would take place peacefully" — such as a generally successful voter registration process, and then the actual vote, which took place largely violence-free.[24] These contradictory developments led many international observers in the territory, and at least some East Timorese, to think that there was a good chance the TNI might actually respect the outcome of the ballot while probably engaging in relatively isolated acts of terror on the margins in its aftermath.[25] Yet there was also a consensus within the East Timorese resistance and among most observers that one could not afford to presuppose such an outcome but, instead, should assume a worst-case scenario. Such a presumption would have required that the international community ensure a far different security arrangement for the East Timorese population than the one that ultimately prevailed.

Although Washington, as represented by Stanley Roth, the assistant secretary of state for East Asian Affairs, did suggest to Canberra at least once (in February 1999) that an international peacekeeping force might potentially be necessary — a position with which Canberra disagreed at the time[26] — it appears that, at best, the United States sent mixed messages to Jakarta and never seriously pursued the option. Thus, while elements of the State Department were pressuring Indonesia to put an end to the TNI/militia terror, the Pentagon — as represented by Admiral Dennis Blair, leader of all U.S. military forces in the Pacific — did nothing to challenge the TNI. In fact, Blair's words to his TNI counterparts seemed to endorse their militia campaign of terror.[27] Even within the U.S. Embassy in Jakarta, the message was ambiguous. The embassy's political section was strongly advocating the pressuring of Jakarta not simply to "control" the militia forces but to disband them. Ambassador Stapleton Roy and others in the embassy, however, were arguing for the need to "stay the course" and avoid pushing the Indonesians too hard lest a nationalist backlash occur, one that would hurt U.S. economic and military interests. In early 1999 Roy actually went to Dili and met with senior militia representatives; Madeleine Albright also met with militia spokespeople during her visit to Jakarta in March 1999. The effect of such meetings was to confer legitimacy on the paramilitary groups and Jakarta's claim that these groups were independent of the TNI and representative of a significant portion of the East Timorese population.[28] Given such mixed messages and the lack of any significant pressure from top-level Clinton administration officials, it was easy for Jakarta to ignore the efforts of State Department officials in Washington and New York, and Jakarta-based U.S. diplomats, working to ensure that it fulfill its obligations under the May 5 accords.[29]

As for Tokyo, the Japanese government pretended through the entire process that the violence occurring in East Timor was the result of a conflict between pro-independence groups (the East Timorese resistance) and anti-independence ones in the form of the militia. Implicitly the TNI was not a party to the conflict but a neutral body mediating between the two warring factions.[30] Needless to say, any sort of serious pressure from Tokyo was not forthcoming.

Even as violence grew in the immediate aftermath of the vote and in anticipation of the announcement of the results, Core Group members still did not make strong statements that might have pressured the TNI to abide by its obligations. On September 3, for example, Deputy U.S. Ambassador to the U.N. Peter Burleigh ruled out the possibility of some sort of international security force entering East Timor in the short term, calling it "not a practical suggestion." Instead, he explained, the United States was "counting on the Indonesian authorities . . . to create a situation of peace and security throughout East Timor." Between the date of the ballot and Burleigh's statement (a five-day period), pro-Indonesia forces had killed at least four local U.N. staff members and three civilians,[31] in addition to burning houses throughout the territory, attacking the UNAMET compound, driving most journalists out of the country, and forcing international observers to evacuate from a majority of the areas outside Dili.

In the days immediately following the announcement, when the TNI-militia campaign of terror, destruction, and forced evacuation was well under way, Clinton administration and high-level Pentagon officials called their Indonesian counterparts and urged them to regain control of the situation in East Timor. On Monday, September 6, following the attack on Bishop Belo's compound, the State Department released a statement that Jakarta had to "either take immediate steps to end the violence or invite the international community to be of assistance." It also stated that good relations between the United States and Indonesia depended on Jakarta's reaction.[32]

On the following day the Clinton State Department and the International Monetary Fund (IMF) both warned Jakarta that it risked the suspension of international loans if it failed to put an end to the terror in East Timor. The State Department called on Indonesia to adopt "a constructive approach towards ending the humanitarian disaster in East Timor," saying that "productive relations" with the international community, including the IMF, depended on such an approach. A few hours later the IMF stated that it was considering delaying a scheduled review of Indonesia's economic situation, without which Jakarta would not be eligible for the next installment of a multibillion-dollar IMF loan package designed to rescue the country's ailing economy.[33]

Clinton himself sent two cables to Habibie. And General Harry Shelton, head of the military's Joint Chiefs of Staff, phoned Wiranto several times in the days following the ballot announcement to discuss the TNI's plan to remove troops from East Timor most closely linked to militias and replace them with soldiers "loyal to the central government in Jakarta."[34] But the effect of such discussion was to lend credence to the TNI's bogus claim that "rogue elements" were responsible—a position belied by Washington's own intelligence resources.

Moreover, assuring words continued to flow from White House officials. Paraphrasing administration sources, for example, *The New York Times* wrote that the Clinton administration had "made the calculation that the U.S. must put its relationship with Indonesia, a mineral-rich nation of more than 200 million people, ahead of its concern over the political fate of East Timor, a tiny, impoverished territory of 800,000 people that is seeking independence." Propagating the "rogue element" canard to the general public, it also quoted a senior administration official saying that General Wiranto needed more time to replace the bad Indonesian troops with ones loyal to the government in Jakarta. "You've got to give him a little time to bring them under control," the official said.[35] And when a reporter asked National Security Adviser Sandy Berger why Washington was not considering intervening in East Timor, given its intervention in Kosovo, Berger flippantly, if not ineloquently, replied, "My daughter has a very messy apartment up in college, maybe I shouldn't intervene to have that cleaned up."[36] Taken together, such words had the effect of letting the TNI know that its actions would exact little international cost.

Nevertheless pressure on the administration from Congress and the American public as a whole was rapidly growing. On September 8 a group of U.S. Senators introduced a bill obligating Washington to cut off all military assistance and block international loans to Jakarta.[37] Columnists and editorials in leading U.S. newspapers called on Washington to cut all military ties and economic assistance to Jakarta.[38] And activists clogged up the phone lines of the White House and members of Congress urging Washington to take decisive action.

Internationally Canberra, no doubt in good part because of massive and rapidly growing public pressure within Australia,[39] had already declared its willingness to lead a multinational military force—a "coalition of the willing"—as long as both Jakarta and the United Nations gave their authorization. It turned up the heat on Washington as well, letting the Clinton administration know that future Australian support for various U.S. military deployments depended, in part, on the administration's commitment to a combat force for East Timor. And on September 7 or 8 Portuguese Prime Minister Antonio Guterres telephoned Clinton and threatened to pull Portugal out of Kosovo unless Washington supported international intervention. To show its seriousness, Lisbon denied permission for sixteen U.S. military flights over the Azores.[40]

In the face of such pressure Clinton announced a suspension of all U.S. "programs of military cooperation" with Jakarta on September 9 and stated that Indonesia had to invite the international community to assist in restoring order. He also delivered an implied threat, predicting "dire" consequences for Indonesia's economy. While it was by far the strongest statement and action to date by the administration, it included a condition that allowed even more time for the TNI to continue its scorched-earth campaign. As Clinton explained, he was calling for such a force *only* (implicitly) "if Indonesia does not end the violence."[41] Finally, less than forty-eight hours later, Clinton announced a suspension of U.S. military sales while in Auckland, New Zealand, for the meeting of the Asia Pacific Economic Cooperation (APEC) forum. The date in Auckland (as well as in Dili), marking the end of U.S. complicity with Indonesian brutality in East Timor, ironically enough, was September 11.[42]

Only hours after Clinton's announcement, London followed suit and announced a suspension of the sale and delivery of Hawk aircraft, in addition to support for a European Union arms embargo and a willingness to contribute to an international military force.[43] Earlier in the week the IMF had informed Jakarta that it was "closely watching" the situation in Indonesia and East Timor, and a few days later it postponed a mission scheduled for mid-September. And World Bank head James Wolfenson had told Indonesia's leaders that "for the international financial community to be able to continue its full support, it is critical that you act swiftly to restore order and that your government carry through on its public commitment to honour the referendum outcome."[44] Meanwhile, Australia threatened to cancel its $1 billion contribution to an international bailout package for Indonesia if Jakarta continued to refuse to invite an international military force into East Timor.[45] And on September 10 Canberra announced that some unspecified, "planned bi-lateral defence activities" with Indonesia would not be taking place and that it would "review all aspects" of its military relationship with Jakarta.[46] On the same day as Canberra's announcement, New Zealand made known that it was suspending bilateral military exercises with Indonesia and military training.[47]

Given the confluence of such developments and others, Jakarta, not surprisingly, announced its willingness to allow an international force into East Timor on September 12.[48] In trying to explain the reluctance of powerful countries to support a suspension of aid or forcefully push for an international intervention in East Timor until that point, the *Financial Times* reported, on September 8, 1999, the words of one Jakarta-based diplomat: "The dilemma is that Indonesia matters and East Timor doesn't."[49] The diplomat was U.S. Ambassador Stapleton Roy.[50]

•

Following the terror surrounding the 1999 ballot, the United Nations came under a good deal of criticism, with many arguing that the vote should not have gone forward and that the world body was naïve not to foresee the horror that ultimately unfolded. And undoubtedly the United Nations — in the form of UNAMET — took a number of questionable actions.

Throughout the weeks leading up to the ballot, UNAMET worked to broker various cease-fire, disarmament, and reconciliation agreements between Falintil and the militia. These efforts climaxed the day before the vote, when the United Nations held a high-profile press conference in Dili, at which a representative from East Timor's guerrilla army and a militia leader, Eurico Guterres, pledged to issue orders to their forces that they not carry any weapons outside their cantonment sites. The massive media coverage gave the event a cachet of historic significance. Hardly anyone in East Timor, however, took the event seriously, mindful that the militia had no functioning cantonment sites and that the TNI-militia had failed to live up to numerous earlier promises to withdraw to barracks (in the case of the TNI) and cantonment areas and to cease its violence. A few hours after the public pledge Eurico Guterres was seen walking around Dili armed with a pistol and an M-16 rifle.[51]

UNAMET head Ian Martin later wrote, "It was the most Unamet could achieve," while acknowledging, "it was not enough."[52] He has also explained that he and his colleagues were under no illusions as to the TNI-militia nexus, one they consistently communicated to headquarters in New York and, by extension, to the members of the Core Group. More than anything, they saw such events as a means to increase the pressure on Jakarta and the TNI to abide by its international commitments.[53] UNAMET's efforts in this area, however, were arguably counterproductive. They had the unintended effect of perpetuating the myth of a conflict that was principally between East Timorese (in the form of Falintil) and the militia, while giving credibility to the empty promises of the militia and their TNI sponsors. In doing so, UNAMET may have weakened efforts to expose internationally what was taking place and to introduce more serious security mechanisms.

One of the sharpest criticisms of Martin and the United Nations concerns UNAMET's quick withdrawal from most areas outside Dili, despite its repeated promise that it would not abandon the East Timorese once violence started following the vote.[54] Martin argues that the mission could not have done more in this regard. Indeed, UNAMET was lucky that the TNI did not kill any international staff, as the Indonesian military had clearly made the decision not to allow the mission to stay in outlying areas.[55] Furthermore, the decision to evacuate came from the security personnel in those areas, not from UNAMET headquarters. Had UNAMET stayed longer, Martin surmises, the result would only have been more casualties among the local and international staff.

Many also contend that Martin and UNAMET denied the validity or underplayed the importance of reports and leaked documents they received or both. Taken together, these reports and documents, at the very least, suggested that Indonesia was planning for large-scale evacuations from East Timor and the destruction of some of East Timor's infrastructure.[56] Indeed, TNI leaders had informed UNAMET of preparations for such evacuations. And, in late August, Indonesia's state secretary Muladi was quoted in the press, speaking of a "strong possibility" of an exodus of 223,000 people — a number supposedly comprised of Indonesian settlers and pro-integration East Timorese — if independence were to win.[57] Around the same time Colonel Nur Muis, who less than two weeks earlier had replaced Tono Suratman as the TNI commander in East Timor, stated that the military would escort East Timorese who wanted to leave to neighboring countries after the ballot. When asked how it would work, the Australia-trained Muis explained: "If the pro-integration side wins and the independence supporters want to leave we are prepared to accommodate them." He also expressed willingness to escort supporters of Indonesia to wherever they desired in the case of a pro-independence outcome.[58] And just before the announcement of the ballot result, Muis reported that the TNI was ready to implement a detailed contingency plan to evacuate 250,000 East Timorese civilians by land, sea, and air in the case of the breakout of a full-scale "civil war."[59]

For Martin, "there was nothing unexpected or inherently unreasonable" about such plans, as they "did not imply the coerced removal of people who would wish to stay in East Timor after the ballot." Perhaps. But such statements — along with the frequent predictions and threats by Indonesian officials and militia leaders of widespread violence in the case of a vote favoring independence — should, at the very least, have raised a huge red flag. In addition, UNAMET's own political analysts had concluded that there was a strong likelihood that something terrible might occur.[60]

On this basis, some have criticized Martin and his top advisers for not envisioning, in their "worst-case scenario," widespread terror by the TNI and its militias,[61] and thus for being ill-prepared for what transpired. But as Ian Martin has argued, worst-case-scenario planning is the purview of the United Nations in New York, not of an individual U.N. mission. In this regard it was the U.N. headquarters that failed—a manifestation of a long-standing tendency *not* to assume worst-case scenarios for fear that planning for such will ruffle diplomatic feathers as it implies that the relevant member-state will not live up to its commitments.[62]

This was not the only instance where New York fell short. The U.N. Secretariat could have done more to raise the international profile of what was taking place in East Timor, while highlighting Indonesia's blatant flouting of its commitment to ensure security. As Tamrat Samuel, an assistant to the U.N. undersecretary-general for political affairs, Kieran Prendergast, and the former head of the East Timor and Indonesia desk in the political affairs department, argues, the Secretariat should have made clear to the Security Council "the need for a major force, and the withdrawal (or scaling down and confinement to barracks) of the TNI." In addition, the Security Council should have sent a delegation to Jakarta and East Timor before the ballot as a show of international will, as Prendergast had suggested.[63] Kofi Annan could also have appealed to international public opinion more effectively prior to the ballot by, among other things, taking advantage of the bully pulpit afforded to him by virtue of his position. Portugal had urged Kofi Annan to be in Dili for the announcement of the ballot result. Instead, he sent his personal representative, Jamsheed Marker, to the East Timorese capital for the August 30 vote, the day after which Marker left for Jakarta.

But, in some ways, the U.N. envoy only added to the problems. Marker, a personal friend of Indonesian foreign minister Ali Alatas, had earned a well-deserved reputation for being far too accommodating toward Jakarta.[64] UNAMET's political affairs division, for example, had formally recommended in June and July that the ballot should *not* go forward, because Indonesia had failed to ensure adequate security as outlined in the May 5 accords. Ian Martin, as head of UNAMET, expressed the same view to New York in mid-July, but U.N. headquarters decided otherwise (based on a number of good reasons). And once it became clear that the vote would go forward, members of UNAMET's political affairs division began to assert to New York and visiting delegations from national governments that some sort of international force had to be in East Timor prior to the ballot.[65] Marker helped to undercut these arguments, expressing weeks before the ballot that no international force would be necessary—either before or after the vote. He repeated this assessment at a UNAMET press conference in Dili on August 30, stating that his position was "proven by the events" of the day.[66]

Regardless of the merit of these various criticisms, they do not erase all the good work that the United Nations and, specifically, UNAMET did, and the very real on-the-ground constraints faced by the U.N. mission. Ian Martin and the UNAMET staff helped to save the lives of many, while the mission as a whole organized and ran — under extremely challenging circumstances — a legitimate act of self-determination, something the people of East Timor had long demanded but that political "realists" had considered impossible.[67] And as the East Timorese population as a whole made perfectly clear, they wanted the vote to go forward, despite their profound worries that a wave of terror would follow the ballot, fearing that any further postponements would result in their losing a once-in-a-lifetime chance. Taking a longer view, it was the dogged determination of a few U.N. officials over a period of more than two decades that helped to keep the East Timor issue alive on the international stage.[68]

In this regard, the United Nations' accomplishments in East Timor in 1999 constituted a success. But it was hardly an unqualified one — especially if one considers that it took decades of U.N. activity to reach the point at which the East Timorese people were able to determine their political status. But these shortcomings, rather than being first and foremost manifestations of individual failings, highlight the profound structural limitations, as well as the opportunities, that the international organization embodies.

The United Nations, like any large organization, is not a monolith. Its myriad divisions, agencies, and personalities represent different strengths and weaknesses, and often divergent interests and visions. In part this explains the failures as well as the successes of the United Nations in East Timor. That said, in matters of international peace and security — the area in which the United Nations has (potentially) the greatest amount of power — the world body is, first and foremost, the creature of the member-states on the Security Council, dominated by the five permanent members (Britain, China, France, Russia, and the United States). But the strongest member by far is the United States, given its overwhelming political-economic and military power on the world stage, and its related ability to effectively blackmail the United Nations partly because a significant percentage of the body's finances is provided by Washington. Hence engaging in after-the-fact analysis of individual U.N. personalities and actions runs the danger of losing sight of the big picture. It also ignores organizational constraints created by these structural factors that even the secretary-general faces. Thus, while Kofi Annan could and should have spoken out more, he would have probably paid a price had he done so. In addition to antagonizing Indonesia, a powerful and influential country within the "Third World" bloc, more important, he would likely have incurred the wrath of the United Nations' most powerful member-states, most notably the United States. Undoubtedly Annan had learned the lesson of his predecessor, Boutros Boutros-Ghali, who, because of U.S. opposition to his reelection owing to his political independence and outspokenness, served only one term.[69]

Despite these obstacles, however, the United Nations was able to advance the East Timor issue. Although little progress was made through the 1970s and 1980s, U.N.-brokered negotiations advanced significantly following the November 1991 Santa Cruz massacre, and, in spite of the massacre, efforts to resolve the East Timor conflict continued. But Jakarta kept insisting that the East Timorese resistance could not participate in any talks, that only state parties (Indonesia and Portugal) had a right to discuss political matters. However, Boutros-Ghali, who had assumed the U.N. leadership one month after the massacre, brokered a compromise to involve the East Timorese, one that satisfied the objective of both Lisbon and the United Nations: the secretary-general's office would consult with the resistance. In this manner the United Nations indirectly involved representatives of the East Timorese people and invigorated diplomatic activity.[70]

The 1996 awarding of the Nobel Peace Prize to José Ramos-Horta and Bishop Belo only added to the United Nations' momentum. This was especially true following Kofi Annan's election as secretary-general in December 1996. Annan and his special representative, Jamsheed Marker, played very active roles in facilitating negotiations between Indonesia and Portugal and, again, indirectly with the East Timorese resistance. Their efforts contributed significantly to the signing of the May 5 accords. These represented a highly important accomplishment, albeit one that would prove woefully and dangerously inadequate from the perspective of the physical security of the East Timorese. But this inadequacy says more about the power relations surrounding the negotiation process and the difficult political context within which U.N. staff had to work than about the shortcomings of specific individuals associated with UNAMET or the United Nations in New York. U.N. officials were not in a position to challenge these power relations in an effort to alter the resulting context. Core Group countries, on the other hand, were in such a position, but they chose not to do much about it.

●

According to James Rubin, spokesperson for the U.S. State Department during the Clinton administration, Washington did the best it could in 1999, given the "extremely difficult circumstances" surrounding East Timor.[71] Even if we accept, for the sake of argument, Rubin's contention, what is striking (but not surprising) about his statement and those of other spokespeople for powerful national governments allied with Indonesia is the lack of any sort of indication of what "we" might have done to have contributed to the making of the "extremely difficult circumstances" in the first place. As the history of military, economic, and diplomatic assistance rendered to Jakarta by various national governments shows, they were effectively partners in Jakarta's war crimes and crimes against humanity in East Timor.

Still the question remains, could Western governments have done more than they did in 1999 to pressure Jakarta? In an academic article examining Australian government policy during that year, Nicholas Wheeler and Tim Dunne argue that critics of Canberra's behavior "overstate the extent to which Australia had a controlling influence over . . . the environment in which [the ballot] was to take place."[72] In terms of pressuring Jakarta to accept some sort of international peacekeeping force prior to the ballot, the authors contend that the political will in the capitals of powerful countries was simply not sufficient to bring about such a result. Also lacking prior to the actual holding of the vote was a "normative context" that framed Indonesia as an international pariah. Only in such a context, they conclude, one that arose solely as a result of the terror campaign following the vote, could material pressure in the forms of cutoffs of various forms of military ties and threats from the World Bank and the IMF have come about and succeeded. In this regard, any efforts on the part of Australia to pressure its Western allies and to force Jakarta's hand prior to September 1999 would have been futile and perhaps counterproductive.[73]

While correct by the standards of the narrow terms around which their analysis is constructed, Wheeler and Dunne make the mistake of limiting their focus to Australia. It seems reasonable to contend that Canberra alone could not have brought about the pressure needed to prevent or significantly limit Jakarta's post-ballot violence. Had Canberra decided to "go it alone," it ran the serious risk of severely damaging relations with Jakarta while producing little of value in terms of an outcome favorable to East Timor. But such a conclusion only points to the need for a concerted approach by Western countries to have pressured Indonesia. Certainly Australia could have worked — behind the scenes — to bring about such a situation (as it did after the announcement of the ballot result). But nothing suggests that Canberra pursued such a course of action. At the same time Wheeler and Dunne assume that the needed normative context could not have come about earlier than it did (accepting the supposition that such a context was absolutely necessary for the material pressure to come about). Had powerful international actors endeavored, for example, to bring attention to Indonesia's myriad pre-ballot atrocities, such a context *could* have arisen in the months preceding the horrors of September 1999. Nevertheless, as Wheeler and Dunne suggest, it is far from clear that Indonesia would have capitulated even had international actors exerted a significant amount of pressure prior to the vote of August 30, 1999. But in framing this observation as they do, the two analysts effectively absolve Australia and other international actors from their responsibility to have tried much harder than they did to ensure that the East Timorese population had adequate security in the weeks and months surrounding the ballot.

Core Group countries—in addition to the likes of Canada, France, and Germany—could have taken actions to ensure or increase the probability that the Indonesian military and its governmental allies would abide by their international agreements and obligations, or, at the very least, could have taken actions to reduce the likelihood of a horrific aftermath to the East Timor vote. For example, Western governments could have insisted that Jakarta disarm and disband the militia groups, thus denying the TNI the thin cover it used to terrorize the population.[74] They also could have threatened Jakarta with a cutoff in military ties and economic aid, and then acted upon such threats as the TNI continued to renege on its promises as the consultation process and the announcement of its result unfolded. These need not have been public threats adding fuel to the fires of nationalist reaction within Indonesia. There were real constraints faced by Indonesia's political leadership, particularly as personified by then president Habibie, whose term would soon end. In any case, given the power relations within the Indonesian state, pressure had to focus on the Indonesian military.

Such pressure might have run the risk of causing Jakarta to dig in its heels or, worse yet, to disallow the ballot to go forward. But had Jakarta pursued this latter course of action, it would likely have led to Jakarta's international isolation, given its pledge to support the U.N.-run process, and thus would have exacted significant costs in terms of aid and loans at a time of significant economic difficulties within Indonesia. In this regard it is difficult to imagine that Indonesia would have taken such radical action, especially had the relevant national governments made public the reasons why they were pressuring Jakarta, and even produced a portion of the large body of proof they possessed showing that the Indonesian government and military were not keeping their international commitments.

Another possible result is that Indonesia could have done nothing in response to the carrying out of threats to cut off aid and military ties, and simply continued the course of action it was pursuing in East Timor. This reaction would have run the risk that the "international community" would have had far less leverage over Jakarta because of the ensuing deterioration of ties that ultimately facilitated Jakarta's acceptance of an international military force. Following this line of thought, the outcome, once mass violence began after the announcement of the ballot result, potentially would have prolonged and deepened the terror campaign, and caused even greater hardship for the East Timorese. But, as in the previous scenario, it is highly unlikely that Jakarta would simply have withstood the severing of economic and military ties and not responded in a manner that sought to address international concerns—largely because it could not have afforded to do so.

Governments, however, do not always make decisions on the basis of a narrow cost-benefit analysis. So it is *possible* (although highly unlikely) that Indonesia's military might have gone forward with its scorched-earth campaign regardless of the pressures coming from its Western patrons. It is for such reasons that Core Group and other powerful countries could and should have ensured that there was a security force able to enter East Timor as soon as the mass violence began in the aftermath of the ballot.

Many argue, however, that an international force could not have entered East Timor without the TNI's permission and cooperation. According to Tim Fischer, who served as deputy prime minister to John Howard and headed Australia's official observer delegation to the ballot, "to go in without the clearance of the Indonesians was tantamount to a declaration of war between Australia and Indonesia. It was simply not on."[75] In addition to obfuscating the responsibility of Core Group and other countries to have pressured Indonesia to provide such clearance — a permission that, as events in September 1999 showed, was not impossible to obtain — such words also exaggerate what most likely would have been minimal Indonesian military resistance had an international force entered East Timor without Indonesia's cooperation.

Given Indonesia's economic dependence on the world's most powerful countries, it is extremely unlikely that the TNI would have engaged in open conflict with an international force — especially one led by Western troops. In any case, Indonesia's military was simply not equipped to take on the likes of the Australian military and the British Gurkhas. Furthermore, the Australians and Americans had very strong intelligence-gathering capacity and were able to effectively monitor Indonesian troop and militia movements within East Timor, and communications within the territory and with Indonesia proper.[76] Although the TNI showed itself to be a capable force for terrorizing civilians and, to a lesser extent, fighting guerrilla insurgencies, it is hardly a world-class military. Also, the nature of the combined TNI-militia scorched-earth campaign made it clear that Indonesia had no intention of staying in East Timor. It is therefore unlikely that any sort of international military intervention without Jakarta's permission would have resulted in significant TNI resistance. With their access to intelligence on the TNI's machinations in East Timor, many of the world's most powerful countries were undoubtedly aware of this well before InterFET entered. But instead of acting on this intelligence in a manner consistent with their political and moral obligations to the East Timorese people, they simply provided the TNI with the space and time to carry out and finish its final campaign of terror and destruction, and then to depart unscathed.

At the very least the various national governments could have had an international force ready to enter East Timor *immediately* once Jakarta agreed to allow one to do so — that is, on September 12, 1999. Western leaders applaud themselves for the speed with which such a force finally did enter the ravaged territory. Nevertheless it was eight days after Habibie agreed to allow an international military force to enter East Timor before foreign troops landed in Dili. And it would be weeks more before they reached some of East Timor's outlying areas, thus allowing time for many more killings and other atrocities. Although there were significant logistical challenges associated with transferring military personnel and resources from abroad, foreign military undoubtedly could have been on the ground much faster than occurred had the political will existed. In the case of the aftermath of the violent overthrow of President Jean-Bertrand Aristide in Haiti on February 29, 2004, for example, U.S. troops began arriving later the same day that Aristide was forced to flee. French and Canadian troops landed soon thereafter.

In summary, the behavior of Jakarta's Western allies in 1999 differed little from that which began in 1975. At both times Jakarta's patrons had multiple and significant options, ones that could have avoided much, if not all, of the carnage experienced in East Timor. In 1999 the governments of the various countries, while officially supportive of the UNAMET-led consultation process — indeed, they provided a great deal of the material resources needed to organize and run the ballot — did not signal to Jakarta nearly as strongly as they could have that they would not tolerate the commission of more crimes. Just as in 1975, the issue then was not what would have happened had these governments militarily intervened to put an end to Jakarta's campaign of terror. Rather, the question is, what would have happened had the various external actors simply stopped enabling Jakarta by cutting off economic and military ties (or at least by threatening to do so)? Because they did not threaten to take such action and then only did so when it was too late, the TNI assumed that it could act in East Timor with impunity, as it had in the past. Had London, Washington, Canberra, Tokyo, and Wellington, among others, behaved in a manner consistent with their international obligations, it is likely that Indonesia's military would not have gone as far as it did in its killings and destruction of East Timor. Even if Jakarta had not complied with its patrons' wishes, its ability to act would have been weaker had the pressures been real (i.e., material) rather than merely rhetorical.

Moral considerations typically are not significant factors in informing the foreign policies of governments. In this light, it is not surprising that political-economic and geostrategic matters were decisive in determining how Core Group members and other governments behaved in 1999. But from both a moral and political perspective, these governments had a responsibility to prevent violence by the TNI, for it was their support for Indonesia for almost two and a half decades that had the cumulative effect of decisively enabling Jakarta to invade East Timor in 1975, to maintain its brutal and illegal occupation of the former Portuguese colony, and to undertake its final act of terror and destruction following the August 30, 1999, ballot. Hence the making of "ground zero" in East Timor in September 1999 was very much a collective effort, one that involved an international community of a different sort than that typically invoked in lofty speeches extolling the virtues of interstate cooperation.

Now that Jakarta's occupation is over, these same governments present their 1999 behavior as largely benign and supportive of the UNAMET process and, when asked, generally claim that they did everything within their power to prevent Indonesian atrocities. At the same time they tend to present themselves as external to the terror that unfolded. If for no other reason than ensuring greater levels of historical accuracy, it is necessary to call into question such representations. More important, it is imperative to challenge such representations because of the considerable implications that they have for present-day efforts to ensure justice for East Timor's suffering and an appropriate level of restitution by those parties responsible for the country's plight.

In order to escape accountability for his crimes, the perpetrator does everything in his power to promote forgetting. Secrecy and silence are the perpetrator's first line of defense. If secrecy fails, the perpetrator attacks the credibility of his victim. If he cannot silence her absolutely, he tries to make sure that no one listens. To this end, he marshals an impressive array of arguments, from the most blatant denial to the most sophisticated and elegant rationalization. After every atrocity one can expect to hear the same predictable apologies: it never happened; the victim lies; the victim exaggerates; the victim brought it upon herself; and in any case it is time to forget the past and move on. The more powerful the perpetrator, the greater is his prerogative to name and define reality, and the more completely his arguments prevail.

—JUDITH HERMAN, Trauma and Recovery: The Aftermath of Violence

Nations have memories, too. And those memories are almost unfailingly self-serving.

—TOBIAS WOLFF, *War Memory*

Forgetting one's participation in mass murder is not something passive; it is an active deed. . . . [W]e can sometimes catch the act of forgetting at the very moment it happens. It is not a moment of erasure, but of turning things upside down, the strange reversal of the victimizer mentally converting himself to victim.

—ADAM HOCHSCHILD, King Leopold's Ghost: A Story of Greed, Terror, and Heroism in Colonial Africa

President Clinton at the U.S. Embassy in Dili on May 20, 2002. Reporter Allan Nairn has his back to camera. *Photo courtesy of Pacifica Radio's* Democracy Now! *(www.democracynow.org).*

His trademark charisma and semblance of sincerity shined through as he spoke. Bill Clinton was there, he proclaimed, "to make a clear and unambiguous statement that America stands behind the people of East Timor in the cause of freedom in the Pacific," something that "is in our nation's best interest and consistent with our deepest values."

Only hours earlier — at midnight as the date changed to May 20, 2002 — East Timor had become the world's newest country. United Nations Secretary-General Kofi Annan formally handed over the reins of government to newly elected president Xanana Gusmão after more than two-and-a-half years of U.N. governance. Clinton — along with Richard Holbrooke — was present, at the invitation of his successor, George W. Bush, to lead the American delegation to the festivities. Now the morning of that same day, the former president was at the official opening of the American Embassy in Dili.

"The United States had an opportunity in 1999 to stand up for the cause of the East Timorese people with Indonesia," Clinton informed the guests at the flag-raising ceremony, "to try to work to support an Indonesia that was more open and more free and to help our friends in Australia and the ASEAN countries to bring their troops in here. And, thanks again to Ambassador Holbrooke who passed a great resolution in the United Nations, we were able to do those things and the rest is history."

He closed his brief statement with a flourish of high-minded words:

For the people who don't know, they may think this is just a small country in a distant part of the world, a long way from America. But the suffering of the East Timorese through hundreds of years of colonial experience and through an oppressive relationship with past Indonesian governments became symbolic of the drama that now dominates the world's stage. One in which America must be heard, not just when we feel it at home, as we did so painfully on September 11, but when we see it around the world. The great question today is whether the world is going to be defined by differences or by common goals. I have argued as long as I could that the only way we can ever respect and celebrate our differences is if we live in a world in which common humanity matters more. Wherever you are from and whatever you are doing here, never think this is a little thing. We raise the American flag today to make a statement that in the 21st century the United States still stands for freedom and the proposition that we cannot have a globalized economy in an interdependent world unless, in that world, our common humanity matters most. I thank you. The world is in your debt and America stands behind you. God bless you all.

As the crowd applauded the former president, Allan Nairn, a journalist and human rights activist from the United States, shouted out a question. It took the form of a detailed overview of Clinton's support for Indonesia's crimes in East Timor.

"Get to the point," Clinton exhorted Nairn as he walked toward the area where the journalist was standing. "You want to make a speech. Give him a hand, he is making a good speech," he stated in an effort to use the crowd to his advantage.

Nairn, an eyewitness to and survivor of the 1991 massacre at the Santa Cruz cemetery, persisted by recounting the unbroken support by Clinton's administration for the TNI in 1999 despite myriad well-documented atrocities by its forces. Finally Nairn asked, "Why did you continue with aid to the Indonesian military if they were killing civilians?" By that time Clinton was only a few feet away from his interrogator.

"I don't believe America or any of the other countries were sufficiently sensitive in the beginning, for a long time, a long time before 1999, going all the way back to the 1970s, to the suffering of the people of East Timor," Clinton responded.

"All I can say is that when it became obvious to me what was really going on and that we couldn't justify not standing up for what the East Timorese wanted, and some decent treatment for them, this under the guise of trying to hold Indonesia together at first and a larger foreign policy issue, I tried to make sure we had the right policy. . . . I can't say that everything that we did before 1999 was right," he continued. "I'm not here to defend everything we did. We never tried to sanction or support the oppression of the East Timorese."

In his final words in response to Nairn, Clinton stated, "I think the right thing to do is to do what the leaders of East Timor said. They want to look forward, and you want to look backward. I'm going to stick with the leaders. You want to look backward. Have at it, but you'll have to have help from someone else."[1]

Refusing to answer any additional questions, Clinton quickly left the gathering. And Richard Holbrooke, despite promises that he would be available for interviews following the ceremony, never appeared.

●

The words of Bill Clinton illustrate how depiction of the past, especially when it involves events of mass violence, is almost always a highly politicized matter. Social groups, and individuals who identify with them, typically employ "memories" or representations of the past to give meaning to their collective life, and to make sense of the world around them. They also utilize these recollections to protect and further their interests.

National memories are especially contentious given the character of allegiance to the nation. They are also particularly selective, effectively editing out of history that which reflects poorly on powerful individuals and hegemonic groups and institutions. Because the nation — or any social grouping to which one has a very strong sense of unquestioning allegiance—supposedly exemplifies the highest of ideals, it is often difficult for adherents to accept criticism of, and admit wrongdoing by, what they see as their particular and ultimate community. For such reasons, George Orwell wrote, "the nationalist not only does not disapprove of atrocities committed by his own side, but he has a remarkable capacity for not even hearing about them."[2]

Memories, and nonmemories—that which we forget or never even learn about—are thus important because, among other reasons, they define who we are. As such, they are powerful forces for shaping the world. In the case of East Timor, competing memories play a decisive role in ongoing struggles over accountability for the country's bloody past.

Battles over the representation of East Timor's past are especially intense within Indonesia, where various human rights organizations, East Timor advocacy groups, and some journalists have played an important role in trying to ensure honesty about Jakarta's history in the now independent country. Nevertheless, within Indonesian officialdom, there is little to suggest that there has been any sort of honest reckoning of the nature and magnitude of crimes the TNI and their political cronies committed in East Timor.

In February 2000 then president Abdurrahman Wahid came closest to displaying such understanding. After laying a wreath at the Indonesian military ceremony in Dili during a three-and-a-half-hour visit to the territory, he offered an apology of sorts to the East Timorese people for the 1999 terror and for previous atrocities.

"I would like to apologize for the things that have happened in the past . . . for the victims, to the families of Santa Cruz, and those friends who are buried here in the military cemetery. These are the victims of circumstance that we didn't want," he said.[3]

Although significant, Wahid's apology was not sufficiently explicit for many. It did not, for example, express remorse for Indonesia's very presence in East Timor, for its 1975 invasion and its nearly twenty-four-year occupation. Nor did the apology represent any kind of consensus on the part of the Indonesian state—a highly fractured entity. Many prominent government officials and military leaders, in fact, continue to present the September 1999 terror and destruction as a spontaneous uprising of disaffected East Timorese in favor of continued "integration" with Indonesia or upset with what they saw as an unfair electoral process run by a United Nations biased toward independence for East Timor.

In doing so they perpetuate the myth that the Indonesian police and military were a neutral party endeavoring to bring about peace between conflicting groups of East Timorese. Maj. Gen. Adam Damiri put forth such an argument in June 2002 while testifying before a Jakarta court looking into the 1999 terror. "There were not enough military and police personnel on the ground to calm heightened tensions between conflicting community groups," asserted Damiri. "We were undertaking mission impossible."[4] A little more than a year later, during his own trial, Damiri characterized as "fantasy" the notion that the TNI was responsible for the atrocities committed in 1999.[5]

Damiri was a central figure in the formation of the militia groups in East Timor in late 1998. In addition, it is believed that he coordinated the terror campaign against pro-independence activists that took place in the early months of 1999, and was also heavily involved in atrocities in the period surrounding the ballot.[6]

●

Although representations of Jakarta's conduct vis-à-vis East Timor within Indonesian society are of great importance, battles over the past that take place outside Indonesia and East Timor as well as those between groups in East Timor and various national governments are, at the very least, of equal significance. These struggles reflect and shape the context within which the international community decides what type of justice, if any, the people of East Timor will receive for their suffering and dispossession.

A key arena in which this struggle unfolds is the international media. Journalists have long played an important role in constructing and perpetuating many of the myths that surround the conflict in the former Portuguese colony. They have done so through a combination of fabrication, half-truths, and omission — phenomena that result from both willful conduct and ignorance.

Such fabrication, half-truths, and omission were very much evident during the UNAMET process. Admittedly many media accounts of what transpired on the ground were outstanding — especially those of journalists who had a strong grasp of East Timor's history or were from countries where there was a high level of interest in and support for East Timor. But many journalists displayed an astonishing level of ignorance of East Timor's reality, uncritically accepting the TNI's fairy tales and reporting events through a highly distorted lens. Some of the American coverage was especially egregious, perhaps because many U.S. reporters had little to no familiarity with East Timor and Indonesia — a legacy of the poor coverage that U.S. media outlets had afforded to the two countries since 1975.

David Lamb, a long-time foreign correspondent for the *Los Angeles Times,* for example, went so far as to incorrectly attribute atrocities committed by pro-Indonesia militia groups in Dili to a "pro-independence militia." Lamb repeatedly referred to this hitherto unknown entity in his reports. For Lamb, pro-independence militia seemingly included Falintil as well as any form of physical resistance to the occupation — including civilians in Dili defending themselves against attacks by the likes of Aitarak. In framing the situation thusly, Lamb helped to confuse his readers, as well as to create a false equation between TNI-directed paramilitary groups (militia) and a national guerrilla army (Falintil).[7]

Such misinformation dovetailed with what was perhaps the most frequent misrepresentation—that which emphasized intra-East Timorese antagonisms as the principle source of the conflict. This depiction has deep roots. From the beginning of the conflict in East Timor, Indonesia contended that what was taking place was a civil war between the vast majority of East Timorese who wanted to be part of Indonesia and a small, well-armed, radical minority in favor of independence. Thus, so went the argument, Indonesia was only present in the country because of the democratic wishes of the East Timorese population.[8] The establishment of militia groups throughout East Timor in late 1998 and 1999 was a concrete manifestation of the attempt to give life to the myth.

Perhaps most egregious among the mainstream media in perpetuating this line was CNN. In the midst of TNI-militia attacks in April 1999, the Atlanta-based network repeatedly reported "clashes between the pro-integration and pro-independence factions"—a wildly inaccurate representation that even the BBC occasionally reproduced. CNN journalist Maria Ressa defended her reporting by explaining that she had to be balanced.[9] Ressa reportedly spent a few days with TNI generals in Indonesia before arriving in East Timor to make contacts and gain knowledge of the reality of the territory. In her subsequent reports, she informed her international viewers that the TNI was serving as a buffer between Falintil and the militias.[10] Even after having spent a good amount of time in the territory, Ressa continued to put forth such TNI-concocted fabrications. In the days following the August 30, 1999, vote, when the TNI and its militia stepped up violent attacks on the civilian population, she framed one attack on a Dili neighborhood as a clash between pro-independence and pro-Indonesia "gangs."[11]

Since that time an abundance of evidence has emerged proving the TNI orchestration of, and direct participation in, the post-ballot terror. But it was plain to any observer on the ground around the time of the vote that TNI members were perpetrating much of the violence.[12] Nevertheless some subsequent accounts in the international press have not been much better than the misleading ones from the period preceding the announcement of the ballot result. A February 2001 report from Agence France Presse, for example, presented the September 1999 violence as caused by "pro-Jakarta militias [who] embarked upon a scorched-earth rampage," without mentioning the role of the TNI.[13] Even U.N. publications have reproduced such misinformation. A 2002 article by a U.N. Public Information Officer working in

East Timor spoke of "the violent fighting that broke out between opponents and supporters of independence after an overwhelming majority of East Timorese had voted for sovereignty" in 1999.[14] Again, the Indonesian military is invisible.

A more subtle form of the "violent East Timorese" argument places emphasis on the role of East Timorese members in the Indonesian military and police. Even some analyses that make clear the responsibility of the Indonesian military for the September 1999 rampage give credence to the contention that East Timorese members of the TNI—supposedly out of their love for Indonesia—were responsible for much of the violence.[15]

East Timorese membership in the military and police present in the territory was limited, however, reaching a high of about 30 percent in the late 1990s.[16] (In the military proper, the percentage was considerably lower.) But those who were in the military and police were all at the lowest ranks, 90 percent being privates and corporals. Further, most of them were not full-time soldiers but, instead, were members of *milsas,* a reserve force of sorts. Of 211 of the territory's top military positions in 1998, not one of the officers had a last name that was identifiably East Timorese. The situation undoubtedly reflected the fact that the TNI could not trust the East Timorese with any position of responsibility.[17] Even within the two TNI battalions that had the most East Timorese—Battalions 744 and 745, actually the only two that were permanently based in the territory—the number of "local" members was small. About 150 out of 600 soldiers in Battalion 745 were East Timorese, for instance.[18] And from the perspective of the Indonesians, they were hardly trustworthy. Present in the main Falintil cantonment area in August 1999, for instance, was the entire marching band of the TNI's Battalion 744, which had defected and joined the guerrilla army.[19]

Among East Timorese militia members the situation was no better. While there were certainly some who were ideologically committed to the cause of the "red and white," many of the rank-and-file militia members were unwilling recruits and had abandoned the paramilitary groups by the time of the vote. This was even true in Bobonaro district, which abutted the West Timor boundary and was supposedly, according to militia and pro-integration spokespersons, one of the most strongly pro-Indonesia of East Timor's thirteen districts.[20]

●

The misinformation is not limited to events that took place strictly in East Timor. It includes deeds that occurred outside the now independent country's boundaries, but ones that significantly impacted upon events in Indonesia and East Timor. It is here that the role of international actors is key. Accounts of violence in East Timor put forth by various national governments and institutions that dominate the "international community" typically serve to mask the role of powerful actors beyond Indonesia's shores that share in the culpability for East Timor's plight.

There is nothing astonishing about such "distancing tactics."[21] States and institutions employ them to represent themselves in the best possible light, while underplaying their nefarious deeds. In employing "memories" or representations of the past, social groups find that the truth does not always satisfy their needs. For this reason they sometimes systematically distort their memories. In doing so, however, outright fabrication is relatively rare. Probably the easiest and most common form of distorting the past is through the selective omission of facts found to be disagreeable, along with exaggeration and embellishment.[22]

In an IMF report on East Timor, for instance, the authors simply state that the territory "was annexed by Indonesia" in 1975, and then they jump to 1999 and the referendum, the outcome of which "triggered widespread violence." There is no indication at all as to who carried out this violence.[23]

Perhaps most remarkable about the discourse of powerful international actors — at least that which is intended for public consumption — is the general silence on the matter of external support for Indonesia's crimes in East Timor, especially on the part of the world's most powerful countries. Instead, the focus is on the supposed generosity of the particular national governments in helping East Timor to rebuild in the post-Indonesia era.

At a June 14, 2000, party in Dili to celebrate Queen Elizabeth's birthday, for example, British diplomats distributed to their compatriots, to the East Timorese, and to international guests a document detailing the United Kingdom's humanitarian assistance to the United Nations and various bodies in East Timor since September 1999.[24] The document said nothing about London's behavior toward East Timor prior to that time, when the British government was one of Indonesia's largest suppliers of military hardware.[25]

The Japanese government, for its part, is now the largest aid donor to East Timor.[26] Like the British, its conduct toward East Timor during the Indonesian occupation is invisible in its official statements and publications. And even the responsibility of the Indonesian government for what transpired in East Timor is missing in its publications. In its depiction of what occurred in 1999, for example, the 2000 *Diplomatic Bluebook* of Japan's Ministry of Foreign Affairs mentions the U.N. ballot and the result of the vote. It then states, "groups dissatisfied with the referendum result stepped up violence and pillaging, plunging East Timor into chaos."[27] Who these "groups" might have been is left to the reader's imagination.

The U.S. government has been only marginally better in this regard. A November 2003 "Background Note" on East Timor from the U.S. State Department's Bureau of East Asian and Pacific Affairs admits that the militia were "organized and supported by the Indonesian military." But in its brief account of what took place following the ballot, the "note" speaks of only the militia as perpetrating the terror. The TNI role is absent. As for international support for Indonesia's crimes, the document states that "many in the West" accepted Jakarta's claims in 1975 that Fretilin was communist in nature and for that reason had to intercede to prevent the party from consolidating power in the former Portuguese colony. As a result, "major powers also had little incentive to confront Indonesia over a territory seen as peripheral to their security interests."[28] Thus the State Department presents the role of the "major powers" as merely a failure to confront Jakarta, and neglects to mention that these unnamed governments actively supported the Indonesian military in myriad and highly significant ways.

In addition to such distortions, the most common manner to bury knowledge of Washington's complicity with Indonesia's wrongdoing is to say nothing. This is exactly what Madeleine Albright does in her autobiographical account of her years as Bill Clinton's secretary of state. The words "East Timor," for example, do not appear in the more than five hundred pages of text. Only in the appended chronology does she refer to the now independent country, noting that, on October 18, 1999, the Indonesian parliament declared the 1976 annexation of East Timor "null and void." As for Indonesia, there are only two brief references totaling a few lines. After admitting that the United States and Suharto's Indonesia "maintained cordial relations," Albright characterizes the longtime dictator as "one of America's least-distinguished partners." But she does so without providing any explanation of the nature of U.S.-Indonesia ties other than to report later that, in 1999, she singled out Indonesia — along with Nigeria, Ukraine, and Colombia — as especially deserving of U.S. assistance.[29]

Of all the governments complicit in Jakarta's crimes in East Timor, the most forthcoming, in terms of providing information about its own role, has been Australia. This apparent openness is a result of many factors, including an unusually strong level of official and popular interest in East Timor; a highly active solidarity movement; a large community of East Timorese refugees and immigrants in Australia; a national sense that Australia owes East Timor a great debt from World War II; the presence of numerous journalists with deep knowledge of the issue and many years of experience covering it; and a core of elected officials and civil servants in the federal bureaucracy (including some willing to leak important documents) who care deeply about justice and accountability vis-à-vis the former Portuguese colony. Nevertheless there is still a strong current of denial in official circles. These denials take two forms; the first is to highlight what Canberra sees as Australia's positive contributions to East Timor.

In an open letter published in the official bulletin of the Australian Agency for International Development (AusAID), for instance, Australian Foreign Minister Alexander Downer wrote that he was "particularly proud of the Australian Government's response to the East Timor crisis." According to Downer, "Australia has long been engaged in efforts to secure peace in the territory."[30] In a separate article in the same issue of the government publication, the author stated that, "because of the generosity of Australians and others, the people of East Timor will slowly be able to get back on their feet."[31] The publication offered nothing regarding how Australia's previous actions might have contributed to the people of East Timor not being on their feet in the first place.

For the occasion of East Timor's formal ascension to independence, Downer explained how Australia had helped "the East Timorese reach 20 May."

> It is worth recalling that the opportunity for change in East Timor came in 1998 with the end of the Soeharto era. A more open-minded president in Jakarta and our own survey of the East Timorese Diaspora in Australia, provided a better appreciation of how East Timorese leaders saw their future, and helped form the basis of our policy change. This was marked by the Prime Minister's letter to President Habibie in December 1998 which outlined a possible new approach to the East Timor.
>
> The Howard–Habibie Summit in April 1999 in Bali helped pave the way for creating the conditions for a popular consultation. Australia's significant diplomatic and political effort helped firm up international support for an act of self-determination and later to restore security.
>
> Australia was involved from the outset. We participated in the first UN monitoring mission, UNAMET. . . . We led the INTERFET mission which restored security in East Timor in the dark days of 1999. And we have contributed a great deal to the UN Transitional Administration in East Timor (UNTAET).[32]

Like Downer, champions and defenders of Australian policy point to Howard's December 19, 1998, letter to Habibie as a decisive development in Jakarta's decision to allow a referendum to take place in East Timor.[33] The letter called upon Habibie to consider "a means of addressing the East Timorese desire for an act of self-determination" while emphasizing that "Australia's support for Indonesia's sovereignty is unchanged." In this regard, Howard suggested that any self-determination process should avoid "an early and final decision on the future status of the province" so that Jakarta would have ample time to convince the East Timorese of the wisdom of staying within Indonesia — an outcome for which he expressed preference.[34] A careful reading of the letter thus makes clear that Howard's letter was hardly the "diplomatic dynamite" that some allege.[35] More important, it ignores developments—especially within the small circle around Habibie—that indicate that Jakarta was well on the way to deciding to allow some sort of vote, as well as the progress taking place in the U.N.-brokered talks between Portugal and Indonesia.[36] In all likelihood Howard's letter made relatively little difference in this process.

The second form of denial is exemplified by the response of Australian Prime Minister John Howard to a question at a May 19, 2002, press conference. A journalist asked Howard upon his arrival in Dili if he had any regret about his own actions while serving Australian governments in the 1976–83 period. The reporter specifically mentioned Canberra's recognition of Indonesia's annexation of the territory and actions that undermined East Timorese efforts to resist Jakarta's aggression.

Unabashedly Howard defended the policies that Canberra adopted during the period in question, suggesting that what had happened in the previous few years—presumably the UNAMET vote and the subsequent transition to independence—would not have happened otherwise. "As to what was done in the past it's possible to criticise governments of both political persuasions in Australia for what has been done in the past," explained the prime minister. "But for my part I'm pleased to say that over the last number of years we have adopted a policy stance which was right, it was fair, it was just, and it's something of which I'm very proud."[37] Thus there was nothing to regret.

In fact, many prominent Australian government officials (past and present) explicitly state that there is nothing for which to apologize.[38] Gareth Evans, for example, Downer's predecessor as foreign minister, dismisses the notion that Australia—specifically the governments he served—has to atone for any sins. "The truth of the matter is that . . . we did as much as we possibly could to advance the East Timor cause within the environment as we found it with the cards that we had. . . . The notion that we had anything to answer for morally or otherwise over the way we handled the Indonesia–East Timor relationship, I absolutely reject."[39]

Meanwhile, a 2000 report from the Australian Senate and the release and publication of formerly classified documents have extensively documented Canberra's complicity in the invasion and occupation of East Timor.[40] While in some ways such openness reflects the non-monolithic nature of the state, it also illustrates the gaping distance between official statements and literature produced for the purposes of public consumption (as in the case of the AusAID publication) and those made for largely internal (to the government) viewing. Although the Senate report is available to the public, it will require great efforts to have its findings reflected in the public discourse and practices of Australian government officials.

The only government that has come close to apologizing is that of New Zealand. In releasing in September 2002 some previously classified papers from the 1975–76 period, Phil Goff, Wellington's foreign minister, spoke of "a failure by the New Zealand government to take a stance which should have been taken" in opposition to the Indonesian invasion. Pointing to similar conduct by the United States and Australia, Goff stated that "the Western world did little to uphold the rights of the East Timorese" and that, as a result, "our countries therefore must share some responsibility for the subsequent suffering endured by the people of East Timor."[41] Wellington's "almost apology" only seems to apply to the several months surrounding the 1975 invasion, however, and not to the many years that followed. And despite this modest beginning of contrition, the New Zealand government still significantly misrepresents what took place in East Timor. A "Country Paper" on East Timor released in April 2003, for example, refers to the pro-independence outcome in the 1999 U.N.-run ballot and then speaks of "widespread violence perpetrated by pro-Indonesian militia groups" in its aftermath—without even mentioning the Indonesian military that Wellington helped to sustain.[42]

●

"Historical memory," journalist Chris Hedges has written, "is hijacked by those who carry out war. They seek, when the memory challenges the myth, to obliterate or hide the evidence that exposes the myth as lie. The destruction is pervasive, aided by the establishment, including the media, which apes the slogans and euphemisms parroted by the powerful."[43] This observation applies not only to those who directly carry out war but also is relevant to the practice of foreign policy more generally. Thus, in the case of Western complicity in Indonesia's invasion and war against East Timor, the media has tended more often than not to "parrot the powerful." The distorted representations of the past that result continue to prevail. Indeed, they were dominant in the flurry of media coverage that surrounded East Timor's independence celebration in May 2002.

In the case of the corporate-owned press in the United States, for example, almost none of the history of American complicity made it into their pages. With the exception of an op-ed piece in *The Baltimore Sun* and articles in the Paris-based *International Herald Tribune* (a paper few in the United States read) and the *Seattle Post-Intelligencer*,[44] no major U.S. newspaper provided anything approaching a full picture of the American role in Indonesia's crimes in East Timor. Although *The New York Times* carried an editorial that mentioned Ford's and Kissinger's explicit authorization for the invasion, it said nothing of the next twenty-three or more years of American complicity.[45] *The Boston Globe* did the same, while also criticizing Clinton for "failing to prevent or stop in time the vengeful campaign of murder, rape, and destruction that Indonesian military officers loosed upon the East Timorese," but not for helping to train and nourish that same military.[46]

A few other major papers did mention the U.S. role, but typically grossly misrepresented it. Thus a *Los Angeles Times* op-ed article spoke of "few objections" from Washington in the face of Indonesia's 1975 invasion.[47] The next day the *Times*, along with *The Washington Post*, reported on Clinton's comment about the United States not being able to "defend everything we did," but said little more.[48] A *Chicago Tribune* editorial also alluded to Clinton's statement, which it favorably characterized as having "added some closure" to East Timor's bloody past. As for the rest of the major newspapers, they were silent about such matters. And all (with the exception of *The Baltimore Sun* op-ed piece) were mute about the need to ensure accountability by Jakarta and Washington for East Timor's suffering.[49]

This is a pattern that has emerged since Indonesia's withdrawal from East Timor. Despite the scale of the atrocities committed in the former Portuguese colony and the flagrant illegality of Indonesia's very presence in the territory, demands for some sort of international judicial mechanism to prosecute war crimes and crimes against humanity on the editorial pages of the mainstream media have been almost nonexistent. *The Christian Science Monitor* — despite TNI soldiers having brutally murdered and mutilated its correspondent in Dili in September 1999[50] — has not carried a single editorial or opinion essay advocating accountability for the crimes committed in East Timor. As for the role of the United States and other Western governments in these crimes, the *Monitor* and other papers have been equally silent.

Such silence is the best approach to obscuring the history of international complicity. This silence, or "forgetting," is a crime of omission of sorts as it facilitates impunity. It also helps to perpetuate myths about the supposed dedication to human rights and principles of international law among the powerful.

The term "forgetting" can be misleading, however, as it suggests passive conduct rather than deliberate behavior. Forgetting is often active in nature. Such intentional burial of the past was on display on May 13, 2000, in Bologna, Italy, at the prestigious Bologna Center of The Johns Hopkins University. The guest speaker was Richard Holbrooke. Introducing him was Paul Wolfowitz, dean of the university's School for Advanced International Studies.

After Wolfowitz's flowery welcome, Holbrooke returned the favor, cracking a joke about how the introduction showed that he gets "better treatment from Republicans than Democrats in some quarters." He then praised the former ambassador to Jakarta as "a continuing participant in the effort to find the right policy for one of the most important countries in the world, Indonesia." Holbrooke proceeded to explain how Wolfowitz's "activities illustrate something that's very important about American foreign policy in an election year and that is the degree to which there are still common themes between the parties. East Timor is a good example. Paul and I have been in frequent touch to make sure that we keep it out of the presidential campaign, where it would do no good to American or Indonesian interests."[51]

It is highly debatable whether a lack of discussion by Democratic and Republican presidential candidates about East Timor serves "American or Indonesian interests" — especially if we understand such "interests" to include the well-being of the citizenries of those countries as a whole, rather than a relatively small group of political, economic, and military elites whose narrow agendas are often couched in terms of the "national interest." But also noteworthy, but hardly unexpected, about the Holbrooke-Wolfowitz conspiracy of silence is the lack of any expression of concern in terms of the implications of the resulting distorted historical record for East Timorese interests.[52] Once again the East Timorese people seem not to matter.

●

Matters of memory, like almost any matter of representation, invite contestation. Honest disagreement over what transpired in the past is certainly one factor that drives such struggles. But, more important, what typically drives them are the ideological and material interests and projects that underlie the competing positions. And while Indonesia's various patrons and allies have done their utmost to recast and bury their past behavior, many in East Timor resist the whitewashing of their history and its implications for accountability for their suffering.

On August 31, 2000, for instance, numerous students at the University of East Timor gathered to confront Alexander Downer to demand an apology for Canberra's support of Indonesia's invasion and occupation at what was supposed to be a question-and-answer session with the Australian foreign minister. For reasons that are unclear, the promised meeting never happened.[53]

The protest took place on the heels of a July 4 demonstration at the U.N. Liaison Office in Dili where a U.S. Independence Day celebration was taking place. More than fifty East Timorese protestors, calling themselves the "1975–1999 Alliance for Justice," gathered to bring attention to what they described as the supporting role of the U.S. government in Indonesia's invasion and occupation of their country, and to demand justice and accountability for U.S. actions.

The demonstrators distributed to all the event's attendees information pamphlets entitled "Honoring the 224th Anniversary of American Independence, 1776–2000 . . . by Remembering 24 Years of U.S. Support for Indonesia's Crimes in East Timor." The Alliance made five demands of Washington: (1) release all government documents relating to East Timor; (2) establish an independent commission to investigate the nature and extent of U.S. complicity in the invasion and occupation; (3) apologize for the U.S. role; (4) make reparations to the people of East Timor; and (5) actively support an international tribunal for war crimes and crimes against humanity committed in East Timor from 1975 to 1999.[54]

A U.S. diplomat at the reception, W. Gary Gray, responded to the demonstration by stating, "It's better to concentrate on the future than rehash the past."[55] William "Jake" Jacobson, who was then the U.S. representative in East Timor, crossed the street to tell the demonstrators how much he respected the East Timorese people for their courage, and then proceeded to speak about America's profound dedication to democracy. When challenged about U.S. complicity in Indonesia's crimes, Jacobson responded that no country had contributed as much as the United States to East Timor's reconstruction. He then turned and walked away.[56]

The words of the U.S. diplomats are manifestations of two different, yet complementary, analytical frameworks. The first asserts that it is not worthwhile to dwell on the past, that it is far better to focus on the future — a similar sentiment to the one put forth by Clinton on May 20, 2002. This suggests that the road ahead (in terms of U.S.-East Timor relations) is a rosy one and that discussing the past will only detour "us" from making progress. The implication of this position is that the future (and the present, for that matter) is not connected to the past. The second analytical framework simply ignores the past — at least the ugly parts of it. From this perspective, the current "generosity" of the United States toward the people of East Timor outweighs any alleged past wrongdoing by Washington.

While those with a vested interest in trying to bury the past will typically endeavor to do so, most striking about countervailing efforts, and their associated memories, is how long they can and do endure, or how they can seemingly rise from the dead after so many years of dormancy. As a character in William Faulkner's *Requiem for a Nun* observed, "The past is never dead. It's not even past." The past is present to the extent that it is embodied in the formation of individuals, institutions, and a host of social relations. It is also in the present to the extent that social actors remember and actively memorialize it. Particular developments can trigger memories of horrific pasts and give rise to social conflict.

Thus, when Japan began efforts to contribute troops to the international peacekeeping force in East Timor, they resurrected painful memories of Japan's crimes in East Timor during World War II. In September 2001 a coalition of East Timorese nongovernmental organizations (NGOs) wrote to

Japan's prime minister Koizumi Junichiro and the foreign minister Tanaka Makiko regarding Tokyo's plans. Recalling the "bitter experience" of the East Timorese people with the Japanese military during the World War II and Tokyo's very strong support for Indonesia over the course of the invasion and occupation, the NGOs urged the Japanese government to abandon its efforts to send troops to East Timor. Instead, they advocated, Tokyo should use the funds that they would have expended on sending the troops "to compensate victims of abuses during World War II and during Indonesia's occupation." In addition, they called upon Tokyo to "publicly acknowledge that past policies have caused great suffering to the East Timorese people." Japan could better assist in enhancing East Timor's security, they wrote, by pressuring Jakarta to stabilize the situation along the West Timor boundary and to institute constructive diplomatic relations with Dili.[57] No response from Tokyo was forthcoming.

When the first group of Japanese military engineers arrived in East Timor in March 2002, more than 50 East Timorese peacefully protested outside the Dili airport. The demonstrators — holding various signs with sayings such as, "Go Home Japanese Self-Defense Force" and "Japanese Troops Are Same as Indonesian Military" — demanded an apology and reparations for the atrocities committed by Tokyo's troops during Imperial Japan's World War II occupation. Among those gathered were two elderly East Timorese women who had been held by Japanese soldiers during the war as sexual slaves. An estimated 800 former "comfort women" are still alive in East Timor. Some elderly male survivors of the war also attended. According to a spokesman for the Foundation for Compensation of Victims of Colonialism in East Timor, his group has registered 3,450 surviving victims.[58]

On the day following the protest against the Japanese government, foreign minister José Ramos-Horta issued a statement calling upon the East Timorese people to forget the tragic events of World War II. Asserting that "Japan has been in the forefront of East Timor recovery efforts since 1999" and that "Japan has atoned in many different ways for its past," Ramos-Horta argued that East Timor needed the technical assistance that the Japanese soldiers would provide. The foreign minister called on people to "celebrate . . . greater and more glorious days" that have come and to "focus on the present and build a better, more prosperous and peaceful future."[59]

Several months earlier, after a second July 4 demonstration in front of the U.S. diplomatic mission, Ramos-Horta also encouraged forgetting about the past. "Presently, the United States is giving strong support to East Timor," he stated. "We shouldn't just look to the past. We need to look at the good relations we have with the U.S. in 2001, not our relationship in 1975."[60]

It is difficult to know exactly why the Nobel laureate made these statements. He is painfully aware, in a highly personal way, of the human costs in East Timor of Japanese and American foreign policies. Ramos-Horta once wrote, for example, about how, as a boy, he had greatly admired much about the United States, including the "moral foundations" of its government institutions. But his "experiences later in life shattered these impressions as the US-backed Indonesian military killed tens of thousands of my people," he continued, "including members of my family. A bomb dropped by an OV-10 Bronco aircraft during the Carter administration killed my sister, Mariazinha. Indonesian soldiers later murdered two of my brothers. And in 1992 my eldest brother, Antonio, died under suspicious circumstances in an Indonesian hospital in Dili."[61]

Like Ramos-Horta, former resistance leaders like Xanana Gusmão (now the country's president) have forcefully spoken in the past about the need for far-reaching accountability for his country's plight. But he no longer publicly mentions it, instead stressing the need for "reconciliation" and to concentrate on the future. Thus, while sharing the stage with Indonesian president Megawati Sukarnoputri at the May 20, 2002, independence celebration, Gusmão did not refer to the crimes of the Indonesian military. Instead, he spoke of "24 years of difficult relations," which he characterized as "the result of a historical mistake which now belongs to history and to the past." And with the likes of Clinton and World Bank president James Wolfenson looking on, he had nothing but praise for the "international community."

Gusmão's silence — one effectively imposed from without — demonstrates the hollow nature of his independence-day proclamation that "today we are a people standing on equal footing with the rest of the world." More than anything it reflects a recognition on his part of an international order that is harshly unfavorable to the relatively small and weak, a reality that East Timor is in a poor position to challenge.

Maintaining such silence must be excruciatingly difficult. Nine years earlier, in his defense plea to an Indonesian court in Dili after his capture, the former guerrilla leader spoke eloquently of how "the concept of *realpolitik* has acquired a new dimension for me. Political realism is political subservience, the denial of the individual conscience, the death of the conscience of a people."[62]

To prevent such a death of East Timor's ideals, actors within the country's civil society endeavor to give substance to Gusmão's claim about the country's "equal footing" and to ensure that "reconciliation" does not become a substitute for justice. Perkumpulan HAK, East Timor's premier human rights organization, issued a statement on independence day, for instance, that characterized "the resistance of the international community of nations and the United Nations to an international tribunal" as "symptomatic of the problems facing East Timor today. Some of our own leaders, in seeing this resistance, have dropped the demand for an international tribunal for fear of angering donor governments," it continued. "Even our own leaders feed us nonsense about 'forgetting the past and looking to the future.' Do we East Timorese have the strength to be true to the principles of our own struggle for independence? How much are we supposed to sacrifice to be a friendly member of the community of nations? For 24 years we asserted our right to self-determination against the international consensus that we were a lost cause. Now that we have independence, are we to do nothing more that obediently follow the new consensus, even when it denies our ideals?"[63]

•

Such words demonstrate that representations of and struggles over the past are not merely a matter of academic interest. The battle to characterize East Timor's history, and thus to shape its present, is inextricably linked to the power struggle involving ongoing efforts to ensure, on the part of some, and to deny, on the part of others, justice for the country's suffering.

The representations of powerful national governments are especially important. Given their influence on the world stage, these governments are in a position to define the international agenda vis-à-vis justice for East Timor. By ignoring East Timor's suffering prior to 1999, by understating the role of the TNI leadership in the making of the country's ground zero, and by dishonestly discussing—indeed, often not even acknowledging—any responsibility for East Timor's plight prior to September 1999, the powerful are effectively relegating important chapters of East Timor's history to official oblivion.[64] At the same time they are helping to construct the geographical, historical, and social boundaries of a process of accountability for East Timor. In doing so they are helping to facilitate and perpetuate the impunity of the Indonesian military as well as their own—one facilitated by their ability to shape the consciousness of their respective constituencies and to play a large role in what we remember and what we forget, and even in what we "know."[65]

Written laws are like spiders' webs; they will catch, it is true, the weak and poor, but would be torn in pieces by the rich and powerful.

—ANARCHASIS, *sixth century B.C.*

One law for the powerful and another for the weak is no law at all.

—STEPHEN SEDLEY, London Review of Books, *2003*

These crimes were committed en masse, not only in regard to the number of victims, but also in regard to those who perpetrated the crime, and the extent to which any of the many criminals was close to or remote from the actual killer of the victim means nothing, as far as the measure of responsibility is concerned. On the contrary, in general the degree of responsibility increases as we draw further away from the man who uses the fatal instrument with his own hands.

—ISRAELI DISTRICT COURT IN JERUSALEM, *judgment against Adolf Eichmann, December 1961*

U.N. Secretary-General Kofi Annan and his wife, Nane Annan, comfort survivors and family members of victims of the April 6, 1999, massacre in Liquiça, while visiting the town in February 2000. *Photo by Eskinder Debebe, courtesy of the United Nations Department of Public Information.*

In addition to various figures of the Indonesian political establishment, the ambassadors of Canada, Finland (representing the European Union), Singapore, and the United Kingdom were gathered at the official residence of Robert Gelbard, the new American ambassador to Jakarta; the date was November 21, 1999. The dignitaries were there to see Richard Holbrooke, who was ending two days of talks in the Indonesian capital.

Holbrooke's visit was the first high-level delegation from the United States since the establishment of the new government of Abdurrahman Wahid. Coming only one month after Wahid's inauguration, the presence of such a prominent member of the Clinton administration was an important sign of Washington's support for the new government in Indonesia and its concern for the country as a whole.

To underline the importance of his visit, Holbrooke informed those present that he had come "not only as the American ambassador to the United Nations but as a member of the cabinet." As such, he would report directly to the American secretary of state and the president on the results of his visit.

As his last act in Jakarta, Holbrooke spoke on the situation in East Timor and U.S.-Indonesia relations, in addition to the ongoing saga of Aceh, an Indonesian province in northern Sumatra where the TNI has committed widescale atrocities in trying to crush a pro-independence movement that enjoys strong local support.

Asserting that "Americans believe profoundly in accountability," the Clinton administration's U.N. ambassador called upon Indonesia to account for its crimes in East Timor. "Accountability is one of the two or three keys to democracy," Holbrooke informed the guests. "You cannot deal with the future unless you also come to terms with the past." When asked what the extent of the accountability should be, Holbrooke drew a comparison to the U.S. investigation of the Watergate scandal in the early 1970s, which eventually implicated the president: "When I talk about accountability, Americans mean full accountability," he explained.[1]

Despite such words, it soon became clear that Holbrooke's notion (and that of Washington and its allies) of "full accountability" applies only to Indonesia, not those countries that aided and abetted Jakarta's crimes. Moreover, "full" seems only to apply to the year 1999—and, even then, only partially.

Since Indonesia's ignominious withdrawal from East Timor in October 1999, the now independent country has received little justice—despite numerous promises that it would. Efforts thus far to ensure judicial prosecution of those responsible for the commission of war crimes and crimes against humanity in East Timor have been seriously flawed and limited to only some of those that took place in 1999, excluding de facto those that occurred in the

1975–98 period. What seemed in the weeks and months following the TNI's post-ballot scorched-earth rampage to be an intense international effort to ensure accountability for the crimes committed against the East Timorese people quickly fizzled out. This result is neither an accident nor a surprise. Rather, it is the predictable outcome of a process shaped disproportionately by the actions of the countries that dominate international affairs, most of which have a vested interest in burying the issue of justice for East Timor given their collective role in the country's plight and maintaining the status quo in terms of their relations with Jakarta.

•

In response to the TNI-militia scorched-earth campaign in September 1999, the United Nations Commission on Human Rights (UNCHR) met in an emergency session in Geneva and called upon the secretary-general to establish an International Commission of Inquiry on East Timor into gross human rights violations in the territory. Nevertheless, behind-the-scenes lobbying by Indonesia (efforts supported by its Western allies) led to a September 27, 1999, resolution that limited the commission's mandate to the period after January 1, 1999, the beginning of the month in which President Habibie first suggested a vote in East Timor. The UNCHR also requested that three Special Rapporteurs carry out missions to East Timor focusing on extrajudicial executions, torture, violence against women, disappearances, and forced displacement.

In a December 10, 1999, report resulting from their mission, the Rapporteurs accused the TNI and its militias of crimes including "murder, torture, sexual violence, forcible transfer of population and other persecution and inhumane acts, including destruction of property," atrocities "committed on a scale that is widespread or systematic or both," thus constituting crimes against humanity. They recommended that the Security Council consider setting up an international tribunal unless Jakarta produced credible results from its own then ongoing investigation and promised prosecution of those responsible for the 1999 terror in East Timor "in a matter of months." At the same time the rapporteurs asserted that the tribunal "should have jurisdiction over all crimes under international law committed by any party in the Territory since the departure of the colonial Power [Portugal, in 1975]."[2]

Less than two months later—on January 31, 2000—the International Commission of Inquiry issued its report, stating that it had found significant evidence to support the contention of extensive Indonesian military involvement in the terror and destruction. As such, it called upon the world body to "establish an international human rights tribunal consisting of judges appointed by the United Nations" for crimes committed in 1999—a step, explained the commission, "fundamental for the future social and political stability of East Timor." That the "actions violating human rights and international humanitarian law in East Timor were directed against a decision of the United Nations Security Council . . . and were contrary to agreements reached by Indonesia with the United Nations to carry out that Security Council decision" made it all the more necessary for international prosecution, according to the commission.[3]

Upon releasing the report, however, Secretary-General Kofi Annan did not endorse the call for an international tribunal in his accompanying letter, stating that he was "encouraged by the commitment shown by President Abdurrahman Wahid to uphold the law and to fully support the investigation and prosecution of the perpetrators." Annan was referring to an investigation that the Indonesian government had established on September 22, 1999, at a time when the international community was beginning to accuse the TNI of crimes against humanity and the U.N. Human Rights Commission was preparing its special session on East Timor.

Annan went on to write that he intended "to pursue various avenues to ensure that [accountability for the crimes] is accomplished adequately, *inter alia*, by strengthening the capacity of UNTAET [United Nations Transitional Administration in East Timor] to conduct such investigations and enhancing collaboration between UNTAET" and the Indonesian government's own investigation.[4]

Given this opening, the dominant members of the Security Council were more than willing to defer to Jakarta's request that it have the right to prosecute its own. In this regard, one of the most important effects of the Indonesian investigation was to forestall momentum toward an international tribunal. The Security Council did state, however, that Indonesia had to bring the perpetrators to justice "as soon as possible" and should "institute a swift, comprehensive, effective and transparent legal process, in conformity with international standards of justice and due process of law."

Only two days after the report's release, Sonia Picado, the head of the commission, stated that she had no faith in the planned Indonesian process, while conceding that she had little hope that the Security Council would support a tribunal. Saying that "East Timor deserves not to be forgotten" and that "the East Timorese deserve compensation — moral and material compensation — because their families and their country have been devastated," she called for the establishment of an international truth commission with the power to pardon or indict those accused. The body, as the Costa Rican lawmaker envisioned it, would include commissioners from both East Timor and Indonesia, as well as some appointed by the United Nations. She expressed hope that Kofi Annan would voice support for her position.[5]

Picado's words had little effect. Kofi Annan never issued a call for an international truth commission. Soon thereafter, however, he reported that Indonesia's foreign minister had "strongly assured" him "of the Government's determination that there will be no impunity for those responsible." The most important thing, Annan explained, was "to send a message" that crimes such as those that took place in East Timor "will not be allowed to stand and that those responsible will be held accountable." If Jakarta were to realize such prosecutions, there would be "no need for the Council or the UN to set up another tribunal to compete with one set up by the Indonesian government that is going to do exactly the same thing."[6]

Not surprisingly Jakarta has not done "exactly the same thing" — or anything remotely approaching it. It was not until March 2002 that Indonesia finally began to prosecute individuals accused of responsibility for atrocities committed in East Timor. But the process was fatally flawed from the start. A decree signed on August 2, 2001, by Indonesian president Megawati Sukarnoputri (who succeeded Abdurrahman Wahid) limited the scope of the ad hoc court for East Timor to crimes committed during the months of April and September 1999, thus excluding the other ten months. At the same time the decree restricted the court's jurisdiction to crimes committed in only three of East Timor's thirteen districts.[7]

In addition to these structural defects, poorly prepared indictments, a lack of prosecutorial skill or desire — including failure to introduce damning evidence uncovered by the Jakarta's own human rights commission — and intimidation of witnesses and judges by the military and its supporters marred the actual proceedings. The result was that, of the court's eighteen verdicts — the final one having been issued on August 5, 2003 — only six were convictions. Two of the six involved the only East Timorese and only civilians tried — bit players who did the bidding of Indonesia's military-political establishment: former East Timor governor Abilio Osorio Soares and Eurico Guterres, the head of the Aitarak militia. Soares received a three-year sentence for failing to "manage his subordinates effectively," and Guterres received ten years from crimes against humanity, the longest sentence of any.[8] In August 2004 the Indonesian Supreme Court had finished passing judgment on all the appeals made by prosecutors and defendants. The court upheld all the acquittals, as well as the three-year sentence of Abilio Soares. (In November 2004, however, the court revisited the case and cleared him of all charges, releasing him from prison.) It also overturned the convictions of the four members of the Indonesian security forces while cutting in half the sentence of Eurico Gutteres, who, as of February 2005, remains free pending one final appeal.[9]

•

Some speculated that Jakarta's less-than-satisfactory performance would invigorate efforts by the world's powerful governments to establish an international tribunal, but that has not happened and there is little evidence that this will change as the dominant countries that comprise the "international community" lack the political will and desire to force the issue. Indeed, it is clear that what truly is at issue is not simply an absence of desire but a common wish among powerful countries that a tribunal *not* take place.[10]

During the presidency of Sukanoputri's predecessor, Abdurrahman Wahid, various representatives of Western governments expressed the fear that too much pressure on Indonesia could hurt efforts to repatriate the tens of thousands of East Timorese that were still at that time in militia-controlled camps in Indonesian West Timor or could destabilize the government in Jakarta or could do both. As one U.N. official in East Timor explained, "Everyone here in East Timor recognises that it's in no one's interests, least of all the refugees, to rock the fragile political position of President Wahid. . . . The worry is that if Mr. Wahid is forced out, Indonesia could very well descend into long-term political instability that might pave the way for a military takeover."[11] Although almost all the refugees have now long been back in East Timor and fears of a military coup have evaporated after Wahid's departure from the presidency, the empty concept of "stability" still seems to govern the thinking of the powerful countries that dominate the United Nations, most of whom maintain close relationships with Indonesia's political and military elites.

Clinton administration officials made some strong statements in 1999 and 2000 calling upon Jakarta to establish a credible and transparent process to prosecute Indonesian citizens charged with gross human rights abuses in East Timor, and threatened to support the establishment of an international tribunal if Jakarta did not do so,[12] but its threats remained empty. The administration of George W. Bush, for its part, has been silent on the matter. Other powerful national governments long friendly to the Indonesian government — such as the United Kingdom, France, Japan, and Germany — have said little to nothing about an international tribunal, presumably because they would prefer that one not happen.[13] As for the office of U.N. Secretary-General Kofi Annan, there has been mostly silence as well. Indeed, despite the end of the sham ad hoc court in Jakarta in August 2003 and previous statements that some sort of tribunal would be established if the Indonesian process was not thorough and serious, there was no official reaction from the U.N. Secretariat until twelve months later when the secretary-general finally expressed his disappointment with the results of the Jakarta court. But rather than advocating any sort of international judicial process, he merely proposed the establishment of a U.N. commission of experts, one that would assess the outcome of the Jakarta trials and other relevant justice mechanisms, and make recommendations on future steps regarding justice for East Timor.

The United Nations has also buried an important report commissioned by the world body's Office of the High Commissioner for Human Rights. Written by Geoffrey Robinson, a well-known international expert on Indonesia and East Timor who served with the UNAMET mission in Dili in 1999, the investigative report was completed and submitted in July 2003.[14] Almost two years later the United Nations had still not released the report. One can only speculate as to why. Robinson's report (which leaked in mid-2004) established that the 1999 violence was part of a widespread and systematic effort targeted principally against the East Timorese civilian population, a campaign that involved individuals at the highest levels of the TNI and Indonesia's civilian leadership, thus implicating them in crimes against humanity. In addition, the report suggests that responsibility lies with the TNI and the Indonesian state as institutions, while arguing that some of the United Nations' most powerful member-states also share in the responsibility for the violence — both in 1999, by failing to take effective steps to stop the predicted terror campaign, and in the more than two previous decades of complicity and acquiescence. The report ends by calling upon the Security Council to act on the recommendations of previous U.N. investigations to establish an international criminal tribunal for East Timor.[15]

The effective burial of the Robinson report and the larger context of silence and inaction would seem to demonstrate that the U.N. Secretariat and the powers-that-be within the Security Council never seriously considered the establishment of an ad hoc international tribunal for East Timor.[16] Many argue that the setting up of such a tribunal was doomed from the start because of the opposition from China and Russia — both having veto power in the Security Council.[17] The governments of the two countries, according to this analysis, were opposed to a tribunal for fear that it would set a precedent for the establishment of similar such judicial mechanisms to prosecute Russia's atrocities in Chechnya and China's crimes in Tibet. The weakness of this perspective, however, is that it fails to explain how such opposition was overcome for the establishment of the international tribunals for Rwanda and the former Yugoslavia. At the same time it does not recognize that Russia and China could and would easily veto any attempt to prosecute their own crimes. As such, the contention that East Timor does not have an international tribunal because of Russia and China does not hold up to scrutiny.[18] In this regard, the China-Russia argument serves as a convenient smokescreen for the opposition and associated inaction of the likes of Washington and London. But, more important, there is no evidence that demonstrates that the Western powers on the Security Council — Britain, France, and the United States — have ever had any desire to see an international judicial mechanism established to prosecute war crimes and crimes against humanity committed against the East Timorese population.

●

There is (or was) another option for the East Timorese to pursue justice: the internationally mandated courts in East Timor known as the "Special Panel

for Serious Crimes." Established by the United Nations during its administration of the territory in the aftermath of the Indonesian occupation, the
courts are "hybrids" made up of East Timorese and international judges. Thus
far these courts — which are scheduled by the United Nations to cease their
existence in May 2005 — have prosecuted and convicted a number of individuals for gross crimes committed in 1999, but all of them have been low-level
East Timorese, typically members of militia groups created and directed by
the TNI. In theory, these courts can try those accused of pre-1999 atrocities,
but they are grossly under-resourced in a material sense. They are also under-
resourced politically. Thus, while Indonesia has signed a memorandum of
understanding with the United Nations obligating both parties to provide
maximum assistance in areas such as the execution of arrests, interviewing arrests, and providing information, Jakarta has failed to live up to its obligations.[19] As of February 2005, Indonesia had not extradited a single individual
under its jurisdiction indicted by the Serious Crimes Unit.[20] And no pressure
of note has been forthcoming from the international community to compel
Jakarta to do so.[21] As all the key players involved in the terror (from 1999 as
well as from before) are in Indonesia, this shortcoming almost has had the
effect of reducing the Serious Crimes process to irrelevance. At the same time
the very existence of such a process makes it appear that the international
community is doing something meaningful, therefore providing an excuse
for the United Nations and its most powerful member-states not to establish a more effective mechanism in the form of, say, an ad hoc international
tribunal.[22] That said, by issuing indictments, the Serious Crimes process
has established a judicial trail — albeit a limited one — that could serve as a
foundation for a more effective process in the future, or at least that is the
hope.

Although major human rights organizations have issued scathing criticisms of legal justice efforts for East Timor, even they seem to have accepted
to a certain extent the limiting of prosecution for war crimes and crimes
against humanity committed in East Timor to 1999 — despite such a parame-
ter having no basis in international law. Amnesty International, for example,
in its July 2001 report criticized the U.N. administration in East Timor for
having no strategy for investigating the "thousands of human rights violations" that took place prior to 1999, which "in the long-run, must be addressed for the sake of truth and justice." Nevertheless, the report said nothing
about addressing pre-1999 crimes in its recommendations to UNTAET and
the international community.[23] Human Rights Watch has more explicitly
criticized the parameters of justice as set forth by the Indonesian government
and the United Nations. In a March 2000 "press backgrounder," the New
York–based organization called upon the international community to "begin

serious preparations for an international tribunal." It also stated that "this focus [on 1999] . . . should in no way foreclose future prosecutions for other crimes committed in the twenty-five years since Indonesia invaded and first occupied East Timor in 1975."[24] Despite these words, Human Rights Watch has said little since that time (as of early 2005) critical of the limited focus on 1999.[25]

As for the United Nations, the world body publicly presents the temporal limits of justice for East Timor as unproblematic. For example, at an August 2000 meeting in Dili with Mary Robinson, U.N. High Commissioner for Human Rights at the time, a number of East Timorese called for prosecution of crimes committed prior to 1999. But, as a press report from that time described,

> Robinson carefully deflected this demand, explaining that though she was aware of "the terrible crimes committed down the years," for which she thought a Truth and Reconciliation Commission might be the best remedy, the UN was concerned only with the events of last September, because the destruction had occurred while the UN was in charge.[26]

Regardless of Robinson's intent, the effect of her words gave substance to the fears of those who worried that the international community had little concern for justice for East Timor. Instead, the powers-that-be, they suspected, were seeking to placate East Timor's demand for such justice by supporting a formal commission charged with establishing an accurate account of the country's traumatic past, a truth that, for most (at least in East Timor), needs, in large part, little clarification.

●

Truth commissions, as they are popularly and generically known, have become almost universal and obligatory components of the process by which national societies attempt to reconstruct and recover from periods of violent, authoritarian rule or war (especially of the civil variety) or both. These formal processes of truth telling typically have multiple goals, possibly including gathering testimony and documentation regarding the period or events covered by the commission; writing a public report based on the information collected; allowing victims an opportunity to recount their experiences; promoting national and community reconciliation while sometimes contributing to the realization of legal justice; recommending institutional reforms; and providing information regarding possible reparations.

Many prefer truth commissions over, or in addition to, formal judicial proceedings. While providing a certain measure of justice (of the law-based variety), trials in the aftermath of wars or regimes responsible for gross atrocities have an inherently symbolic aspect, as a relatively small number of individuals are tried as a way of holding accountable a much larger number that such conflicts or regimes typically implicate.[27] Trials are also limited in what they can accomplish because of their high cost, time- and resource-consuming nature, and the difficulties of obtaining convictions. It is partly owing to these limits and "partly out of a recognition that even successful prosecutions do not resolve the conflict and pain associated with past abuses" that authorities in countries transitioning from conflict-ridden or authoritarian societies have increasingly opted for truth commissions as part of a larger effort to come to terms with an ugly past.[28]

In one sense, truth commissions are far more limited than a formal judicial process given the latter's legal power. In other ways, however, truth commissions are more ambitious. Because their mandate is broader, commissions examine events as part of a larger history of conflict or repression or both along with the causes and consequences of the violence. This enables and obligates commissions to conduct more encompassing investigations and to draw broader conclusions than do judicial processes.[29]

Proponents of truth commissions see them as indispensable to a transition to a more just, democratic, and peaceful political order as well as an important component to nation (re)building, in addition to facilitating the construction of a viable state. It is for these reasons and others that such bodies have become so popular: by 2000 twenty-one had completed their work since 1974, and numerous other commissions were active in countries ranging from Sierra Leone to Panama.[30]

East Timor is one of the most recent countries to adopt such a mechanism, formally establishing a Commission for Reception, Truth, and Reconciliation (CAVR) with the swearing-in of its seven national commissioners in January 2002, a time when the country was still under U.N. administration.[31] Like any such commission, it had a defined mandate in terms of its investigations, the historical record it would construct, and the recommendations it would make.

The CAVR was charged with establishing an authoritative historical record regarding human rights violations that took place between 1974 and 1999, while reporting these violations and the factors that contributed to their occurrence. In this regard the commission investigated not only individual cases of rights violations but also the extent to which the violations were part of a systematic pattern of abuse. Allegations of war crimes and crimes against humanity thus formed part of the commission's investigations. The CAVR also was charged with examining the role of international actors — such as foreign governments — in its attempt to provide a full picture of why gross human rights abuses occurred.

The commission had limited resources for investigations, however. And it did not have the power to bring charges against those who refused to co-operate nor to compel testimony or evidence from any individuals, the government of Indonesia, or other national governments. Consequently the possibility that those most responsible for gross human rights violations from 1975 to 1999 — Indonesia's military and political leaders and their foreign backers — would participate in the truth-telling process was left to the highly unlikely event that they possessed sufficient goodwill.[32]

The CAVR also assisted "in restoring the human dignity of victims," in part by providing them with the opportunity to tell their stories publicly. It also sought to promote reconciliation among East Timorese by "supporting the reception and reintegration of individuals who have caused harm to their communities" for what were deemed as relatively minor acts of violence (such as killing a few livestock or burning one or two houses). This entailed holding perpetrators of such crimes accountable to their victims. The commission did this through Community Reconciliation Procedures (CRPs) by which perpetrators agreed to perform acts of restoration that are meaningful to the survivors and their communities. For example, the crime of burning a house down might have required the offender to rebuild that house.[33] The resulting "community reconciliation agreement" was registered at a district court, which was supposed to ensure that acts of reconciliation were proportionate to the original crimes, were carried out, and did not violate human rights. The commission was charged with referring to the country's general prosecutor for possible prosecution crimes defined as "serious" (genocide, war crimes, torture, and crimes against humanity — regardless of when they were committed — as well as murder and sexual offenses perpetrated between January 1 and October 25, 1999), which were ineligible for CRPs. Finally, the commission was charged with issuing a report of its findings, one that would include recommendations concerning reforms and other measures to respond to the needs of victims of human rights violations. The commission, having formally begun its work in early 2002, was required to do all this in a two-year period, with the possibility of extensions, which it received, resulting in a delay in the report's release until July 2005.[34]

•

Many present truth telling, as embodied by the various commissions, and justice in the form of trials and tribunals as distinct, and sometimes mutually exclusive, processes.[35] And, indeed, this has often been the case as many commissions possess or have had the power to grant amnesty to political architects and perpetrators of atrocities (as, most famously, in South Africa) or are the result of a political compromise between the ancien régime or the perpetrators of terror and the forces of change. Such compromises typically trade justice for truth by decreeing a blanket amnesty in exchange for the establishment of a truth commission (e.g., in Sierra Leone).[36]

But such trade-offs are not necessarily inherent in the realization of truth commissions. To the contrary, truth commissions can actually facilitate justice by gathering information that prosecutors can later use to try those accused of committing or directing atrocities — as has happened in the cases of Argentina and Chad.[37] And it is this more positive relationship between truth gathering and legal justice that the commission in East Timor hoped to embody. Indeed, the commission explicitly presented its work as complementary to that of the formal justice system.[38]

Nevertheless, even where there is no explicit quid pro quo in terms of exchanging truth telling and justice (again, as typically understood), there does often appear to be a de facto trade-off. Not surprisingly, those who would potentially be judged in would-be criminal proceedings frequently have a preference for a truth-telling process that excludes the possibility of trials since the latter are deemed more punitive. Further, various international actors often favor truth commissions over trials. In the case of Haiti in the mid-1990s, for example, international donors explicitly stated that they would not fund a special prosecutor's office because they had already funded a truth commission, one that merely confirmed what was generally already known about coup-era atrocities.[39]

A variety of reasons account for why international actors might support such a trade-off but undoubtedly an important one is that truth commissions are generally far less threatening to the powerful (or the formerly powerful) than are trials. Such a motivation is especially relevant when important international actors have somehow been involved in the acts and period in question or have strong ties to those who would face prosecution or both. In this regard truth commissions have become a manner by which to avoid legal justice.[40]

Thus far this has proven to be the case in East Timor.

East Timor's predicament is emblematic of the often present trade-off of truth for law-based justice. The promise of truth commissions like that of East Timor, however, is that they provide a form of justice that is arguably more appropriate to societies attempting to recover from wars or despotism than that of a conventional judicial mechanism, in large part through the attempt to realize reconciliation.

•

"Reconciliation" is a slippery term. For some, it seems to mean a simple burying of the past with the goal of erasing any real or would-be tensions related to the period and actions under scrutiny.[41] In its more serious forms, one hears terms like "healing" and "coming to terms with the past" as definitions, with the goal implicitly being one of forgiveness between former adversaries.[42] Behind such explanations seems to be the notion that "reconciliation" means an acknowledgment of wrongdoing by the guilty party along with some sort of appropriate reparative actions—ranging from a formal apology to material reparations—as a concrete manifestation of that acknowledgment. This would entail an agreement by the aggrieved that the acknowledgment and reparation are sufficient. In this regard, truth telling, reconciliation, and restitution—defined here not simply as the return of that which has been taken but as something that includes "the entire spectrum of attempts to rectify historical injustices"[43]—are inherently linked. The goal of reconciliation, ideally, is thus not to forget the past but to make it possible for those wronged and those who have committed wrongs to live together in a manner that is peaceful, respectful, and healthy through the provision of justice, one broadly conceived.[44]

For many, South Africa's Truth and Reconciliation Commission (TRC) is the model.[45] Undoubtedly the TRC accomplished much in producing an authoritative account of the horrors of Apartheid, allowing many survivors to confront their victimizers, and destroying myths of the past held by many of Apartheid's beneficiaries and champions. At the same time the TRC was an important component of a delicate and, in many ways, highly successful process of transition from a racist, authoritarian country with a formidable repressive apparatus—one long supported by the world's wealthiest and most powerful countries—to a multiracial democracy. Given the profound injustices that characterized Apartheid South Africa, the relative lack of bloodshed during the transition is of historic proportions. But the TRC is also a manifestation of the serious limitations of this transition.

The nature of the power relations within South Africa and a larger global political-economic context unfavorable to radical social transformation severely limited the ability of the African National Congress and the larger freedom movement to affect the types of changes that they would have tried to realize had they had greater space to do so. Hence the TRC did not offer justice in either a legalistic or a material manner of significance. Nevertheless some argue that it provided another form of justice, a restorative one, a form of justice that is more appropriate to the new South Africa. According to former Archbishop Desmond Tutu, who chaired the commission, this restorative type of justice is "characteristic of traditional African jurisprudence. Here the central concern is not retribution or punishment . . . [but rather] the healing of breaches, the redressing of imbalances, the restoration of broken relationships, a seeking to rehabilitate both the victim and the perpetrator, who should be given the opportunity to be reintegrated into the community he has injured by his offense."[46]

Whether the resulting form of justice is either retributive or restorative, truth commissions tend to focus on individual acts or events of violence while ignoring systematic forms of injustice that also caused great harm. In doing so, they help to reify the notion that the worst injustices are those brought about by individual atrocious acts perpetrated by the state or by anti-state actors. In the case of South Africa, for example, one effect of the commission's focus on individual acts and events was to downplay (by default) the fact that Apartheid was a system, one in which certain groups and individuals — within South Africa but also abroad — accrued great socioeconomic benefits while helping to dispossess and impoverish a far greater number. Although a few thousand victims, or families of those killed during the Apartheid regime, have received some monetary compensation as a form of reparation,[47] the TRC's form of justice did not help to "restore" the very real socioeconomic deficiencies experienced by millions of South Africans as a result of Apartheid as a political-economic system. This limits the realization of "restorative justice" for those who continue to suffer from "post-Apartheid" Apartheid — that is, Apartheid not simply as a political regime but as a socioeconomic system.[48]

The South African commission, however, did look into how certain institutions — the business sector and some Christian churches, for example — benefited from or helped to construct the larger environment that gave rise to the myriad human rights atrocities of the Apartheid regime.[49] In addition, the TRC's final report asserted that "reconciliation requires a commitment, especially by those who have benefited and continue to benefit from past discrimination, to the transformation of unjust inequalities and dehumanizing poverty."[50] But in making the argument, the commission stated that such a task was beyond its mandate.[51]

In not putting such structural injustice at the center of the commission's work, the South African truth and reconciliation process might have limited the possibilities for the type of sociopsychological/spiritual forgiveness championed by Desmond Tutu, among others.[52] Thus, by default, the TRC relegated to official oblivion important, if not key, components of the "truth" embodied by the period treated by the commission. In this regard, what such commissions omit from history contributes to official forgetting, a form of "remembering to forget."[53]

Addressing structural inequalities and material needs underlying and flowing from the conflict or period addressed by a commission is not only necessary in terms of a fuller conception of justice; it is also an important factor in improving intergroup relations.[54] In this sense we cannot reduce reconciliation to a sociopsychological or emotional process. Reconciliation — in order to lead to successful reconstruction of a society — requires an approach that moves beyond a paradigm of criminal justice, one that focuses on individual perpetrators and victims. What is needed is a paradigm of social justice that is concerned more with beneficiaries and victims (in a collective sense).[55]

Such a paradigm would embrace the notion that reconciliation and redistributive justice are inherently linked.

While East Timor's commission did not typically use the language of restorative justice, such a conception of justice significantly informed its work — at least implicitly. The restoration was to flow from the commission's efforts to provide dignity to individual victims by granting them an opportunity to tell their stories and by rebuilding frayed social ties through the formal reconciliation mechanisms. At the same time the commission was supposed to help restore various forms of loss through the provision of justice — by establishing local community reconciliation procedures and, for so-called serious crimes (e.g., murder, rape, systematic destruction), by referring them to the country's general prosecutor for formal trials. In this regard the justice foreseen by the commission's architects was both retributive and restorative in nature.

East Timor's commission, however, was unique in that it covered a period and set of events for which all those in positions of military responsibility, and the vast majority of direct perpetrators of atrocities and their political architects and directors, resided outside the national territory, in Indonesia. This was the case because what took place in East Timor was the result of an international conflict. Thus, to the extent that the CAVR saw itself as facilitating reconciliation between former adversaries, in fact it was only between the victimized population and relatively low-level perpetrators within East Timor's national territory, people who committed nonserious crimes — in other words, the reconciliation was only between East Timorese. Moreover, as its mandate made clear, East Timor's commission was intended to focus almost exclusively on personal or direct forms of violence. It is too early to say whether the CAVR will have any significant positive effects on East Timorese society. Regardless of the outcome, we should not exaggerate the impact of its work, nor should we pretend that it is an adequate substitute for a far-reaching process of accountability and justice.

●

It is hardly an accident that East Timor has not received justice through U.N. mechanisms. While the United Nations has had a great deal of success in setting international human rights standards, it has been largely ineffective in enforcing those standards.[56] This failure is largely one of design as the lack of effective enforcement mechanisms is inherent in the structure of the United Nations, which was designed to maintain the global status quo. The World War II victors ensured that the new international body would allow them to pursue their narrow national interests on the global stage without collective constraints.

In 1945 a number of countries had advocated the establishment of a world legislature and a world court with compulsory jurisdiction. Such proposals had strong public support throughout the world, including in the United States. A 1946 Roper Poll, for example, showed that 63 percent of the U.S. public supported the creation of a democratically elected world congress with binding decision-making power.[57] The key postwar powers, such as the United States, France, the United Kingdom, and the Soviet Union, however, ignored this post-nationalist sentiment and laid the basis for a U.N. oligarchy. As the Mexican delegate to the founding convention in San Francisco in 1945 noted, the U.N. Charter assured that "the mice would be disciplined, but the lions would be free."[58] But as the recent history of East Timor has shown, those with whom the lions are on good terms, such as Indonesia's military and political leaders, are also free.

The Allied powers had the clear goal of ensuring that those who had won World War II would dominate the emerging world order. A total of fifty countries were present at the 1945 Conference on International Organization in San Francisco, the meeting that drew up the architecture of the United Nations. The fifty countries were mostly from the industrialized North. The other participants included a handful of Latin American countries (most of whom were diplomatically subservient to the United States), India (still under British colonialism), Egypt, Iran, Lebanon (under the control of France), Saudi Arabia, Turkey, and the Philippines. The overall balance of forces at the conference was one in which thirty-five of the participating countries were closely allied to the United States, five to the Soviet Union, and only ten were nonaligned. Although both the United States and the Soviet Union were in favor of the Security Council provision granting veto power to each of the permanent members, their reasons were quite different: given the balance of forces between the capitalist and communist camps within the United Nations, Moscow wanted to ensure that it could prevent Washington and its allies from dictating the decisions of the new body; the United States, on the other hand, wanted just what the Soviets feared — namely, the ability to dominate the council. What all the great powers shared, however, was a desire to prevent any small countries from having an effective voice in the running of the new international organization. At the urging of the Roosevelt administration during a meeting in Dumbarton Oaks, just outside Washington, D.C., in mid-1944, China, Great Britain, and the Soviet Union agreed to the veto of what was to become the Security Council. Hence the founding of the United Nations did not represent a challenge to the post–World War II order but, instead, a strengthening of it — especially in terms of its most powerful members, the United States being by far the most potent and thus the greatest beneficiary.[59]

The establishment of a regime of effective international law has long been difficult. Before 1945, for example, there was no clear international legal prohibition of crimes against humanity.[60] Prior to the Second World War it was mainly the United States and the major European powers that wrote the international treaties and legal precedents regarding war crimes and what came to be known as crimes against humanity. As such, these laws tended to favor their authors and protected them from prosecution for horrific state violence against indigenous or colonized peoples.[61] International legal mechanisms during this period were thus purposively designed not to have jurisdiction over conflicts between colonized peoples and imperialist powers. Instead, they concerned relations only between sovereign states.[62] They thus facilitated impunity for the myriad atrocities committed by Western powers. In the years preceding World War I, for example, Belgium was responsible for the deaths of millions in its colony of the Congo. France, proportionally speaking, slaughtered the same amount in its colonies in Equatorial Africa. And the United States killed hundreds of thousands in the Philippines in a brutal counterinsurgency war against a pro-independence movement.[63]

Despite the weakness and selectivity of international legal mechanisms during this period, they proved to be too much for some when they had the potential to apply not only to the defeated but to the victorious. At the Paris Peace Conference that marked the end of World War I, the French delegation actually proposed the establishment of a permanent international criminal court associated with the League of Nations, but Washington, London, and the other powers present gave the matter "little consideration." Similarly "the German offer to submit cases of accused war criminals to preliminary judgment of an international court of neutral jurists, if the Allies would do the same, was not considered at all." Had they done so, "it is possible that the peace conference could have made provisions for punishment of war crimes a permanent part of international relations."[64]

Many decades later, although prohibitions against genocide and crimes against humanity exist on paper, and ad hoc tribunals are in place for the former Yugoslavia and Rwanda, effective international legal mechanisms and institutions are woefully lacking. Again, probably more than any other country, the United States has worked to prevent the permanent establishment of such mechanisms and institutions. Although Washington played a key role in the shaping of the *Universal Declaration of Human Rights,* for example, the United States insisted that the document be nonbinding. Such resistance by Washington to any attempt to limit U.S. sovereignty, combined with the subordination in U.S. policy-making circles of human rights to putative national security concerns, continued throughout the Cold War decades[65] and persist today. And even though an international criminal court is now a reality — in part because of a growing acceptance by most Western countries to an international legal regime — the body is much weaker than it might have been, largely because of a watering down of its mandate to enlist Washington's support. (Despite all the concessions made to satisfy Washington, the Clinton and G. W. Bush administrations opposed ratification of the treaty creating the court.) As such, it is difficult to foresee the permanent international tribunal as it currently stands ever prosecuting officials from Washington, London, or Tel Aviv.

The United States has not been alone in trying to prevent the realization of binding international human rights covenants. Although the *Universal Declaration of Human Rights* is supposedly a "common standard of achievement for all peoples and all nations," almost all national governments at the time the declaration was created expressed their desire that the standards not be legally binding, claiming that human rights were a matter of "internal" concern for each country.[66] But although other countries — especially powerful ones — have been guilty at times of intransigence similar to that of the United States, none are in a position of power to have as detrimental an effect on democratic, international legal mechanisms as is Washington. Furthermore, numerous governments, including many in the West, have shown themselves increasingly open to strong and democratic international legal mechanisms, whereas the United States has not. Although Washington has long paid lip service to the need for an effective United Nations and regime of international law, it is clear that the U.S. position toward the United Nations has changed little since the establishment of the international body in 1945. For Washington, the United Nations is largely only desirable to the extent that it serves as an international means to a highly national end, one that is generally dismissive of any true internationalism. John Bolton, who would later serve as Undersecretary of State for Arms Control and International Security in the George W. Bush administration, described the world body at a conference in Washington, D.C., in 1994 as follows:

> There is no United Nations. There is an international community that occasionally can be led by the only real power left in the world, and that is the United States, when it suits our interest, and when we can get others to go along. . . . When the United States leads, the United Nations will follow. When it suits our interests to do so, we will do so. When it does not suit our interests we will not.[67]

Such thinking is not limited to high-level Republicans. Many powerful Democrats think similarly. Madeleine Albright, Bill Clinton's ambassador to the United Nations during his first presidential term before she became secretary of state, for example, informed the world body in 1994 while speaking menacingly about Iraq that the United States would "behave multilaterally when we can and unilaterally when we must."[68] The next year Albright declared the United Nations "a tool of American foreign policy."[69]

Given such perspectives and the power of the United States to influence U.N. action, it is of little wonder that the United Nations was never able to compel Indonesia to accede to the demands of the international community as embodied by the various U.N. resolutions on East Timor during the twenty-four-year occupation. And it is hardly surprising that the promised international criminal tribunal for East Timor, or some adequate variant thereof, has not materialized.

•

The resulting lack of justice has very real consequences for East Timor. First, it undermines sociopolitical reconstruction within the territory as victims, survivors, and their loved ones see insufficient likelihood of those responsible for their suffering—especially those within Indonesia—having to admit to and atone for their crimes. Thus it potentially inhibits local and national reconciliation between the vast majority of East Timorese who supported independence and those who worked in support of the Indonesian occupation. It also clearly undermines the foundation for improving relations between various sectors of society within Indonesia and those in East Timor.

On a more concrete level, the lack of accountability means that many East Timorese families still do not know what happened to their loved ones or remain separated from their children or siblings. Indonesia's crimes include the "disappearance" of countless East Timorese—individuals arrested by Indonesian authorities during the occupation who were never released or seen again in public, and for whom there has never been an adequate accounting[70]—and the kidnapping of many hundreds of East Timorese children, ones taken from their families during September 1999 and still held in Indonesia.[71]

Regarding a broader accountability, the impunity enjoyed by the world's powerful for their complicity in the violence perpetrated by the Indonesian military increases the likelihood that such shameful conduct will reoccur (indeed, it already is in many parts of the world), thus further undermining international peace and justice. It also allows these powerful nations to rewrite their histories (and, by extension, that of East Timor), presenting themselves as (implicitly longtime) supporters of the country whose present-day assistance to its reconstruction is an act of generosity, rather than an extremely modest beginning at amends from those who share in the responsibility for East Timor's suffering over almost a twenty-four-year period. Thus representatives of the international community have characterized the transfer of reconstruction funds to East Timor as "charity"—as did Peter Galbraith, who at the time was head of the U.N. administration's Office of Political, Constitutional, and Electoral Affairs.[72] A report in *The New York Times,* in addition to exaggerating the importance of international "handouts" to East Timor's survival, went so far as to describe East Timor as "the ultimate welfare state — a ward of the international community subsisting almost entirely on handouts from abroad."[73]

The lack of justice also has profoundly detrimental implications for the populations of restive regions in Indonesia such as Aceh (in northern Sumatra) and West Papua/Irian Jaya, areas where the TNI has been implicated in widespread and ongoing atrocities. Major General Adam Damiri, who, during 1999, was in charge of a military region that encompassed East Timor, embodies the dangers. Damiri was the last person tried by the ad hoc court, which found him guilty (sentencing him to three years for failure to prevent troops under his command from committing crimes against humanity) — a surprise to many observers, especially because the prosecutor himself had recommended that the court acquit Damiri.[74] Damiri missed a number of his court dates — causing significant delays in the process — because he was, at the time, the senior military commander for Jakarta's brutal counterinsurgency war in the province of Aceh.[75] Similarly, in another highly contested region of Indonesia, West Papua, where the indigenous population has long contested its incorporation into Indonesia, individuals who carried out atrocities in East Timor have been present. Eurico Guterres, the former militia head in Dili, announced in December 2003 the establishment of a militia group in West Papua to fight against local pro-independence forces.[76] Around the same time as the news of Guterres's activities emerged, the Indonesian government announced the appointment of General Timbul Silaen as head of the police force in West Papua. Silaen was Indonesia's police chief in East Timor throughout 1999. Jakarta's own investigation had implicated him for having taken no action to control those under his command and thus failing to prevent a number of massacres. Nevertheless the ad hoc court acquitted him.[77]

In addition to facilitating further state terror in Aceh and West Papua, the impunity reigning in Indonesia serves to weaken the country's fragile democratic institutions and to restrict the space for the country's pro-democracy and human rights activists. It also allows the country's military establishment and its political allies to whitewash their ugly history in East Timor.

Such impunity was on display on September 27, 2002, in New York City when, in that city, East Timor became the 191st member-state of the United Nations. While East Timorese president Xanana Gusmão vowed to build a "tolerant and just" country, the ambassadors of various nations offered their congratulations. One of those nations was Indonesia, whose representative spoke glowingly of the progress the two countries had made in the area of reconciliation.[78] Given that the Indonesian government has at no time even acknowledged the criminal nature of its actions against the East Timorese people going back to 1975 — never mind having apologized — it is clear that the ambassador's notion of reconciliation is one in which former protagonists simply forget the past, at least officially. It is a forgetting imposed by the strong on the weak, one aided and abetted by an "international community" that seems to accept Jakarta's vacuous notion of what constitutes reconciliation and has abandoned all but the thin appearance of concern for accountability for East Timor's suffering.

All this has the effect of erasing a history of collective responsibility for the territory's current poverty-stricken state, and thus obscuring the shared obligation to ensure that East Timor has sufficient resources to build a society in which its citizens can attain all their basic needs. In this regard the failure to realize justice has serious material implications by lessening the likelihood that East Timor will receive reparations for its suffering, thus perpetuating the territory's impoverishment. Indeed, much of the international community working in East Timor is proceeding under the assumption that East Timor is and will remain a poverty-stricken country. As an Australian government official in Dili explained in June 2000 in justifying the insufficient resources for reconstruction provided by the "international community," the United Nations "knows it can only establish the basic services that East Timor is then able to maintain. This is going to be a very poor country for a very long time and we cannot build what the East Timorese cannot then afford to run."[79] In one of the world's poorest countries, a country in which people still commonly die from preventable diseases such as malaria, tuberculosis, and diarrhea, such a justification has potentially fatal consequences.

In May 2002 the United Nations Development Program issued a report designating East Timor as Asia's poorest country and one of the twenty poorest countries in the world. According to the report, East Timor's annual per capita gross domestic product is U.S.$478, and more than 40 percent of the population lives below the national poverty line of 55 cents per day. More than half the adult population of East Timor is illiterate, and approximately 45 percent of its children less than five years of age are underweight, a factor that has dangerous implications for the children's future development. East Timor also has one of the world's highest rates of maternal mortality.[80] Such factors are the concrete manifestations of the "silent violence" or the "violence of everyday life" that structure and are rooted in East Timorese society,[81] factors that, while also in some measure the legacy of centuries of Portuguese colonial neglect and exploitation, are largely the product of Indonesia's actions and those of its international supporters from 1975 to 1999. And hence the failure to realize justice for East Timor for the full extent of the violence committed against its people ensures that a violence of a different sort will endure, one embedded in the very social fabric and landscape of the new country.

We must do more to reach out to our children and teach them to express their anger and to resolve their conflicts with words, not weapons.

—BILL CLINTON, *in reaction to the Columbine High School massacre in Littleton, Colorado, April 20, 1999*

By aiding and abetting murder, the Taliban regime is committing murder.

—GEORGE W. BUSH, *September 20, 2001*

Family in front of the ruins of their home in Suai, June 2000. *Photo by the author.*

"**D**o you have any photos of my husband?," the middle-aged woman asked. She was dressed entirely in black, a sign in East Timor of mourning the death of a loved one. Olinda Quintas posed the question when I met her in August 2000 at her home in Lospalos, in the eastern portion of Indonesia's former province. I had met her spouse, Verissimo, during my 1992 visit. Unfortunately I did not have any such photos, nor did Senhora Quintas. Indonesian military-backed militia had burned her home on August 27, 1999, destroying all her family's possessions and mementos.[1]

Armed Indonesian soldiers and militia had surrounded the family compound that night, where the local office of the National Council of Timorese Resistance (CNRT) was also located and where a celebration was taking place to mark the end of the campaign period, less than three days before the start of the August 30 U.N.-run referendum. When the armed men fired into the family home, Olinda escaped through a window. Her husband did not. Members of the militia then rushed inside where they hacked Verissimo Dias Quintas to death with machetes.

Their home had a couple of rooms off the front porch that they rented out. I had stayed in one of them about seven years before the deadly attack. The only other place to stay in town was a *wisma* (guesthouse) owned by the Indonesian police. As the *liurai,* or traditional king, of the area, and because he knew how to play the game with the Indonesians, Verissimo enjoyed a certain level of immunity. In his living room was a photo of Verissimo shaking hands with Suharto during a meeting in Jakarta between the Indonesian dictator and a contingent of East Timorese *liurais.* Next to the photo was another showing Verissimo as a Falintil commander in East Timor's mountains from the late 1970s. Although Verissimo could give the appearance of having acquiesced to Indonesia's annexation of his homeland, he privately displayed his true sentiments behind closed doors.[2] Those sentiments became public when the CNRT emerged above ground, with Verissimo positioned as the local head of the pro-independence body.

I never saw Verissimo Quintas after I left his home in 1992. I had always intended to return but was unable to do so during my 1996 and 1998 trips. Anticipating a victory for the pro-independence option, I had planned to visit him after the ballot in 1999 and very much looked forward to that day. I took the call in the IFET-OP office in Dili on the morning of Saturday, August 28, 1999, when a Canadian volunteer working with our team in the Lospalos area called to report what had happened to Verissimo the previous evening.

Returning to Lospalos in July 2000, I found a town that had been devastated. Similar to towns throughout East Timor, most of the buildings in Lospalos lay in ruin. All the streets, now silent, were littered with rubble.

Both the scene, and the sorrow of Olinda and her family, were explicit images of the aftermath of the making of a ground zero.

●

A ground zero is a location of extreme violence and devastation that involves the killing of large numbers of civilians and profound destruction of the human landscape. All ground zeros share a certain equality in terms of the gross human suffering they embody. But the very different responses they receive internationally demonstrate that not all such sites of horror, and the war crimes and crimes against humanity they comprise, are equal — at least in the eyes of the global powers-that-be, despite all the high-minded words we hear from world leaders.

Whereas the reaction of the Western powers to the crimes of September 11, 2001, has been one of firm resolve to ensure accountability (and also to ensure that the perpetrators and their supporters are not in a position to repeat their crimes), those same parties have responded to East Timor largely through an ethic of charity, providing poverty-level resources for reconstruction while ignoring matters of accountability except in a most superficial fashion. The reason for this unequal response seems clear: most of the powerful countries that dominate international relations were complicit in the making of East Timor's suffering and devastation in 1999, and were also complicit in the almost twenty-four years of war crimes and crimes against humanity that preceded it.

These different responses are also partially fueled by how the powerful represent, and how we remember, what took place. Struggles over such representations are important for informing responses to the tragedies they embody. But memory battles are not so much about the past as they are about the present and the future.[3] Memories shape what we see as possible, plausible, good and bad. In that regard they have profound implications for how we react to past, present, and future atrocities, to the practices, individuals, and institutions that give rise to them, and to the responses in their aftermath by the powers-that-be.

In writing about the connection between memory and horrific events, historian Tzvetan Todorov draws a distinction between two types of memories — literal memories and exemplary ones. Literal memories of horror, he argues, are those that lead nowhere beyond the event itself. In other words, literal memories limit their focus to the event(s) relating to the particular horrific experience without making any connections of empathy to other horrendous occurrences. Purveyors of such memories are only interested in connecting individuals, groups, and other events to the specific suffering in question and, in the process, condemning all those associated with the authors of the original trauma. The horror defines to a significant degree the victimized group, and the consequences of the original terror continue to do so as time passes.

In contrast, purveyors of exemplary memories are not so interested in using the past to enhance their identity and interests but, rather, to open it up to analogy and, in the process, derive benefits for humanity as a whole. As in the case of literal memories, those employing exemplary memories acknowledge the singular nature of the horrific experience, but they do not stop there. Instead, they seek to make connections between the suffering they recollect and other events of horror, thus opening their memories to analogy and generalization and making it possible to extract lessons that can inform present and future practices aimed at combating injustices. A universal ethic of solidarity with other victims of horrific violence informs and emerges from exemplary memories.[4]

All memories have a geography. We recall memories through specific sites and attach our recollections to particular places. We see this most clearly in memorialized spaces such as the ground zeros of Hiroshima and New York City. And just as there are literal and exemplary memories of gross atrocities, so, too, are there literal and exemplary memorialized spaces of horror and tragedy.

Memories of atrocities are also linked to specific dates. Like December 7 — the date in 1941 when Imperial Japan launched a surprise attack against the U.S. naval base in the territory of Hawaii — September 11 is now "a day that will live in infamy," one remembered in a literal sense in the collective memory of the United States. While the differences are many, the two dates are undoubtedly alike in important ways: both involved attacks against important sites of American power on national territory, caused the deaths of thousands, and prompted major American war efforts, in part, to avenge the original attacks.

What we recall about these dates, however, is perhaps not as important as what we do not remember about them. What the vast majority of us tend to forget — or do not even know at all — is that the dates December 7 and September 11, respectively, also mark the beginning (in 1975) and the end (in 1999) of U.S. complicity in one of the worst set of atrocities in the post–World War II era, those that took place in East Timor.

Like so many dates, these "days of infamy" could apply to a number of events across the world over the course of the last century. September 11, for instance, in addition to marking a day of horror and tragedy in New York City, is also the day in 1973 when the American-backed Chilean military, led by army commander Augusto Pinochet, overthrew the democratically elected socialist government of Salvador Allende.[5] What followed were fifteen years of military dictatorship, and the terror and violence that such a regime typically employs to seize and maintain power. The regime brutally killed and "disappeared" about three thousand people, while imprisoning and sadistically torturing many more, in an effort to eliminate any challenges to its rule.

Writer Ariel Dorfman, who lived through the coup, has written about the tragic parallels between what he witnessed in his native Chile and what he viewed on television from his home in North Carolina in the aftermath of September 11, 2001:

> I see hundreds of relatives wandering the streets of New York, clutching the photos of their sons, fathers, wives, lovers, daughters, begging for information, asking if they are alive or dead, the whole United States forced to look into the abyss of what it means to be *desaparecido* [disappeared], with no certainty or funeral possible for those beloved men and women who are missing. And I also recognize and repeat the sensation of extreme unreality that invariably accompanies great disasters caused by human iniquity so much more difficult to cope with than natural catastrophes. Over and over again I hear phrases that remind me of what people like me would mutter to themselves during the 1973 coup and the days that followed: "This cannot be happening to us, we have only known this form of destruction through movies and books and remote photographs. If it's a nightmare, why can't we awaken from it?"[6]

Dorfman employs memory in an exemplary fashion. In doing so he shows that New York City—where he spent ten years of his youth in exile—and Chile are tied together not only by dates of tragedy but also by a community of human pain and suffering. That he has suffered because of U.S.-orchestrated brutality in his homeland does not prevent the Chilean expatriate from identifying with the victims of lower Manhattan. On the contrary, it empowers him and seems to obligate him morally to do so.

The question is, do those who identify most strongly with the victims of lower Manhattan—the American people as a whole—identify with those of Dorfman's Chile or of East Timor? Undoubtedly a number of them do. But most striking about the renowned writer's effort to draw parallels is how little it seems to have resonated within the United States—at least among the political elites who dominate public discussion.[7] Thus far, there is nothing in official behavior to suggest a willingness and desire to empathize with the suffering of others, to work for a more peaceful and just world, and to look into the national mirror and examine how our own sins have inexcusably brought about ground zero–like tragedies. To the contrary, the political establishment has framed the World Trade Center tragedy as a literal memory, as a definitive and exceptional crime that deserves, indeed demands, an ultimate but unfortunately not-so-unique response: virtually unchallenged U.S. military power, one that largely ignores international law and its associated mechanisms.[8]

It makes sense that people in the United States identify with, and thus feel in an extraordinary manner, the suffering embodied by what took place on September 11, 2001, as opposed to what occurred eighteen years earlier in

Chile or only two years prior in East Timor — and not simply because Washington has effectively buried its role in the suffering of both countries. After all, that which is shared among Americans is more profound than the ties between the people of the United States and those of East Timor and Chile. Yet membership in the imagined community that is the United States (imagined in the sense that all countries and all communities — except very small ones in which all members have face-to-face relations — require the concerted construction of a sense of unity) does not satisfactorily explain the reaction.[9] Americans responded to September 11 in the way that they did and continue to do not simply because of their identification with the victims as fellow members of the national community but arguably more so because the tragedy made them realize that, just as the victims died, so could they.[10] The attack shattered the notion of American exceptionalism that saw the country's citizenry as invulnerable, beyond the threats of suffering and terror that have long plagued so many throughout the world.[11]

Similar factors explain why ordinary citizens and national leaders in places such as Tokyo, Auckland, Paris, and London commemorated the World Trade Center tragedy on the one-year anniversary. Tony Blair, for example, attended a solemn memorial mass in London, and the French prime minister Jacques Chirac, his eyes moist, proclaimed at a ceremony at the American Embassy that France's citizenry stands "with all their hearts at the side of the American people."[12] These undoubtedly heartfelt expressions of sympathy and solidarity are, in one sense, very touching. At the same time it is too simplistic to perceive them as expressions of a universal human family. (After all, Blair and Chirac have not expressed anything approaching similar levels of sorrow and solidarity for the people of East Timor.) While transcending territorial boundaries and reflecting an entity larger than the nation, they still reflect an exclusive community: one that does not equally embrace the poor and nonwhite, nor those subjugated by the West and its allies. Rather than mere Chechens, Rwandans, or East Timorese, the victims were like us — people living among the rich and powerful. In this regard the memory of September 11 is still literal. Similarly New York's ground zero — although its official memorialization is still in the process of becoming — has, for many, become a literal space.

●

The term "ground zero" first appeared in an article by Hanson W. Baldwin in *The New York Times* on July 7, 1946.[13] Baldwin used the words to characterize the geographical expression of the horror caused by the atom bombs dropped on Hiroshima and Nagasaki: "The intense heat of the blast started fires as far as 3,500 feet from 'ground zero' (the point on the ground directly under the bomb's explosion in the air)," he wrote; "and charred telephone poles were observed as far as 13,000 feet [more than two miles] away." The article reported on the findings of a U.S. government study conducted in post–atom-bomb Japan published the previous week and the results of an atomic bomb test conducted by the U.S. military around the same time on Bikini, a now uninhabited atoll in the Marshall Islands, its population relocated by American authorities in anticipation of the atomic explosion.[14] The title of the article referred to the atom bomb as the "most terrible weapon." And, for the Japanese, the results were undoubtedly "most terrible." As Baldwin reported, the atom bombs dropped on Japan "produced the greatest casualty rate per square mile in human history. *One* bomb dropped from *one* plane caused 15,000 deaths per square mile in Hiroshima; another bomb from one plane caused 20,000 deaths per square mile in Nagasaki."[15] Between the two cities, an estimated 210,000 perished immediately, and another 130,000 died of radiation poisoning over the five years that followed.[16]

Much of the popular opinion in the United States continues to perceive the dropping of the two bombs as just, a position reinforced by a strong consensus within the highest levels of Washington officialdom.[17] The standard argument underlying this opinion is that half a million American soldiers would have lost their lives invading Japan and that it was necessary to force Tokyo's capitulation. However, the historical record shows that top American authorities thought otherwise at the time.[18]

The U.S. military estimated that the number of American soldiers that would have been killed had the Pentagon launched a land invasion would have been considerably less than half a million—about forty thousand. But far more important, the U.S. military hierarchy did not perceive such an invasion as necessary, seeing the surrender of Imperial Japan as imminent. It was for these reasons that General Douglas MacArthur, supreme commander of Allied forces in the Pacific, called the dropping of the atomic bombs "completely unnecessary from a military point of view"—a position shared by General Eisenhower.[19] The decision to drop the bomb was a political one—made by President Truman and his advisers—one of the key goals being to intimidate and send a message to the Soviet Union, thus ensuring that the United States could dictate the terms on which the war ended.[20] In other words, Washington sacrificed hundreds of thousands of Japanese lives for political reasons, not out of military necessity.[21] Further proof of the low value accorded by the Pentagon to the lives of Japanese civilians was on deadly display five days after the bombing of Nagasaki. On August 14, 1945—the last day of the war—about one thousand American planes bombed a number of Japanese cities. It was during this mission that Truman announced the war's end.[22] Amid the corpses, survivors found U.S. government leaflets—written in Japanese—that had been dropped along with the bombs. "Your government has surrendered," they stated. "The war is over."[23] Such gross cruelty, and the logic underlying the creation of the first ground zero only days earlier, were not unlike that which would produce the horrors of East Timor and New York City decades later.

The expression "ground zero" evolved over the decades that followed Hiroshima and Nagasaki to signify a location of tremendously violent activity and devastation. In other words, it became exemplary, a term to describe a location of extreme violence and suffering, not a single, specific geographic site. In evolving in this fashion, "ground zero" became a term and concept that allowed for comparison between sites of severe human suffering. In the aftermath of the September 11, 2001, attack in New York City, however, the term has become one used by many (often as a proper noun) to signify a single place and associated set of events. "Ground Zero" now represents the site of the attack against the World Trade Center, and nowhere else[24] — at least as framed by Washington and a cooperative media establishment. The term — along with the associated memorialized site and the practices associated with it — is in the process of becoming literal to the extent that it underlies a U.S.-framed global "war on terror" rather than an effort to eradicate and seek accountability for horrific violence in all its roots and manifestations.

There are those who reject the use of collective memories of mass atrocities as part of a larger struggle for justice that makes linkages between events of terror, arguing that the particular memory of horror that they embrace is totally unique and absolutely extraordinary and that, in making comparisons, we commit a sacrilege and display insufficient appreciation for the episode in question. Similarly many will surely argue against the use of memorial spaces in an exemplary manner. But to utilize recollections and memorial sites of gross atrocities as a tool for closing down discussion and comparison, to further a particular agenda specific to the interests of one group, while refusing to see the commonality with people and places that have also suffered horribly, is to abuse such memories and memorial sites.[25] That lower Manhattan has come to embody ground zero speaks more to the power of the United States than it does any sort of uniquely horrific nature of the New York City attacks. Like all individual events, the attacks against the World Trade Center were distinctive — in addition to being horrific. But to say that they are unique is to speak a truism as no two events are exactly alike. More than that, however, it is an attempt, regardless of intent, to raise the violence and the associated horror and suffering to a level above those of all other ground zero–like atrocities, including what transpired in East Timor two years earlier. And, as the preeminent horror, it implicitly demands and deserves an extraordinary response in comparison with other ground zeros.

●

It is not that the so-called international community — in this case shorthand for the small group of countries that dominate international affairs given the unequal power relations within the United Nations and the world more gen-erally—did not respond to East Timor's ground zero. It did, but only after failing to prevent what it most probably could have thwarted. And the re-sponse has been largely in the form of (woefully inadequate) material and financial help for the country to rebuild. In the case of the United States, such international assistance was not necessary in the aftermath of the September 11, 2001, attacks, given the country's wealth. In this sense the two cases are not comparable.

Where they may be compared is in matters of justice and accountability. Both involved heinous crimes against humanity, leading to the deaths of thousands of noncombatants. And both were attacks against the "interna-tional community," albeit in different forms. In the case of the World Trade Center, hundreds of non–U.S. nationals—from dozens of different coun-tries—lost their lives given the multinational character of the workforce of the complex (and of New York City more broadly). In the case of East Timor, although only a handful of non–East Timorese were among those killed, the terror was—among other things—an attack, in effect, against the authority of the United Nations and the international community it is supposed to rep-resent. In this regard both cases would seem to demand *active* international support for accountability. Yet the reactions of the international community have been markedly different.

The response to ground zero in New York City has been one of strong re-solve to hold accountable the perpetrators of the crime and their supporters. In many ways it has been an ethic of vengeance more than one of justice that has informed these efforts. The United States, as one might expect, has spent billions of dollars trying to hunt down the architects of September 11, 2001, and their networks of support, with countries ranging from Britain to Japan to Australia providing significant and various forms of assistance in this mil-itaristic quest, one that has led to the deaths of thousands of civilian non-combatants in Afghanistan.

Australian prime minister John Howard, Indonesian president Megawati Sukarnoputri, and British prime minister Tony Blair were all present in Wash-ington in the days following the September 11 attacks against the World Trade Center and the Pentagon. All three offered solemn words of solidarity and ex-pressed their resolve to support Washington's declaration of war on terror.

While the White House threatened to "end states" that support terrorists and to "rid the world of the evil-doers," Tony Blair vowed to give his full back-ing to the fight "between the civilized world and fanaticism."[26] And John Howard promised that Australia would stand "shoulder-to-shoulder" with the United States in the aftermath of what he characterized as "not just an as-sault on America . . . [but] an assault on the way of life that we hold dear in common."[27]

Megawati Sukarnoputri's visit resulted in a joint statement condemning the September 11 attacks and an agreement "to cooperate with the international community in combating terrorism," but it was short on specifics as to the role Indonesia might play in the evolving Washington-led alliance.[28] In return, Jakarta received significant pledges of aid, while requesting a resumption of U.S. military ties, something the Bush administration was eager to put into place.[29]

Knowing that the irony of Indonesia's head of state pledging support for a war against terrorism would not be lost on some, the White House had to ensure that the Indonesian government offer something as repentance for its own crimes. Thus Megawati reportedly made a tepid promise to "resolve outstanding issues relating to past human rights violations, especially in conflict zones," without specifically mentioning East Timor.

Since that time Jakarta has made no serious effort to "resolve outstanding issues" related to atrocities committed against East Timor. This lack of accountability is a reflection of, among other things, a double standard in terms of how the actors that dominate world affairs pursue gross violators of international law. As for the impunity enjoyed by Jakarta's supporters (largely the same actors that have allowed Jakarta to escape prosecution), it exemplifies — in addition to the obvious — a tendency to conceive of violence in narrow terms, a conceptualization that manifests itself in the content of international law.

•

Violence against human beings takes many forms — direct, physical acts of brutality, such as those that created the various ground zeros, are only the most obvious ones. Less evident are the supporting actors and accompanying social relations that contribute to such violence, or the social structures and actions that also cause injury to people. We have a propensity to focus our critical attention far more on the first type — an outgrowth of a narrow conceptualization of violence, one that impoverishes our understanding of the social actors and complex processes that contribute to the harming of people.

For such reasons Johan Galtung, the renowned Norwegian peace studies scholar, includes in his definition of "violence" anything that prevents us from achieving *realizable* social goals deemed by most people in the world to be desirable. Such goals might include a healthy diet, access to potable water, or adequate health care and housing for all. Thus hunger in a world in which there is more than enough food produced to provide everyone with an adequate diet is a manifestation of violence, as is homelessness in wealthy countries such as Britain and the United States. When an identifiable actor commits violence, it is direct or personal. When there is no actor present — or when violence is the outgrowth of the seemingly acceptable, institutionalized practices of organizations deemed legitimate — then the violence is indirect or structural.

Although neither type of violence is inherently worse or more important than the other, many of us consider shooting and killing someone an act of violence, but not the creation and reproduction of social conditions that inevitably result in deaths. Part of the reason that we tend to focus our outrage on direct or personal violence is because it is visible as action; there is no question among the victims and witnesses of such violence that what has brought about the resulting suffering is *violence*. Structural or institutionalized violence, on the other hand, is often hidden or seemingly "natural" — inherent in our regular surroundings. It is part of the social fabric, the status quo. Such "violence" seems normal, rather than extraordinary, so we do not really notice it, or, if we do, it doesn't disturb us — partly, perhaps, because seeing it as violence might disrupt our comfortable lifestyles.[30]

Similarly representations of mass violence are often far too narrow with regard to whom they ascribe culpability. Structural violence that underlies or enables the direct or personal violence to take place usually receives relatively little attention. The lack of visible agency for the human suffering that results from structural violence usually means not only that it goes unnoticed but also that it is not challenged. This structural violence is not hidden simply because it occurred "behind the scenes" — indeed, for most people, so did the direct violence — but because powerful actors reproduce its hidden nature or construct it as something legitimate or other than violence through various representations. To the extent that such depictions serve to obscure or legitimize direct and structural forms of violence, we can consider them examples of what we might call *representational violence*.[31]

The strength of such a conceptualization of violence is its wide scope. Rather than reducing violence to singular, visible acts or events, it pushes us to appreciate that violence — like any other social act — does not take place in a vacuum. It emerges out of a complex web of social relations that involves individual acts, structures or processes, and discourse, or expressions of communication. One might argue, however, that this strength is also a potential weakness in that it makes violence seem to be almost everywhere and in everything, thus creating analytical complexity and hence, perhaps, confusion. This analytical challenge is also potentially a practical one as it could complicate efforts to achieve accountability for acts of gross violence. But to suggest that isolated acts or events of violence emerge out of a complex web of social relations is not to say that all factors within the web are equally significant or guilty (politically, morally, or legally). Nor does it necessarily prevent us from taking concrete actions to redress gross violence. To the contrary, it positions us to be more effective: such a conceptualization allows us to better understand how and why individual acts and events of horrific violence happen and, in doing so, to critique the limits of conventional approaches to accountability for atrocities. It thereby points the way to more effective politico-legal practices and mechanisms to ensure justice and accountability for war crimes and crimes against humanity. It is also empowering in that it facilitates a wider array of interventions by individuals, groups, and institutions to fight against the myriad factors that give rise to and enable gross atrocities and mass violence and that allow for subsequent impunity for the perpetrators.

In this regard the targets must include the body of international humanitarian law, the content of which reflects very narrow notions of responsibility for gross violence. As legal scholar Roger Clark contends, "International criminal responsibility proceeds on the basis of the pithy aphorism of the Nuremberg Tribunal that crimes are committed by people rather than by abstract entities" (such as states or military organizations).[32] Similarly complicity in international crimes against humanity and war crimes is narrowly defined, drawing on Anglo-American notions of law that limit accountability to anyone who agrees to the commission of a crime or to anyone who *intentionally* encourages or aids in the commission of a crime.[33] Thus international law restricts its scrutiny to acts of direct violence as demonstrated by its focus on intent. In that regard it is necessary to distinguish between violence that is intended and that which is unintended. According to Galtung, this is a significant distinction under Judeo-Christian ethics and Roman jurisprudence, both of which decide guilt based more on the intent than on the consequence, thus potentially resulting in impunity for some.

> This connection is important because it brings into focus a bias present in so much thinking about violence, peace, and related concepts: ethical systems directed against *intended* violence will easily fail to capture structural violence in their nets — and may hence be catching the small fry and letting the big fish loose.[34]

In the case of responsibility for East Timor's suffering, the "big fish" remain free not only in the legal sense but also largely in terms of scrutiny.

To highlight the importance of indirect or structural violence is not to suggest that one should not be concerned with personal or direct violence. To the contrary, if the concern is with peace — as well as with justice — then the focus of critical attention and associated actions must be on both direct and structural forms of violence,[35] and the individuals, groups, and institutions that carry it out. At the same time the focus must not merely be on violence that is intended as such. If one accepts the premise that people should be held responsible primarily for the likely or predictable consequences of their actions, intent is not so important.[36] Ultimately one should be far more concerned with outcomes, as Galtung suggests.

Of course, this is not purely an intellectual project. There are profound political reasons why international law allows so much impunity: it generally reflects the interests of relatively powerful countries, and effectively shields them from the possibility of prosecution, or even having to account for their actions.[37]

The resulting double standard became highly visible following the September 11, 2001, attacks against the United States. As illustrated by President George W. Bush's speech nine days later and his administration's subsequent behavior, Washington (rightfully) contends that those that support the commission of crimes against humanity and war crimes — in the form of aiding and abetting the activities of the perpetrators — are equally guilty. Following this logic, the United States introduced, and the Security Council approved, two resolutions that overcome the typically limited form of accountability that defines complicity in the most narrow of terms. Resolution 1368, adopted the day following the attacks, *stresses* that "those responsible for aiding, supporting or harbouring the perpetrators, organizers, and sponsors of these acts will be held accountable." Resolution 1373, adopted on September 28, 2001, states that "all States shall . . . [e]nsure that any person who participates in the financing, planning, preparation or perpetration of terrorist acts or in supporting terrorist acts is brought to justice."[38]

Just as complicity in war crimes and crimes against humanity is an occasional standard of behavior for accountability, so, too, are reparations a required measure of contrition — at least when the culpable party is an enemy of the powerful. Thus Iraq under Saddam Hussein was required to provide restitution to Kuwait for Baghdad's 1990 invasion and brief, but destructive, occupation.[39] No such demand has been made of Indonesia nor of its powerful supporters — at least in the international halls of respectable debate — despite the equally illegal nature of the invasion and occupation, and the far greater levels of associated destruction and human suffering.

●

Such uneven-handed behavior by the world's powers notwithstanding, there is a perception among many — especially in the United States — that countries whose systems of government are based on liberal principles of electoral democracy and respect for the law tend to be overwhelmingly law-abiding in their approach to international affairs.[40] According to this view, it is countries like the United States, Britain, France, and Australia that most strongly and consistently support a legalist approach to international relations.

And undoubtedly there are instances in which Western countries have supported a law-based approach — such as in the aftermath of wars and atrocities as in the cases of post–World War II Nuremberg prosecutions and the still active international criminal tribunals on Yugoslavia and Rwanda. But such cases do not prove nearly as much as some contend. What matters more in trying to measure the level of support a state renders to legalistic mechanisms is how it behaves when it is not a mere witness to crimes or a victor with legitimate postwar grievances but, rather, when its citizens or government institutions have been a perpetrator of atrocities or complicit in them. As the case of East Timor demonstrates, the commitment to international law on the part of the powerful is not nearly as profound as their rhetoric suggests. But East Timor is certainly not the only example.

In 1984, for instance, the Nicaraguan government filed a case at the International Court of Justice (ICJ) against the United States for acts of aggression against the Central American country. The response of the Reagan administration, after failing to convince the ICJ to drop the case on the grounds that the court did not have jurisdiction to decide cases involving ongoing armed conflict, was to announce that it would simply ignore the court's verdict. In 1986 the ICJ found in Nicaragua's favor, determining that U.S. direct aggression and aid to the "Contras" were illegal, and enjoining Washington to immediately cease such acts and to provide reparations to Nicaragua. As promised, the Reagan White House rejected and ignored the court's decision.[41]

Despite such disdain for effective international legal mechanisms, perceptions of the United States, and the West more generally, as law-abiding persist. One of the dangers of such misperceptions is that they fuel an approach to the world that facilitates a double standard and an associated view that the United States and the West have the right to judge others — others who do not effectively have the same right. Witness, for instance, calls by Washington insiders and the mainstream media for prosecution of Khmer Rouge leaders for their horrific crimes against the people of Cambodia.[42] These same proponents of justice, however, are silent about the need for accountability for the U.S. crimes that preceded the atrocities of the Khmer Rouge and laid the basis for its seizure of power.[43]

Such views also dovetail with a double standard toward violence, judging it on the basis of who employs it, not on its effects or legitimacy. The result is a perception of our violence as good or more legitimate than that of those we abhor. Michael Ignatieff, director of the Carr Center for Human Rights at Harvard University, for example, argues that we should make a distinction between terror and brutality. Terror, he writes, is violence against civilians carried out by non-uniformed groups who seek to cause panic or inflict revenge, not to achieve military victory (i.e., terrorists). Brutality is also violence against civilians, but committed by national militaries under regular command with clear politico-military objectives as part of a larger effort that is often just (e.g., self-defense).[44]

The first problem with such an argument is the assumption that we can easily determine intentions. A second relates to the rejection of the notion that "[state] brutality in winning just wars is equivalent to terrorist brutality in an unjust cause."[45] The quandary here is who determines what is "just" and what is not, and how is that done.

Furthermore, how should we define state violence against civilians when carried out for unjust reasons (e.g., perpetuating an illegal occupation, pursuing extra-national political and economic interests, etc.)? Or what about when nonstate groups wage war to end such injustice? By Ignatieff's logic, fighting against colonial occupation could be construed as terrorism, but the illegal U.S. bombing of Cambodia is mere brutality.

Finally, such a view inevitably sides with established powers and the violence they employ. After all, it is national governments that can utilize standard militaries whereas those with relatively little power—especially those outside state structures—are compelled to use unconventional methods. Thus the violence of states is generally depicted as inherently more legitimate than that of nonstate actors. Nonstate actors who employ violence against civilians are, by definition, terrorists. State actors who employ violence against civilians, on the other hand, are just that: state actors, albeit ones guilty of brutality. Their violence does not define who they are. We do not refer to them as "brutalists," for example.

Such intellectual acrobatics show why United Nations member-states have failed to reach a consensus on a definition of terrorism: it is a highly politicized term that is user-friendly (typically meaning whatever the party employing it wants it to mean). Thus, for Washington, terrorism can apply only to those outside the confines of state power or to a handful of "rogue states." Meanwhile, state actors, especially the United States and its allies, can only be guilty of "excesses" or a failure to exercise "restraint"—no matter how horrific their crimes. As Azmi Bishara, a dissident Palestinian member of the Israeli Knesset has written, the powerful now define terrorism not on the basis of what you do but who you are.[46]

It is for such reasons that "terrorism" has become an almost worthless concept for serious analytical inquiry and, more important, for practical politics guided by universal principles of justice and accountability.[47] It is a term for political polemics. Despite their narrowness with regard to assigning culpability, internationally agreed-upon legal concepts—such as crimes against humanity and war crimes—are far more useful, in addition to being more just.

●

Abuse of language, in addition to memory, is commonplace among nationalists. Nationalists—broadly defined here—have a tendency to see the world as they like, as opposed to the way it is, and they represent it accordingly. Nationalists, as discussed by George Orwell, are those whose self-identity is based on a form of unquestioning group-think that perceives the world as divided between "good" and "evil," and sees one's ultimate duty to promote the interests of one's (always "good") group.[48] In the case of countries, this leads to a national self-righteousness that, when combined with a disproportionate amount of political-economic and military power, is a dangerous chemistry in world affairs. It is a recipe for imperialism, one made all the more perilous when informed by a deluded national memory.

Given the violent process through which its territorial expanse took place and the almost constant projection of its political-economic and military power abroad since the end of the nineteenth century, the United States has long been an imperialist country. Presently, the United States has 725 military bases in at least 38 different countries, to say nothing of bases in the various U.S. territories in the Pacific and elsewhere. And, during 2003, U.S. military personnel were present in 153 of the 189 member-states of the United Nations, with large-scale deployments in twenty-five countries.[49] Nevertheless "imperialist" has rarely been a term applied to the United States by political commentators within the country over the last several decades. Although some on the isolationist Right have disparagingly spoken of American imperialism, it has largely been Left-leaning critics of the United States — both at home and abroad — who have employed the term "imperialism" to characterize U.S. foreign policy and practice in an unflattering manner. They see the primary goal and effect of U.S. foreign policy as one of preserving and enhancing a world marked by gross inequality, an institutionalization and furthering of injustice from which the United States profits greatly. American political elites have typically denied such characterizations. To the contrary, mainstream commentators and politicians have tended overwhelmingly to reject such an adjective to describe American practices overseas.

Much more recently, however, some prominent conservatives as well as liberals in the United States have also begun to describe their country, given its global reach and effectively unchallenged international supremacy, as an imperial power or advocate that the United States play such a role. When used by such individuals, the label of "imperialist" is not a criticism but merely a statement of perceived fact or necessity. They see the United States as a benign empire, one of liberty and democracy, an empire that should be maintained and enhanced. Sebastian Mallaby, for example, an editorial writer and columnist for *The Washington Post,* argues that the United States and the West, more generally, must reluctantly take on the imperialist yoke to rescue "failed states." Mallaby perceives this to be a "rich man's burden" of sorts.[50] From the conservative internationalist end of the political spectrum, Max Boot, the former head of the opinion page of the *Wall Street Journal* and now a Senior Fellow at the New York City–based Council on Foreign Relations, similarly champions American imperialism. It is one guided by a narrow sense of the national interest and an almost messianic mission to spread American influence and values (in the form of liberal democracy and, especially, capitalism) abroad. By bringing such "freedoms" to places where they do not yet exist, Washington can enlarge America's (informal) "empire of liberty." The United States has long attempted to do this, argues Boot—from the pacification of the Philippines at the end of the nineteenth century to the occupations of Haiti and Nicaragua in the early decades of the twentieth to the failed efforts in Vietnam—and Americans need to recognize this. "Freedom" does not come cheaply, he contends. Its maintenance and enhancement require a willingness to employ U.S. military power abroad. In this regard Boot quotes Thomas Friedman, columnist for *The New York Times:* "The hidden hand of the market will never work without a hidden fist. McDonald's cannot flourish without McDonnell Douglas, the designer of the U.S. Air Force F-15."[51] Richard Holbrooke, reflecting the lack of any significant differences between mainstream Democrats and Republicans about the right of the United States to dominate world affairs,[52] calls Boot's book "ground-breaking," stating that it "could change your views on one of the most important issues facing our nation: the use of military force as a policy instrument."[53]

One of the reasons that an American empire enjoys such support across the elite political spectrum within the United States is because of the widespread view that American imperialism is of a very different nature from those of traditional imperial powers. Unlike imperial Britain, Japan, or France—so the thinking goes—the United States has generally not been interested in, nor pursued, territorial conquest. Instead, it has achieved its global influence through relatively benign means. Eminent historian John Lewis Gaddis argues in focusing largely on spheres of imperial influence in Europe, for example, that the United States realized its empire through invitation whereas the Soviet Union constructed its empire through imposition.[54]

In the case of the so-called Third World, however, there was nothing benign about U.S. empire building, and it cannot be explained to a significant degree by Cold War competition with the Soviets[55]—not least because such conduct preceded the outbreak and continued after the demise of East-West tensions. Nevertheless American imperialism is distinct from those that emerged in the eighteenth, nineteenth, and early twentieth centuries but not out of any special American dedication to the principles of national self-determination as Gaddis and others have claimed.

The American empire is predicated on a global market—one over which the United States has a disproportionate amount of influence—rather than on a sub-global economic sphere made up of colonized areas ruled by and centered on a single "mother country." It is a "nationalist globalism," in the words of geographer Neil Smith. As such, partnerships with other countries are an important component of American imperialism as are global institutions such as the International Monetary Fund and the World Bank. Together these partnerships (with other wealthy countries and with "Third World" elites) and international institutions help to resolve the geographical contradiction between a world of national territorial states and an increasingly globalized economy.[56] Because the power of the United States is exercised largely indirectly—although bloody episodes, such as the American attack against Vietnam or the most recent war with Iraq, demonstrate that Washington is more than willing to employ old-style violence when deemed necessary—the American empire has the appearance of a relatively benign endeavor. But the profound (and growing) socioeconomic inequalities that underlie it and that it helps to produce, and the political (and sometimes military) bullying employed to maintain and further it, illustrate that appearances can be deceiving.

Imperial powers have always relied on proxies, subordinates, partners, or all three, to help realize their politico-geographical projects. The U.S. empire is unique given the extent to which it relies on partner countries—ones that are nominally equal but, in reality, are inferior in terms of political, military, and economic power on the international stage—to maintain and further its interests. Given the team-like nature of the U.S.-led empire, the benefits it produces for those who maintain it are not limited to the United States but also flow to its partners. As such, the embracing of this empire has an unusual international aspect to it. In fact, one of its intellectual progenitors—at least in terms of its most recent manifestation—is found across the Atlantic. Conservative British historian Paul Johnson championed this latest call for imperialism in 1993 in *The New York Times Magazine*. In the aftermath of the Cold War, Johnson saw chaos breaking out across the globe, especially in countries such as Haiti, Liberia, and Somalia. For Johnson, these seemingly intractable situations suggested that large parts of the world had actually regressed, leading him to call for the reinstitution of colonialism, a trusteeship system of sorts run by the world's "civilized powers," for countries "not fit to govern themselves." Such an enterprise, Johnson argued, is very different from imperialist adventures whose concern is economic; rather, it is moral: "Their continued existence, and the violence and human degradation they breed, is a threat to the stability of their neighbors as well as an affront to our consciences. There is a moral issue here: the civilized world has a mission to go out to those desperate places and govern."[57]

A little more than a year after the attack of September 11, 2001, on the World Trade Center, Johnson situated his bring-back-colonialism call in the new war-on-terror paradigm championed by Washington and its allies. Writing on Max Boot's op-ed page in the *Wall Street Journal*, Johnson informed readers that the West, in addition to having to wage war against states that sponsor terrorism, might have to occupy and administer them as well. "Countries that cannot live at peace with their neighbors and that wage covert war against the international community cannot expect total independence," he wrote. In addition to Afghanistan, Johnson named Iraq, Sudan, Libya, Iran, and Syria (the usual cast of "rogue state" characters) as possible candidates for colonization by the "great civilized powers"—America and its allies.[58]

While all the marked states have, at times, engaged in or supported horrific violence, most striking about Johnson's list are the countries that it does not include. It is also noteworthy that Johnson compares the states that he categorizes as sponsors of modern-day terrorism to nineteenth-century pirates, a comparison with a lineage of which he is probably unaware.

Writing approximately sixteen centuries ago, the renowned theologian St. Augustine related a story about a pirate captured by Alexander the Great, who asked his prisoner "how he dares molest the sea." "How dare you molest the whole world?" responded the pirate. "Because I do it with a little ship only, I am called a thief; you, doing it with a great navy, are called an Emperor."[59]

Such a parable has strong relevance to contemporary constructions of "pirates" and "emperors" in the form of "terrorists" and "great civilized powers." Although the term "terrorism" first came into use in the late eighteenth century to designate government violence employed to subjugate restless populations, it is applied today largely to nonstate groups or individuals who employ violence.[60] Washington and Tel Aviv, for example, characterize almost any act of Palestinian violence—whether directed against Israeli civilians or military personnel—as terrorism, whereas Israeli state violence aimed at subjugating Palestinians fighting against or even nonviolently resisting their dispossession and the occupation of their homeland (defined as illegal under international law through multiple U.N. Security Council resolutions) is typically represented as "defense," "security," "retaliation," or the like.[61]

For such reasons it is far too simple to divide the world into "terrorists"—those whose violence we do not like—and the civilized (we and our allies). Once again, unless we can employ internationally agreed-upon terms, their use is inherently selective and hence their legitimacy dubious. After all, how can we label Al Qaeda and the Taliban as terrorist, but not apply the same moniker to the Indonesian military and the various states that have supported an entity responsible for the slaughter of many hundreds of thousands over the last few decades? The answer is, only through the applications of double standards—one standard of behavior for us, and another for those we oppose.

Robert Cooper, an adviser to Tony Blair's government and a senior British diplomat, comes close to endorsing such a double standard. Cooper sees the contemporary world as divided between premodern states ("failed states" located primarily in the global South); modern states (e.g., China, India, and Pakistan), which behave in traditional state fashion according to interests and power, and thus somewhat predictably; and postmodern and postimperial states (e.g., Canada and countries in Western Europe), whose security no longer depends on territorial conquest and who thus reject the use of force as a means to resolve international disputes, instead relying on the conventions and mechanisms associated with international governance.

While Cooper sees modern states as a potential threat to the postmodern world, his greatest concern are the premodern states, which, even though they are typically extremely weak, can serve as operational bases for nonstate terrorists and international drug syndicates, thus threatening the well-being of the "more orderly parts of the world." Thus,

> The postmodern world has to start to get used to double standards. Among ourselves, we operate on the basis of laws and open cooperative security. But, when dealing with old-fashioned states outside the postmodern continent of Europe, we need to revert to the rougher methods of an earlier era—force, pre-emptive attack, deception, whatever is necessary to deal with those who still live in the nineteenth century world of every state for itself.

"Among ourselves," Cooper argues, "we keep the law but when we are operating in the jungle, we must also use the laws of the jungle." Thus, when the "premodern" threatens the modern and postmodern, "defensive imperialism"—military action—is in order. After that, "what is needed is a new kind of imperialism, one compatible with human rights and cosmopolitan values: an imperialism which aims to bring order and organisation but which rests today on the voluntary principle." International membership organizations such as the World Bank and the International Monetary Fund are models that Cooper invokes, along with U.N.-type protectorates as in the cases of Bosnia and Kosovo.[62]

Once again, the West becomes the standard by which all others are judged, and should rightfully play the role of maintaining global order. Thus some argue that countries like the United States have a duty to take the lead in preventing mass atrocities from occurring by taking unilateral action (in the form of "humanitarian intervention") when necessary.[63] But there is clearly a problem with Washington taking the lead in fighting something it has helped to perpetrate on numerous occasions, and for which it has never atoned, apart from, on one occasion, a half-hearted admission of wrongdoing (but not an apology, by Clinton in the case of Guatemala).[64]

Nevertheless simply because the United States has been complicit in gross atrocities in the past does not mean it is therefore incapable of doing good, if even at times for the wrong reasons. But it does mean that we should remain extremely skeptical of American leadership on the global stage. Myriad examples of U.S. antipathy toward international law and political institutions means that "humanitarian intervention" could turn out to be just another instrument in Washington's empire-maintenance tool kit. The same could be said of the West in general.

This is not to imply that if we could get the American and Western houses in order, the world would be fine. To use George W. Bush's language, there are plenty of "evildoers" in the world. Something must be done to stop gross atrocities, genocides, and the commission of crimes against humanity, yes, but it should be a truly international project. The best place to start is at home, but not by first and foremost asking Washington and its allies to intercede abroad. Demanding that their foreign policies are consistent with international law and human rights standards, as well as that there be international accountability for their own government officials who may have engaged or have been complicit in war crimes and crimes against humanity, is the first step. Doing so will also increase the likelihood of international cooperation in cases they advocate.

Various analysts within the U.S. political mainstream and on the Left-leaning margins have warned of the dangers of U.S. imperialism. But, in doing so, some analysts have focused on the perils for the imperial power, not those on the receiving end of the empire's practices.[65] Others offer advice as to how to make the American empire more moral, moderate, and thus successful.[66] And then there are those that call for a benign imperialism,[67] seeing the choice as an unfortunate but realistic one between barbarism and an imperialism that minimizes such barbarism.[68]

Embracing imperialism — even a supposedly benign one — is a dangerous enterprise. It is important to remember that empire, as Chalmers Johnson teaches us, has costs and consequences — ones that are often unseen as such and typically unanticipated.[69] And in terms of the subject population, it is true that some imperial powers have been historically more beneficent, less physically violent than others, just as some dictators can be relatively benign. But it is a mistake to think that any global imperial power can be benign in an absolute sense.

Imperial powers have long purported to be benevolent.[70] But, as J. A. Hobson observed more than a century ago, the claim by imperialist powers that they engage in empire-building practices "for the purpose of rendering services to the conquered equal to those which she exacts is notoriously false: she neither intends equivalent services nor is capable of rendering them, and the pretence that such benefits to the governed form a leading motive or result of Imperialism implies a degree of moral or intellectual obliquity so grave as itself to form a new peril for any nation fostering so false a notion of the nature of its conduct."[71]

Hobson was writing about the old-style imperialism, one in which colonial empires were central. But the observation also applies to the present-day world order dominated by the United States and, to a lesser degree, its powerful allies. This domination is a more indirect form than the empires of old, but it is also a more profound and ultimately more effective one. Like any imperialism, it is inherently barbaric as it is predicated upon the existence and maintenance of severe socioeconomic inequalities (structural violence) that are inherent in all empires, and occasionally necessitates the employment of direct physical violence when those unhappy with the injustices of empire attempt to rebel. Barbarism versus imperialism is thus a false dichotomy.

●

East Timor's tragic history and its ground zero are inextricably tied to the history of empire. Whether that history becomes part of our collective memory is another matter.

It is said that the victors are the ones who write history. "It might also be said," in the words of Peter Burke, "that history is forgotten by the victors. They can afford to forget, while the losers are unable to accept what happened and are condemned to brood over it, relive it, and reflect how different it might have been."[72] But perhaps instead of thinking in terms of "victors" and "losers," we should conceive of the matter in terms of beneficiaries and victims, or the powerful and less powerful.

Although the East Timorese people ultimately won their struggle, they paid an extremely high price for it — and continue to do so in myriad ways. As for the Indonesian military and its supporters, although they ultimately failed in their efforts to conquer and pacify East Timor, they have suffered relatively little for their crimes. The East Timorese population is condemned to remember: they will live with the physical, social, and psychological effects of the horrific war and occupation for decades. Meanwhile, the Indonesian elite and its international partners-in-crime have the luxury of forgetting.

While power may afford such luxuries, ethics and morality do not. Indeed, there is an ethical responsibility for those implicated in the suffering of others to remember,[73] and not simply to create a "cult of memory for the sake of memory."[74] While there are numerous reasons to remember — not least the needs of the victims — remembering is important as part of a larger social struggle against unjust power. To alter somewhat the words of Milan Kundera, the struggle of memory against forgetting is the struggle against power,[75] a struggle that must extend beyond the boundaries of a specific set of atrocities.

The responses of Washington, Canberra, London, Tokyo, and Jakarta to the ground zeros of East Timor and New York exhibit a double standard that underlies a world order in which there is rarely accountability by those who victimize the relatively weak (unless those responsible are also relatively marginal within the global political-economic and military hierarchy), while the rich and powerful either enjoy impunity for their own crimes or can bomb and kill those they accuse of criminality. Like the pursuit of security, revenge — couched in the language of righteousness — seems to be the privilege only of the powerful. The dispossessed, the occupied and colonized, are typically not allowed to use force to secure what is theirs; if they do try, their actions are often labeled terrorism. What is worse, the weak, as a way of endearing themselves to the powerful, often have to pretend that the injustices for which they crave justice and accountability never happened. This, too, is a manifestation of violence. It is folly to pretend that the world which this reflects, one predicated on massive inequality and its maintenance, is sustainable, just, or secure. Pervasive instability, ubiquitous violence, and profound insecurity for the global majority are the inevitable results.

Crises such as those of the various ground zeros present challenges, as well as opportunities. We can utilize the crisis for various and vastly different ends. As Ariel Dorfman writes regarding the tragedy of September 11, 2001, it "can lead to renewal or destruction, it can be used for good or for evil, for peace or for war, for aggression or for reconciliation, for vengeance or for justice, for the militarization of a society or its humanization." But in order for justice, peace, reconciliation, and humanization to be the outcomes, Americans and others traumatized by the attacks will first have to "admit that their suffering is neither unique nor exclusive, that they are connected, as long as they are willing to look at themselves in the vast mirror of our common humanity, with so many other human beings who, in apparently faraway zones, have suffered similar situations of unanticipated and often protracted injury and fury." Only in this way can we all work together to create a world in which another terrifying September 11 — or another ground zero — never happens again.[76]

Making sure memories and memorials of atrocities are exemplary — in other words, by not abusing them — while striving for historical accuracy, is one step in this process.[77]

Some are guilty, but all are responsible.

—RABBI ABRAHAM J. HESCHEL, *"The Religious Basis of Equality of Opportunity — The Segregation of God"*

Reality is not destiny, it is a challenge.

—EDUARDO GALEANO, Democracy Now! *(radio show),* *December 29, 2000*

Dili, August 1999. *Photo by the author.*

East Timor has officially been an independent country since May 20, 2002, when the United Nations Transitional Administration in East Timor (UNTAET) handed over the reins of government to the country's democratically elected political leadership.[1] The reality of the world's newest country is multifaceted — one of joy borne of new-found freedom but also one of great pain given the difficulties of everyday life for the country's majority. Independence has brought opportunities that were previously nonexistent for many, if not most, of East Timor's citizens. But at the same time East Timor faces formidable and often daunting obstacles in terms of efforts to create a just society in which all its members are able to satisfy their basic human needs. These factors reflect the strengths and weaknesses of the transition process and, to a far greater extent, the legacy of terror experienced by East Timor during Indonesia's war and occupation. They also exemplify the unjust terms upon which it was integrated into a global political-economy that disproportionately favors a relatively small percentage of the world's population, one largely concentrated in the countries of the West, at the expense of the global majority.

UNTAET assumed authority in the territory following Indonesia's withdrawal from its former province in October 1999. While laying the groundwork for East Timor's formal independence, there were serious deficiencies in UNTAET's work, and, more broadly, in the work of the international community, in the territory; for example, insufficient attention was given to the provision of justice and to providing the foundation for the long-term socioeconomic sustainability of the society, to name just two areas. Nonetheless there were also many noteworthy accomplishments. In the area of humanitarian relief, for instance, the international community was very successful (despite some shortcomings) in meeting the most urgent needs of East Timor's population in terms of providing emergency shelter, preventing food emergencies and averting the outbreak of epidemics. The United Nations and its peacekeeping force also effectively protected East Timor from extraterritorial threats, namely, the militia and TNI.[2]

Just how far East Timor had come in the short time since the end of Indonesia's occupation struck me in mid-2000, only several months after UNTAET had established itself, while I was living and working in Dili. The date was July 17 — what the Indonesian government used to refer to as Integration Day (the official holiday commemorating Indonesia's formal annexation of East Timor). Yet almost none of my East Timorese neighbors, friends, or colleagues recalled the significance of the date without prompting. For them it was just another day, albeit one in a radically new era.

During that first trip back to East Timor following the September 1999 terror, the hardship that resulted from the dying days of the Indonesian occupation was palpable and ubiquitous. Although several months had passed since the last Indonesian soldiers had left the territory, devastation was everywhere. The vast majority of the population lacked gainful employment, and many were still relying on various forms of international humanitarian assistance to survive. Hunger was common. Nevertheless there was a level of collective joy and relaxation that many (the relatively young) had never experienced in their lives and many others had not felt for more than two decades. As many East Timorese told me at the time, they may not have a house or a job but at least they could talk freely and walk down the street without fear. Almost everyone had a story or stories they wanted to share — tales of terror, atrocities, and death, but many more of bravery, human ingenuity, and survival in the last days of the Indonesian occupation.[3] These stories were accounts of pain and pride but were also efforts to ensure the remembrance of East Timor's collective suffering and courage in a time of relative peace and freedom.

The importance of this new reality was evident when I visited Ana Lopes in mid-2000 at the ruins of her family home in one of Dili's most devastated neighborhoods. She laughed as she spoke, expressing herself with confidence and comfort. Unlike during my many visits with her in July and August of 1999, Ana talked to me for the first time in a voice louder than a faint whisper. Unlike in 1999, when militia regularly terrorized her, she no longer nervously rocked back and forth in her chair during our discussion. Nor did she cry when we spoke.

When I left, she walked me out of the house and onto the street — something she had never done during my visits the previous year for fear of enraging the militia types who stalked the neighborhood. This time Ana crossed the road and proudly showed me the corn she was growing in a garden opposite her house, amid the ruins of the militia post.

•

Although one should not underestimate how far East Timor has come in a brief time, one should not exaggerate it either. East Timor's experiences since Indonesia's withdrawal illustrate the painful limitations of independence. More than five years later many public facilities still lie in ruins, much of the country's social infrastructure is below pre-September 1999 levels, and unemployment and underemployment are massive as a result of the very low levels of economic development. In addition, East Timor — like relatively small, low-income countries throughout the world — faces formidable obstacles in a global order of profound and growing socioeconomic inequality and deep differences in political power on the international stage. The continuing charade regarding justice and accountability for East Timor's suffering — and the inability of the country's elected leadership to forcefully advocate for such—is only one of the more striking manifestations of the limits of the country's formal independence.

Another is the ongoing rewriting of the country's tortured history as powerful individuals and institutions erase the complicity of Indonesia's partners in the invasion and mass killings in East Timor. In late 2002, for example, former U.S. president Jimmy Carter received the Nobel Peace Prize, despite his administration's provision of weaponry to Jakarta that helped enable the TNI to kill what were probably tens of thousands of East Timorese in the late 1970s. Such behavior—and Carter's overall less-than-stellar human rights record overall during his presidency (which included strong support for the Shah of Iran, the brutal Somoza government of Nicaragua, and the military-dominated regime in El Salvador)—received almost no attention in the mainstream media coverage surrounding the 2002 award.[4] To the contrary, analysts typically lauded Carter's White House years. Jonathan Steele, a British journalist, for example, described Carter as "the only US president since 1945 never to order American soldiers into combat" and contended that "he made human rights a top priority" during his presidency.[5]

Several months after the awarding of the Nobel Prize, East Timorese president Xanana Gusmão received UNESCO's 2002 Félix Houphouët-Boigny Peace Prize, the committee chairman for which was Henry Kissinger. In his remarks on the occasion, Kissinger noted that East Timor's struggle had taken place "amidst nations following imperatives they considered more immediate"—nations that went unnamed. Nevertheless, Kissinger continued, the former Portuguese colony succeeded "against all odds—against overwhelming military power, against indifference abroad." As part of the historical whitewash, the former State Department head opined that "Americans can take pride in the role their country has played in the ultimate culmination of these efforts."[6]

In addition to erasing the fact that many Western powers were complicit in Indonesia's crimes in East Timor until almost the bitter and bloody end, various policy makers and pundits are framing the past in such a way as to suggest that these powers were actually the saviors of the newborn country. Even before Jakarta agreed to allow international troops to enter East Timor, some were presenting Western efforts to pressure Indonesia to put an end to the terror as an example of Western righteousness. Framing Washington's role in these efforts as part of a larger project of peace brokering, Walter Russell Mead of the Council on Foreign Relations in New York City, for instance, gushed, "It is as though an industry of peace is our greatest export."[7] Even among those who are critical of Washington's behavior in 1999 for not doing enough to stymie the TNI's crimes, many present the terror and destruction that engulfed East Timor in 1999 as a paradigmatic case necessitating U.S. and

Western "humanitarian intervention" to save lives abroad, rather than an example of the depravity of U.S. foreign policy and that of many other Western governments and how they have frequently brought about or facilitated mass atrocities.[8]

In addition to having to endure such historical distortions, East Timor also remains occupied in a sense: the Australian government continues to hold on to and exploit deposits of oil and natural gas contained in seabed areas in the Timor Sea, areas that, on the basis of international law, appear to belong to East Timor. Australia gained control of these areas through a combination of what appears to be an incorrect drawing of East Timor's east-west sea boundaries during the Portuguese colonial period and a subsequent infamous agreement signed with Indonesia during the occupation.[9] Although East Timor contests Australia's control, the newly independent country lacks the power to compel Canberra to respect its claim. What makes these seabed areas so important is that the deposits of oil and natural gas are worth billions of dollars.

International legal mechanisms are available to adjudicate such disputes. But Canberra, fearing that it would lose, has changed the terms upon which it accepts international dispute resolution mechanisms as they relate to maritime boundaries. Previously Australia had declared its acceptance of the International Court of Justice and the International Tribunal for the Law of the Sea as venues for the compulsory settlement of disputes under the United Nations Convention on the Law of the Sea (UNCLOS). In March 2002, however, Canberra announced that it was taking advantage of a clause contained in UNCLOS that allows parties to the treaty to exclude certain areas from compulsory dispute resolution. On this basis Canberra decided to exclude sea boundaries, contending that negotiation rather than litigation is the best manner in which to resolve such disputes. Such negotiations, inevitably infused with various forms of power, greatly favor Australia because of its much greater economic, military, and political strength. Whereas the Australian government sought to exploit Indonesia's war of conquest and effectively steal East Timor's resources during the course of Jakarta's occupation, it now seeks to do so through diplomatic methods. On its face, such diplomacy is nonviolent, but to the extent that it draws upon, takes advantage of, and reinforces East Timor's political-economic marginality, one borne, in part, of an extremely violent Indonesian occupation supported by Australia (among others), the line between political negotiation and war is a fuzzy one at best.[10]

Given East Timor's endemic material poverty and the profound destruction the country experienced in the aftermath of the Indonesian withdrawal in 1999, East Timor is in desperate need of the contested revenue resulting from the Timor Sea. The income lost to the newly independent country could make a huge difference in the quality of life of its citizenry, whereas in the case of Australia, such revenues will only add to the treasury of an already wealthy country. These differences are ones with literally life and death implications. According to *The State of the World's Children 2004* put out by UNICEF, 126 of every 1,000 children in East Timor will die before their fifth birthday, 89 before their first. In contrast, only 6 children per 1,000 in Australia die within their first year, a figure that does not change for those under five years of age.[11] As a further example, two consecutive years of drought have led to a significant reduction in crop yields in East Timor. An investigation in late 2003 by the United Nations World Food Program and Food and Agriculture Organization revealed that more than 100,000 people in East Timor (out of a population of less than 1 million) faced serious food shortages causing widespread hunger. Only international food aid helped to avert a larger crisis.[12]

A May 8, 2004, article in *The Age* (Melbourne) put a human face to these statistics. The article reported on Julmira Babo, a twelve-year-old East Timorese girl who choked to death on October 1, 2003, on hundreds of 20- to 30-centimeter roundworms. The worms had crawled up from her infested lower intestine through her stomach, and clogged the esophagus or food passage. The medicine needed to prevent this tragedy would have cost 10 cents.[13]

It is for such reasons that the Timor Sea conflict is so significant. In 2004 East Timor's annual government spending was $74.6 million. In May of the same year East Timor's government announced cuts of $40.5 million over the next four years in its already measly national budget. As of May 2004 the Australian government was taking in more than $700,000 per day from oil fields in a disputed area of the Timor Sea, one that lies twice as close to East Timor as it does to Australia.[14] While Canberra frequently speaks of Australian "generosity" in providing humanitarian and developmental assistance for East Timor's reconstruction, the total cost of such assistance is a fraction of the revenues Australia has thus far secured from the disputed areas of the Timor Sea. The money East Timor would gain through a settlement of the dispute consistent with international law—estimates range from $12 billion to more than $20 billion over the next three decades—would provide the country with far more effective means than it has at present to achieve a standard of living for the population consistent with basic human rights standards and notions of human dignity, and make tragedies such as that of Julmira Babo far less likely.[15]

Conventional wisdom says that there is little East Timor can do about such matters. In terms of international justice, many argue that East Timor should just put the matter behind and let bygones be bygones. To do otherwise would antagonize its former occupier as well as its powerful patrons in the West. Similarly, regarding the sea controversy, numerous "pragmatists" contend that Dili should just settle for less than it deserves and work on trying to improve upon its relationship with Canberra. Given the power imbalance between East Timor and Australia, and the need for Dili to maintain good relations with its southern neighbor—for reasons ranging from military and defense ties (especially if threats from the TNI were to resurface) to trade relations in the form of preferential treatment for East Timorese goods to multilateral support for the country's multifaceted reconstruction—it makes sense, these pragmatists argue, to try to make the best out of an admittedly unfair situation. Such conventional wisdom has long been an important current in discussions around the world about East Timor—and it has often proved to be wrong. Many key and influential policy makers in the West, for example, long dismissed the possibility of East Timorese independence—up until 1999.

Going back several decades, some leading officials, in fact, envisioned East Timor remaining under imperial Portuguese control almost indefinitely. As Sumner Welles, an undersecretary of state during the U.S. presidential administration of Franklin D. Roosevelt opined in 1943, "it would certainly take a thousand years" before the territory and its people would achieve independence.[16]

Such "realistic" assessments were also common during the Indonesian era, when many in Washington, London, Canberra, and other capitals argued that championing East Timorese self-determination was a lost cause. A "Top Secret" analysis by the U.S. Central Intelligence Agency, issued only five days after Jakarta's full-scale invasion of Portuguese Timor, envisaged that Fretilin would "probably make a maximum effort to publicize its own cause and attempts at spectacular shows of resistance." But over the long run, the CIA memorandum predicted, "such actions are unlikely either to seriously disturb Indonesian control or to arouse much foreign interest."[17] And certainly there were times when such an analysis seemed correct—owing to, among other reasons, the West's willingness to support the Suharto regime and, not least, Jakarta's determination to maintain East Timor within the Indonesian fold. As Indonesian Defense Minister General Benny Murdani told a gathering of East Timorese civil servants on February 3, 1990:

> Don't dream about having . . . a state of Timtim [the Indonesian phrase for East Timor]. . . . There is no such thing as a Timtim nation, there is only an Indonesian nation. . . .
>
> [I]f you try to make your own state . . . it will be crushed by ABRI [TNI]. . . . [T]here have been bigger rebellions, there have been greater differences of opinion with the government than the small number calling themselves Fretilin, or whoever their sympathizers are here. We will crush them all! I repeat, we will crush them all![18]

Benny Murdani, like Sumner Welles and the CIA, turned out to be incorrect. The question is why?

●

That East Timor, given the country's tiny size, its geographical isolation, and the power of those who had a vested interest in seeing it remain part of Indonesia, would ultimately win its struggle for self-determination was anything but a foregone conclusion. How and why East Timor was able to overcome daunting odds is a huge matter to which I cannot do justice within the scope of this book. Another book is needed. Nevertheless a few thoughts on this important issue are in order.

The determination and sophistication of the East Timorese resistance was clearly a key factor in its ultimate success.[19] But larger structural factors ("structure" here referring to the activities of large collectivities of people and associated institutions) and changes in structural power were also crucial. These included pressures in the mid- and late 1990s exerted by pro-democracy, labor, human rights, and other political movements, ranging from mildly reformist to radical, within Indonesia;[20] efforts by foreign capitalists and international financial institutions to liberalize and make more transparent Indonesia's economy; and the activities of numerous actors within Indonesia and abroad who helped to bring about the country's economic crisis. These pressures provided openings for East Timor and its allies, opportunities they effectively exploited but without which their struggle for formal national self-determination would probably still be ongoing.[21]

Part of the shift in power involved a weakening of the collective resolve of various Western governments supporting Indonesia. In part, this was arguably a function of the end of the Cold War and the diminishing of Indonesia's geopolitical importance in terms of the so-called East-West conflict.[22] The shift was also very much related to the rise of an international solidarity movement in the aftermath of the 1991 Santa Cruz massacre that effectively organized in a transnational manner and pressured various national governments and international institutions to take positions more amenable to East Timorese self-determination.[23] Many governments and elected officials who had hitherto shown very little sympathy or concern for the East Timorese shifted toward positions more favorable to the East Timor cause over the course of the 1990s, resulting in important policy initiatives and providing further openings for the international solidarity movement. The resulting pressures on Jakarta did not escape notice there. When the U.S. State Department, for example, blocked the transfer of a handful of U.S.-made F-5 fighter jets from Jordan to Indonesia for, among other reasons, human rights concerns, *The Jakarta Post* editorialized that the move "resounded like [a] sonic boom" in Indonesia's capital.[24] In addition to demonstrating the importance of nonstate actors and various forms of organizing in shaping international politics and the potential for using morality-laden arguments to move policy makers, the case of East Timor also illustrates the significance of marketing human rights causes:[25] the East Timorese resistance and its supporters abroad internationalized the issue of East Timor to an unusually successful degree. That East Timor is predominantly Catholic and thus was able to exploit formal and informal international institutional links not enjoyed — at least to the same extent — by other religions (and thus provide the Catholic Church in East Timor with an unusually high level of institutional autonomy in the occupied country) was also undoubtedly an important factor.[26]

Thus, by 1999, many key actors within the governments of Jakarta's allies had made an assessment that it was time for Indonesia to get out of East Timor — or, at the very least, they were ambivalent about the matter. Domestically — within the countries represented by those governments — East Timor had become an issue of debate, largely as a result of the growing effectiveness of solidarity and human rights groups and the resulting activism within national legislative bodies. This led to various pressures on the bilateral relationships between Western countries and Indonesia. And, internationally, East Timor's cause had become increasingly validated over the course of the 1990s (e.g., the 1996 Nobel Peace Prize going to two East Timorese), the result of the collective efforts of the various national groups and the sophisticated work of the East Timorese resistance. Hence it had become more difficult for government officials in Western countries to act dismissively or apathetically toward Jakarta's occupation of the Connecticut-size territory. Thus, while support for Indonesia's invasion and occupation had exacted relatively little cost prior to the early 1990s, such support was proving increasingly costly and damaging to the various bilateral relationships in the years that followed. And in terms of Indonesia itself, its economic meltdown in 1998 and the associated political instability made all the more evident the costs on many fronts of maintaining an occupation. These and other factors came together to produce a situation where Western governmental actors wanted to see a resolution to the conflict and, on that basis, provided various forms of support to the U.N.-run popular consultation in East Timor in 1999.

It is important to keep in mind the significance of past international activism around East Timor at a time when the prospects for legal justice for the country and its people seemed close to dead. As the cases of Argentina and Chile demonstrate, such matters have a remarkable capacity to become resurrected — even after many years have passed. But what makes the case of East Timor more difficult is the international dimension of the atrocities; it was not primarily a civil war — as in Rwanda and El Salvador, for example — but one involving the invasion of one country by another. There is thus an extra set of power dynamics at work that stymie efforts to realize justice and accountability.

East Timor's political leadership is severely constrained by the need to maintain a working relationship with Indonesia — on a variety of matters including trade, security along their common land and sea boundaries, and movement of people and goods between the enclave of Oecussi and the rest of East Timor—and to avoid alienating powerful members of the international community. It is for such reasons that the political leadership has made clear that the pursuit of justice is, first and foremost, an international responsibility, as opposed to being the task of the tiny and highly vulnerable East Timorese government.[27]

International responsibility to pursue justice is more than one of strategy. It is primarily one of politico-legal obligation. As international solidarity activists wrote to the CNRT Congress in August 2000, "the issue of justice goes beyond the scope of East Timor. The crimes committed by the TNI in East Timor are not ordinary crimes. They are crimes against Humanity. As such, they . . . concern Humanity as a whole. Not addressing these crimes will undermine the international efforts for accountability and prevention of further such crimes." In this regard, justice is important not only for East Timorese society itself but also for the promotion of human rights and the rule of law in Indonesia and throughout the world.

This justice must be one that seeks full accountability for war crimes and crimes against humanity committed from 1975 to 1999. To realize this requires challenging the United Nations but, more important, the powerful countries that supported Indonesia, especially the United States, Britain, and France, given their positions as permanent members of the U.N. Security Council.

An uncountable number of crimes against humanity and war crimes were committed during the 1975–99 period in East Timor. Although an international court could not pursue anything approaching them all, it could prosecute a limited number of the worst crimes—such as the 1975 invasion, the mass killings at Lacluta in 1981 and Kraras in 1983, the 1991 massacre at the Santa Cruz Cemetery, and a handful of the most horrible atrocities committed in 1999. Such an approach would have the advantage of limiting the duration and costs of the tribunal while covering the entire period of the Indonesian invasion and occupation, thus increasing the likelihood that many of the principal architects and perpetrators would be held accountable.

It would also confirm that the invasion, occupation, and destruction of East Timor by Indonesia was a long-standing, systematic, criminal conspiracy, planned and ordered at the highest levels of government. Many of the perpetrators continue to wield authority and influence in neighboring Indonesia. Hence the future of peace, justice, and democracy in both East Timor and Indonesia depends on removing those people from power.

●

Just how significant the implications of truth and justice for East Timor are beyond the boundaries of Indonesia and its former twenty-seventh province became intensely clear to me on December 14, 2003, when I first learned of the U.S. military's capture of Saddam Hussein in Iraq, and read President George W. Bush's promise that the former Iraqi dictator would "face the justice he denied to millions." I had just completed reading a friend's manuscript for a book on the events preceding the bloody seizure of power in Indonesia by General Suharto, a man responsible for the deaths of hundreds of thousands.[28] But unlike in the case of Hussein, Washington and its wealthy and militarily powerful allies have no desire that Suharto and his accomplices be held accountable for their crimes.

Thus, today, the retired Suharto resides comfortably in Jakarta, and the brutal military he helped to build remains intact, free to commit atrocities throughout the Indonesian archipelago. Similarly officials from the United States, Britain, and Australia, who were complicit in the 1965–66 slaughter in East Timor and in Indonesia's twenty-four-year reign of terror there, continue to lead their lives unhindered.

In October 2003 *The Toledo Blade,* a newspaper based in Toledo, Ohio, published an extraordinary four-day series about U.S. soldiers in Vietnam in 1967, a forty-five-member elite paratrooper group called "Tiger Force." The soldiers deliberately killed hundreds of unarmed men, women, and children in a seven-month period. They tortured and executed prisoners, raped villagers, kicked out the teeth of the dead for gold fillings, and cut off their victims' ears and scalps, keeping them as souvenirs.

William Doyle, a former Tiger Force sergeant, explained to the *Blade* how he and his fellow soldiers were able to carry out their actions: "You can do any damn thing you want to, anywhere you want to. . . . Who's going to check you? What's the checks and balances? There's not any. You're calling all the shots." He went on to say that his only regret was that he didn't kill more.[29]

Despite the shocking revelations and the fact that the reporters responsible for the series received the prestigious Pulitzer Prize several months later, most major newspapers and television networks in the United States gave the reports short shrift or ignored them. Similarly Washington officialdom responded with silence. Thus, for most people in the United States, the events effectively never happened.

Such disregard is part of a pattern of postwar behavior, one that has allowed U.S. political structures, modes of behavior, and individual actors responsible for Vietnam-era crimes to remain unscathed. In the specific case reported by the *Blade,* for example, a Pentagon investigation substantiated that Tiger Force members had committed twenty war crimes. However, no one was prosecuted.

Yet to focus on the individual soldiers who committed the atrocities or the officers that encouraged them is to miss a larger issue of accountability regarding the illegitimacy of the very U.S. presence in Vietnam and the systematic death and destruction that accompanied it.[30] Whereas about 58,200 U.S. soldiers tragically lost their lives, the Vietnamese suffered an estimated 2 million to 3 million deaths. Since the war's end, U.S. land mines and unexploded ordnance have killed or maimed at least 100,000. And about 500,000 Vietnamese children have been born with birth defects believed to be related to Agent Orange, with many second- and third-generation children currently feeling the effects of U.S chemical warfare.[31]

Today most people in the United States have little knowledge of the true nature of the U.S. involvement in Vietnam and the human toll it exacted and continues to incur.[32] Similarly most people in the relevant Western countries have little to no knowledge of the role of their governments in aiding, abetting, or facilitating Indonesia's crimes. In both cases, the ignorance and "forgetting" have facilitated an absence of accountability. From aiding and abetting Indonesian atrocities in East Timor from 1975 to 1999 to the current debacle in Iraq—one that, although U.S-led, not so coincidentally involves troops from Britain, Australia, and Japan—to the painful material poverty experienced by so many in contemporary East Timor, the ill effects of forgetting and allowing impunity for the crimes and complicity of the West in these events continue to endure.

Regarding the importance of remembering and forgetting, let us recall Bill Clinton's words to a journalist questioning his administration's policies toward East Timor in Dili on May 20, 2002: "I think the right thing to do is to do what the leaders of East Timor said. They want to look forward, you want to look backward. I'm going to stick with the leaders. You want to look backward. Have at it, but you'll have to have help from someone else."

Clinton's words and, more important, the practices they serve to shield and the associated unjust privilege they seek to perpetuate are an inextricable part of the horror experienced by the people of East Timor. The horror is not limited to East Timor's territory. Nor is it distant from places such as Washington, London, Canberra, and Tokyo. Although we are relatively insulated from its most shocking manifestations and most pernicious effects—a manifestation of what we might call imperial privilege, one that derives from and reproduces the unjust structures of the global political economy—the horror and many of the agents responsible for it are among us.

It is for these reasons, and for the sake of the people of East Timor and Indonesia, for others throughout the world who face the direct or indirect violence of Washington and its allies, as well as for our own sake, that we have to be that "someone else" to whom Bill Clinton inadvertently issued a challenge to remember and to fight for accountability for past atrocities. Accepting this challenge is a critical component of efforts to realize a world free of ground zeros and the underlying and resulting injustices.

NOTES

1. ENCOUNTERING GROUND ZERO

The sources of the epigraphs to the chapter are, respectively, James E. Young, *The Texture of Memory: Holocaust Memorials and Meaning* (New Haven: Yale University Press, 1993), 1; and John Lindsay-Poland, "Soft-Peddling American Intervention," *Peace Review* 8, no. 2 (June 1996): 181.

1. Seth Mydans, "U.N. Peacekeepers Stake Timor Claim," *The New York Times,* September 21, 1999, A1+.
2. TNI became the acronym of the Indonesian military in mid-1999. Prior to that time its acronym was ABRI. President Habibie changed the name as a way of suggesting a break with ABRI's ugly past. Herein I use the acronym TNI regardless of the time period in which I am referring to the military.
3. Maggie O'Kane, "Enter the Peacekeepers: Calm, Efficient—And Two Weeks Too Late," *The Guardian Weekly,* September 23–29, 1999, 1–2.
4. For an analysis of the debate surrounding the death toll in East Timor, see Ben Kiernan, "The Demography of Genocide in Southeast Asia: The Death Tolls in Cambodia, 1975–79, and East Timor, 1975–80," *Critical Asian Studies* 35, no. 4 (2003): 585–597.
5. See James Dunn, "Genocide in East Timor: The Attempt to Destroy a Society and Its Culture," in *The East Timor Problem and the Role of Europe,* ed. Pedro Pinto Leite (Leiden: International Platform of Jurists, 1998), 83–94. Also see Roger S. Clark, "Does the Genocide Convention Go Far Enough?: Some Thoughts on the Nature of Criminal Genocide in the Context of Indonesia's Invasion of East Timor," *Ohio Northern University Law Review* 8:2 (1981): 321–328. For a thoughtful analysis of the complexities of, and problems with, applying the term "genocide" (as an international legal concept) to East Timor, see Derrick Silove, "Conflict in East Timor: Genocide or Expansionist Occupation?" *Human Rights Review* 1, no. 3 (April–June 2000): 62–79; see also Ben Saul, "Was the Conflict in East Timor 'Genocide' and Why Does It Matter?" *Melbourne Journal of International Law* 2, no. 2 (October 2001): 477–522.

Regardless of whether the mass killings in East Timor meet the strict guidelines of the genocide convention, which defines genocide as acts aimed at destroying "in whole or in part, a national, ethnic, racial or religious group," the scale and nature of the killings were undoubtedly genocide-like, similar to the bulk of the Khmer Rouge's crimes in Cambodia.

6. Human Rights Watch, "East Timor: Serious Obstacles to Justice Remain" (press release), September 2, 2000. The organization estimates that the TNI and its militia killed an estimated additional one thousand people in the months preceding the ballot. Regarding rapes and sexual enslavement during this period, see Seth Mydans, "Sexual Violence as Tool of War: Pattern Emerging in East Timor," *The New York Times,* March 1, 2001, A1+.

7. For an analysis of the various forms that denial can take and the reasons for them, see Stanley Cohen, *States of Denial: Knowing about Atrocities and Suffering* (Malden, Mass.: Blackwell Publishing, 2001).

8. See Agence France Presse, "US Gave Silent Blessing to Taliban Rise to Power: Analysts," October 7, 2001; available online at http://www.etan.org/. Also see Stephen Zunes, *Tinderbox: U.S. Middle East Policy and the Roots of Terrorism* (Monroe, Maine: Common Courage, 2003).

9. Peter Novick, *The Holocaust in American Life* (New York: Houghton Mifflin, 2000), 9. Also see Norman G. Finkelstein, *The Holocaust Industry: Reflections on the Exploitation of Jewish Suffering* (New York: Verso, 2000).

10. Sven Lindqvist, *"Exterminate All the Brutes": One Man's Odyssey into the Heart of Darkness and the Origins of European Genocide* (New York: The New Press, 1996).

11. Ibid., x. See also Finkelstein, *Holocaust Industry.*

12. Adam Hochschild, *King Leopold's Ghost: A Story of Greed, Terror, and Heroism in Colonial Africa* (New York: Houghton Mifflin, 1998), 294.

13. Eqbal Ahmad, "Terrorism: Theirs and Ours," presentation at the University of Colorado, October 12, 1998. Speech available online at http://www.irr.org.uk/terrorism/index.htm. A brief biography of Eqbal Ahmad is available online at http://www.bitsonline.net/eqbal/biography.asp/.

14. See Colin Tatz, *Genocide in Australia* (Canberra: Australian Institute of Aboriginal and Torres Strait Islander Studies, 1999).

15. There are many excellent works on the Rwanda genocide. Two of the most authoritative are Gérard Prunier, *The Rwanda Crisis: History of a Genocide* (New York: Columbia University Press, 1997); and Alison Des Forges, *Leave None to Tell the Story: Genocide in Rwanda* (New York: Human Rights Watch, 1999). Also see Peter Uvin, *Aiding Violence: The Development Enterprise in Rwanda* (West Hartford: Kumarian, 1998). Most well known is Phillip Gourevitch, *We Wish to Inform You That We Will Be Killed with Our Families: Stories from Rwanda* (New York: Farrar, Straus and Giroux, 1998).

16. See Ward Churchill, *A Little Matter of Genocide* (San Francisco: City Lights Books, 2000).

17. See Elizabeth Olson, "U.N. Says Millions of Children, Caught in Poverty, Die Needlessly," *The New York Times,* March 14, 2002, A11. See also Paul Farmer, *Infections and Inequalities: The Modern Plagues* (Berkeley: University of California Press, 1999).

18. See Johan Galtung, "Violence, Peace, and Peace Research," *Journal of Peace Research* 6, no. 3 (1969): 167–191.

19. Regarding nations as imagined communities, see Benedict Anderson, *Imagined Communities: Reflections on the Origin and Spread of Nationalism* (London: Verso, 1991).

20. See, for example, Samantha Power, *"A Problem from Hell": America and the Age of Genocide* (New York: Basic Books, 2002). Also see William Shawcross, *Deliver Us from Evil: Peacekeepers, Warlords and a World of Endless Conflict* (New York: Simon and Schuster, 2000).

21. See Stephen Lukes, *Power: A Radical View* (London: The MacMillan Press, 1974); and

John Gaventa, *Power and Powerlessness: Quiescence and Rebellion in an Appalachian Valley* (Urbana: University of Illinois Press, 1980). Also see Cohen, *States of Denial,* 2001.

22. See Avishai Margalit, *The Ethics of Memory* (Cambridge, Mass.: Harvard University Press, 2002).

23. See Eric Wolf, *Europe and the People Without History* (Berkeley: University of California Press, 1982).

24. See Richard C. Lewontin, *Biology as Ideology: The Doctrine of DNA* (New York: Harper Perennial, 1991).

25. See Howard Zinn, "Objections to Objectivity," *Z Magazine,* October 1989, 58–62.

26. For a noteworthy compilation of both classic and new articles on the relationship between states and violence, see Catherine Besteman, ed., *Violence: A Reader* (New York: New York University Press, 2002).

27. Most important among these assumptions are that states are selfish, unified actors, that the international system of states is competitive and anarchic (not in the sense of chaos but rather the absence of effective governance on the global level and hence a lack of security), and thus that states need to put national security concerns at the center of their international policies.

There are differences among these elites, but they are limited to the narrow spectrum defined by the realist-liberal split. The realists understand anarchy to be a constant in history and tend to be suspicious of international institutions and their ability to protect the well-being of individuals and collectivities from external threats. Therefore they advocate that states put security concerns at the center of their international policies. Typically realists see unilateralism as a better guarantor of the national interest than multilateralism, and embrace the national territorial state as the best protector of individual rights. Liberals differ to the extent that they perceive anarchy as ameliorable and are more hopeful about international cooperation. In this regard, they see international institutions as having the potential to reduce international anarchy and bring about a better context in which states can pursue their interests and resolve interstate conflict. See Peter J. Katzenstein, "Introduction: Alternative Perspectives on National Security," in *The Culture of National Security: Norms and Identity in World Politics,* ed. Peter J. Katzenstein, 1–32 (New York: Columbia University Press, 1996). For various perspectives within the (neo)realist school, see J.D.B. Miller and R. J. Vincent, eds., *Order and Violence: Hedley Bull and International Relations* (Oxford: Clarendon, 1990).

Realists characteristically see balances of power between potent states, and strategic alliances among like-minded polities as the answer to this quandary. Meanwhile, liberals in their various forms champion international institutions or the democratization of states or both, under the supposition that authoritarian and militaristic polities are more warlike than democratic ones, which, these analysts argue, have a tendency to extend their domestic norms to the international arena. See K. J. Holsti, *The State, War, and the State of War* (Cambridge: Cambridge University Press, 1996).

28. See Mary Kaldor, *New and Old Wars: Organized Violence in a Global Era* (Stanford, Calif.: Stanford University Press, 2001); and Holsti, *State of War,* 1996.

29. See, for example, David J. McCraw, "Idealism and Realism in the Foreign Policy of the Fourth Labour Government," *Political Science* (New Zealand) 53, no. 2 (December 2001): 21–37.

A problem with using the notion of "national interest" to explain a government's behavior is that it ignores the process by which specific groups construct that very "national interest" as a politico-ideological device to advance particular agendas. See Jutta Weldes, *Constructing National Interests: The United States and the Cuban Missile Crisis* (Minneapolis: The University of Minnesota Press, 1999).

30. Proponents of this argument apply it to Western Europe, and to countries such as the United States, Australia, and Canada. However, this contention ignores the fact that

all these countries have engaged in bloody bouts of ethnic and political cleansing, and social and territorial boundary making, as part of the process in building their own nation-state — but in an earlier time. Such bloodletting, apparently, is a tragically normal element of modern territorial state making. See Michael Mann "The Dark Side of Democracy: The Modern Tradition of Ethnic and Political Cleansing" *New Left Review*, no. 235 (May/June 1999): 18–45.

As another commentator has written, "If indeed Western Europe has become a kind of Switzerland writ large, a place where war never interrupted business and it was safe to dream utopian dreams undisturbed by the sound of cannon fire or fighter-bombers shrieking across the sky, that is at least partly because Western Europe has already *had* its wars of religion, its genocides, its 'ethnic cleansing' — year after year, century after century" (David Rieff, *A Bed for the Night: Humanitarianism in Crisis* [New York: Simon and Shuster, 2002], 73).

31. See Daniele Archibugi, "So What If Democracies Don't Fight Each Other?" *Peace Review* 9, no. 3 (September 1997): 379–384.

32. The leader in this undeclared war against the Third World has long been the United States. See Gabriel Kolko, *Confronting the Third World: United States Foreign Policy, 1945–1980* (New York: Pantheon, 1988).

33. See John Agnew and Stuart Corbridge, *Mastering Space: Hegemony, Territory and International Political Economy* (London: Routledge, 1995).

34. Tarak Barkawi and Mark Laffey, "The Imperial Peace: Democracy, Force and Globalization," *European Journal of International Relations* 5, no. 4 (1999): 403–434.

35. See Lakshman Yapa, "What Causes Poverty? A Postmodern View," *Annals of the Association of American Geographers* 86, no. 4 (December 1996): 707–728; and Tim Mitchell, "America's Egypt: Discourse of the Development Industry," *Middle East Report* (March–April 1991): 18–36.

36. Barkawi and Laffey, "The Imperial Peace," 1999.

37. See ibid.

38. See, for example, Martin Shaw, "The State of Globalization: Towards a Theory of State Transformation," *Review of International Political Economy* 4, no. 3 (autumn 1997): 497–513. These states are almost synonymous with the member-states of the Organization for Economic Cooperation and Development (OECD), an entity made up of thirty countries that, according to the OECD website, share "a commitment to democratic government and the market economy."

In making his case about the rise of a kind of Western global state, Shaw argues, "Despite undoubted economic rivalries and political tensions between national elites, and deep social conflicts, these have not taken the form of serious violence. The coherence and stability of the western state bloc have been problematic, internally in the relations of its component states and in their relations with society, and externally in their relations with other centers of state power. But its coherence has been developed and its stability managed, overall with considerable success" (501).

39. See Barbara Stallings, "International Influence in Economic Policy: Debt, Stabilization, and Structural Reforms," in *The Politics of Economic Adjustment: International Constraints, Distributive Conflicts, and the State,* ed. Stephen Haggard and Robert R. Kaufman, 41–88 (Princeton, N.J.: Princeton University Press, 1992).

International relations are those between states, whereas transnational relations include extra-national involvement on the part of nonstate actors. See Thomas Risse-Kappen, ed., *Bringing Transnational Relations Back In: Non-state Actors, Domestic Structures, and International Institutions* (Cambridge: Cambridge University Press, 1995).

40. A classic example of this school of thought is Noam Chomsky and Edward S. Herman, *The Washington Connection and Third World Fascism,* Vol. 1, *The Political Economy of Human Rights* (Cambridge, Mass.: South End Press, 1979).

One can also apply a political-economy perspective to conflicts within nation-states or local communities. See Geoffrey Robinson, *The Dark Side of Paradise: Political Violence in Bali* (Ithaca, N.Y.: Cornell University Press, 1995); and Uvin, *Aiding Violence,* as examples of such an approach to cases of mass violence.

41. See Johan Galtung, "A Structural Theory of Imperialism," *African Review* 1, no. 4 (1972): 93–138. Also see Barkawi and Laffey, "The Imperial Peace," 1999.

42. At the same time countries regularly "outsource" terror, to use the words of Israeli political scientist Neve Gordon. Drawing on the activities of his own country's political and military establishment, Gordon shows that national governments — mimicking the practices of corporations — frequently subcontract out (to collaborators, proxy military forces, private sector businesses, etc.) the commission of human rights violations so as to mask their own moral and political responsibility. See Neve Gordon, "Outsourcing Violations: The Israeli Case," *Journal of Human Rights* 1, no. 3 (September 2002): 321–337.

43. For some classic and path-breaking writings on these matters, see Maurice Halbwachs, *On Collective Memory,* ed. and trans., and with an introduction by, Lewis A. Coser (Chicago: University of Chicago Press, 1992).

   Fentress and Wickham argue that the term "social memory" is more appropriate. They contend that Halbwachs and others have emphasized the collective at the expense of the individual, reducing the latter to a sort of automaton shaped by the larger society and neglecting the matter of individual consciousness and its relation to the group(s) of which the individual is part. See James Fentress and Chris Wickham, *Social Memory* (Oxford: Blackwell, 1992).

44. In discussing collective memory versus history, I draw upon Robert D. Benford, "Whose War Memories Shall Be Preserved?" *Peace Review* 8, no. 2 (June 1996): 189–194; Fentress and Wickham, *Social Memory;* Elliot J. Gorn, "Professing History: Distinguishing between Memory and the Past," *Chronicle of Higher Education* (April 28, 2000): B4–B5; Jerry Lembcke, *The Spitting Image: Myth, Memory, and the Legacy of Vietnam* (New York: New York University Press, 1998); and Novick, Holocaust, 2000.

2. PRE-BALLOT EAST TIMOR

The sources of the epigraphs to the chapter are, respectively, Richard Wright, "The Psychological Reactions of Oppressed People," *White Man, Listen!* (New York: Harper Perennial, 1995), 21; Carolyn Forché, introduction to *Against Forgetting: Twentieth-Century Poetry of Witness,* ed. Carolyn Forché (New York: Norton, 1993), 46; and Nina Ognianova, "I thought . . . my tapes! How can they be safe?" International Journalists Network online, October 17, 2003; available at http://www.ijnet.org/FE Article/newsarticle.asp?UILang=1&CId=151310&CIdLang=1.

1. Fretilin is the Portuguese-language acronym for the Revolutionary Front for an Independent East Timor. In independent East Timor it is now the party of government.

   The East Timorese elite founded a number of political parties within a few weeks of the April 1974 coup that overthrew the Portuguese military dictatorship and initiated a process of democratization and decolonization in Lisbon's colonies in Asia and Africa. Only three of these parties played a significant role in shaping the decolonization process in what was then known as Portuguese Timor: the UDT (Timorese Democratic Union); the ASDT (Association of Timorese Social Democrats, later to become Fretilin); and Apodeti (Timorese Popular Democratic Association).

   The UDT, the first party founded, quickly became the most popular. Generally conservative and pro-Portugal, the UDT's most prominent members represented East Timor's wealthiest citizens, many of whom were senior administrative officials in Dili or leading plantation owners, and some indigenous elites. The UDT started out strongly in favor of a continued association with Portugal, but, in the face of significant opposition among the populace and within its own party, it quickly evolved to support eventual total independence.

Established soon after the UDT's founding, the ASDT based its program on "the universal doctrines of socialism and democracy" and "the rejection of colonialism." Fully committed to independence, the ASDT envisioned an eight- to ten-year period of decolonization during which time the East Timorese could develop the appropriate political and economic structures necessary for national independence. Populist in its approach, Fretilin's program emphasized the need for literacy campaigns, agrarian reform, a Timorese-oriented educational system, as well as the promotion of local culture, women's and workers' rights, health, and agriculture.

Apodeti was originally called the "Association for the Integration of Timor into Indonesia" and favored an "autonomous integration" with Indonesia. The group, however, quickly changed its name for public relations purposes. By far the smallest of the three major political parties, Apodeti's followers never numbered more than a few hundred, but its influence well exceeded its small membership. Apodeti appears to have been largely a project of Indonesian intelligence. Three of its key leaders all had been cooperating for a number of years with Bakin, the Indonesian army's intelligence service, which had decided in the late 1960s that, for reasons of national stability and security, Indonesia could not permit an independent East Timor. Immediately after Apodeti's founding, Indonesia began providing financial support to its East Timorese agents within the party.

While the UDT began as the largest political group, it quickly began to lose ground to the ASDT. The UDT's initial wavering on the question of independence, the concentration of its political activities in the major towns, and the identification of many of its more prominent members with the old elite worked to the ASDT's favor. In the few months following its creation, the ASDT worked to increase its popularity, winning the support of a number of key *liurais* throughout the country and solidifying its base in rural areas. In September 1974 the ASDT leadership changed the group's name to Fretilin and demanded an immediate declaration of de jure independence from the Portuguese and the establishment of a transitional government that would carry East Timor through a rapid process of decolonization. By early 1975 Fretilin was, by most accounts, including that of the Portuguese administrators, the group that enjoyed the most popular support.

For information on these various political parties, see James Dunn, *Timor: A People Betrayed* (Sydney: ABC Books, 1996); Helen Hill, *Stirrings of Nationalism in East Timor: FRETILIN 1974–1978: The Origins, Ideologies and Strategies of a Nationalist Movement* (Otford, New South Wales, Australia: Otford Press, 2002); Jill Jolliffe, *East Timor: Nationalism and Colonialism* (St. Lucia, Queensland: University of Queensland Press, 1978); José Ramos-Horta, *Funu: The Unfinished Saga of East Timor* (Trenton, N.J.: Red Sea, 1987); and John Taylor, *East Timor: The Price of Freedom* (London: Zed, 1999).

2. See Dunn, *A People Betrayed*; and Geoffrey C. Gunn, *Timor Loro Sae: 500 Years* (Macau: Livros do Oriente, 1999). For oral histories of the brutality suffered at the hands of the Japanese occupiers, see Michele Turner, *Telling: East Timor, Personal Testimonies 1942–1992* (New South Wales, Australia: New South Wales University Press, 1992). Turner's book also contains information regarding atrocities committed by Australian troops against East Timorese whom they suspected of betraying them.

3. Falintil is the Portuguese-language acronym for the Armed Forces of National Liberation of East Timor. At the time it was the military wing of Fretilin. In September 1989 Falintil separated from Fretilin and became the guerrilla army of a unified resistance composed of various political parties and organizations, of which Fretilin was only one

member, albeit a dominant one. Now that East Timor is independent, Falintil no longer exists as a guerrilla army, but many of its soldiers have become members of the national military, called Falintil-FDTL, which has about fifteen hundred active personnel. The head of the force is Taur Matan Ruak, the last head of Falintil before its disbandment.

4. Fretilin's appropriation of the term *maubere* (*bibere* in its feminine form), a term used by the Portuguese to express contempt for the East Timorese masses and to convey to the Portuguese colonialists the idea of East Timorese inferiority, reversed the colonial nuance to one of cultural identity and pride. Thus Fretilin named its ideology *mauberismo*.

Critics often characterized Fretilin as a communist movement — indeed Jakarta used this characterization to justify its invasion. According to James Dunn, however, despite Fretilin's assuming "the mantle of a revolutionary front, it remained essentially a populist, Catholic party whose leaders' attitudes were attuned more to the socialist aims and experiences of similar movements in Third World countries, but especially in Africa, than to those of any communist state" (*A People Betrayed*, 62). See also Hill, *Stirrings of Nationalism*; Jolliffe, *East Timor*; Ramos-Horta, *Funu*; and Taylor, *Price of Freedom*, 1999.

5. Once the Portuguese abandoned its colony, and fearing an imminent full-scale invasion, Fretilin unilaterally declared the Democratic Republic of East Timor independent on November 28, 1975. Fretilin hoped that a relatively high level of recognition of its declaration would protect East Timor from the feared invasion. But despite promises of "certain recognition" within ten days of the declaration from twenty-five countries, including China, the USSR, Norway, Brazil, Sweden, East Germany, and Cuba, only Mozambique, Angola, Guinea Bissau, and Cape Verde quickly granted official recognition (Jolliffe, *East Timor*, 216–217). A total of fifteen countries eventually extended recognition. See Roger Clark, "The 'Decolonisation' of East Timor and the United Nations Norms on Self-Determination and Aggression," in *International Law and the Question of East Timor*, ed. Catholic Institute for International Relations and International Platform of Jurists for East Timor (London: Catholic Institute for International Relations, 1995), 65–102.

The United Nations never recognized Indonesia's invasion and annexation as legitimate. Instead, it perceived the territory and its people as having a still unrealized right to self-determination. It thus recognized Portugal as the administering authority of East Timor.

6. Quoted in the *Tapol Bulletin* (London), September 1983.

7. Taylor, *Price of Freedom*, 1999.

8. Dunn, *A People Betrayed*; Taylor, *Price of Freedom*. Rape and sexual enslavement by Indonesian troops of East Timorese women were common occurrences during the war and the occupation. See Miranda E. Sissons, *From One Day to Another: Violations of Women's Reproductive and Sexual Rights in East Timor* (Fitzroy, Australia: East Timor Human Rights Centre, 1997); Turner, *Telling*; George Aditjondro, "The Silent Suffering of Our Timorese Sisters," in *Free East Timor: Australia's Culpability in East Timor's Genocide*, ed. Jim Aubrey, 243–265 (Sydney: Vintage, 1998); and J. Modvig et al., "Torture and Trauma in Post-Conflict East Timor," *The Lancet* 356:9243 (November 18, 2000): 1763.

9. Carmel Budiardjo and Liem Soei Liong, *The War against East Timor* (London: Zed, 1984).

10. "Jakarta's Timor Dead . . . ," *The Washington Post*, January 9, 1976.

11. Taylor, *Price of Freedom*, 70.

12. Budiardjo and Liem, *The War against East Timor*, 23; see also Dunn, *A People Betrayed*; and Taylor, *Price of Freedom*.

13. Taylor, *Price of Freedom*.

14. Budiardjo and Liem, *The War against East Timor.*
15. Noam Chomsky and Edward S. Herman, *The Washington Connection and Third World Fascism,* Vol. 1, *The Political Economy of Human Rights* (Cambridge, Mass.: South End Press, 1979).
16. Budiardjo and Liem, *The War against East Timor;* and Taylor, *Price of Freedom.*
17. Dunn, *A People Betrayed;* and Taylor, *Price of Freedom.*
18. Taylor, *Price of Freedom;* and Budiardjo and Liem, *The War against East Timor.*
19. Taylor, *Price of Freedom.*
20. Budiardjo and Liem, *The War against East Timor.*
21. Arnold Kohen and John Taylor, *An Act of Genocide: Indonesia's Invasion of East Timor* (London: TAPOL, 1979).
22. Quoted in Taylor, *Price of Freedom,* 97. Politically induced famine-like conditions continued to plague much of East Timor through the early 1980s. See Rod Nordland, "Hunger: Under Indonesia, Timor Remains a Land of Misery," *The Philadelphia Inquirer,* May 28, 1982; reprinted in *East Timor: The Struggle Continues,* ed. Torben Retbøll, 60–80 (Copenhagen: International Work Group for Indigenous Affairs, 1984).
23. For a firsthand account of a participant in the "fence of legs," see Turner, *Telling.*
24. Taylor, *Price of Freedom.*
25. Ibid., 102. Also see Dunn, *A People Betrayed;* Dunn spells Kraras as "Creras." The Australian government assembled a top-secret report on Indonesian atrocities committed in the early years of the war. Based on electronic intelligence and completed in January 1979, only eighteen copies of the report were printed, some of which were distributed to national intelligence agencies in countries allied with Australia. According to a 2002 newspaper account, the report remains highly classified (Hamish McDonald and Desmond Ball, "Blue Book of Horrors Makes a Diplomatic Time Bomb," *Sydney Morning Herald,* February 15, 2002).
26. Asia Watch, *Human Rights in Indonesia and East Timor* (New York: Human Rights Watch, 1989); and Amnesty International, *Power and Impunity: Human Rights under the New Order* (New York: Amnesty International, 1994).
    The death toll has been disputed, with some arguing that an estimate of 200,000 is excessive. For an overview of the debate, see Ben Kiernan, "The Demography of Genocide in Southeast Asia: The Death Tolls in Cambodia, 1975–79, and East Timor, 1975–80," *Critical Asian Studies* 35, no. 4 (2003): 585–597. In the end, Kiernan states that "a toll of 150,000 is likely close to the truth" for the 1975–80 period. But if one adds the numbers of victims killed post-1980 and from the 1981–82 famine, "the figure is substantially higher" (594). One could thus infer from Kiernan that the 200,000 figure is credible if applied to the war and occupation through the 1980s.
27. For a recounting of the politics surrounding the Pope's visit and a firsthand account of the resistance demonstration at the mass, as well as an overview of the various events that made up what some came to characterize as the Timorese intifada, see Constâncio Pinto and Matthew Jardine, *East Timor's Unfinished Struggle: Inside the Timorese Resistance* (Cambridge, Mass.: South End Press, 1997). Also see Andrew McMillan, *Death in Dili* (Rydalmere, Australia: Hodder and Stoughton, 1992).
28. John G. Taylor, *Indonesia's Forgotten War: The Hidden History of East Timor* (London: Zed, 1991); updated and released in late 1999 as *East Timor: The Price of Freedom.*
29. Matthew Jardine, "East Timor: Media Turned Their Backs on Genocide," *Extra!* 7, no. 7 (November/December 1993): 23–24.
30. For an extensive analysis of media coverage of East Timor from the time of the invasion until the late 1980s, see Edward S. Herman and Noam Chomsky, *Manufacturing Consent: The Political Economy of the Mass Media* (New York: Pantheon, 1988). The poor coverage was not limited to the United States. Regarding the situation in Canada, see Peter Eglin, "East Timor, *The Globe and Mail* and Propaganda: The 1990s — Saving In-

donesia from East Timor with 'Maoist Shields' and 'Tragic Destiny,'" *Portuguese Studies Review* 11, no. 1 (2003): 67–84.

31. Media coverage increased noticeably in the aftermath. But the coverage was often misleading and perpetuated a variety of myths about the nature of the conflict. See Jardine, "Media Turned Their Backs on Genocide"; Will Carey, "East Timor: The Making of an International Issue, 1974–99," *Brock Review 1998/99* 7, no. 29 (1998–99): 29–56; and Eglin, "*The Globe and Mail* and Propaganda."

32. See Pinto and Jardine, *East Timor's Unfinished Struggle.*

33. For eyewitness accounts by Western journalists, see Allan Nairn, *The New Yorker,* December 9, 1991; Max Stahl, "Massacre among the Graves," *Independent on Sunday,* November 17, 1991; and Russell Anderson, "The Massacre of 12 November 1991," in *Free East Timor: Australia's Culpability in East Timor's Genocide,* ed. Jim Aubrey (Sydney: Vintage, 1998), 145–152. Also see Pinto and Jardine, *East Timor's Unfinished Struggle.*

34. Matthew Jardine, "Forgotten Genocide: A Little Attention, at Last, for East Timor," *The Progressive* 56, no. 12 (December 1992): 19–21.

35. See Pinto and Jardine, *East Timor's Unfinished Struggle.*

36. Max Stahl, "Dili, the Bloody Aftermath," *Sydney Morning Herald,* February 12, 1994.

37. United Nations Commission on Human Rights, *Report by the Special Rapporteur, Mr. Bacre Waly Ndiaye, on his Mission to Indonesia and East Timor from 3 to 13 July 1994* (E/CN.4/1995/61/Add.1), November 1, 1994.

38. See Hannah Arendt, *Eichmann in Jerusalem: A Report on the Banality of Evil* (New York: Viking, 1973 [1963].

39. In June 2000 I did see Eduardo again. Like many high-level members of the resistance, Eduardo and his longtime girlfriend married not long after the Indonesian withdrawal. They had a daughter soon thereafter, whom they named *Vitoria,* or "Victory." Eduardo now lives in Dili and works with former members of the resistance, trying to help them find employment and to adapt to the realities of an independent East Timor.

40. Alfred Russel Wallace, *The Malay Archipelago: The Land of the Orang-utan, and the Bird of Paradise,* 2 vols. (London: MacMillan, 1869), 1:307.

41. Dunn, *A People Betrayed.*

42. Taylor, *Indonesia's Forgotten War;* and Dunn, *A People Betrayed.*

43. Glen Francis, "Slavery in Timor," *The Observer* (Sydney, Australia) 3, no. 22 (October 29, 1960): 12–13.

44. Taylor, *Indonesia's Forgotten War.* For a thorough history of East Timor prior to the time of the Indonesian invasion, see Gunn, *Timor Loro Sae.*

45. A. Diaz de Rábago, "Portuguese Timor," *New Catholic Encyclopedia,* Vol. 14 (New York: McGraw-Hill, 1967), 165–166.

46. Dunn *A People Betrayed;* and Jill Jolliffe, *East Timor: Nationalism and Colonialism* (St. Lucia, Queensland: University of Queensland Press, 1978).

47. Robert Archer, "The Catholic Church in East Timor," in *East Timor at the Crossroads: The Forging of a Nation,* ed. Peter Carey and G. Carter Bentley (Honolulu: University of Hawaii Press, in association with the Social Science Research Council, New York, 1995), 120–133. Also see Arnold Kohen, *From the Place of the Dead: The Epic Struggles of Bishop Belo of East Timor* (New York: St. Martin's, 1999). Kohen's book is the most comprehensive history of the Catholic Church in the former Portuguese colony.

48. Quoted in Taylor, *Indonesia's Forgotten War,* 157.

49. The official press release is available online at http://www.nobel.se/peace/laureates/1996/press.html.

50. Matthew Jardine, "In East Timor, Teetering on the Edge of More Bloodshed," *The Washington Post,* March 2, 1997, C3.

51. The trip is recounted in Matthew Jardine, "The U.S.-Indonesia Alliance against East Timor," *The Christian Science Monitor,* January 14, 1997. A longer, more detailed version

appears as "For East Timor's Guerrillas, the Struggle Continues . . . ," *Estafeta* (newsletter of the East Timor Action Network/U.S.), vol. 2, no. 4/vol. 3, no. 1 (winter 1996–97): 6–7.

52. See Matthew Jardine, "The Life and Death of David Alex and the Ongoing Struggle for East Timor," *Cultural Survival Quarterly* 21, no. 3 (fall 1997): 42–45.

　　In the aftermath of Indonesia's withdrawal in 1999, some individuals in Dili inspected the grave in which the Indonesian authorities had supposedly buried David Alex. It was empty.

53. See John Martinkus, *A Dirty Little War* (Sydney: Random House Australia, 2001), 70–73. José Antonio Belo currently lives in Dili with his wife and children. He works as a cameraman and reporter for a number of foreign media outlets, including the Australian Associated Press. In 2003 José traveled to Washington, D.C., to receive the Knight International Press Fellowship Award for his journalistic work in Indonesian-occupied East Timor. For an article about José's life and work, see Nina Ognianova, "I thought . . . my tapes! How can they be safe?" International Journalists Network online, October 17, 2003; available online at http://www.ijnet.org/FE_Article/newsarticle.asp?UILang=1&CId=151310&CIdLang$

54. The two most important languages in East Timor during this time were Tetum—the indigenous lingua franca—and Indonesian. Like most people of his generation, João Guterres spoke both.

55. The East Timor Action Network/U.S. published an action alert on the arrests of João Guterres and José Antonio Belo in *Estafeta* 3, nos. 2–3 (autumn 1997): 9.

56. The information about João comes from José Antonio Belo who related it to journalist John Martinkus. Martinkus recounts the information but refers to João as John Malanno (*A Dirty Little War,* 71).

3. MEANWHILE IN WASHINGTON . . . AND OTHER CAPITALS

The sources of the epigraphs to the chapter are, respectively, Noam Chomsky, "Nefarious Aggression," *Z Magazine,* October 1990, 19; Reuters, "Australian Warships Sail for Persian Gulf Amid Protests," August 13, 1990.

1. U.S. Congress, "United States Policy toward Indonesia," hearing before the Subcommittee on Asia and the Pacific of the Committee on International Relations, House of Representatives, 105th Congress, May 7, 1997 (Washington, D.C.: U.S. Government Printing Office, 1998), 1.

2. Ibid., 18.

3. Ibid., 58. The spellings "Suharto" and "Soeharto" are interchangeable.

　　For an analysis of Wolfowitz's position on Indonesia and East Timor, and his post-1999 efforts to present himself as a critic of the Suharto regime, see Tim Shorrock, "Paul Wolfowitz: A Man to Keep a Close Eye On," *Asia Times,* March 21, 2001; available online at http://www.atimes.com/se-asia/CC21Ae01.html.

4. U.S. Congress, "United States Policy toward Indonesia," 8–9.

5. Ibid., 11.

6. Ibid., 8–9.

7. Sidney Lens, *The Forging of the American Empire: From the Revolution to Vietnam, a History of U.S. Imperialism* (London: Pluto Press, in conjunction with Haymarket Books [Chicago], 2003). Also see Thomas Schoonover, *Uncle Sam's War of 1898 and the Origins of Globalization* (Lexington: University Press of Kentucky, 2003).

8. Peter Hayes, Lyuba Zarsky, and Walden Bello, *American Lake: Nuclear Peril in the Pacific* (Ridwood, Victoria, Australia: Penguin, 1986).

In a key (formerly top-secret) document from 1948, George Kennan, director of the Policy Planning Staff at the U.S. State Department, laid out what many regard as a key component of the thinking that informed post–World War II U.S. policy in the region, if not throughout much of the world. Noting that the United States had "about 50% of the world's wealth but only 6.3% of its population," Kennan advised:

Our real task in the coming period is to devise a pattern of relationships which will permit us to maintain this position of disparity without positive detriment to our national security. . . .

We should make a careful study to see what parts of the Pacific and Far Eastern world are absolutely vital to our security, and we should concentrate our policy on seeing to it that those areas remain in hands which we can control or rely on. . . . To do so, we will have to dispense with all sentimentality. . . . We should cease to talk about vague and . . . unreal objectives such as human rights, the raising of living standards, and democratization.

From George F. Kennan, "Review of Current Trends, U.S. Foreign Policy," PPS/23, Top Secret. Included in U.S. Department of State, *Foreign Relations of the United States, 1948,* vol. 1, part 2 (Washington, D.C.: Government Printing Office, 1976), 524–525.

9. See, for example, Henry Cabot Lodge, "We Can Win in Vietnam," *The New York Times Magazine,* January 17, 1965, 15+.

10. "Why the U.S. Risks War for Indo-China," *U.S. News & World Report,* April 16, 1954, 23.

11. See Audrey R. Kahin and George McT. Kahin, *Subversion as Foreign Policy: The Secret Eisenhower and Dulles Debacle in Indonesia* (New York: New Press, 1995).

12. The convention defines as genocide acts aimed at destroying "in whole or in part, a national, ethnic, racial or religious group." The architects of the genocide convention made the explicit decision to exclude political groups. They did so in order to insure the support of many countries, largely those of the Soviet bloc and some from Latin America as well, which feared that the inclusion of political groups would inhibit the ability of states to suppress armed rebellions within their boundaries. See Samantha Power, *"A Problem from Hell": America and the Age of Genocide* (New York: Basic Books, 2002).

13. Noam Chomsky, *Year 501: The Conquest Continues* (Cambridge, Mass.: South End Press, 1993), 122–123.

14. *Time,* July 15, 1966. Also see Chomsky, *Year 501,* 123–131.

15. Quoted in John Roosa, *Pretext for Mass Murder: The September 30th Movement and Suharto's Coup d'Etat in Indonesia* (Madison: University of Wisconsin Press, forthcoming in 2005).

16. For a discussion of the U.S. role, see Geoffrey Robinson, *The Dark Side of Paradise: Political Violence in Bali* (Ithaca, N.Y.: Cornell University Press, 1995); Kahin and Kahin, *Subversion as Foreign Policy;* and Roosa, *Pretext for Mass Murder.*

17. Kathy Kadane, "Ex-agents say CIA Compiled Death Lists for Indonesians," *San Francisco Examiner,* May 20, 1990; available online at http://www.pir.org/kadane.html.

18. See James Dunn, *Timor: A People Betrayed* (Sydney: ABC Books, 1996); and John Taylor, *East Timor: The Price of Freedom* (London: Zed, 1999).

19. Quotes from William Burr and Michael L. Evans, eds., *East Timor Revisited: Ford, Kissinger and the Indonesian Invasion, 1975–76, National Security Archive Electronic Briefing Book,* no. 62, Document 1, December 6, 2001; available online at http://www.gwu.edu/~nsarchiv/NSAEBB/NSAEBB62/.

20. Hamish McDonald, *Suharto's Indonesia* (Honolulu: University Press of Hawaii, 1981).

21. Text of cable available in Wendy Way, Damien Browne, and Vivianne Johnson, eds., *Australia and the Indonesian Incorporation of Portuguese Timor, 1974–1976* (Carlton, Victoria: Melbourne University Press, 2000), 313–314.

22. Taylor, *Price of Freedom*, 1999; José Ramos-Horta, *Funu: The Unfinished Saga of East Timor* (Trenton, N.J.: Red Sea, 1987); and Jill Jolliffe, *East Timor: Nationalism and Colonialism* (St. Lucia, Queensland: University of Queensland Press, 1978). Also see Australian Senate Foreign Affairs, Defence and Trade References Committee, *East Timor: Final Report of the Senate Foreign Affairs, Defence and Trade References Committee* (Canberra: Parliament of the Commonwealth of Australia, December 2000), chap. 6.

23. Dunn, *A People Betrayed;* Taylor, *Price of Freedom;* and Jolliffe, *East Timor.*

24. Taylor, *Price of Freedom;* Jolliffe, *East Timor;* and Dale Van Atta and Brian Toohey, "The Timor Papers," parts 1, 2, *National Times* (Australia), May 30–June 5, 1982, and June 6–12, 1982.

25. Ibid.

26. Taylor, *Price of Freedom;* and Carmel Budiardjo and Liem Soei Liong, *West Papua: The Obliteration of a People* (Surrey [UK]: TAPOL, the Indonesia Human Rights Campaign, 1988 [1983]). Also see Michele Turner, *Telling: East Timor, Personal Testimonies 1942–1992* (New South Wales, Australia: New South Wales University Press, 1992).

27. Quoted in Burr and Evans, *East Timor Revisited*, Document 4.

28. U.S. House of Representatives, "Human Rights in East Timor," Hearings before the Subcommittee on International Organizations of the Committee on International Relations, June 28 and July 19, 1977 (Washington, D.C.: U.S. Government Printing Office, 1977), 62.

29. Text of agreement reprinted in U.S. Congress, House of Representatives, "Human Rights in East Timor and the Question of the Use of U.S. Equipment by the Indonesian Armed Forces," hearing before the Subcommittees on International Organizations and on Asian and Pacific Affairs of the Committee on International Relations, March 23, 1977 (Washington, D.C.: U.S. Government Printing Office, 1977), 76.

30. Quoted in Burr and Evans, *East Timor Revisited*, Document 4.

31. *Congressional Record*, March 3, 1976: H 1551–53, reprinted in *East Timor, Indonesia, and the Western Democracies*, ed. Torben Retbøll (Copenhagen: International Working Group on Indigenous Affairs, 1980), 86–87.

32. Tom Harkin, "Our Proxy War in East Timor: The U.S. Abets a Brutal Annexation," *The Progressive* (December 1980): 46.

33. See U.S. Congress, "Human Rights in East Timor and the Question of the Use of U.S. Equipment by the Indonesian Armed Forces," 5.

34. Quoted in Burr and Evans, *East Timor Revisited*, Document 6.

35. U.S. Congress, "Human Rights in East Timor and the Question of the Use of U.S. Equipment by the Indonesian Armed Forces," 8.

36. Ross Waby, "Aid to Indonesia Doubled as U.S. Shrugs Off Timor," *The Australian*, January 22, 1976.

    A significant component of that "business" involved oil. Formerly classified documents show that Indonesia's oil wealth was an underlying reason for American support for Jakarta. In a formerly secret memorandum (circa November 21, 1975) to President Gerald Ford regarding their then upcoming trip to Indonesia, Kissinger wrote in the section entitled "Background and Strategy":

> In the post-Vietnam environment, U.S. interests in Indonesia are based both on its present position in the region and, especially, on its anticipated future role. . . . It is potentially one of the richest [countries in Southeast Asia]. Its geographic location and resources are of major strategic importance in the region. Flanking the Southeast Asian mainland, Indonesia controls the sea passages between the Pacific and Indian Oceans, including Japan's life line to Middle East oil; its own oil fields provides a significant portion of Japan's oil consumption and a small but increasing part of our own oil imports. Its other major resources — rubber, tin and tropical products — are also of some significance to the United States.

Later, in a section entitled "Issues and Talking Points," Kissinger wrote more on oil-related matters:

> The Indonesians place considerable emphasis on solidarity with OPEC [Organization of Petroleum Exporting Countries]. Nevertheless they have played a passive moderate role at OPEC meetings and during the latest round kept their price increases significantly below those of other OPEC countries. They did not participate in the Arab oil embargo. The United States accounts for the bulk of Indonesia's oil investment (about 86%) and an increasing amount (about 11%) of our crude oil imports are from Indonesia. (Quoted in Burr and Evans, *East Timor Revisited*, Document 3)

37. U.S. Department of State, *American Foreign Policy Basic Documents, 1977–1980* (Washington, D.C.: U.S. Government Printing Office, 1983), 1315.
38. See U.S. Congress, "Human Rights in East Timor and the Question of the Use of U.S. Equipment by the Indonesian Armed Forces," 8, 18.
39. George McArthur, "Indonesia Anxious to Replace Decrepit Arms," *International Herald Tribune*, December 5, 1977.
40. See Terence Smith, "Mondale Is a Nonexpert Who Matters," *The New York Times*, May 14, 1978, sec. 4.
41. Tapol, "Bartering Human Rights," *Tapol Bulletin*, no. 27 (June 1978): 1.
42. Dunn, *A People Betrayed*, 298; and Taylor, *Price of Freedom*, 73–74.
43. Hamish McDonald, "Staging the Rites of Integration," *Far Eastern Economic Review* (June 18, 1976): 22.
44. Daniel Southerland, "US Role in Plight of Timor: An Issue That Won't Go Away," *The Christian Science Monitor*, March 6, 1980, 7.
45. E-mail communication from James Dunn to the author, January 6, 2003.
46. U.S. Congress, House of Representatives, "Famine Relief for East Timor," Hearing before the Subcommittee on Asian and Pacific Affairs of the Committee on Foreign Affairs, December 4, 1979 (Washington, D.C.: U.S. Government Printing Office, 1979), 17.
47. U.S. Congress, "Human Rights in East Timor," 48.
48. Quoted in Southerland, "US Role in Plight of Timor."
49. U.S. Congress, House of Representatives, "Recent Developments in East Timor," Hearings before the Subcommittee on Asian and Pacific Affairs of the Committee on Foreign Affairs, September 14, 1980 (Washington, D.C.: U.S. Government Printing Office, 1980), 11.
50. Jimmy Carter, *Keeping Faith: Memoirs of a Presidency* (New York: Bantam, 1982), 143.
51. The role of Ronald Reagan and his administration in the suffering of East Timor was lost in the largely hagiographic U.S. press coverage in the weeks following Reagan's death in June 2004. One exception was a June 6, 2004, Associated Press article entitled "East Timorese Say Reagan Responsible for Indonesian Massacres." According to Mericio Akara, one of those interviewed for the piece, "With Reagan's passing, another witness to the crimes of America in East Timor has gone. . . . The Indonesians killed tens of thousands in East Timor using American-made weapons. So the American government under Ronald Reagan should be considered morally responsible for their deaths" (article available online at http://www.etan.org/).
52. William D. Hartung and Jennifer Washburn, "U.S. Arms Transfers to Indonesia, 1975–1997: Who's Influencing Whom?" (New York: World Policy Institute, March 1997).
53. "East Timor: The Shame Endures" (editorial), *The New York Times*, December 7, 1990.
54. Allan Nairn, foreword to *East Timor's Unfinished Struggle: Inside the Timorese Resistance* by Constâncio Pinto and Matthew Jardine (Cambridge, Mass.: South End Press), 1997), xx.
55. Matthew Jardine, "Forgotten Genocide: A Little Attention, at Last, for East Timor," *The Progressive* 56, no. 12 (December 1992): 20.

56. Charles Scheiner, "No US Military Aid to Indonesia in Fiscal Year 1993!" *Bulletin of Concerned Asian Scholars* (July–September 1992): 51

57. Jardine, "Forgotten Genocide."

58. Bill Clinton and Al Gore, *Putting People First: How We Can All Change America* (New York: Times Books, 1992), 138.

59. See Matthew Jardine, "APEC, the United States & East Timor," *Z Magazine,* January 1995, 34–39.

60. IRIP News Service, "Timor: No Longer a Sideshow," *Inside Indonesia,* no. 41 (December 1994): 5.

61. Andrew Pollack, "Students Scale Fence to Seek Clinton's Help over Human Rights," *The New York Times,* November 13, 1994, 10. An earlier edition of the paper had a front-page photo of the occupation with the story on page 6. The final edition buried the story even further inside.

62. Quoted in David E. Sanger, "Real Politics: Why Suharto Is in and Castro Is Out," *The New York Times,* October 31, 1995, A3.

63. Allan Nairn, "Indonesia's Killers," *The Nation,* March 30, 1998, 6–7. The program under which the Pentagon conducted the training is known as Joint Combined Exchange Training (JCET). For information on and analysis of the origins and nature of JCET, see Chalmers Johnson, *Blowback: The Costs and Consequences of American Empire* (New York: Henry Holt, 2000).

64. Nairn, "Indonesia's Killers."

65. Arnold Kohen, *From the Place of the Dead: The Epic Struggles of Bishop Belo of East Timor* (New York: St. Martin's, 1999), 24.

66. Ibid., 24. For a discussion of the lukewarm response of the Australian government to the awarding of the 1996 Nobel Peace Prize to Ramos-Horta and Belo, see Clinton Fernandes, *Reluctant Saviour: Australia, Indonesia and the Independence of East Timor* (Melbourne: Scribe Publications, 2004).

67. Regarding Canadian policy, see Sharon Scharfe, *Complicity: Human Rights and Canadian Foreign Policy: The Case of East Timor* (Montreal: Black Rose, 1996); Jeffery Klaehn, "Canadian Complicity in the East Timor Near-Genocide: A Case Study in the Sociology of Human Rights," *Portuguese Studies Review* 11, no. 1 (fall–winter 2003): 49–65; and the Canadian documentary (circa 1997) *Bitter Paradise: The Sell-Out of East Timor,* produced and directed by Elaine Brière. As for the complicit or enabling conduct (or both) of France, Germany, Sweden, Denmark, and other European countries, see Gabriel Defert, *Timor Est: Le Génocide Oublié — Droit d'un people et raisons d'État* (Paris: Éditions L'Harmattan, 1992); Retbøll, *East Timor, Indonesia, and the Western Democracies;* Torben Retbøll, ed., *East Timor: The Struggle Continues* (Copenhagen: International Work Group for Indigenous Affairs, 1984; and Taylor, *Price of Freedom.*

68. See Fernandes, *Reluctant Saviour.*

69. See Dunn, *A People Betrayed;* Fernandes, *Reluctant Saviour;* and Hamish McDonald, "The Price of Betrayal," *Sydney Morning Herald,* September 13, 2000. Also see the collection of official Australian government documents published in Way, Browne, and Johnson, *Australia and the Indonesian Incorporation of Portuguese Timor.* For an analysis of the documents, see Paul M. Monk, "Secret Intelligence and Escape Clauses: Australia and the Indonesian Annexation of East Timor, 1963–76," *Critical Asian Studies* 33, no. 2 (2001): 181–208.

70. The diplomat was James Dunn. Quoted in Dunn, *A People Betrayed,* 124.

71. Quoted in Noam Chomsky, *East Timor and the Western Democracies* (Nottingham, UK: Russell Peace Foundation, 1979), 3.

72. Rob Wesley Smith, "Radio Maubere and Links to East Timor," in *Free East Timor: Australia's Culpability in East Timor's Genocide,* ed. Jim Aubrey, 83–102 (Sydney: Vintage, 1998).

73. Quoted in Scott Burchill, "East Timor, Australia and Indonesia," in *Guns and Ballot Boxes: East Timor's Vote for Independence,* ed. Damien Kingsbury, 169–184 (Victoria, Australia: Monash Asia Institute, Monash University, 2000), 171.

74. Geoffrey Gunn, *East Timor and the United Nations: The Case for Intervention* (Lawrenceville, N.J.: Red Sea, 1997); and Sasha Stepan, *Credibility Gap: Australia and the Timor Gap Treaty* (Fitzroy, Australia: Australian Council for Overseas Aid, 1990).

75. Kenneth Davidson, "We're All Dressed Up, Please Tell Us Where to Go" and "The Wrong Signal" (editorial), *The Age,* September 16, 1993; see also Martin Daly, "PM Washes Blood from Other Hands, *The Age,* September 18, 1993.

76. Michael Richardson, "Fraser Given Blunt Warning at Washington Talks: 'Don't Anger Jakarta,'" *The Age,* August 3, 1976.

77. Roosa, *Pretext for Mass Murder;* and Mark Curtis, *Web of Deceit: Britain's Real Role in the World* (London: Vintage, 2003). See also John Pilger, *Hidden Agendas* (New York: New Press, 1998).

78. Way, Browne, and Johnson, *Australia and the Indonesian Incorporation of Portuguese Timor,* 295.

79. J. R. Walsh and George Munster, *Documents on Australian Defence and Foreign Policy, 1968–1975* (Hong Kong: J. R. Walsh and G. J. Munster, 1980), 192–193.

80. Mark Curtis, *The Ambiguities of Power: British Foreign Policy since 1945* (London: Zed, 1995), 221.

81. *Death of a Nation,* documentary directed by John Pilger, Channel Four (UK), February 1994. Quote also in John Pilger, "Journey to East Timor: Land of the Dead," *The Nation,* April 25, 1994, 550–552.

82. Robin Cook, "The Tragic Cost of Britain's Arm Trade," *New Statesman,* June 30, 1978, 874. Regarding Indonesia's war against West Papua/Irian Jaya, see Budiardjo and Soei Liong, *West Papua.* See also John Saltford, *The United Nations and the Indonesian Takeover of West Papua: The Anatomy of Betrayal* (London: Routledge Curzon, 2003).

83. John Pilger, "We Helped Them Descend into Hell," *New Statesman,* September 13, 1999.

84. Ibid.

85. Quoted in Paul Hainsworth, "New Labour, New Codes of Conduct? British Government Policy towards Indonesia and East Timor after the 1997 Election," in *The East Timor Question: The Struggle for Independence from Indonesia,* ed. Paul Hainsworth and Stephen McCloskey (London: Tauris, 2000), 97.

86. Hainsworth, "New Labour," 100.

87. Ibid.; and TAPOL, Indonesian Human Rights Campaign, "Ethics, Investments and Repression — Britain and Indonesia: The Test for Government and Business," London, March 31, 1998. Also see Curtis, *The Ambiguities of Power;* and idem, *Web of Deceit.*

88. Ed Vulliamy and Antony Barnett, "U.S. Aided Butchers of Timor," *The Observer,* September 19, 1999.

89. Hainsworth, "New Labour." See also Paulo Gorjão, "New Labour and the United Kingdom's Foreign Policy towards the Self-determination of East Timor, 1997–2002," *Asian Survey,* forthcoming.

90. Robin Cook, "Britain Is Ready to Pursue Justice in East Timor," *The Observer,* September 19, 1999; available online at http://www.guardian.co.uk/ethical/article/0,2763,191998,00.html.

91. Defert, *Timor Est.*

92. Quoted in Akihisa Matsuno, "Japan and the East Timor Issue: The Government, Citizens' Movement and Public Opinion," paper prepared for the Fifth Symposium of Oporto University on East Timor, Portugal, July 22–29, 1993.

93. Matthew Jardine, *East Timor: Genocide in Paradise* (Monroe, Maine: Common Courage Press, 1999).

94. Quoted in Free East Timor Japan Coalition, letter to Japanese Defense Agency, July 16, 2001, on file with author.
95. Ibid.
96. The diplomat Alison Stokes issued a report that Wellington did not make public for twelve years. According to Stokes, she received on the flight to Dili a pamphlet announcing the result of the vote in advance. See Maire Leadbeater, "The Timor Gap," *The Listener* (New Zealand), October 5, 2002.
97. Quoted in Leadbeater, "The Timor Gap."
98. Phil Goff, "East Timor: Lessons and Implications," *New Zealand International Review* 24, no. 2 (July/August 1999): 2–5.
99. Leadbeater, "The Timor Gap."
100. Quoted in Goff, "Lessons and Implications."
101. Maire Leadbeater, "Pussyfooting Record No Source of Pride," *New Zealand Herald*, October 13, 1999; Gordon Campbell, "Peace in Our Time: Can New Zealand Wash the Blood from Its Hands in East Timor?" *The Listener*, September 24, 1999; and Free East Timor Coalition, New Zealand, "East Timor Overview," online at http:// homepages.ihug.co.nz/~stu/fret/bulletin/nz.html.
102. Jill Jolliffe, "Murdered Timor Reporter Disowned, Documents Show," *The Age* (Melbourne), September 21, 2002.
103. See Jill Jolliffe, *Cover-Up: The Inside Story of the Balibo Five* (Melbourne: Scribe Publications, 2001); and Desmond Ball and Hamish McDonald, *Death in Balibo, Lies in Canberra* (St. Leonards, New South Wales: Allen and Unwin, 2000).
104. Leadbeater, "The Timor Gap."
105. Roger Clark, "The 'Decolonisation' of East Timor and the United Nations Norms on Self-Determination and Aggression," in *International Law and the Question of East Timor*, ed. Catholic Institute for International Relations and International Platform of Jurists for East Timor (London: Catholic Institute for International Relations and International Platform of Jurists for East Timor, 1995).
106. During this time Indonesia emphasized on a number of occasions that it had no territorial claim to the territory. See Dunn, *A People Betrayed*.
107. Quoted in Dunn, *A People Betrayed*, 322.
108. Dunn, *A People Betrayed*.
109. Ibid.
110. For the text of the resolution, see Gunn, *East Timor and the United Nations*, 107–108.
111. Ramos-Horta, *Funu*.
112. For the text of the resolution, see Gunn, *East Timor and the United Nations*, 109–110.
113. See Ramos-Horta, *Funu*.
114. Benin also voted against the resolution, but because it merely "deplored" rather than "categorically condemned" Indonesia's aggression (Clark, "The 'Decolonisation' of East Timor," 71). According to José Ramos-Horta, Algeria's resolution intentionally employed the word "deplore" instead of the much stronger word "condemn" in the hope of winning the votes of countries that otherwise might not have approved the measure. Still, this "compromise" was not sufficient for most of Indonesia's supporters. See Ramos-Horta, *Funu*. Also see Dunn, *A People Betrayed*.
115. Dunn, *A People Betrayed*, 325.
116. For the text of the resolution, see Gunn, *East Timor and the United Nations*.
117. Dunn, *A People Betrayed*.
118. By the late 1980s, however, China's priorities had changed; its greater concern was to improve relations with Suharto's Indonesia. In addition, important countries like Japan and India provided very strong support for Indonesia's position at the United Nations. See ibid.
119. This argument is made by Roger Clark, international legal specialist and longtime East Timor observer. Interview with author, August 17, 1993.

120. Daniel Moynihan (with Suzanne Weaver), *A Dangerous Place* (Boston: Little, Brown, 1978), 247.
121. A summary of the voting records of individual member-states on each of the eight General Assembly resolutions is available online at http://etan.org/etun/UNvotes .htm.
122. For an interesting insider's view of the cynical power politics that inform the voting behavior of U.N. delegations, see Ramos-Horta, *Funu*.
123. This was because the United Nations never deemed East Timor as having undergone a proper process of decolonization. As such, it was still theoretically — at least under international law — under Portuguese administration.
124. See Dunn, *A People Betrayed;* also see Ramos-Horta, *Funu*.
125. Ramos-Horta, *Funu*.
126. Ibid., 57. Fretilin's U.N. Representative in the post-invasion period described Portugal's role through the mid-1980s as follows:

    Portuguese attitudes toward East Timor ranged from condescending paternalism to outright disrespect for the rights of the people of East Timor to self-determination. From early 1974, the preference in Lisbon was for handing over the country and its people to Indonesia, bearing in mind only the Portuguese image.

    For a discussion of Portuguese diplomacy and East Timor, see Dunn, *A People Betrayed;* Ramos-Horta, *Funu;* Taylor, *Price of Freedom;* and Estêvão Cabral, "Portugal and East Timor: From a Politics of Ambivalence to a Late Awakening," *Portuguese Studies Review* 11, no. 1 (2003): 29–47.
127. See Clark, "The 'Decolonisation' of East Timor."
128. For the text of the letter, see Gunn, *East Timor and the United Nations,* 236.
129. Regarding Belo's letter, see Kohen, *From the Place of the Dead.* Arnold Kohen, a longtime student of, and activist on, East Timor, reported the potential for a deal between Portugal and Indonesia. Interview with the author, June 12, 2002.
130. See Pinto and Jardine, *East Timor's Unfinished Struggle.*
131. See, for example, Theodore Friend, *Indonesian Destinies* (Cambridge, Mass.: Harvard University Press, 2003), 172–173.
132. See Way, Browne, and Johnson, *Australia and the Indonesian Incorporation of Portuguese Timor,* esp., 306–309, 313–314, 327–328. See also Dunn, *A People Betrayed.*
133. Van Atta and Toohey, "The Timor Papers."
134. Although the U.S. Embassy warned the Indonesian military against using American equipment, U.S. officials in Jakarta also made clear that they were not in favor of an independent East Timor for fear that it might allow the Soviet Union to establish a "foothold" in the region, according to the Australians. The U.S. Embassy reportedly also told military leaders in Jakarta that any merger with Indonesia should take place in a peaceful manner that reflected the desires of the East Timorese population.

    The Australian Embassy reported such matters based on its viewing of a cabled report from U.S. Ambassador Newsom. The Americans allowed their Australian counterparts to take notes on the report. The Australian cable is reprinted in Walsh and Munster, Documents on Australian Defence and Foreign Policy, 203–207.
135. Quoted in Nairn, Foreword to *East Timor's Unfinished Struggle,* xiii–xiv.
136. These options are adopted and adapted from Fernandes, *Reluctant Saviour.*
137. Telegram 286596 from the State Department to U.S. Delegation Secretary's Aircraft, December 7, 1975, NSA Country Files, East Asia and the Pacific, Indonesia Box 6, Gerald Ford Library. Cited and quoted in Brad Simpson, "Solidarity in an Age of Globalization: The Transnational Movement for East Timor and U.S. Foreign Policy," *Peace and Change* 28, no. 3–4 (July 2004), 453–482.
138. Richard Nixon, "Asia after Viet Nam," *Foreign Affairs* (October 1967): 111.
139. Quoted in Peter Dale Scott, "Exporting Military-Economic Development: America and the Overthrow of Sukarno," in *Ten Years' Military Terror in Indonesia,* ed. Mal-

colm Caldwell (Nottingham (U.K.): Bertrand Russell Peace Foundation for Spokesman Books, 1975), 241.

4. UNAMET DAYS

The source for the epigraph to this chapter is Steven Mufson and Colum Lynch, "E. Timor Failure Puts U.N. On Spot," *The Washington Post,* September 26, 1999, A1.

1. "E. Timor Integration Day '99: The Last to be Celebrated?" Antara, July 17, 1999.
2. Don Greenlees and Robert Garran, *Deliverance: The Inside Story of East Timor's Fight for Freedom* (Crows Nest, Australia: Allen and Unwin, 2002), 27.
3. John Martinkus, *A Dirty Little War* (Sydney: Random House, 2001); and Lansell Taudevin, *East Timor: Too Little Too Late* (Sydney: Duffy and Snellgrove, 1999).
4. Martinkus, *A Dirty Little War;* and Taudevin, *Too Little Too Late.*
5. Regarding the myriad factors that informed Habibie's decision, see Thomas Ambrosio, "East Timor Independence: The Changing Nature of International Pressure," in *Transforming East Asian Domestic and International Politics: The Impact of Economy and Globalization,* ed. Robert W. Compton (Hants, U.K.: Ashgate, 2002), 115–137; Theodore Friend, *Indonesian Destinies* (Cambridge, Mass.: Harvard University Press, 2003); Greenlees and Garran, *Deliverance;* Mark Rolls, "Indonesia's East Timor Experience," in *Ethnic Conflict and Secessionism in South and Southeast Asia,* ed. Rajat Ganguly and Ian Macduff (Thousand Oaks, Calif.: Sage, 2003), 166–194; and John Taylor, *East Timor: The Price of Freedom* (London: Zed, 1999).
6. U.N.-led negotiations had greatly intensified beginning in 1997, when Kofi Annan took over as U.N. secretary-general and decided to give priority to the East Timor issue.
7. Taudevin, *Too Little Too Late.*
8. Quoted in Greenlees and Garran, *Deliverance,* 109.
9. "Besi Merah Putih" is Indonesian for "Red and White Iron" — red and white being the colors of the Indonesian flag. For information on the various militia groups, see Taudevin, *Too Little Too Late.*
10. Lindsay Murdoch, "Indonesian Riot Squad 'Took Part in Massacre,'" *Sydney Morning Herald,* April 9, 1999; "Mass Killings Sweep across East Timor," *Tapol Bulletin* (May 1999), no. 152; available online at http://tapol.gn.apc.org/bulletin152.htm; Statement of Father Rafael dos Santos, *Suara Timor Timur,* April 8, 1999; translated version available online at http://www.etan.org/. Also see Agence France Presse, "Man Cited in Timor Church Attack a Soldier, District Military Chief Says," June 6, 2002; available online at http://www.etan.org/.
11. Ian Martin, *Self-Determination in East Timor: The United Nations, the Ballot, and International Intervention* (Boulder, Colo.: Lynne Rienner, 2001).
12. BBC, "Timor Bishop's Convoy Attacked," April 11, 1999; available online at http://www.etan.org/. Also see Irena Cristalis, *Bitter Dawn: East Timor, A People's History* (London: Zed, 2002).
13. See Cristalis, *Bitter Dawn.* Cristalis provides an eyewitness account of much of the day's events.
14. *Tapol Bulletin,* May 1999.
15. Allan Nairn, "License to Kill in Timor," *The Nation,* May 31, 1999.
16. Martin, *Self-Determination in East Timor,* 29–31. Also see Cristalis, *Bitter Dawn.*
17. Available online at http://etan.org/etun/agreemnt.htm.
18. Agence France Presse, "Annan Remarks after East Timor Accords Signing," May 5, 1999; available online at http://www.etan.org/.
19. See Neil King Jr. and Jay Solomon, "Diplomatic Gambles at the Highest Levels Failed in East Timor," *Wall Street Journal,* October 21, 1999.

20. See Martin, *Self-Determination in East Timor*. Text of memorandum available online at http://etan.org/etun/UNmemo.htm.

21. May 28, 1999; report available online at http://etan.org/.

22. Mark Dodd, "Caught Red-Handed: Jakarta's Assassins," *Sydney Morning Herald*, May 21, 1999.

23. Quoted in Agence France Presse, "UN Rights Chief Demands Action against Timor Militia," July 10, 1999; available online at http://www.etan.org/.

24. International Federation for East Timor Observer Project (IFET-OP), "Report on the Militia Attack on the Humanitarian Team in Liquiça," July 8, 1999; available online at http://etan.org/ifet/.

25. See Martin, *Self-Determination in East Timor*; Taudevin, *Too Little Too Late*; John Aglionby, "Secret Papers Reveal Timor Pledge as Sham," *The Sunday Observer*, June 13, 1999; and Mark Dodd, "Army Defies UN in Autonomy Rally," *Sydney Morning Herald*, June 14, 1999. Also see "Blood Money," *Dateline*, SBS-TV (Australia), broadcast on February 16, 2000; transcript available online at http://www.etan.org/.

26. Voter registration was scheduled to commence on June 22, 1999. For an understanding of the debate within the United Nations surrounding the delays, see Tamrat Samuel, "East Timor: The Path to Self-Determination," in *From Promise to Practice: Strengthening UN Capacities for the Prevention of Violent Conflict*, ed. Chandra Lekha Sriram and Karin Wermester (Boulder, Colo.: Lynn Rienner, 2003), 197–230.

27. Greenlees and Garran, *Deliverance*, and Martin, *Self-Determination in East Timor*.

28. See Samuel Moore, "The Indonesian Military's Last Years in East Timor: An Analysis of Its Secret Documents," *Indonesia* 72 (October 2001): 9–44; Greenlees and Garran, *Deliverance*; and Clinton Fernandes, *Reluctant Saviour: Australia, Indonesia and the Independence of East Timor* (Melbourne: Scribe Publications, 2004).

29. Quoted in Lindsay Murdoch, "Militia May Try to Sink Ballot," *The Age*, August 5, 1999; available online at http://www.etan.org/.

30. Mark Dodd, "Indonesian Militia 'Cuts Off 60,000 from Outside Help,'" *Sydney Morning Herald*, July 10, 1999.

31. Stephen Steele, "E. Timorese Bishop Threatened by Pro-Indonesia Militias," Catholic News Service (New York), August 25, 1999.

32. Lindsay Murdoch, "Timor Militias Massing for War, US Told," *Sydney Morning Herald*, August 23, 1999.

33. Agence France Presse, "US Sees No Prospect for Sending Armed UN Peacekeepers to East Timor," August 23, 1999; available online at http://www.etan.org/.

34. Associated Press, "Clashes Kill Six in East Timor," August 27, 1999; available online at http://www.etan.org/.

35. Oecussi is where the first Portuguese settlement on the island was located. It appears that the Portuguese first arrived on the island in 1511. Along with Portuguese traders, the Dutch were occasionally visiting the territory to obtain sandalwood and slaves by the early 1600s. Eventually conflict ensued between the two groups as they both tried to extend their influence on the island and throughout the region. The Netherlands ultimately prevailed, leaving Lisbon with tiny East Timor, including the Oecussi enclave located in part of what became the much larger Dutch East Indies, the colony out of which Indonesia emerged. See C. R. Boxer, "Portuguese Timor: A Rough Island Story, 1515–1960," *History Today* 10, no. 5 (May 1960): 349–355; and idem, *Fidalgos in the Far East, 1550–1770* (New York: Oxford University Press, 1968). Also see William Burton Sowash, "Colonial Rivalries in Timor," *The Far Eastern Quarterly* 7, no. 3 (May 1948): 227–235.

36. IFET-OP, "Campaign Ends in Wave of Pro-Integration Terror," August 28, 2002; available online at http://etan.org/ifet/. See Martinkus, *A Dirty Little War*, for an eyewitness account of the attack on Memo.

37. CNRT media release, "Indonesia and Militias Will Murder UN Observers or Interna-

tional Media Then Slaughter East Timorese Independence Supporters," August 29, 1999. Regarding the United Nations in Rwanda, see Alison Des Forges, *Leave None to Tell the Story: Genocide in Rwanda* (New York: Human Rights Watch and the International Federation of Human Rights, 1999).

5. FROM GUARDED EUPHORIA TO "GROUND ZERO"

The source of the epigraph to this chapter is Steven Mufson and Colum Lynch, "E. Timor Failure Puts U.N. on Spot," *The Washington Post,* September 26, 1999, A1.

1. There were five polling places in Indonesia, four in Australia, and one each in Macau, New York City, Lisbon, and Maputo (Mozambique) to accommodate the East Timorese diaspora. A total of 446,666 people registered to vote: 433,576 in East Timor and 13,090 overseas.
2. A press release from the Indonesian government explaining its reasoning for not allowing Ramos-Horta to return is available online at http://www.prica.org/news/Timtim/PR-31-DEPLU.htm.
3. Ian Martin, *Self-Determination in East Timor: The United Nations, the Ballot, and International Intervention* (Boulder, Colo.: Lynne Rienner, 2001); Keith B. Richburg, "E. Timor Militia Resume Violence after Vote," *The Washington Post,* September 1, 1999; Geoffrey Robinson, "'If You Leave Us, We Will Die,'" *Dissent* (winter 2002): 87–99; and "Ominous Signs Only Two Days after Historic East Timor Vote; Militia Roadblocks, and Widespread Threats against Local Population, International Observers, and UNAMET Personnel," IFET-OP Report #8, September 1, 1999; available online at http://etan.org/ifet/.
4. Associated Press, "Militiamen Attack outside U.N. Headquarters in East Timor," September 1, 1999, available online at http://www.etan.org/; Richard Lloyd Parry, "As Police Stand and Watch, the Timor Militia Go on a Rampage," *The Independent,* September 2, 1999; Don Greenlees and Robert Garran, *Deliverance: The Inside Story of East Timor's Fight for Freedom* (Crows Nest, Australia: Allen and Unwin, 2002).
5. See Peter Bartu, "The Militia, the Military, and the People of Bobonaro District," *Bulletin of Concerned Asian Scholars* 32, nos. 1, 2 (2000): 35–42; and Stephen Steele, "The Widows of Maliana," *Florida Catholic,* September 21, 2000.
6. Earl Candler, the CivPol, survived his wounds. See Candler, "It Was Like Being Lost in Paradise," *Peoria Journal Star,* August 13, 2000; available online at http://www.etan.org/.
7. Also see Irena Cristalis, *Bitter Dawn: East Timor, A People's History* (London: Zed, 2002).
8. John Roosa, "Scorched Earth, Betrayed Hope," *Indonesia Alert!* 2, no. 2 (fall 1999): 1+.
9. Agence France Presse, "Deported American Activist Says Military Chief behind Timor Killings," September 20, 1999; available online at http://www.etan.org/. Also see Lansell Taudevin, *East Timor: Too Little Too Late* (Sydney: Duffy and Snellgrove, 1999).
10. See John Martinkus, *A Dirty Little War* (Sydney: Random House, 2001).
11. The IFET-OP was among the countless targets. Within fifteen minutes of the forced evacuation of the international observer project from its headquarters on the night of September 6, 1999, Indonesian soldiers and militia entered the building and began stealing all the furniture and equipment, and then set the premises on fire shortly thereafter.
12. Bhimanto Suwastoyo, "East Timorese 'Feigned Death to Survive Army-backed Attack,'" Agence France Presse, June 20, 2002; available online at http://www.etan.org/; Agence France Presse, "Indonesian Troops Disguised as Militiamen Joined in East Timor Attack," June 25, 2002; available online at http://www.etan.org/.

13. Two other women who were present on the wharf at the time told me a similar story independent of each other. When the ship finally departed, one of them heard that all thirty-two students had been slain. Such a number seems highly unlikely, but, based on the reports of the three witnesses, it does appear that there were at least some fatalities at the harbor that day. As of this writing no independent investigation of the incident has been conducted, so there is no authoritative account of what transpired nor is there an estimate of the death toll.

14. See Martinkus, *A Dirty Little War.*

15. See Cristalis, *Bitter Dawn;* Martin, *Self-Determination in East Timor;* and Martinkus, *A Dirty Little War.*

16. Asfané Bassir Pour, "Le Combat Solitaire de Kofi Annan," *Le Monde,* October 31–November 1, 1999; Greenlees and Garran, *Deliverance.*

17. David Usborne, "The Puppet Leader Grants an Audience," *The Independent,* September 10, 1999; David Usborne, "A Front-row Seat to Watch the Limits of Diplomacy, *The Independent on Sunday,* September 12, 1999. Also see Greenlees and Garran, *Deliverance.*

18. Sander Thoenes, "What Made Indonesia Accept Peacekeepers," *The Christian Science Monitor,* September 14, 1999.

19. Martin, *Self-Determination in East Timor;* Martinkus, *A Dirty Little War;* Greenlees and Garran, *Deliverance.* Also see Bassir Pour, "Le Combat Solitaire de Kofi Annan."

20. SWAPO is the acronym for the South West African People's Organization, the national resistance body formed in 1959 in Namibia to challenge Apartheid South Africa's rule of the country. SWAPO, now a political party, won the newly independent country's first election in 1989.

21. David Usborne, "A Chilling Meeting with Dr. Strangelove of Jakarta," *The Independent,* September 11, 1999; Also see Basir Pour, "Le Combat Solitaire de Kofi Annan"; and Martin, *Self-Determination in East Timor.*

22. David Usborne, "UN Mission—General Croons as His Soldiers Preside over the Death of Dili," *The Independent,* September 13, 1999.

23. David Usborne, "'When You Are Gone, They Will Kill Us,'" *The Independent,* September 12, 1999.

24. Martin, *Self-Determination in East Timor.*

25. Usborne, "'When You Are Gone, They Will Kill Us.'"

26. Usborne, "UN Mission."

27. Ibid.

28. See John Anglioby, "General's 'Songs for Timorese' Branded a Sick Stunt," *The Guardian,* October 24, 2000; and "Indonesia's Ex-military Chief Sings Love Songs for Nation's Refugees," CNN, November 2, 2000; available online at http://www.cnn.com/2000/ASIANOW/southeast/11/01/indonesia.singing.general/.

29. See Thoenes, "What Made Indonesia Accept Peacekeepers."

30. See Greenlees and Garran, *Deliverance.*

31. Regarding Rwanda and the United Nations, see Alison Des Forges, *Leave None to Tell the Story: Genocide in Rwanda* (New York: Human Rights Watch and the International Federation of Human Rights, 1999); and Gérard Prunier, *The Rwanda Crisis: History of a Genocide* (New York: Columbia University Press, 1997); also see Linda Melvern, *A People Betrayed: The Role of the West in Rwanda's Genocide* (London: Zed, 2000). Regarding Srebenica as well as Rwanda, see Samantha Power, *"A Problem from Hell": America and the Age of Genocide* (New York: Basic Books, 2002).

32. Some journalistic accounts of what transpired in the UNAMET compound have sharply criticized UNAMET head Ian Martin for deciding to evacuate all U.N. staff, while leaving behind the East Timorese refugees. Such accounts report that a petition by dozens of foreign journalists—along with an international outcry and protests by

the refugees — played a significant role in convincing the United Nations to reverse the decision. See, for example, Martinkus, *A Dirty Little War;* and Cristalis, *Bitter Dawn.*

According to Ian Martin, however, the petition played no role in the reversal of the decision to evacuate as it came about well after events overtook the original decision. It was indeed Martin's decision to evacuate, one he made on the recommendation of his security staff. The situation, they surmised, had passed the point of acceptable risk. Martin's greatest concern was for the local (East Timorese) staff. Had the evacuation taken place as originally proposed, Martin stated, UNAMET would have tried to obtain guarantees from the TNI for the safety of the nonstaff East Timorese in the compound (IDPs, or internally displaced persons). Upon announcing the evacuation to the UNAMET staff on September 8, a number of the staff people immediately stated that they would not leave. Martin thus asked them to draw up a list of volunteers among UNAMET staff who would stay behind. That same evening Martin went to speak with Colonel Muis, the TNI commander of East Timor at the time; Major General Adam Damiri, head of the TNI's regional command; and Major General Kiki Syahnakri, who was the martial law administrator for East Timor. Muis asked UNAMET to stay, to give the military more time to make martial law work. At the same time Muis stated that there was no way the evacuation could happen the next day as the TNI needed adequate time to secure the route. Muis did not want to evacuate in the dark, so, logistically speaking, the earliest the evacuation could take place would have been on the morning of September 10. When Martin later returned to the UNAMET compound a viable list of international UNAMET volunteers was already in place. In retrospect, Martin wishes he had asked for a list of volunteers to stay behind from the start. He also argues that the whole sequence of events played out rather well as the "threat" to evacuate forced the TNI's hand and eventually resulted in the military's allowing an evacuation of everyone in the compound. Of course, this was an unintended outcome. Interview with Ian Martin, New York City, September 2, 2002.

33. See Greenlees and Garran, *Deliverance.*
34. See, for example, Cameron Barr, "The 745 Convoy Encounters an Adversary That Fires Back," *The Christian Science Monitor,* March 16, 2000; Martinkus, *A Dirty Little War;* and Greenlees and Garran, *Deliverance.*
35. See Greenlees and Garran, *Deliverance;* and Martinkus, *A Dirty Little War.* Also see Cristalis, *Bitter Dawn.*
36. Martinkus, *A Dirty Little War.*
37. See ibid.; and Taudevin, *Too Little Too Late.*
38. See Australian Broadcast Corporation, *Four Corners,* "A License to Kill," broadcast on March 15, 1999, transcript available online at http://www.abc.net.au/4corners/stories/s20270.htm. Also see East Timor Human Rights Centre, "Urgent Situation in East Timor," January 27, 1999; available online at http://www.etan.org/.
39. Martinkus, *A Dirty Little War,* 387.
40. Cameron Barr, "Post-Referendum Backlash in Los Palos: Near Their Base, Soldiers Target the Referendum Victors" and "A Pattern of Violence," *The Christian Science Monitor,* March 14, 2000.
41. Cameron Barr, "A Brutal Exit: A Deadly Highway Rendezvous," *The Christian Science Monitor,* March 13, 2000.
42. Cameron Barr, "A Brutal Exit: Their Orders? Destroy Everything. Shoot Anything," *The Christian Science Monitor,* March 16, 2000.
43. Barr, "The 745 Convoy Encounters an Adversary That Fires Back."
44. Cameron Barr, "A Brutal Exit: Welcome to Dili. 'Don't Even Tell Your Wives' What You Did," *The Christian Science Monitor,* March 17, 2000.
45. The official account held that no shots were exchanged between the TNI and InterFET. However, there may well have been at least one clash between the two forces — near

Suai. And there were certainly a number of clashes between InterFET and the militias. See Martinkus, *A Dirty Little War.*

46. For a defense of this approach, see Nicholas J. Wheeler and Tim Dunne, "East Timor and the New Humanitarian Intervention," *International Affairs* 77, no. 4 (2001), 805–827.

47. See Samuel Moore, "The Indonesian Military's Last Years in East Timor: An Analysis of Its Secret Documents," *Indonesia* 72 (October 2001): 9–44; and Clinton Fernandes, *Reluctant Saviour: Australia, Indonesia and the Independence of East Timor* (Melbourne: Scribe Publications, 2004).

6. THE INTERNATIONAL COMMUNITY AND EAST TIMOR IN 1999

The source of the epigraphs to this chapter are, respectively, Neil King Jr. and Jay Solomon, "Diplomatic Gambles at the Highest Levels Failed in East Timor," *The Wall Street Journal,* October 21, 1999, A1+; Robin Cook, "Speech to the Royal Institute of International Affairs," Chatham House, London, January 28, 2000, reprinted in *Human Rights: Foreign and Commonwealth Office Annual Report 2000* (London: Foreign and Commonwealth Office, July 2000), 132–137; available online at http://www.fco.gov.uk/Files/kfile/HRPD 00 human rights.pdf; and "Australia's East Timor Secret," *Dateline,* SBS TV (Australia), broadcast on May 9, 2001; transcript available at http://www.sbs.com.au/dateline/index .php3?archive=1&artmon=5&arty=2001#.

1. Interview with Geoffrey Robinson, March 2002, University of California, Los Angeles. Also see Robinson, "'If You Leave Us, We Will Die,'" *Dissent* 49, no.1 (winter 2002): 87–99.

2. The Core Group was a subset of a much larger East Timor "Support Group," an entity made up of about twenty-five countries. The purpose of the Support Group was to provide assistance to the United Nations regarding the implementation of the agreements pertaining to the vote. The U.N. Secretariat occasionally briefed the members of this larger group. The members of the Core Group were, by far, the most actively engaged countries in events relating to the East Timor vote. See Tamrat Samuel, "East Timor: The Path to Self-Determination," in *From Promise to Practice: Strengthening UN Capacities for the Prevention of Violent Conflict,* ed. Chandra Lekha Sriram and Karin Wermester (Boulder, Colo.: Lynn Rienner, 2003), 197–230.

3. Much of the material in this chapter is adapted from my article "The Making of 'Ground Zero' in East Timor in 1999: An Analysis of International Complicity in Indonesia's Crimes," *Asian Survey* 42, no. 4 (July/August 2002): 623–641.

4. Interviews with Mark Quarterman, Special Assistant to the Undersecretary-General for Political Affairs, March 31, 2000, U.N. Headquarters, New York; and with Tamrat Samuel, Assistant to the Undersecretary-General for Political Affairs, U.N. Headquarters, New York, February 27, 2001.

   According to Geoffrey Robinson, Marker played an important role in convincing New York that Indonesia could be trusted in this regard ("'If You Leave Us, We Will Die,'").

5. See Jamsheed Marker, *East Timor: A Memoir of the Negotiations for Independence* (Jefferson, N.C.: McFarland, 2003). See also Samuel, "The Path to Self-Determination"; Steven Mufson and Colum Lynch, "East Timor Failure Puts U.N. in Dock," *The Guardian Weekly,* September 30–October 6, 1999, 31; and Asfané Bassir Pour, "Le Combat Solitaire de Kofi Annan," *Le Monde,* October 31–November 1, 1999.

   Kofi Annan did attach to the final accord a private memorandum to the Indonesian and Portuguese governments outlining the major security measures needed for the ballot to take place. These included the redeployment of Indonesian troops in East Timor and the laying down of arms by all armed groups, a process that was to be completed well before the vote. See Samuel, "The Path to Self-Determination." The memorandum is available online at http://etan.org/etun/UNmemo.htm.

6. Text of letter available online at http://www.etan.org/.

7. Author interview with José Ramos-Horta, May 15, 2001, San Francisco, California.

8. Aniceto Guterres Lopes, "East Timor's Bloodiest Tradition," *The New York Times,* May 5, 1999.

9. Official at the U.S. Mission to the United Nations, author interview, New York, February 26 and 27, 2001.

10. Alexander Downer, "East Timor—Looking Back on 1999," *Australian Journal of International Affairs* 54, no. 1 (April 1, 2000): 6–7.

11. Robinson, "'If You Leave Us, We Will Die,'" 90–91.

12. Geoffrey Robinson, "With UNAMET in East Timor: An Historian's Personal View," in *Bitter Flowers, Sweet Flowers: East Timor, Indonesia, and the World Community,* ed. Richard Tanter, Mark Selden, and Stephen R. Shalom (Lanham, Md.: Rowman & Littlefield, 2001), 55–72.

13. Bassir Pour, "Le Combat Solitaire de Kofi Annan."

14. Official at the U.K. Mission to the United Nations, author interview, New York, March 1, 2001.
   Despite such inaction, an academic analysis of the "Blair doctrine" contends that, "when it became obvious that the Indonesia military was active in derailing the transition to democracy in East Timor, the UK government broke with the policy of quiet dialogue with Indonesia over human rights. . . . [T]he United Kingdom effectively used all the instruments available to it . . . to put a halt to the barbarism" (Tim Dunne and Nicholas J. Wheeler, "The Blair Doctrine: Advancing the Third Way in the World," in *New Labour's Foreign Policy: A New Moral Crusade* ed. Richard Little and Mark Winkham-Jones [Manchester, U.K.: Manchester University Press, 2000], 66).

15. Official at the U.S. Mission to the U.N. José Ramos-Horta met with Stanley Roth, the U.S. undersecretary of state for Asia and the Pacific, in July 1999 and asked him to urge President Clinton to make such a statement (José Ramos-Horta, author interview, San Francisco, May 15, 2001).

16. For an excellent overview of this period, see John Martinkus, *A Dirty Little War* (Sydney: Random House, 2001).

17. See Jeffrey T. Richelson, *The U.S. Intelligence Community* (Boulder, Colo.: Westview, 1999).

18. See John Lyons, "The Timor Dossier," *The Bulletin* (Sydney), October 12, 1999, 24–29. In addition, an Australian aid worker in East Timor had been providing detailed accounts to his supervisors in Jakarta about the TNI's creation and direction of, and support for, the militia groups since at least mid-1998. Australian officials reportedly tended to treat the reports with disdain. See Lansell Taudevin, *East Timor: Too Little Too Late* (Sydney: Duffy and Snellgrove, 1999).

19. See Desmond Ball, "Silent Witness: Australian Intelligence and East Timor," *Pacific Review* 14, no. 1 (March 1,2001): 35–62; and John Birmingham, "Appeasing Jakarta: Australia's Complicity in the East Timor Tragedy," *Quarterly Essay* (Melbourne), no. 2 (2001): 1–87. Also see Hamish McDonald, "Silence over a Crime against Humanity, *Sydney Morning Herald* and *The Age,* March 14, 2002; available online at http://www.etan.org/. For a devastating analysis of how the Howard government's public diplomacy provided cover for the TNI-militia terror in the run-up to the ballot and of the ineffectiveness of its private diplomacy, see Clinton Fernandes, *Reluctant Saviour: Australia, Indonesia and the Independence of East Timor* (Melbourne: Scribe Publications, 2004).

NOTES TO PAGES 121–122

20. See the press release put out by the New Zealand navy on the military maneuvers at http://www.navy.mil.nz/rnzn/article.cfm?article_id=177&article_type=news.

21. "Australia's East Timor Secret," *Dateline*, SBS-TV (Australia), broadcast on May 9, 2001; transcript available at http://www.sbs.com.au/dateline/index.php3?archive=1&artmon=5&arty=2001#. See also Jill Jolliffe, "Canberra Accused over Militia's Bloody Plan," *The Age*, May 9, 2001; available online at http://groups.yahoo.com/group/berita-bhinneka/message/33068?source=1.

22. See Brendan Nicholson, "Silent Shame, Silent Witness," *The Age*, December 24, 2000; available online at http://www.etan.org/.

    According to Edmund McWilliams, who worked as the political counselor in the U.S. Embassy in Jakarta until July 1999,

    Reporting from all sources which I saw, and some of which I generated on behalf of the U.S. Embassy left no doubt about the origins of the militias, or their purpose: i.e., as creations of the Indonesian military and as agents of provocation and intimidation vis-à-vis the people of East Timor and organized pro-independence elements. During a June 1999 visit which carried me alone from Dili to Attambua and on to Suai (with return by the same overland route), I encountered a meeting of senior Indonesian military officers and East Timorese militia at a major hotel in Attambua. I was also informed while in West Timor of Indonesian military plans to compel the movement of large numbers of people from East Timor to West Timor. ("Statement for the Truth and Reconciliation Commission—Dili," March 5, 2004)

23. Desmond Ball, Australia National University, telephone interview, February 20, 2002.

24. Downer, "East Timor—Looking Back on 1999," 7. Eric Schwartz, who served the Clinton White House as Special Assistant to the President for National Security Affairs and, from June 1998 to June 2001, as Senior Director for Multilateral and Humanitarian Affairs, makes a similar argument. He contends that, as of late August 1999, based on the body of intelligence received in Washington, it was not clear that the Indonesian military would do what they did in the aftermath of the ballot (Eric Schwartz, telephone interview with author, May 30, 2002).

25. Within the East Timorese population as a whole, however, there was widespread fear of what the TNI would do. As IFET-OP wrote in its August 17, 1999, Report (#5): "Based on IFET-OP's numerous field visits, it appears that a significant portion of the East Timorese population believes that the time of the vote will be a time of war." Report available online at http://etan.org/ifet/.

26. See Lyons, "The Timor Dossier."

27. Allan Nairn, "U.S. Complicity in Timor," *The Nation*, September 27, 1999. Blair was supposed to tell his TNI counterpart to shut down the militia terror campaign, but instead, according to a classified cable on the April 8, 1999, meeting obtained by Nairn, Admiral Blair "told the armed forces chief that he looks forward to the time when [the army will] resume its proper role as a leader in the region. He invited General Wiranto to come to Hawaii as his guest in conjunction with the next round of bilateral defense discussions in the July–August '99 time frame. He said Pacific command is prepared to support a subject matter expert exchange for doctrinal development. He expects that approval will be granted to send a small team to provide technical assistance to police and . . . selected TNI personnel on crowd control measures."

    Such behavior by Blair is indicative of the rising power of regional commanders-in-chief within the U.S. military structure vis-à-vis civilian policy makers in the executive branch of the government, a development that has significant implications for the conduct of U.S. foreign policy. See Andrew J. Bacevich, *American Empire: The Realities and Consequences of U.S. Diplomacy* (Cambridge, Mass.: Harvard University Press, 2002). Regardless, President Clinton could have reprimanded and sanctioned Blair for contravening the administration's instructions, but he did not do so.

28. According to Edmund McWilliams,
    The United States Government accepted the transparently fraudulent Government of Indonesia contention that these militias were representative of factions within East Timor and that their genesis was in some sense democratic and popularly based. . . . Such meetings [those of Roy and Albright] conferred an aura of legitimacy on these murderous militias and on their creation by the Indonesian military. ("Statement for the Truth and Reconciliation Commission—Dili," March 5, 2004)
29. Edmund McWilliams, Head of the Political Section, U.S. Embassy in Jakarta (June 1996–July 1999), author interview, Washington, D.C., June 10, 2001.
30. Free East Timor Japan Coalition, letter to Japanese Defense Agency, July 16, 2001, on file with author.
31. "U.S. Rejects Call for U.N. to Send Peacekeepers to East Timor," Cable News Network, September 3, 1999, http://www.cnn.com/ASIANOW/southeast/9909/02/e.timor.05/index.html.
32. Don Greenlees and Robert Garran, *Deliverance: The Inside Story of East Timor's Fight for Freedom* (Crows Nest, Australia: Allen and Unwin, 2002), 242.
33. David Sanger, "Indonesia Is Warned It Could Lose Western Aid," *The New York Times*, September 7, 1999, A12.
34. Greenlees and Garran, *Deliverance*, 243.
35. Elizabeth Becker and Philip Shenon, "With Other Goals in Indonesia, U.S. Moves Gently on East Timor," *The New York Times*, September 9, 1999.
36. National Security Adviser Sandy Berger and National Economic Adviser Gene Sperling, Press Briefing, the White House, Office of the Press Secretary, September 8, 1999; available online at http://clinton4.nara.gov/WH/New/APEC1999/brief6.html.
37. Agence France Presse, "Outraged US Senators Urge Cut Off Military Aid, Loans to Indonesia," September 8, 1999; available online at http://www.etan.org/.
38. See, for example, Anthony Lewis, "The Fruits of 'Realism,'" *The New York Times*, September 7, 1999; "Pressure Indonesia to Halt Killings" (editorial), *The Atlanta Constitution*, September 9, 1999, A14; and "And Now, Kosovo East" (editorial), *The Christian Science Monitor*, September 7, 1999, 10.
39. See Fernandes, *Reluctant Saviour*.
40. José Ramos-Horta, author interview. Also see Greenlees and Garran, *Deliverance;* and Paulo Gorjão, "The End of a Cycle: Australian and Portuguese Foreign Policies and the Fate of East Timor," *Contemporary Southeast Asia* 23, no. 1 (April 2001): 101–121.
41. *Public Papers of the Presidents of the United States: William J. Clinton, 1999*, vol. 2 (Washington, D.C.: U.S. Government Printing Office, 2000), 1511–1517. Also see Agence France Presse, "Clinton Demands Indonesia Accept International Force," September 9, 1999; available online at http://www.etan.org/; and CNN, "Clinton Warns Indonesia as U.S. Severs Military Relations," September 9, 1999; available online at http://www.cnn.com/US/9909/09/us.east.timor/.
42. Steve Holland, "Clinton Suspends U.S. Military Sales to Indonesia," Reuters, September 11, 1999; available online at http://www.etan.org/. The Department of State press release announcing the suspension of military sales is also available online at http://secretary.state.gov/www/briefings/statements/1999/ps990910a.html. The press release is dated September 10, 1999—most likely because Auckland is sixteen hours ahead of Washington, D.C.
43. Agence France Presse, "Britain Suspends Sale of Hawk Jets to Indonesia," September 11, 1999; available online at http://www.etan.org/; and Patrick Wintour, John Gittings, and Eduardo Goncalves, "UK Blocks Hawks for Indonesia; Blair Suspends Arms Sale," *The Observer*, September 12, 1999. Despite the announcement, the Blair government continued to deliver Hawks to Indonesia until September 23, 1999. See Noam Chomsky, *A New Generation Draws the Line: Kosovo, East Timor and the Standards of the West*

(London: Verso, 2000), 68; Mark Curtis, *Web of Deceit: Britain's Real Role in the World* (London: Vintage, 2003; and Michael White, "Jakarta Gets Its Three Hawk Jets," *The Guardian,* September 20, 1999; available online at http://www.etan.org/.

44. Greenlees and Garran, *Deliverance,* 244–245. Also see Agence France Presse, "IMF Suspends Talks on Economic Program with Indonesia," September 10, 1999; available online at http://www.etan.org.

45. Sander Thoenes, "East Timor: Martial Law — Habibie's Last Card," *Financial Times,* September 8, 1999.

46. The official press release announcing these changes is available online at http://www.minister.defence.gov.au/1999/index.html.

47. The New Zealand government's announcement of the suspension is available online at http://www.scoop.co.nz/stories/PA9909/S00257.htm.

Japan, for its part, proved unwilling to take any steps of even minor significance, such as threatening to withhold part of its huge bilateral aid monies. (Japan provides the majority of Indonesia's international development assistance funds.) Instead, Tokyo issued weak statements that it was the responsibility of Indonesia to restore order and that, if Jakarta could not fulfill that obligation, it should accept international support. See Paulo Gorjão, "Japan's Foreign Policy and East Timor, 1975–2002," *Asian Survey* 45, no. 2 (2002): 754–771.

48. See Thoenes, "What Made Indonesia Accept Peacekeepers."

49. Thoenes, "East Timor: Martial Law — Habibie's Last Card."

50. Historian John Roosa learned this from one of the journalists present at the interview. E-mail communication with author, July 1, 2000.

Sometime in late September 1999 Australian foreign minister Alexander Downer met privately with Indonesia's ambassador to Canberra, Sastrohandoyo Wiryono. Employing logic similar to that of Stapleton Roy, Downer assured Jakarta's ambassador that Indonesia was "one hundred times more important than East Timor" (quoted in Lyons, "The Timor Dossier," 26).

Since retiring from diplomatic service at the end of the Clinton administration, Roy has been the managing director of Kissinger Associates, Inc. — Henry Kissinger's international consulting firm.

51. See Irena Cristalis, *Bitter Dawn: East Timor, A People's History* (London: Zed, 2002).

52. Ian Martin, *Self-Determination in East Timor: The United Nations, the Ballot, and International Intervention* (Boulder, Colo.: Lynne Rienner, 2001), 212.

53. Interview with Ian Martin, 2002. For a discussion of the efforts and explanation of the thinking behind the strategy they embodied, see Samuel, "The Path to Self-Determination."

54. On a similar note, UNAMET and Martin also came under heavy criticism for almost leaving behind the East Timorese civilians (nonlocal staff) seeking refuge in the U.N. compound (see chapter 5, above).

55. That the TNI and the militia did not kill any international U.N. staffers was most likely a result of deliberate policy. As its conduct showed, the military wanted to scare internationals so they would flee. Had they begun to murder foreigners, the reaction of the international community — especially the West — would have been far more intense. In this regard, the murder of Sander Thoenes was probably the result of truly "rogue elements." In any case, the killing happened after InterFET began to arrive.

56. For a report on one of these documents, see Australian Associated Press, "Indonesia Expects Timor Poll Loss, Plans Evacuation," July 25, 1999; available online at http://www.etan.org/.

57. Martin, *Self-Determination in East Timor,* 82.

58. Lindsay Murdoch, "Freedom Flight to Darwin," *Sydney Morning Herald,* August 24, 2001, 1.

59. Hamish McDonald et al., *Masters of Terror: Indonesia's Military and Violence in East Timor in 1999* (Canberra: Strategic and Defence Studies Centre, Australian National University, 2002).
60. See Martin, *Self-Determination in East Timor;* Martinkus, *A Dirty Little War;* Greenlees and Garran, *Deliverance;* and Cristalis, *Bitter Dawn.*
61. See, for example, Cristalis, *Bitter Dawn.*
62. Interview with Martin, 2002. Martin argues that the United Nations should conduct worst-case-scenario planning as a matter of practice so that it does not appear to be anything extraordinary. Also see Martin, *Self-Determination in East Timor.*
63. Samuel, "The Path to Self-Determination," 226.
64. One of Ian Martin's political advisers later characterized Marker as a "diplomat of the old school" who was "a firm believer in the value of cordial face-to-face discussion." Marker had a tendency to accept the empty promises of the Indonesian authorities and "to understate the seriousness of the security situation and to let the Indonesians off the hook far too easily." In this regard, he helped to give "a skewed impression of what UNAMET actually knew and thought about security and political conditions" (Robinson, "'If You Leave Us, We Will Die,'" 92).
65. Robinson, "'If You Leave Us, We Will Die.'"
66. Quoted in Cristalis, *Bitter Dawn,* 215.
67. See Robinson, "'If You Leave Us, We Will Die.'"
68. Two officials who stand out in this regard are Francesc Vendrell and Tamrat Samuel.
69. See Phyllis Bennis, *Calling the Shots: How Washington Dominates Today's UN* (New York: Olive Branch, 2000). Also see Boutros Boutros-Ghali, *Unvanquished: A U.S.– U.N. Saga* (New York: Random House, 1999).
70. Greenlees and Garran, *Deliverance.*
71. Neil King Jr. and Jay Solomon, "Diplomatic Gambles at the Highest Levels Failed in East Timor," *Wall Street Journal,* October 21, 1999.
72. Nicholas J. Wheeler and Tim Dunne, "East Timor and the New Humanitarian Intervention," *International Affairs* 77, no. 4 (2001): 805–827.
73. Ibid., 818.
74. Edmund McWilliams argues:

> [The post-ballot] violence could have been prevented had the international community, and especially the United States taken prudent action in the Spring and Summer of 1999. . . . [T]he United States Government was gravely mistaken insofar as it failed to demand that the Indonesian military disarm and disband the various East Timor militias whose criminal behavior and legal impunity for the behavior was readily apparent as early as Spring 1999. . . . [Instead], the United States Government urged only that the Indonesian military exercise greater control over these bands. Even that limited objective was never realized. ("Statement for the Truth and Reconciliation Commission—Dili," March 5, 2004)

75. Tim Fischer, *Ballots and Bullets: Seven Days in East Timor* (St. Leonards, NSW, Australia: Allen and Unwin, 2000), 131.
76. See Ball, "Silent Witness"; and Andrew Clark, "The Untold Story of Australia's Debt to the United States," *Australian Financial Review,* December 31, 2003.

7. REPRESENTING THE PAST

The sources of the epigraphs to this chapter are, respectively, Judith Herman, *Trauma and Recovery: The Aftermath of Violence: From Domestic Abuse to Political Terror* (New York: Basic Books, 1997), 8; Tobias Wolff, "War Memory" (op-ed), *The New York Times,* April 28,

2001, A15; and Adam Hochschild, *King Leopold's Ghost: A Story of Greed, Terror, and Heroism in Colonial Africa* (New York: Houghton Mifflin, 1998), 295.

1. Full text of Clinton-Nairn exchange contained in "Transcript: Peace, Democracy in East Timor Long-Term U.S. Goals," May 20, 2002, distributed by the Office of International Information Programs, U.S. Department of State; available online at http://usinfo.state.gov/products/pdq/pdq.htm.
2. George Orwell, "Notes on Nationalism," in *Collected Essays, Journalism and Letters of George Orwell*, ed. Sonia Orwell and Ian Angus, 4 vols. (London: Secker and Warburg, 1969), 3:370.
3. Agence France Presse, "Cheers and Anger Greet Indonesian President in East Timor," February 29, 2000; available online at http://www.etan.org/.
4. Tertiani ZB Simanjuntak, "UN Clipped Out Power in E. Timor: Witnesses," *The Jakarta Post,* June 20, 2002. Also see "'TNI Not Responsible for Abuses,'" *The Jakarta Post,* January 9, 2003.
5. Agence France Presse, "Claims That Army Fuelled E.Timor Atrocities Are 'Fantasy': General," *The Jakarta Post,* July 1, 2003; available online at http://www.etan.org/.
6. See Hamish McDonald et al., *Masters of Terror: Indonesia's Military and Violence in East Timor in 1999* (Canberra: Strategic and Defence Studies Centre, Australian National University, 2002).
7. See, for example, David Lamb, "Militia Warfare Threatens Vote in East Timor," *Los Angeles Times,* August 29, 1999, A1+; and idem, "E. Timorese Flood Polls during Lull in Violence," *Los Angeles Times,* August 30, 1999, A1+
8. See, for example, Ali Alatas, "De-Bunking the Myths around a Process of Decolonization," remarks by Indonesian Foreign Minister Alatas before members of the National Press Club, Washington, D.C., February 20, 1992, distributed by the Embassy of Indonesia, Washington, D.C.; and the Department of Foreign Affairs, Republic of Indonesia, *East Timor: Building for the Future,* July 1992.
9. Irena Cristalis, *Bitter Dawn: East Timor, A People's History* (London: Zed, 2002), 149.
10. Hernâni Carvalho, *Os Dias da UNAMET: Crónicas de uma Reportagem em Timor* (Lisbon: Hugin Editores, 2000).
11. Keith Richburg of the *The Washington Post* also fell into this trap. A September 3, 1999, article that he wrote ("Jakarta Suggests UN Force in Timor," *The Washington Post* and *International Herald Tribune*) characterized attacks by the militia and TNI against civilian areas of Dili in the days following the ballot as "factional fighting." His subsequent reports avoided this error.

    Reporting by Canada's most prestigious newspaper, *The Globe and Mail,* in the several months preceding the ballot was also frequently highly flawed. See Robert Everton and James Winter, "Media Coverage of an Imminent Bloodbath in East Timor: What Was Known, and When?" *Portuguese Studies Review* 11, no. 1 (fall–winter 2003): 85–101.
12. See, for example, Ian Martin, *Self-Determination in East Timor: The United Nations, the Ballot, and International Intervention* (Boulder, Colo.: Lynne Rienner, 2001). See also testimony of Allan Nairn. U.S. Congress, International Operations and Human Rights Subcommittee of the House Committee on International Relations, "Hearing Monitoring the Humanitarian Crisis in East Timor," September 30, 1999; transcript available online at http://etan.org/legislation/999bhear.htm#ALLAN%20NAIRN. In another account Nairn, who was arrested by Indonesian police in Dili on September 14, 1999, reported that he shared a military-chartered flight from Dili to Kupang, West Timor, with dozens of Indonesian police intelligence agents who were dressed as militia members, what he interpreted as further proof that the "militias are a tightly coordinated police and military operation in East Timor." Quoted in Dennis Bernstein,

"Doing Time in Timor," *San Francisco Bay Guardian,* September 22, 1999; available online at http://www.flashpoints.net/fNairnGuardian.html.

13. Agence France Presse, "Australia Thanks Italy for East Timor Deployment," February 11, 2001; available online at http://www.etan.org/.

14. See Taric Jasarevic, "Reviving Fisheries in East Timor: Casting Nets for Development," *UN Volunteers News,* no. 93 (August 2002); available online at http://www.unv.org/publications/index.htm.

15. See, for example, Don Greenlees and Robert Garran, *Deliverance: The Inside Story of East Timor's Fight for Freedom* (Crows Nest, Australia: Allen and Unwin, 2002), chap. 11.

16. Until April 1999 the police were a formal part of the military.

17. Samuel Moore, "The Indonesian Military's Last Years in East Timor: An Analysis of Its Secret Documents," *Indonesia* 72 (October 2001).

18. Cameron Barr, "Post-Referendum Backlash in Los Palos: Near Their Base, Soldiers Target the Referendum Victors" and "A Pattern of Violence," *The Christian Science Monitor,* March 14, 2000. Also see Lansell Taudevin, *East Timor: Too Little Too Late* (Sydney: Duffy and Snellgrove, 1999).

19. John Martinkus, *A Dirty Little War* (Sydney: Random House, 2001).

20. See Peter Bartu, "The Militia, the Military, and the People of Bobonaro District," *Bulletin of Concerned Asian Scholars* 32, nos. 1, 2 (2000): 35–42.

21. Paul Farmer, "Pathologies of Power: Rethinking Health and Human Rights," *American Journal of Public Health* 89, no. 10 (October 1999): 1486–1496.

22. R. Baumister and S. Hastings, "Distortions of Collective Memory: How Groups Flatter and Deceive Themselves" in *Collective Memory of Political Events: Social Psychological Perspectives,* ed. James W. Pennebaker, Dario Páez, and Bernard Rimé (Mahwah, N.J.: Lawrence Erlbaum, 1997), 277.

23. See Luis M. Valdivieso et al., *East Timor: Establishing the Foundations of Sound Macroeconomic Management* (Washington, D.C.: International Monetary Fund, 2000), 1.

24. See British Office in East Timor, "British Support for East Timor," June 14, 2000; copy on file with author.

25. TAPOL, Indonesian Human Rights Campaign, London, "Ethics, Investments and Repression—Britain and Indonesia: The Test for Government and Business," March 31, 1998.

26. For an overview of Japanese aid to East Timor, see *The La'o Hamutuk Bulletin* (August 2002); available online at www.etan.org/lh.

27. The document is available online at http://www.mofa.go.jp/policy/other/bluebook/2000/III-a.html.

28. U.S. Department of State, Bureau of East Asian and Pacific Affairs, "Background Note: East Timor," November 2003; on file with author.

29. Madeleine Albright, *Madam Secretary: A Memoir* (New York: Miramax, 2003), 518, 351, and 443, respectively.

30. Alexander Downer, "From the Minister," *Focus* (March 2000) (inside front cover).

31. Kirsten Hawke, "Survivors Rebuild Their World," *Focus* (March 2000): 5–6; quote at 6.

32. "East Timor: Birth of a Nation," Statement by Hon. Alexander Downer, Minister for Foreign Affairs, Australia, May 15, 2002.

33. See, for example, Tim Fischer, *Ballots and Bullets: Seven Days in East Timor* (St. Leonards, NSW, Australia: Allen and Unwin, 2000).

34. Text of letter contained in Fischer, *Ballots and Bullets.*

35. Fischer, *Ballots and Bullets,* 14.

36. See Greenlees and Garran, Deliverance; and Clinton Fernandes, *Reluctant Saviour: Australia, Indonesia and the Independence of East Timor* (Melbourne: Scribe Publications, 2004).

37. Transcript of the Prime Minister the Hon John Howard MP, Press Conference on Arrival in Dili, East Timor, May 19, 2002.
38. Even the current governing party's main opposition, the Australian Labor Party, does not favor an apology. See Rob Taylor and Denis Peters, "Federal Oppn Denies Supporting Apology for E Timor," Australian Associated Press, September 5, 2000.
39. Quoted in Paul Daley, "Man for a Crisis," *The Age* (Melbourne), March 5, 2001. For a critical response to Evans's claims, see Scott Burchill, "Not Guilty on Timor? Explain This Then," *The Age* (Melbourne), March 12, 2001. More recently Evans has acknowledged somewhat the problematic nature of Australia's role in Indonesian-occupied East Timor, stating, "I am one of those who has to acknowledge, as Australia's foreign minister at the time, that many of our earlier training efforts helped only to produce more professional human rights abusers." See Gareth Evans, "Indonesia's Military Culture Has to Be Reformed," *International Herald Tribune*, July 24, 2001.
40. See Australian Senate Foreign Affairs, Defence and Trade References Committee, *East Timor,* chaps. 6–7; Wendy Way, Damien Browne, and Vivianne Johnson, eds., *Australia and the Indonesian Incorporation of Portuguese Timor, 1974 — 1976* (Carlton, Victoria: Melbourne University Press, 2000). Also see Paul M. Monk, "Secret Intelligence and Escape Clauses: Australia and the Indonesian Annexation of East Timor, 1963–76," *Critical Asian Studies* 33, no. 2 (2001): 181–208.
41. The words are contained in a press release available online at http://www.beehive .govt.nz/ViewDocument.cfm?DocumentID=14842.
42. The document is available online at http://www.mfat.govt.nz/foreign/regions/sea/ countrypapers/timorlestepaper.html.
43. Chris Hedges, *War Is a Force That Gives Us Meaning* (New York: Public Affairs, 2002), 141.
44. Ben Terrall, "The Price of Independence" (op-ed), *The Baltimore Sun*, May 20, 2002; available online at http://www.etan.org/; Michael Richardson, "How U.S. Averted Gaze When Indonesia Took East Timor," *International Herald Tribune,* May 20, 2002; and Larry Johnson, "A Reminder of What America Owes East Timor," *Seattle Post-Intelligencer,* May 20, 2002.
45. "A Nation Is Born" (editorial), *The New York Times,* May 20, 2002.
46. "Newborn East Timor" (editorial), *The Boston Globe,* May 20, 2002.
47. Mark Lee, "The Hard Work of Forgiveness," *Los Angeles Times,* May 19, 2002.
48. Richard C. Paddock, "E. Timor Celebrates Its Birth," *Los Angeles Times,* May 20, 2002; and Rajiv Chandrasekaran, "East Timorese Wave Their Flag as Independence Is Proclaimed," *The Washington Post,* May 20, 2002, A16.
49. The British press was little better. See David Edwards and David Cromwell, "East Timor and the British Press: The British Press Bury Western Complicity in East Timor Genocide," *Media Lens* (U.K.), May 31, 2002.
50. See chapter 5, above.
51. Richard Holbrooke, Speech to the Bologna Center of The Johns Hopkins University, May 13, 2000; available online at http://www.un.int/usa/00holo513.htm.
52. Despite this performance and Holbrooke's work over the years to support the Indonesian occupation, Portuguese president Jorge Sampaio awarded Holbrooke the Order of Henry the Navigator for his efforts on behalf of East Timorese independence and reconstruction. See Lusa, "Lisbon Honors ex-US Ambassador to UN for Pro-Timor Efforts," July 7, 2004; available online at http://www.etan.org/.
53. Rod McGuirk, "East Timorese Students Want Australian Apology," Australian Associated Press, August 31, 2000; available online at http://www.etan.org/.
54. The full text of the flyer is available online at http://etan.org/news/2000a/alljust .htm#Pamphlet. Similar demonstrations have taken place every year since then.
55. Associated Press, "Timorese Protesters Demand US Apology for '75 Invasion," July 4, 2000; available online at http://www.etan.org/. Gray served as a political officer for the

U.S. Embassy in Jakarta during the late 1990s, through the time of the UNAMET ballot. Despite his words on July 4, 2000, during Indonesia's occupation Gray was very sympathetic toward and supportive of the East Timorese struggle (within the limits of his capacity as a member of the U.S. diplomatic corps under the Clinton administration).

56. Witnessed by the author.

57. *The La'o Hamutuk Bulletin* 2, nos. 6–7 (October 2001).

58. Joanna Jolly, "Japan Military Arrives in East Timor," Associated Press, March 4, 2002; available online at http://www.etan.org/; and Joanna Jolly, "Sex Slave Protests Confront Japanese Army," *The Age,* March 5 2002. Also see Nao Shimoyachi, "East Timorese Recalls Wartime Sex-Slave Experience," *The Japan Times,* December 14, 2002.

59. José Ramos-Horta, "East Timor Must Forget the Tragic Events of World War II," Media Release, Department of Foreign Affairs, March 5, 2001.

60. Quoted in *The La'o Hamutuk Bulletin* 2, no. 4 (July 2001).

61. José Ramos-Horta, "Clinton's Indonesia Policy Split," *The Christian Science Monitor,* April 16, 1997.

62. Xanana Gusmão, Defense Plea, May 17, 1993.

63. Copy of statement on file with author.

64. See Eviatar Zerubavel, "Social Memories: Steps to a Sociology of the Past," *Qualitative Sociology* 19, no. 3 (1996): 283–299.

65. Regarding the power of the state to shape the worldviews of its citizenry, see Katherine Beckett, *Making Crime Pay: Law and Order in Contemporary American Politics* (New York: Oxford University Press, 1997). Also see Joseph Nevins, *Operation Gatekeeper: The Rise of the "Illegal Alien" and the Re-Making of the U.S.-Mexico Boundary* (New York: Routledge, 2002).

8. ACCOUNTING FOR THE PAST

The sources of the epigraphs to this chapter are, respectively, Stephen Sedley, "No More Victors' Justice?" *London Review of Books* 25, no. 1 (January 2, 2003): 17; Hannah Arendt, *Eichmann in Jerusalem: A Report on the Banality of Evil* (New York: Viking, 1973 [1963]), 246–247.

1. Richard Holbrooke, Transcript from November 21, 1999, press conference, Embassy of the United States of America, Jakarta, Indonesia; available online at http://www .usembassyjakarta.org/news/holbrooke-roth.html.

2. U.N. General Assembly, "Situation of Human Rights in East Timor" (New York: United Nations, December 10 1999), 20–21; available online at http://www.jsmp.minihub.org/ Reports/special%20rapp%20report.pdf.

3. U.N. Office of the High Commissioner for Human Rights, "Report of the International Commission of Inquiry on East Timor to the Secretary-General" (New York: United Nations, January 2000); available online at http://www.unhchr.ch/huridocda/ huridoca.nsf/(Symbol)/A.54.726,+S.2000.59.En.

4. Annan wrote these words in identical letters that accompanied the report to the heads of the General Assembly, the Security Council, and the U.N. Commission on Human Rights. The letter is available online at http://www.unhchr.ch/huridocda/huridoca .nsf/(Symbol)/A.54.726,+S.2000.59.En.

5. Mark Riley, "UN Scorn for Jakarta Justice for Timor," *Sydney Morning Herald,* February 2, 2000.

6. *India Times,* February 15, 2000. Quoted in David Cohen, "Seeking Justice on the Cheap: Is the East Timor Tribunal Really a Model for the Future," *Asia Pacific Issues,* no. 61 (August 2002): 2–3.

7. See *The La'o Hamutuk Bulletin* (October 2001); available online at www.etan.org/lh/bulletin.html.
8. The most comprehensive analysis of the court is David Cohen, "Intended to Fail: The Trials before the Ad Hoc Human Rights Court in Jakarta" (New York: International Center for Transitional Justice in New York City, 2003); the full report is available online at http://www.ictj.org/downloads/Intended_to_Fail — FINAL.pdf. See also International Crisis Group, "Indonesia: The Implications of the Timor Trials," May 8, 2002 (report available online at http://www.crisisweb.org/projects/asia/indonesia/reports/A400643_08052002.pdf); and the reports of the Institute for Policy Research and Advocacy (ELSAM) of Indonesia (available online at http://www.elsam.or.id/txt/english/publications/index.htm).
9. Indonesia's parliament provided a potential loophole for those appealing convictions when it passed a constitutional amendment in August 2000. The legislation prohibits prosecution for crimes that did not constitute an offense at the time of their commission, thus potentially disallowing trying individuals for war crimes or crimes against humanity committed in East Timor or Indonesia prior to the passage of the amendment. See Slobodan Lekic, "Indonesia's Military Win Concessions from Top Assembly," Associated Press, August 18, 2000; available online at http://www.etan.org/; and Amnesty International. "Indonesia: Retroactivity Amendment Regressive for Human Rights" (press release), August 18, 2000; available online at www.amnesty.org. Regarding the 2004 acquittals and overturning of convictions, see Human Rights Watch, "Indonesia: Court Sanctions Impunity for East Timor Abuses," August 7, 2004; available online at http://www.hrw.org/English/docs/2004/08/06/indone9205.htm.
10. In the case of Australia, for example, it appears that government officials deliberately downplayed the scale of the atrocities in September 1999 in order to avoid embarrassing Jakarta. According to an Australian army intelligence officer who led investigations of atrocities during the InterFET mission, officials in Australia made it clear to him that an international tribunal was undesirable. See "Australia's East Timor Secret" (2001); and "See No Evil," Dateline, SBS-TV (Australia), broadcast on May 9, 2001; transcript available at http://www.tip.net.au/~wildwood/01maysbs2.htm.
11. John Aglionby, "Timorese Pay the Price for Stability," *The Guardian* (London), November 15, 2000.
12. See, for example, Agence France Presse, "International Tribunal for East Timorese 'Bloodbath' Possible: Albright," May 5, 2000; available online at http://www.etan.org/.
13. At the last several meetings on East Timor of the U.N. Security Council, not one of the speakers representing the various member-states has even mentioned an international tribunal or prosecution of crimes committed prior to 1999.

    In August 2004 New Zealand's government broke with the ranks of the West and called for an international tribunal for the crimes committed in 1999 in East Timor, "notwithstanding the opposition which might exist to this path being followed." See Phil Goff, Minister of Foreign Affairs and Trade, New Zealand Government, "Latest Verdicts Blow for East Timor Justice — Goff," Media Release, August 8, 2004; available online at http://www.etan.org/.
14. See Jill Jolliffe, "Australia Blamed in East Timor Report," *Sydney Morning Herald,* April 5, 2004; and Jill Jolliffe, "Evidence Damns Indonesians, UN Refuses to Publish Timor Report, *The Gazette* (Montreal), April 7, 2004, A16. Both articles are available online at http://www.etan.org/.
15. Geoffrey Robinson, "East Timor 1999: Crimes against Humanity" (A Report Commissioned by the United Nations Office of the High Commissioner for Human Rights), July 2003. A copy of the report is on file with this author.

16. See Noam Chomsky, *A New Generation Draws the Line: Kosovo, East Timor and the Standards of the West* (London: Verso, 2000).

17. See Joe Lauria, "UN Tribunal on Timor Is Called Unlikely," *The Boston Globe,* January 15, 2000, A04.

18. Nevertheless, at least two U.N. officials and someone from Human Rights Watch asserted to me that it is not worthwhile to champion an international tribunal for exactly this reason.

19. See Caitlin Reiger, "The East Timor Experiment with International Justice," paper delivered at a conference on "Justice in the Balance: Military Commissions and International Criminal Tribunals in a Violent Age," University of California, Berkeley, March 16, 2002; Joseph Nevins, "(Mis)Representing East Timor's Past: Structural-Symbolic Violence, International Law, and the Institutionalization of Injustice," *The Journal of Human Rights* 1, no. 4 (December 2002); and various issues of *The La'o Hamutuk Bulletin.*

Jakarta now repudiates the memorandum of understanding, arguing that it has no legal standing because Indonesia's parliament never ratified it. The United Nations in East Timor does not accept this argument as valid.

20. The Serious Crimes Unit (SCU) describes itself as "responsible for conducting investigations and preparing indictments to assist in bringing to justice those responsible for Crimes Against Humanity and other serious crimes committed in East Timor in 1999." According to a March 9, 2004, press release from East Timor's Office of the Deputy General Prosecutor for Serious Crimes, the SCU had indicted "a total of 369 persons with 281 of those accused presently outside the jurisdiction of Timor Leste including 37 Indonesian TNI Military Commanders and Officers, 4 Indonesian Chiefs of Police and 60 East Timorese TNI members."

21. The Serious Crime Unit has issued many warrants for the arrest by Interpol (were they ever to leave Indonesia) of those indicted. But in January 2004 Longuinhos Monteiro, East Timor's chief prosecutor, accused the United Nations of blocking the issuance of Interpol arrest warrants for General Wiranto and seven other senior TNI officers for political reasons. See Jill Jolliffe, "UN Accused of Blocking East Timor Warrants," *The Age,* January 14, 2004.

22. On January 15, 2004, the East Timor National Alliance for an International Tribunal — "a coalition of organizations representing local and international NGOs, churches, students and victims" of Indonesia's crimes — wrote to the United Nations to express its disappointment with international efforts thus far regarding justice and to offer suggestions for improving the situation. In addition to calling for the establishment of an international tribunal, the Alliance stated that, if "the UN and the governments of the world continue to be unwilling to support meaningful justice for crimes against humanity and East Timor," a continuation of the Special Crimes Unit (SCU) and the Special Panels (SP) in their current forms is "unwarranted." In addition to focusing on low-level East Timorese perpetrators, the SCU and SP provide "an excuse for East Timor's government and the international community to avoid meaningful action for justice." This the Alliance characterized as a "cruel charade perpetrated by those for whom justice is a weapon of realpolitik, rather than a basic human right," and argued that "it would be better to do nothing than to perpetuate the lie." Text of letter available online at http://www.etan.org/.

Despite limiting its work to 1999, the SCU had only investigated half the murders committed during that year as of mid-2004. Nevertheless the United Nations has been cutting back on the number of criminal investigators (from thirty-six to seventeen). As envisioned by the U.N. Security Council, the SCU was scheduled to finish its investigations by November 2004, and the Special Panels (along with the U.N. assistance mission in East Timor as a whole) would cease to exist as of May 20, 2005, thus putting an end to prosecutions. According to East Timor's Judicial System Monitoring Project (JSMP), "The serious crimes process is a vital aspect of providing justice for the crimes against humanity committed in East Timor. To not give full support, particularly in terms of investigation, is to back down on a commitment made by the UN in 1999 to bring those responsible to justice." See JSMP press release of May 6, 2004, "UN Sacrifices Justice for Dollars," available online at http://www.jsmp.minihub.org/News/May04/06may04_jsmppress_unsacrifices_eng.htm/.

23. Amnesty International, "East Timor: Justice Past, Present and Future" (AI-index: ASA 57/001/2001), July 27, 2001; available online at www.amnesty.org.

In an April 14, 2004, joint report issued with the East Timor–based Judicial System Monitoring Program, Amnesty International called upon the United Nations to consider the establishment of an international tribunal among other options to prosecute the 1999 crimes. In doing so, Amnesty and the JSMP stated, "All those responsible for committing crimes in Timor-Leste in 1999, and eventually for the whole period of Indonesia's occupation, should be brought to justice." Report available online at http://www.jsmp.minihub.org/Reports/jsmpreports/jsmp_amnety_report_justiceforET_

24. See Human Rights Watch, "Justice for East Timor," Press Backgrounder, March 2000; available online at www.hrw.org.

25. The only instance of such criticism/advocacy I was able to locate was a May 17, 2002, press release that spoke of the need to bring "perpetrators to justice for serious human rights abuses committed in East Timor in 1999 and previously." See Human Rights Watch, "East Timor: Stronger Judiciary Needed," May 17, 2002; available online at www.hrw.org.

26. Daniel Nelson, "Robinson Grilled over Justice in East Timor," One World News Service, August 16, 2000; available online at http://www.etan.org.

27. Gary Jonathan Bass, *Stay the Hand of Vengeance: The Politics of War Crimes Tribunals* (Princeton, N.J.: Princeton University Press, 2000).

28. Priscilla B. Hayner, *Unspeakable Truths: Confronting State Terror and Atrocity* (New York: Routledge, 2000), 14.

29. Ibid.

30. For an overview of the various commissions, see ibid.

31. The website of the CAVR is located at http://www.easttimor-reconciliation.org/.

32. *The La'o Hamutuk Bulletin* (October 2001).

33. For a journalistic account of one such Community Reconciliation Procedure, see "East Timor's Example," *The Times of India,* January 5, 2004; available online at http://timesofindia.indiatimes.com/articleshow/404228.cms.

Although most participants expressed satisfaction with the CRPs, some victims felt that the punishments meted out were not sufficiently strong. See Geoffrey Robinson, "Forgiveness in East Timor, but Where Is the Justice?" published online by the International Institute of the University of California, Los Angeles; available at http://www.international.ucla.edu/print.asp?parentid=11589, May 28, 2004.

34. The founding regulation of the commission is located at http://www.un.org/peace/etimor/untaetR/Reg10e.pdf.

35. See, for example, Amy Gutman and Dennis Thompson, "The Moral Foundations of Truth Commissions," in *Truth v. Justice: The Morality of Truth Commissions,* ed. Robert Rotberg and Dennis Thompson (Princeton, N.J.: Princeton University Press, 2000), 22–44.

36. Reed Brody, "Justice: The First Casualty of Truth?" *The Nation,* April 30, 2001, 25–28+. Also see Aryeh Neier, *War Crimes: Brutality, Terror, and the Struggle for Justice* (New York: Times Books, 1998).

37. Hayner, *Unspeakable Truths;* and Brody, "Justice: The First Casualty of Truth?"

38. See the commission's website at http://easttimor-reconciliation.org/justicesystem.htm.

39. Brody, "Justice: The First Casualty of Truth?"

40. See Jonathan D. Tepperman, "Truth and Consequences," *Foreign Affairs* 81 (March/April 2002), 128+.

41. See Neier, *War Crimes*.

42. Martha Minow, *Between Vengeance and Forgiveness: Facing History after Genocide and Mass Violence* (Boston: Beacon, 1998); and Desmond Tutu, *No Future without Forgiveness* (New York: Doubleday, 1999).

43. Elazar Barkan, *The Guilt of Nations: Restitution and Negotiating Historical Injustices* (New York: Norton, 2000), xix.

44. I would like to acknowledge and thank Harvey Weinstein of the Human Rights Center at the University of California, Berkeley, for numerous conversations on related matters. His insights and criticisms helped greatly in my effort to improve my analysis of reconciliation in theory and practice.

45. Robert I. Rotberg, "Truth Commissions and the Provision of Truth, Justice, and Reconciliation," in *Truth v. Justice: The Morality of Truth Commissions,* ed. Robert I. Rotberg and Dennis Thompson (Princeton, N.J.: Princeton University Press: 3–21).

46. Tutu, *No Future without Forgiveness,* 54–55. A frequent misconception about truth commissions is that they lead to group and personal "healing." For proponents of this position, participation in a truth commission is almost akin to therapy. Research on the "healing" effects of commissions is far from conclusive, however. In fact, there is much evidence that such bodies can actually heighten intergroup tensions (see Hayner, *Unspeakable Truths;* also see Richard A. Wilson, *The Politics of Truth and Reconciliation in South Africa: Legitimizing the Post-Apartheid State* (Cambridge: Cambridge University Press, 2001). Regarding the difficulties of "healing" in East Timor, see Margot Cohen, "Survivors in East Timor Find It Hard to Forgive," *Far Eastern Economic Review,* March 28, 2002; available online at http://www.etan.org/.

47. See Hayner, *Unspeakable Truths;* and Ginger Thompson, "South African Commission Ends Its Work," *The New York Times,* March 22, 2003.

48. See Hein Marais, *South Africa: Limits to Change: The Political Economy of Transition* (London: Zed, 2001); and Terry Bell, with Dumisa Buhle Ntsebeza, *Unfinished Business: South Africa, Apartheid and Truth* (London: Verso, 2003).

49. Wilson, *The Politics of Truth and Reconciliation in South Africa.*

50. Quoted in Hayner, *Unspeakable Truths,* 164–165.

51. Hayner, *Unspeakable Truths.*

52. Tutu is well aware of these structural injustices and the need for South Africa to address them in order to build a just and peaceful South Africa. Speaking on the day marking the formal end of the TRC's work, Tutu asked rhetorically,

> Can you explain how a black person wakes up in a squalid ghetto today, almost 10 years after freedom? Then he goes to work in town, which is still largely white, in palatial homes. And at the end of the day, he goes back home to squalor?
>
> I don't know why those people don't just say, "To hell with peace. To hell with Tutu and the truth commission." (Quoted in Thompson, "South African Commission Ends Its Work")

53. Barbara Zelizer, *Remembering to Forget; Holocaust Memory through the Camera's Eye* (Chicago: University of Chicago Press, 1998).

54. Hayner, *Unspeakable Truths.* In making this argument, Hayner draws on Mahmood Mamdani, "Degrees of Reconciliation and Forms of Justice: Making Sense of the African Experience," paper presented at the conference "Justice or Reconciliation," at the Center for International Studies, University of Chicago, April 25–26, 1997.

55. Hayner, *Unspeakable Truths;* also see Mamdani, "Degrees of Reconciliation and Forms

of Justice"; Wilson, *The Politics of Truth and Reconciliation in South Africa;* and Roy Brooks, ed., *When Sorry Isn't Enough: The Controversy over Apologies and Reparations for Human Injustice* (New York: New York University Press, 1999).

56. Ramesh Thakur, "Amnesty International and the United Nations," *Journal of Peace Research* 31, no. 2 (May 1994): 143–160.

57. Greg Guma, "Beyond the New World Order: A Post-Nationalist Perspective," *Toward Freedom* (August/September 2001); available online at http://www.towardfreedom .com/2001/aug01/newworld.htm.

58. Quoted in Abba Eban, "The U.N. Idea Revisited," *Foreign Affairs* 74, no. 5 (September/October 1995): 43.

59. Phyllis Bennis, *Calling the Shots: How Washington Dominates Today's UN* (New York: Olive Branch, 2000). See also Peter Gowan, "US: UN," *New Left Review,* no. 24 (November–December 2003): 5–28.

An important weapon in Washington's arsenal was an operation named "Ultra," which permitted the United States to intercept confidential foreign diplomatic traffic in the six months preceding and two months during the San Francisco conference that drafted the U.N. Charter. These intercepted cables significantly aided Washington in its quest to establish a Security Council controlled by the five Allies, a largely impotent General Assembly, and a pliable Secretariat. See S. Schlesinger, "Cryptanalysis for Peacetime: Codebreaking and the Birth and Structure of the United Nations," *Cryptologia* 19, no. 3 (July 1995): 217–235.

60. Christopher Simpson, *The Splendid Blond Beast: Money, Law, and Genocide in the Twentieth Century* (Monroe, Maine: Common Courage, 1995).

61. Ibid.

62. Calvin DeArmond Davis, *The United States and the Second Hague Peace Conference: American Diplomacy and International Organization, 1899–1914* (Durham, N.C.: Duke University Press, 1975); and Simpson, *The Splendid Blond Beast.*

63. Adam Hochschild, *King Leopold's Ghost: A Story of Greed, Terror, and Heroism in Colonial Africa* (New York: Houghton Mifflin, 1998). Regarding the U.S. war in the Philippines, see Sidney Lens, *The Forging of the American Empire: From the Revolution to Vietnam, a History of U.S. Imperialism* (London: Pluto Press, in conjunction with Haymarket Books [Chicago], 2003).

64. James F. Willis, *Prologue to Nuremberg: The Politics and Diplomacy of Punishing War Criminals of the First World War* (Westport: Greenwood, 1982), 86.

65. Diane Orentlicher, "The United States Commitment to International Human Rights," in *Human Rights in the World Community: Issues and Action,* ed. Richard Pierre Claude and Burns H. Weston, 2nd ed. (Philadelphia: University of Pennsylvania Press, 1992), 340–357.

66. Philip Alston, "The UN's Human Rights Record: From San Francisco to Vienna and Beyond," *Human Rights Quarterly* 16, no. 2 (May 1994): 375–390.

67. Bennis, *Calling the Shots,* xxii. From 1989 to 1993 Bolton was Undersecretary of State for International Organization in the George H. W. Bush administration.

68. Mark Tran, "US Tells Iraq to Pull Back Troops or Face Air Strikes," *The Guardian,* October 17, 1994, 20; quoted in Noam Chomsky, "US Iraq Policy: Motives and Consequences," in *Iraq under Siege: The Deadly Impact of Sanctions and War,* ed. Anthony Arnove (Cambridge, Mass.: South End Press, 2000), 47–56.

69. From an article by Catherine Toups, *The Washington Times,* December 13, 1995; quoted in Bennis, *Calling the Shots,* 245.

70. See, for example, Neil Barrett, "The Truth of the Matter," *The Age,* June 17, 2004; available online at http://www.etan.org/.

71. See Lindsay Murdoch, "Timor Parents Beg for Their Stolen Children," *The Age,* April 24, 2001; available online at http://www.etan.org/. See also "East Timor's Stolen Chil-

dren," *Dateline,* SBS-TV (Australia), broadcast on September 4, 2002 (transcript on file with author); and Simon Elegant, "Timor's Lost Boys," *Time* (Asia edition), December 23, 2002 (available online at http://www.etan.org/). Although many of the children have been reunited with their parents, at least a few hundred of them still remain in Indonesia separated from their families, according to a January 2004 report from the U.N. High Commissioner for Refugees.

72. *The La'o Hamutuk Bulletin,* July 17, 2000.
73. Seth Mydans, "A Tonic for East Timor's Poverty," *The New York Times,* October 19, 2000.
74. Despite his conviction, Damiri, now retired, continued to serve as Assistant for Operations to the Chief of the General Staff of the TNI.
75. The war has deep roots, but its intensity dramatically escalated with Megawati Sukarnoputri's declaration of martial law in May 2003. Following the declaration the TNI in Aceh has committed large-scale atrocities, including extrajudicial executions and forced disappearances (Human Rights Watch, "Aceh under Martial Law: Inside the Secret War," report released on December 18, 2003; available online at http://hrw .org/reports/2003/indonesia1203/indonesia1203.pdf.
76. Matthew Moore, "Guterres Says Papuan Force Ready to Fight," *The Age,* December 20, 2003; available online at http://www.westpapuanews.com/articles/publish/article _219.shtml.
77. Matthew Moore, "Rights Group Attacks Papua Police Chief's Timor Record," *The Age,* December 2, 2003; available online at http://iiasnt.leidenuniv.nl:8080/DR/2003/12/ DR_2003_12_02/2. Regarding the sordid history of Indonesia and the international community in West Papua, see Carmel Budiardjo and Liem Soei Liong, *West Papua: The Obliteration of a People,* Surrey (UK): TAPOL, the Indonesia Human Rights Campaign, 1988 [1983]); and John Saltford, *The United Nations and the Indonesian Takeover of West Papua: The Anatomy of Betrayal* (London: Routledge Curzon, 2003).
78. The statement is available online at http://www.indonesiamission-ny.org/speeches/ ga/plenary/ga-092702–57.htm.
79. Peter Alford, "A Nation Built on Ashes," *The Australian,* June 26, 2000.
80. See United Nations Development Programme (UNDP), *Ukun Rasik A'an — The Way Ahead* (East Timor: Human Development Report) (Dili: UNDP, 2002).
81. See Michael Watts, *Silent Violence: Food, Famine and Peasantry in Northern Nigeria* (Berkeley: University of California Press, 1983); and Nancy Scheper-Hughes, *Death without Weeping: The Violence of Everyday Life in Brazil* (Berkeley: University of California Press, 1993).

9. DOUBLE STANDARDS OR JUSTICE AT GROUND ZERO?

The sources of the epigraphs to this chapter are, respectively, *Public Papers of the Presidents of the United States: William J. Clinton, 1999,* Book 1, January 20 to July 31, 1999 (Washington, D.C.: U.S. Government Printing Office, 2000), 587; and George W. Bush, "Address to a Joint Session of Congress and the American People," September 20, 2001. Text of speech available online at http://www.whitehouse.gov/news/releases/2001/09/20010920-8 .html.

1. Olinda and her family eventually received a photo of Verissimo. One taken by a foreign journalist appeared in a book published and distributed by UNTAET on the occasion of the one-year anniversary of the August 30, 1999, ballot. See UNTAET, *Timor Lorosa'e: Tinan Importante Ida / One Momentous Year* (Dili: Publications Unit, Office of Communication and Public Information, United Nations Transitional Administration in East Timor, 2000), 18.

2. Even seasoned observers of occupied East Timor were sometimes fooled by his behavior. See John Martinkus, *A Dirty Little War* (Sydney: Random House, 2001), 60. The author suggests that Verissimo (whom he refers to as "Vincente") was a spy for the Indonesian military.

3. See Seumas Milne, "The Battle for History," *The Guardian Weekly,* September 19–25, 2002, 11.

4. Tzvetan Todorov, "The Abuses of Memory," *Common Knowledge* 5, no. 2 (spring 1996): 6–26.

5. Regarding the role of the United States in Pinochet's coup, see Christopher Hitchens, *The Trial of Henry Kissinger* (New York: Verso, 2001). Also see Peter Kornbluh, *Chile and the United States: Declassified Documents Relating to the Military Coup, September 11, 1973,* National Security Archive Electronic Briefing Book No. 8 (Washington, D.C.: National Security Archive, September 11, 1998); available online at http://www.gwu.edu/~nsarchiv/NSAEBB/NSAEBB8/nsaebb8i.htm.

6. Ariel Dorfman, "The Last September 11," in *Chile: The Other September 11,* ed. Pilar Aguilera and Ricardo Fredes (Melbourne: Ocean Press, 2003), 2–3.

7. An abridged version of Dorfman's essay appeared in one of the largest and most influential newspapers in the United States only ten days after the World Trade Center attack. See Ariel Dorfman, "America Looks at Itself through Humanity's Mirror," *Los Angeles Times,* September 21, 2001.

8. See Phyllis Bennis, *Before & After: U.S. Foreign Policy and the September 11th Crisis* (Brooklyn: Olive Branch, 2003).

9. Regarding nations as imagined communities, see Benedict Anderson, *Imagined Communities: Reflections on the Origin and Spread of Nationalism* (London: Verso, 1991).

10. See Mark Slouka, "A Year Later: Notes on America's Intimations of Mortality," *Harper's Magazine* 305, no. 1828 (September 2002): 35–43.

11. Dorfman, "The Last September 11."

12. Brian Knowlton, "On a Day of Remembrance, Sept. 11 Vigils and Prayers," *International Herald Tribune,* September 11, 2002.

13. William Safire, "On Language," *The New York Times Magazine,* November 11, 2001, 46.

14. See JoAnn Wypijewski, "From a Tropical Paradise to a Nuclear Hell" (op-ed), *Los Angeles Times,* March 1, 2004.

15. Hanson W. Baldwin, "Atom Bomb Is Proved Most Terrible Weapon," *The New York Times,* July 7, 1946, 10E.

16. Howard Zinn, *Hiroshima: Breaking the Silence* (Westfield, N.J.: Open Media, 1995).

17. See Evelyn Tan Powers, "Most in Poll Say Bombing Was Justified," *USA Today,* August 4, 1995; and Robert J. Lifton and Greg Mitchell, "The Bomb's Divisive Legacy," *The Toronto Star,* August 9, 1996. No sitting U.S. president has ever called into question Truman's decision to drop the atomic bombs. On the contrary, they have typically expressed strong support. In 1995 President Bill Clinton, for example, voiced his backing for Truman's course of action, which "we did not believe then and I do not believe now was the wrong one" (quoted in Lifton and Mitchell, "The Bomb's Divisive Legacy").

18. For an excellent discussion of the Pacific War and U.S. actions during and after, see Stephen R. Shalom, "V-J Day: Remembering the Pacific War," *Z Magazine,* July–August 1995.

19. Quoted in Ronald Takaki, *Hiroshima: Why America Dropped the Atomic Bomb* (Boston: Little, Brown, 1995), 30.

20. See ibid.; and Zinn, *Hiroshima.*

21. Columnist Nicholas Kristof of *The New York Times* has argued that the dropping of the atomic bombs was necessary nevertheless. Drawing on work by Japanese scholars, Kristof contends that the Japanese military was not on the verge of surrender on the eve of the bombings. To the contrary, they were ready to sacrifice millions of Japanese lives to prevent Tokyo's capitulation. The atomic bombs actually strengthened the hand

of the peace faction within the country's ruling circles by demonstrating just how high the costs would be if Japan were to continue the war. See Nicholas D, Kristof, "Blood on Our Hands?" *The New York Times,* August 5, 2003.

What Kristof's analysis assumes, however, is that the hard-line faction would have prevailed over the peace faction had Washington not dropped the bombs. This is far from clear. Furthermore, and more important, Washington had good reason to believe that the Japanese military was ready to surrender, especially provided that Japan could retain the emperor system. Although the Japanese refused to surrender after the bombings of Hiroshima and Nagasaki, Japan (and the war faction within) agreed to lay down its arms once the United States offered a conditional surrender—one that allowed Tokyo to retain the emperor. Had Washington made such an offer earlier, there is a distinct possibility that Japanese hard-liners would have agreed to a surrender before the bombings of Hiroshima and Nagasaki. In addition, we cannot know what Tokyo— or, more specifically, the hard-line faction—would have done had Washington not dropped the atomic bombs. Given the rapidly deteriorating situation for Japanese forces in Manchuria at the time, and the possibility of the Soviet Union entering into the Pacific War, there were important factors that, had they been allowed to run their course, might very well have led to a Japanese surrender. Finally, Kristof fails to consider that it might have been possible to end Japan's occupation of various parts of Asia without conquering Japan proper and slaughtering huge numbers of civilians in the process.

I thank historian Ronald Takaki of the Department of Ethnic Studies at the University of California, Berkeley, and Stephen Shalom of the Department of Political Science at William Paterson University for sharing with me their critiques of Kristof's article (e-mail communications with author on September 1, 2003, and September 14, 2003, respectively).

22. The wanton disregard for Japanese lives manifested by such bombings reflected the strength of racism on the part of the United States. For a discussion of the effects of racism on the conduct of the Pacific War by both the Japanese and the Americans, see John Dower, *War Without Mercy: Race and Power in the Pacific War* (New York: Pantheon, 1986).

23. Zinn, *Hiroshima,* 17.

24. Safire, "On Language."

25. See Todorov, "The Abuses of Memory."

26. CNN, "Bush Vows to Rid the World of 'Evil-doers,'" September 16, 2001, and "Blair: We Are All at Risk," September 16, 2001; both available online at http://www.cnn.com.

27. Louise Dodson, "We'd Fight with US Against Terror: PM," *The Age* (Melbourne), September 14, 2001.

28. Many in Jakarta questioned the wisdom of the Indonesian president's going forward with her planned visit to Washington, coming only days after the attacks. But the Bush administration insisted that she do so. As leader of the country with the world's largest Islamic population, Megawati's presence was seen as important to help undercut accusations of anti-Muslim bias and a framing of the conflict as one between the West and Islam as Washington was preparing for war.

29. The pledges of aid included $130 million to promote judicial and legal reform in Indonesia. In addition, the Bush administration agreed to grant duty-free status to eleven Indonesian products worth $100 million under the Generalized System of Preferences. Perhaps the biggest beneficiary, however, were U.S.-based energy corporations. The Bush administration pledged that three U.S. agencies—the Export Import (Exim) Bank, the Overseas Private Investment Corporation (OPIC), and the U.S. Trade and Development Agency—would endeavor to provide a total of $400 million to promote trade and investment in Indonesia, especially in the oil and gas sector. In response, ten

U.S. companies—mostly oil and gas companies—made a commitment to the visiting Indonesian delegation for a new investment totaling $2 billion. See "Joint Statement between the United States of America and the Republic of Indonesia," Office of the White House Press Secretary, September 19, 2001; available online at http://www .whitehouse.gov/news/releases/2001/09/20010919–5.html.

Washington is now providing millions of dollars in assistance and training to an "antiterror" unit of troops from the Indonesian Mobile Brigade police (Brimob). That said, efforts to prevent the resumption of IMET and other forms of military assistance have been unsuccessful as a result of the work of human rights and solidarity organizations and ongoing congressional opposition. See Ben Terrall, "Ashcroft in Indonesia: Bloodshed and Terror with U.S. Connivance," *CounterPunch* 11, no. 4 (February 16–29, 2004): 4–5.

30. Johan Galtung, "Violence, Peace, and Peace Research," *Journal of Peace Research* 6, no. 3 (1969): 167–191.

31. Galtung refers to such violence as "cultural violence": "Any aspect of a culture that can be used to legitimize violence in its direct or structural form." See Johan Galtung, "Cultural Violence," *Journal of Peace Research* 27, no. 3 (1990): 291.

32. Roger S. Clark, "East Timor and the International Criminal Court," in *The East Timor Problem and the Role of Europe*, ed. Pedro Pinto Leite (Leiden: International Platform of Jurists for East Timor, 1996), 97.

33. See Christopher Kutz, *Complicity: Ethics and Law for a Collective Age* (Cambridge: Cambridge University Press, 2000). Also see Jessica Howard, "Invoking State Responsibility for Aiding the Commission of International Crimes—Australia, the United States and the Question of East Timor," *Melbourne Journal of International Law* 2, no. 2 (October 2001): 1–47.

34. Galtung, "Violence, Peace, and Peace Research," 172.

35. Ibid.

36. Noam Chomsky characterizes this premise as a truism. See Noam Chomsky, *The New Military Humanism: Lessons from Kosovo* (Monroe, Maine: Common Courage, 1999), 39.

37. For a discussion of the origins of international law in terms of shielding the powerful, see Christopher Simpson, *The Splendid Blond Beast: Money, Law, and Genocide in the Twentieth Century* (Monroe, Maine: Common Courage, 1995).

38. The two resolutions are available online at http://www.un.org/Docs/scres/2001/ sc2001.htm. I thank Roger Clark for bringing them to my attention.

39. Office of the Iraq Program, United Nations, "Oil-for-Food—The Basic Facts, 1996 to 2002," August 2002; available online at http://www.un.org/Depts/oip/background/ basicfacts.html. Also see Anthony Arnove, ed., *Iraq under Siege: The Deadly Impact of Sanctions and War* (Cambridge, Mass.: South End, 2000).

40. See, for example, Gary Jonathan Bass, *Stay the Hand of Vengeance: The Politics of War Crimes Tribunals* (Princeton, N.J.: Princeton University Press, 2000).

41. See Paul Lewis, "World Court Supports Nicaragua after U.S. Rejected Judges' Role," *The New York Times,* June 28, 1986, 1+; and Noam Chomsky, *Necessary Illusions: Thought Control in Democratic Societies* (Boston: South End Press, 1989).

42. See, for example, David J. Scheffer, "Justice for Cambodia" (op-ed), *The New York Times,* December 21, 2002; and "Killing Fields Unavenged" (editorial), *Los Angeles Times,* April 17, 1998. Scheffer was Ambassador-at-Large for War Crimes Issues during the second half of the Clinton administration. He was also the chief U.S. negotiator in the talks to establish the International Criminal Court

43. See John Pilger, "The Friends of Pol Pot," *The Nation,* May 11, 1998. According to a study by the Inquiry Commission of the Finnish government, the U.S. bombing of Cambodia from 1969 to 1973 caused the deaths of 600,000 Cambodians and created 2

million refugees. See Kimmo Kiljunen, ed., *Kampuchea: Decade of the Genocide: Report of a Finnish Inquiry Commission* (London: Zed, 1984). Ben Kiernan estimates that the bombing caused the deaths of somewhere between 50,000 and 150,000 deaths. See Ben Kiernan, "The American Bombardment of Kampuchea, 1969–1973," *Vietnam Generation* 1, no. 1 (winter 1989): 4–41.

44. See Michael Ignatieff, "'The Lessons of Terror': All War against Civilians Is Equal," *The New York Times Book Review,* February 17, 2002.

45. Ibid.

46. Azmi Bishara, "Twin Towers of Horror," *Al-Ahram Weekly Online,* no. 573, February 14–20, 2002.

47. See Daniel Lazare, "We Are All Terrorists," *Radical Society* 29, no. 4 (2002): 13–20; and John V. Whitbeck, "'Terrorism': A World Ensnared by a Word" (op-ed), *International Herald Tribune,* February 18, 2004.

48. See George Orwell, "Notes on Nationalism," in *Collected Essays, Journalism and Letters of George Orwell,* ed. Sonia Orwell and Ian Angus, Vol. 3 (London: Secker and Warburg, 1969); and Chris Hedges, *War Is a Force That Gives Us Meaning* (New York: Public Affairs, 2002). Also see Joseph Nevins, "Letting Out the (War) Dogs," *The Nation,* vol. 275, no. 17, November 18, 2002, 50+.

49. Chalmers Johnson, *The Sorrows of Empire: Militarism, Secrecy, and the End of the Republic* (New York: Metropolitan Books, 2004).

50. Sebastian Mallaby, "The Reluctant Imperialist," *Foreign Affairs* 81, no. 2 (March–April 2002): 2+.

51. Quote taken from Thomas Friedman, *The Lexus and the Olive Tree: Understanding Globalization* (New York: Farrar, Straus and Giroux, 1999), 373.

52. For a substantiation of this point, see Andrew J. Bacevich, *American Empire: The Realities and Consequences of U.S. Diplomacy* (Cambridge, Mass.: Harvard University Press, 2002).

53. Holbrooke's comments are contained on the jacket of the book. See Max Boot, *The Savage Wars of Peace: Small Wars and the Rise of American Power* (New York: Basic Books, 2002).

54. John Lewis Gaddis, *Now We Know: Rethinking Cold War History* (Oxford: Oxford University Press, 1997).

55. This is not to suggest that Cold War tensions did not significantly help to shape specific U.S. actions in the "Third World." But the Cold War does not explain, in any decisive way, the overall empire-like behavior of the United States in Latin America, Asia, and parts of Africa throughout the twentieth century.

56. See Neil Smith, *American Empire: Roosevelt's Geographer and the Prelude to Globalization* (Berkeley: University of California Press, 2003).

57. Paul Johnson, "Colonialism's Back—and Not a Moment Too Soon," *The New York Times Magazine,* April 18, 1993, 44. Also see Niall Ferguson, *Empire: The Rise and Demise of the British World Order and the Lessons for Global Power* (New York: Basic Books, 2003).

58. Paul Johnson, "The Answer to Terrorism? Colonialism," *Wall Street Journal,* October 6, 2001.

59. Quoted in Noam Chomsky, *Pirates and Emperors: International Terrorism in the Real World,* 2nd ed. (Cambridge, Mass.: South End, 2002), vii. A translation of the original is contained in Saint Augustine, *The City of God* (London: J. M. Dent, 1931), book 4, chap. 4. The translation differs slightly from that used by Chomsky, but the meaning is identical.

60. Chomsky, *Pirates and Emperors.*

61. For a critical Israeli perspective on the double standards employed when using the term "terrorist" in relation to the Palestinian-Israeli conflict, see Amira Hass, "Always a

Fighter, Always a Terrorist," *Ha'aretz,* October 9, 2002; available online at http://www
.haaretzdaily.com/hasen/pages/ShArt.jhtml?itemNo=217634. Also see Joel Beinin, "Is
Terrorism a Useful Term in Understanding the Middle East and the Palestinian-Israeli
Conflict?" *Radical History Review,* no. 85 (winter 2003): 12–23.

62. Quotes taken from Robert Cooper, "Why We Still Need Empires," *The Observer* (London), April 7, 2002; available online at http://www.observer.co.uk/worldview/story/
0,11581,680117,00.html. For an expanded version of the article, see idem, "The Post-
Modern State," in Mark Leonard, *Reordering the World: The Long-Term Implications of
11 September* (London: Foreign Policy Centre, 2002), 11–20. Also see Robert Cooper,
The Post-Modern State and the World Order, 2nd ed. (London: Demos and the Foreign
Policy Centre, 2000).

63. See, for example, Samantha Power, *"A Problem from Hell": America and the Age of Genocide* (New York: Basic Books, 2002). For a critical analysis of the book, see Joseph
Nevins, "On Justifying Intervention," *The Nation,* vol. 274, no. 19, May 20, 2002, 32+.

64. In Guatemala more than two hundred thousand — most of them indigenous Mayans —
lost their lives in the context of a brutal conflict between a U.S.-backed military oligarchy and a guerrilla force during the 1970s and 1980s. The 1999 report of the internationally supported Guatemalan Commission for Historical Clarification concluded
that the state was responsible for more than 90 percent of the deaths and had committed "acts of genocide." The commission found that American training of members
of Guatemala's intelligence apparatus and officer corps in counterinsurgency "had
significant bearing on human rights violations." It also found that Washington, largely
through its intelligence agencies, "lent direct and indirect support to some illegal state
operations." See *Guatemala: Memory of Silence, Report of the Commission for Historical
Clarification,* February 1999; available online at http://shr.aaas.org/guatemala/ceh/
report/english/toc.html. The roots of American involvement in the Guatemalan military's reign of terror run deep, Washington having played a key role in the overthrow
of a democratically elected government there in 1954. See Stephen C. Schlesinger and
Stephen Kinzer, *Bitter Fruit: The Story of the American Coup in Guatemala* (Cambridge,
Mass.: Harvard University Press, 1999); and Kate Doyle and Peter Kornbluh, *CIA and
Assassinations: The Guatemala 1954 Documents,* National Security Archive Electronic
Briefing Book No. 4 (Washington, D.C.: National Security Archive, n.d.); available
online at http://www.gwu.edu/~nsarchiv/NSAEBB/NSAEBB4/index.html. Also
see Kate Doyle, *The Guatemalan Military: What the U.S. Files Reveal,* National Security
Archive Electronic Briefing Book No. 32 (Washington, D.C.: National Security
Archive, June 2001); available online at http://www.gwu.edu/~nsarchiv/NSAEBB/
NSAEBB32/index.html; and Daniel Wilkinson, *Silence on the Mountain: Stories of Terror, Betrayal, and Forgetting in Guatemala* (Boston: Houghton Mifflin, 2002).

While visiting Guatemala on March 10, 1999, Clinton stated, "For the United
States, it is important that I state clearly that support for the military forces and intelligence units which engaged in violence and widespread repression was wrong, and the
United States must not repeat that mistake. We must, and we will, instead continue to
support the peace and reconciliation process in Guatemala." Regarding Clinton's expression of regret, see BBC, "Clinton: Backing of Dictators Was Wrong," March 11,
1999; available online at http://news.bbc.co.uk/1/hi/world/americas/294590.stm.
Also see Jim Lobe, "Time for a U.S. Truth Commission?" InterPress Service, March 14,
1999.

65. See, for example, Michael Ignatieff, "The Burden," *The New York Times Magazine,* January 5, 2003, 22–27+. (For an interesting critique of Ignatieff's article, see Lewis H.
Lapham, "Light in the Window," *Harper's Magazine* 306, no. 1834 [March 2003]: 7–
9.) At the liberal-Left end of the spectrum of respectable debate, Todd Gitlin has also
strongly criticized the imperialism embodied by the G. W. Bush doctrine. In the end,

however, his greatest concern is not the implications of imperialism for those targeted by the empire but the United States itself. The Bush doctrine, he argues, will only fuel anti-Americanism, which will lead to more harm for Americans. See Todd Gitlin, "America's Age of Empire," *Mother Jones* 28, no. 1 (January/February 2003): 35–37.

66. See Bacevich, *American Empire;* and James Chace, "Imperial America and the Common Interest," *World Policy Journal* 19, no. 1 (spring 2002): 1–9.

67. See Christopher Hitchens, "Imperialism: Superpower Dominance, Malignant and Benign," *Slate Magazine,* December 10, 2002; available online at http://slate.msn.com/id/2075261/.

68. David Rieff, comments at conference on "Communities in Crisis: Human Rights, Reconstruction, Tolerance," University of California, Berkeley, November 10, 2000. Also see idem, "A New Age of Liberal Imperialism?" *World Policy Journal* 16, no. 2 (summer 1999).

69. Chalmers Johnson, *Blowback: The Costs and Consequences of American Empire* (New York: Henry Holt, 2004).

70. See David Rieff, *A Bed for the Night: Humanitarianism in Crisis* (New York: Simon and Schuster, 2002); and Noam Chomsky, *Hegemony or Survival: America's Quest for Global Dominance* (New York: Metropolitan Books, 2003).

71. J. A. Hobson, *Imperialism: A Study* (Ann Arbor: University of Michigan Press 1965), 368.

72. Peter Burke. "History as Social Memory," in *Memory, History, Culture and the Mind,* ed. Thomas E. Butler (New York: Basil Blackwell, 1989), 106.

73. See Avishai Margalit, *The Ethics of Memory* (Cambridge, Mass.: Harvard University Press, 2002).

74. Todorov, "The Abuses of Memory," 15.

75. Kundera's quote reads, "The struggle of man against power is the struggle of memory against forgetting" (Milan Kundera, *The Book of Laughter and Forgetting* [New York: HarperPerennial 1994], 3).

76. Dorfman, "The Last September 11," 3–4.

77. There are many examples of exemplary memorial sites. The memorial at the Alfred P. Murrah Federal Building in Oklahoma City, USA—bombed by Timothy McVeigh on April 19, 1995, resulting in 168 deaths—is one such site (see http://www.oklahomacitynationalmemorial.org/). The site of the massacre at My Lai, Vietnam, where U.S. soldiers killed hundreds of unarmed civilians on March 16, 1968, is another. See CNN, "'Blood and Fire' of My Lai Remembered 30 Years Later," CNN Online, March 16, 1998. Available online at http://www.cnn.com/WORLD/9803/16/my.lai/.

10. EPILOGUE

The source of the epigraphs to the epilogue are, respectively, Rabbi Abraham J. Heschel, "The Religious Basis of Equality of Opportunity—The Segregation of God," in Mathew Ahmann, *Race: Challenge to Religion* (Chicago: Regnery, 1963), 64; and *Democracy Now!* radio show, Pacifica Radio, December 29, 2000; available online at www.democracynow.org.

1. The official name of the country is the Democratic Republic of Timor-Leste.

2. UNMISET (United Nations Mission of Support in East Timor) replaced UNTAET with East Timor's ascension to formal independence in May 2002. UNMISET's mandate was to assist the new government until May 2004 (later extended to May 2005) by supporting the long-term stability and security of the country.

   The nature and extent of the United Nation's work in post-occupation East Timor is multifaceted and complex, and to discuss it adequately is far beyond the scope of this book. For an analytical overview, see various issues of *The La'o Hamutuk Bulletin;* available at http://www.etan.org/lh.

3. For accounts of the post-ballot terror and individual stories of survival, see John Martinkus, *A Dirty Little War* (Sydney: Random House, 2001); and Irena Cristalis, *Bitter Dawn: East Timor, A People's History* (London: Zed, 2002).

4. The one exception I could find was Tariq Ali, "The Ignoble Nobel," *The Guardian* (London), December 7, 2002. For an overview of the gap between the human rights rhetoric and the actual practice of the Carter presidency, see Stephen Shalom, "Remembering the Carter Administration," *Z Magazine,* October 1988 (part 1), and November 1988 (part 2).

5. Jonathan Steele, "Salute to President Who Sent No Soldiers into War," *The Guardian Weekly,* October 17–23, 2002, 3.

6. Henry Kissinger, "Remarks for 2002 Félix Houphouët-Boigny Peace Prize Award Ceremony," June 10, 2003; available online at http://www.etan.org/et2003/june/15–21/10kisnger.htm.

7. Jane Perlez, "America Talks and (Some) Others Listen," *The New York Times,* September 12, 1999, sec. 4, 4.

8. See, for example, Nicolaus Mills, preface to *The New Killing Fields: Massacre and the Politics of Intervention, ed.* Nicolaus Mills and Kira Brunner (New York: Basic Books, 2002), ix–xi.

9. Regarding the dubious legality of the agreement, see Roger S. Clark, "Timor Gap: The Legality of the 'Treaty on the Zone of Cooperation in an Area between the Indonesian Province of East Timor and Northern Australia,'" *Pace Yearbook of International Law* 69, no. 4 (1992): 69–95.

10. For background and analysis of the dispute, see *The La'o Hamutuk Bulletin* (various issues); available online at http://www.etan.org.lh/; Democratic Republic of Timor-Leste, Timor Sea Office website; available at http://www.timorseaoffice.gov.tp/; Joseph Nevins, "Contesting the Boundaries of International Justice: State Countermapping and Offshore Resource Struggles between Australia and East Timor," *Economic Geography* 80, no. 1 (2004): 1–22; Quinton Temby, "Timor's Tutorial in Oil Politics," *Asia Times Online,* May, 21, 2003; available online at http://www.atimes.com/atimes/Southeast_Asia/EE21Ae06.html; and Jonathan Holmes, "Rich Man, Poor Man," *Four Corners* (Australian Broadcasting Corporation current affairs television show), May 10, 2004; transcript available online at http://www.abc.net.au/4corners/content/2004/s1105310.htm.

11. The report is available online at http://www.unicef.org/sowc04/15579_contents.html.

12. International Organisation for Migration (IOM), IOM Press Briefing Notes" Timor-Leste, January 13, 2004, on file with author. Also see Australian Broadcasting Corporation, "East Timor Drought Causes Food Crisis," *PM* (radio program), December 9, 2003; transcript available online at http://www.abc.net.au/pm/content/2003/s1006766.htm.

13. Rochelle Mutton, "Girl, 12, Chokes to Death on Worms," *The Age,* May 8, 2004; article available online at http://www.etan.org/et2004/may/01–08/08girl12.htm. Also see ABC Radio, "East Timor: Girl's Death Highlights Poor Healthcare," May 14, 2004; transcript available online at http://www.abc.net.au/ra/asiapac/programs/s1108744.htm.

14. Oxfam Community Aid Abroad (Australia), "Two Years On . . . What Future for an Independent East Timor?" May 2004; report available online at http://www.oxfam.org.au/campaigns/easttimor/. The figure of more than U.S.$700,000 is derived from Oxfam Community Aid Abroad's estimate of AUD$1 million.

A December 2003 statement by the East Timorese organization *La'o Hamutuk* estimated that Australia had received $1 billion in revenues from one disputed oil field since 1999. Given the illegitimacy of Australian control of the oil field, the revenues, according to the organization, make East Timor "the largest foreign contributor to Australia's national budget." See La'o Hamutuk, "Statement to the Development Partners Meeting," December 2003; text available online at http://www.etan.org/lh/misc/dpconf.htm.

15. See *La'o Hamutuk Bulletin,* esp. vol. 3, no. 8 (December 2002); available online at http://www.etan.org/lh. Also see Pamela Bone, "Generous Aid Equals Greater Security," *The Age* (Melbourne), May 31, 2004.

In a May 2004 radio interview about the seabed controversy, Australian foreign minister Alexander Downer characterized East Timor as "a country which we helped to bring to independence and to which we have been enormously generous and supportive over recent years." Radio Australia, "East Timor: Australia Accused of Trying to Steal Oil Reserves," May 3, 2004; transcript available at http://www.abc.net.au/ra/asiapac/programs/s1100516.htm.

For a perspective from East Timorese civil society on this matter, see the founding statement (April 2004) of the Movement Against the Occupation of the Timor Sea; available online at http://www.etan.org/.

16. Quoted in Neil Smith, *American Empire: Roosevelt's Geographer and the Prelude to Globalization* (Berkeley: University of California Press, 2003), 356.

17. National Intelligence officer for Japan and Pacific Asia, Memorandum to Thomas Barnes, Central Intelligence Agency, December 12, 1975. Photocopy of document obtained from Gerald R. Ford Library. Thanks to Brad Simpson for providing me with the document.

18. Speech translated and distributed by TAPOL.

19. See Constâncio Pinto and Matthew Jardine, *East Timor's Unfinished Struggle: Inside the Timorese Resistance* (Cambridge, Mass.: South End Press, 1997).

20. These movements included groups working in solidarity with the cause of East Timorese self-determination. Indonesian solidarity activists continue to support East Timor in various ways—from within Indonesia and within East Timor itself. See, for example, "Meet Titi Irawati: An Indonesian Human Rights Worker in East Timor," *Inside Indonesia,* no. 71 (July–September 2002): 13.

Numerous Indonesians living in East Timor during the time of the occupation—like the father of Liliana (introduced in chapter 1)—worked with the resistance in various ways. According to Liliana, he worked with the clandestine front. A small number of Indonesians even joined Falintil, the guerrilla army. See Nug Katjasungkana, "The Indonesian Who Joined Falintil," *Inside Indonesia,* no. 71 (July–September 2002), 14–15.

21. James F. Glassman, "Structural Power, Agency and National Liberation: The Case of East Timor," *Transactions of the Institute of British Geographers* 28, no. 3 (2003): 264–280.

22. Thomas Ambrosio, "East Timor Independence: The Changing Nature of International Pressure," in *Transforming East Asian Domestic and International Politics: The Impact of Economy and Globalization,* ed. Robert W. Compton, 115–137. But perhaps more so it reflected the consolidation of American power in Southeast Asia to such an extent that Washington no longer felt as compelled as it once did to curry Jakarta's favor lest Indonesia's ruling elites turn elsewhere.

23. David Webster, "Non-State Diplomacy: East Timor, 1975–99," *Portuguese Studies Review* 11, no. 1 (fall–winter 2003): 1–28; and Brad Simpson, "Solidarity in an Age of Globalization: The Transnational Movement for East Timor and U.S. Foreign Policy," *Peace and Change* 28, no. 3–4 (July 2004): 453–482.

Transnational advocacy networks, such as that supporting East Timor, typically employ, among other things, "moral leverage" and a concomitant "mobilization of shame" by highlighting that targeted governments, institutions, and policy makers are failing to live up to their obligations and their own claims. See Margaret E. Keck and Kathryn Sikkink, *Activists beyond Borders: Advocacy Networks in International Politics* (Ithaca: Cornell University Press, 1998).

24. "Self-defence and Reality" (editorial), *The Jakarta Post*, August 11, 1993. Cited and quoted in Charles Scheiner, "The United States: From Complicity to Ambiguity," in *The East Timor Question: The Struggle for Independence from Indonesia*, ed. Paul Hainsworth and Stephen McCloskey (London: I. B. Tauris, 2000), 123.

25. See Clifford Bob, "Overcoming Indifference: Internationalizing Human Rights Violations in Rural Mexico," *Journal of Human Rights* 1, no. 2 (June 2002): 247–261.

26. See Arnold Kohen, *From the Place of the Dead: The Epic Struggles of Bishop Belo of East Timor* (New York: St. Martin's, 1999); and Will Carey, "East Timor: The Making of an International Issue, 1974–99," *Brock Review 1998/99* 7, no. 29 (1998–99): 29–56.

27. There is strong support within East Timor for the position that the international community has a duty to ensure that those responsible for the country's suffering be held accountable. See Piers Pigou, "Crying without Tears: In Pursuit of Justice and Reconciliation in Timor-Leste: Community Perspectives and Expectations," International Center for Transitional Justice, August 2003; report available online at http://www.ictj.org/downloads/Crying_Without_Tears_designed.pdf/.

28. John Roosa, *Pretext for Mass Murder: The September 30th Movement and Suharto's Coup d'Etat in Indonesia* (Madison: University of Wisconsin Press, forthcoming in 2005).

29. The series and subsequent articles related to Tiger Force are available on the *The Toledo Blade*'s website at http://www.toledoblade.com/apps/pbcs.dll/section?Category=SRTIGERFORCE.

30. The accord ending the war made it clear that the United States was the aggressor. A secret protocol to the 1973 Paris treaty stipulated that Washington would provide funds to reconstruct Vietnam. Washington, however, has never followed through. President Jimmy Carter summarized the U.S. position in 1977, explaining that there was no need to dispense monies to Vietnam or even to apologize, as "the destruction was mutual." Washington still pretends it has nothing for which to atone.

31. See Robert Dreyfuss, "Apocalypse Still," *Mother Jones* (February 2000): 42–51+.

32. Misinformation on the U.S. war in Vietnam and the efforts to recast American involvement in Vietnam in a manner that sheds favorable light on Washington vilifies and misrepresents the antiwar movement and portrays the United States more as a victim than a victimizer. See Jerry Lembcke, *The Spitting Image: Myth, Memory, and the Legacy of Vietnam* (New York: New York University Press, 1998); and H. Bruce Franklin, *Vietnam and Other American Fantasies* (Amherst: University of Massachusetts Press, 2000).

INDEX

Page numbers in italics refer to photographs.

INDEX

Mallaby, Sebastian, 195
Mantiri, General, 33
Mario, Father, 27
Marker, Jamsheed, 117, 128, 130, 244n64
Martin, Ian, 100, 101, 126–127, 128–129,
    237–238n32, 244n62
Martinkus, John, 255n2
mauberismo, 223n4
Maununu massacre, 108
May 5 Agreement, 86–87, *113*
    Kofi Annan and, 86, *113,* 117, 239–240n5
    negotiations over security measures,
        116–120
    violations of, 89
    See also referendum
McWilliams, Edmund, 241n22, 242n28,
    244n74
Mead, Walter Russell, 207
media
    influence of, 11
    misinformation and misrepresentation
        by, 32, 59–60, 142–143, 149–150,
        245n11
    Santa Cruz massacre and, 33, 34
    TNI/militia attacks on, 68, 99, 109–110
    See also specific media
Megawati Sukarnoputri, 89, 162, 188–189,
    254n75, 256n28
Memo massacre, 92
memorial sites, exemplary, 260n77
memories, 20–21
    distortion of, 140–141, 149–150
    link to specific dates, 183
    literal versus exemplary, 182–185
militia
    East Timorese membership, 144
    IFET-OP, attacks on, 236n11
    looting by, 101, 102, 107
    media, attacks on, 99
    Red Cross, attacks on, 102–103
    scorched-earth campaign, *1,* 3–4, 100–
        103, 108–110, 237n13
    terror campaign against pro-indepen-
        dence supporters, 84–85, 88, 91–93,
        218n6
    TNI coordination of, 101–102, 241n22,
        245n12
    UNAMET, attacks on, 97–101
    See also TNI
modernity, social distance and, 12
modern states, 199
Mondale, Walter, 53–54

Monjo, John, 57
Monteiro, Longuinhos, 250n21
Moynihan, Daniel Patrick, 72
Muis, Muhammad Noer, 110, 127, 238n32
Muladi, State Secretary, 127
Murdani, Benny, 210
Murphy, Morgan, 52
Mydans, Seth, 4

Nagasaki, 186
Nairn, Allan, 33, *137,* 139–140, 241n27,
    245n12
Namibia, 237n20
National Council of Timorese Resistance
    (CNRT), 82–83, 90, 92–93, 181
National Intelligence Daily, 51
nationalism, 194–195
NBC news, 32
Ndiaye, Bacre Waly, 34–35
Netherlands, 235n35
Newsom, David D., 50
New York Times, 56, 124, 176–177, 255–
    256n21
    misinformation and misrepresentation,
        54, 59–60, 149
New Zealand, 122
    call for international tribunal, 249n13
    Indonesia relations, 67–69, 125
    occupation, complicity in, 62, 67–69
    occupation, distortion of complicity in,
        149
    See also East Timor Core Group
Nicaragua, 193
Nixon, Richard, 77
Novick, Peter, 9

Oakley, Robert, 54
Oecussi, 102, 235n35
O'Kane, Maggie, 4
Operation Komodo Dragon, 49, 63
Operation Security, 30
Orwell, George, 141, 194–195
Owen, David, 65

Pacific War, 25, 152–153, 186
Paris Peace Conference, 174
Pearl Harbor, 10, 183
People's Representative Assembly (East
    Timor), 54
Peren, Roger, 68
Pérez de Cuellar, Javier, 73
Perkumpulan HAK, 154–155

270